JOHN BROWN

AND THE

LEGEND OF FIFTY-SIX

JOHN BROWN

AND THE

LEGEND OF FIFTY-SIX

BY

JAMES C. MALIN

Professor of American History
University of Kansas

HASKELL HOUSE PUBLISHERS Ltd.

Publishers of Scarce Scholarly Books

NEW YORK, N. Y. 10012

1971

First Published 1942

HASKELL HOUSE PUBLISHERS Ltd.
Publishers of Scarce Scholarly Books
280 LAFAYETTE STREET
NEW YORK, N. Y. 10012

Library of Congress Catalog Card Number: 70-117588

Standard Book Number 8383-1021-4

Printed in the United States of America

To the Memory

OF

FRANK HEYWOOD HODDER

PROFESSOR OF AMERICAN HISTORY AT THE
UNIVERSITY OF KANSAS
1891–1935

PREFACE

In Italy in 1698 occurred an execution in punishment for murder, and it was the record of that case that inspired Robert Browning's *The Ring and the Book*. The point at issue was the eternal question of truth and how it can be determined. The procedure of the poet was to permit each point of view to be told in turn: Half-Rome, the Other Half-Rome, Tertium Quid, each of the principals, the lawyers' arguments and finally the summation on review of the case by the Pope. This emphasized the extent to which the subjective element enters into what is ordinarily regarded as fact.

In early Kansas, during the controversy between anti-slavery and pro-slavery factions, murders and other crimes were committed, and not the least of these were lying and hate and the intimidation of truth—all in the name of humanitarian idealism and in defense of an accustomed way of life. The passage of years, instead of resolving differences, brought intensification of hates and embitterment of controversy, and truth was forgotten altogether in the battle among rival cults. Even now few can discuss the John Brown question except in terms of trying to prove something. Not many seem capable of attaining that objectivity which made it possible for Emily Dickinson to write under other circumstances, "I had no time for hate. . . ."

The problem arising out of the Kansas Troubles involves more than the determining and ordering of the facts of 1856. In origin and evolution, the Legend about John Brown was primarily subjective. John Brown and his contemporaries all had their own ideas of the ultimate goal of society as well as the means by which it could be attained. Who has the Authority to sit in judgment upon this man and his age? The aim of this book is not to prove, to praise, or to condemn; it is to establish facts as objectively as possible. But it is something more than that, and it would fall short of its purpose did it not contribute somewhat toward an understanding of the larger problem of human behavior.

There is no such thing as a definitive historical study in any case and no pretensions are made that the final word on John Brown has been written. So far as can be determined at this time, however, all available Kansas materials have been utilized and much is altogether new. There is a fairly representative coverage of eastern materials, the most important of which are the records of the General Land Office which have been used for the first time in connection with the Brown question. When placed in the broad framework of cultural history, it is evident that the John Brown theme is far from exhausted—the study of it is only begun. Many suggestions of important problems appear in the pages of this book. There is a Southern Legend that deserves systematic treatment. The impact of the Brown tradition on Europe is unexplored.

Too often the function of historical research is considered in terms of settling specific questions and writing Q.E.D. at the end of the discussion—definitiveness. The spirit of the closed mind is thus emphasized and research becomes a tool for stopping the last chinks through which a fresh impulse might break. Historical wisdom cannot be gained by sealing conclusions in closed compartments. Instead, one of the principal objects of research should be to generate curiosity. It is a contribution, therefore, to present a significant body of unsolved problems which may direct the spirit of creative inquiry along new paths and encourage reexploration of the old.

What is the meaning of the Legend about John Brown? Is it an endorsement of the application of direct action to social change, an approval of the overthrow of institutions by violence? A review of three-quarters of a century of the growth of the Kansas phase of the Legend emphasizes the fact that John Brown has had his strongest hold among conservative classes of society. It has never been conspicuous as an inspiration of industrial wage workers or even of Marxian revolutionaries. It has served rather, perhaps, as a sort of psychological compensation for people otherwise most respectable and conservative socially. And it must be remembered that even during Brown's lifetime this aspect of his influence was more significant than is generally recognized. Is it merely a strange paradox, or is it a form of practical or even a necessary balancing of social forces, that such a national Legend, grounded in a doctrine of violence, should become to such a degree an escape mechanism for a class of society which would be most injured by its application?

For the reading of the entire manuscript the author is indebted to Professor John H. Nelson of the University of Kansas and to Mr. Kirke Mechem, Secretary of the Kansas State Historical Society. He is grateful to Mr. Boyd B. Stutler of New York for many courtesies in pursuit of elusive material, to Professor N. W. Storer of the University of Kansas for astronomical calculations which were useful in historical analyses, and to Miss Maud Smelser, who is in charge of Kansas books in the Library of the University of Kansas. It is a particular pleasure to express appreciation to the staff of the Kansas State Historical Society for unrivaled reference services for beyond the call of duty, and especially to Mrs. Lela Barnes, while in charge of the manuscripts division, and to Mr. Nyle Miller, director of research. Acknowledgments of indebtedness are due to Professor John D. Hicks of the University of California, representing the American Historical Association, to Professor Avery Craven of the University of Chicago, and to Professors William E. Lingelbach and Roy Nichols of the University of Pennsylvania for their interest and help in planning for the publication of this book. The University of Kansas contributed a grant-in-aid from the Graduate Research Fund toward the cost of research, but the author's primary obligation is to the American Philosophical Society for publication. The author alone is responsible for the contents of the book.

JAMES C. MALIN

TABLE OF CONTENTS

PART THREE. A CRITIQUE, THE JOHN BROWN AND THE
KANSAS QUESTIONS RESTATED

DOCUMENTS

MAPS

PART I

THE CONTEMPORARY PRINTED RECORD

CHAPTER I

INTRODUCTION

More than seventy-five years have passed since the execution of John Brown but no strictly scientific study of him has been made; that is, one which applies to the problem in full measure the critical technique of modern historiography. The fact seems to pass unnoticed that no professional historian has written a biography of the Old Hero, and more significant still, that the profession has produced scarcely an important monograph on any phase of the question.[1] Interest has centered too narrowly in the man himself, too little or none has been directed toward the associates of Brown, toward the broader ramifications of the problem in this period of national crisis, and toward the Brown Legend as national folklore. The task is too great, in fact, for any one scholar, and requires minute and mature research on the part of many persons, but it is not only a problem in volume of materials, but more important, true understanding can be achieved only by the combined efforts of many minds, each of which lights up a different facet of the whole.

Brown's career turned most largely around two episodes, his Kansas exploits of 1856 and the Harpers Ferry raid, although other phases of his life should not be neglected. An accumulation of new materials has led to this reconsideration of his Kansas career and the history of the Legend of 1856. In the light of new facts and a quite different approach it is possible to rewrite much of both the history and legend of that one memorable year. The re-examination raises the question which has had the greater influence on the course of history, the man John Brown, or the legend about John Brown, and no satisfying treatment of the Brown problem is possible which does not recognize clearly this distinction between the fact and the fable.

[1] The most important recent contribution which may serve as the exception that emphasizes the generalization is the article by R. V. Harlow, "Gerrit Smith and the John Brown raid," *American Historical Review*, 37 (October, 1932), 32–60, and a book by the same author, *Gerrit Smith* (1939).

One of the most loyal admirers of John Brown was James Hanway of Dutch Henry's Crossing, renamed Lane, Kansas, who, writing about 1875, despaired of restoring facts and displacing fancy:

> Kansas history dates from 1854 and 1855, twenty to twenty-one years ago. And the most important epoch of its existence to eighteen to nineteen years.
>
> Those who are known as "old settlers," who lived here at the time of her troubles, and had opportunity to know something of the real conditions of things as they transpired are often astonished to find that events should be published for history which are not history.
>
> Let us take for illustration a single case which there is no doubt about with those who had an opportunity of knowing the truth at the time it transpired. We refer to the "Potawatomie tragedy" as it has been called.
>
> Redpath in his Life of Capt. John Brown, Holloway in his history of Kansas, and the late interesting articles which appeared in the Jan'y and Feb. numbers of the *Atlantic* for 1875, by F. B. Sanborn, on John Brown.
>
> These are all of one type. We are told that, "all free statesmen agree" that John Brown, Sr. was absent at the time, and knew nothing of the event until the following day. This is the stereotyped history of that transaction and no doubt will be handed down as one of the best established facts in Kansas history. Those on the other hand, who were acquainted with this tragical event, know very well that old Cap Brown commanded the company which dispatched these five proslavery border ruffians, consequently he was not twenty miles away as Sanborn and others have stated.
>
> Col. Phillips our present member of Congress, was the correspondent of the N. Y. *Tribune;* he pub. the first version for the *Tribune,* this was copied into a thousand papers. Horace Greeley when he issued the *Tribune Almanac* for 1857 recorded it as history. Writers like Holloway and others have followed "copy" adding here and there a few ideas or comments to make the picture more attractive: hence if anyone who knows these published statements to be incorrect, and attempts to correct them, he is met with all the accumulated evidence which newspapers and books for years have been busy circulating.
>
> The question naturally suggests itself, if what is regarded as history of such recent date, is so full of error, what must be the details of history which have been handed down to us for several thousand years.[2]

Hanway had already written his version of the history to which he referred and published it several times in the local papers over a period of seven years, and was to continue to write for another seven years without experiencing the satisfaction of having secured the general acceptance of his point of view. It was left to others to force the issue, and eventually to revise the John Brown story, but

---

[2] Undated paper in *Hanway MSS.*, in possession of the Kansas State Historical Society. The approximate date is fixed, however, by the context as 1875.

in a direction which was far more distasteful to Hanway than the first. Even though he hated legendary versions, Hanway proved to be one of the leading purveyors of Brown legends.

With one possible exception, John Brown's biographers have had a special defense or plea to make. Redpath, Sanborn and Hinton were associates of Brown and in that sense were writing not only a eulogy of their hero, but were making a defense of themselves. Others who wrote on the subject, or gave aid or comfort to those who did, occupied much the same position: Gerrit Smith, T. W. Higginson, George Stearns, S. G. Howe, Theodore Parker, Thoreau and Emerson. Somewhat different were the champions of the non-resistant abolitionists; the sons of William Lloyd Garrison and the grandson, Oswald Garrison Villard, but John Brown, with all his shedding of blood, emerged a hero, not of arms and blood, but of the spirit. On the opposite side were other special pleaders: Eli Thayer, Charles Robinson, G. W. Brown, F. W. Blackmar and Hill P. Wilson. Hanway felt that the case was practically hopeless after only twenty years of accumulation of fable, but the modern historian faces three-quarters of a century of it.

John Brown was born May 9, 1800, at Torrington, Connecticut. Soon after he was twenty-one he became the father of the first of a family of twenty children. During the thirty-five years that elapsed between the birth of his first child and his migration to Kansas he engaged in more than twenty distinct business ventures in at least six different states. Most of these were unsuccessful, some ended in bankruptcy, and two or more in crime. Judging from the number of litigations on record against him, he must have been almost constantly a defendant in court for failure to meet his obligations in payment of notes, or wages, or in fulfillment of other contracts. Several of the cases in question leave no doubt of flagrant dishonesty on his part in both business and family relations. To the historian, this record of unreliability proven in court and in correspondence, is of vital importance, because it is, to some extent at least, an index to the reliability of John Brown as a witness after he became a public character. On the other side of the account were his enduring friendships, formed among people of his own station in life as well as among those where he would be least expected to find welcome, and the loyalty he inspired among them in spite of the inescapable facts of his repeated failures.

Prior to his migration to Kansas there are only four authentic episodes in which he was connected with the negro question. The first is a proposal to take one negro boy into the family and raise him as his own, and this plan was linked with a proposal to establish a school for negroes. The line of argument in support of these plans was that education of negroes was the most effective weapon which could be used to undermine slavery. The authority for this episode is a letter written by John Brown to his brother Frederick, dated November 24, 1834, and on account of its importance, a part of the letter is quoted here:

Since you left I have been trying to devise some means whereby I might do something in a practical way for my poor fellow-men . . . in bondage, and having fully consulted the feelings of my wife and my three boys, we have agreed to get at least one negro boy or youth, and bring him up as we do our own. . . . I will just mention that when the subject was first introduced, Jason had gone to bed; but no sooner did he hear the thing hinted, than his warm heart kindled, and he turned out to have a part in the discussion. . . . I have for years been trying to devise some way to get a school a-going here for blacks, and I think that on many accounts it would be a most favorable location. . . . This has been for me a favorite theme of reflection for years. . . . If you will join me in this undertaking, I will make you any arrangement of our temporal concerns that shall be fair.[3]

Except for the fact that neither phase of the proposals in this letter materialized, nothing further is known of the course of the negotiations. The second authentic case is the preparation of an article entitled ''Sambo's Mistakes'' about 1848–1849 for publication in an abolition paper, *The Ram's Horn*. The third is his letter of advice to the Gileadites at Springfield, Massachusetts, in 1851, which was called forth by the agitation following the enactment of the federal fugitive slave law of 1850. The fourth episode in the group is the arrangement by which he secured a farm or farms near North Elba, New York, that by example he might aid and teach the negroes on Gerrit Smith's land the more effective practice of agriculture and management of their personal affairs. Brown indicated his interest in this region in a letter to his father January 10, 1849:

We feel a good deal of spirit about the oppressions, & cruelties that are done in the land, but in regard to other verry important interests we are quite too indifferent. I suppose it may well be questioned whether any one duty can be acceptably performed; while most others are neglected. I was on some of the Gettit Smith lands lying opposite Burlington Vt; last fall that he has given away to the blacks & I found no objection to them but the high northern Latitude in which they lie. They

[3] Villard, *John Brown*, 43–44.

are indeed rather inviting on many accounts. There are a number of good colored families on the ground; most of them I visited. I can think of no place where I would sooner go; all things considered than to live with those poor despised Africans to try, & encourage them; & show them a little so far as I am capable how to manage. You kneed not be surprised if at some future day I should do so. . . .[4]

Brown moved his family to North Elba during the same year. They occupied the farm until 1851, when he removed them again to Ohio. Then in 1855, just before the migration to Kansas, he returned them to North Elba.

Unless it be the taking of a negro into the family circle, there is nothing in these instances to indicate any activity or views on slavery that differed materially from those of any number of the active anti-slavery or abolition people of the time. The North Elba project has one point of possible interest that historians have not pointed out. If Brown is to be credited with sincerity at the time he undertook it, this might be in the nature of a revival, in a somewhat different form, of the negro plans of 1834 with Smith rather than Frederick Brown supplying the capital. There is no evidence, however, that Brown remained at North Elba to fulfill any plan regarding the negroes during either of the periods that his family resided there.[5]

Among the stories that go to make up the Brown Legend, there is one to the effect that John Brown, together with certain members of his family, pledged themselves by a most solemn oath to wage by force and arms eternal warfare against slavery. This is made the key to John Brown's career, "his greatest or principal object." The primary difficulty with the story is that there is no contemporary evidence to support it. Against this the argument might be presented that as this was a secret oath no contemporary record would have been made of it, but such an answer does not meet the difficulty. The authority for the story is in the nature of reminiscences after Harpers Ferry when the justification of Brown's life was being formulated. The witnesses and eulogists, being involved with Brown, however, were making defense of themselves as well, and they failed to agree on either the circumstances or the date of the alleged family pact. John Brown, Jr., men-

[4] This letter was written from Springfield, Massachusetts. The original is in the possession of the K. S. H. S., of Topeka.

[5] At the time of the Harpers Ferry excitement the New York *Evening Post*, December 20, 1859, published a series of letters all written by Brown in 1849 to Willis A. Hodges, one of the negroes on the Smith lands. These letters give the most intimate record available about that episode.

tioned three separate dates, while Jason did not make mention of force and arms.[6]   The version given to Sanborn by John Brown, Jr., contains the following:

Father, mother, Jason, Owen and I were, late in the evening [1839], seated around the open fire-place of the kitchen, in the old Haymaker house where we then lived,—and there he first informed us of his determination to make war on slavery . . . by force and arms. He said that he had long entertained such a purpose—that he believed it his duty to devote his life, if need be, to this object, which he made us fully to understand. After spending considerable time in setting forth in most impressive language the hopeless condition of the slave, he asked who of us were willing to make common cause with him . . . , naming each of us in succession, are you Mary, John, Jason, and Oliver? Receiving an affirmative reply from each, he kneeled in prayer, and all did the same. . . . After prayer he asked us to raise our right hands, and then he administered to us an oath, the exact terms of which I cannot recall, but in substance it bound us to secrecy and devotion to the purpose of fighting slavery by force and arms to the extent of our ability.[7]

Attention is here called to the similarity of this version to the project set forth by his father in the letter of 1834, except for the glosses of the son in the light of the Harpers Ferry justification. The persons involved in both cases were the father, mother and three sons who discussed the respective plans late in the evening and agreed on them.   The contemporary record of 1834, as distinguished from the reminiscent version, applied the family agreement to the question of a negro boy as an approach to the overthrow of slavery through education.   There is a strong suggestion from the above that the family pact never went any further, except in retrospective imagination.

A table of ages of the children of John Brown who figured in the Kansas discussions aids in visualizing the family group at different

    6 Later treatment of the growth of the Brown Legend will help to explain the rigid insistence on contemporary evidence on every event in Brown's career. The mere fact of absence of such contemporary evidence does not constitute proof that an event did not occur, but it does place more positively the burden of proof upon those who contend that it did. The history of the legend, to be developed later in this book, demonstrates without question that many of the stories about Brown told by persons directly associated with him were pure fabrications. The serious contradictions in the family pact stories therefore place this episode in the class of those which must be rejected unless or until positive evidence of validity is forthcoming.

    For a critical examination of contemporary evidence see especially W. P. Garrison, "John Brown, Practical Shephard," Andover Review, 14 (December, 1890) 579–587. Comment in the Nation, 51 (December 4, 1890) 443. Sanborn's reply is in the Nation, 51 (December 25, 1890) 500. W. P. Garrison, "John Brown, Guerilla," Andover Review, 15 (January 1891) 55–66.

    7 Villard, John Brown 45–46.

periods critical to the major controversies.[8] At the time of the
letter of 1834 the three boys mentioned were thirteen, twelve and
ten years of age and the pledges must be viewed as involving children. If the date 1839 is taken as the point of reference, the boys
were at an age when such an oath might carry some weight, although
even then they were just boys in their teens.

Another contention basic to the John Brown Legend is that when
he went to Kansas he had no intention of settling there and that he
migrated for the express purpose of waging war against slavery.
A specific statement which is pretty much representative on the
matter of the Brown family came from Annie Brown Adams in a
letter to F. G. Adams, secretary of the Kansas State Historical Society in September 1886, when she said that her father, Salmon,
Oliver, and the son-in-law Henry Thompson went to Kansas to make
it a free state, but the others John, Jr., Jason, Owen and Frederick
went to settle. She insisted further that there was a big difference
between fighting in self-defense when attacked as the latter group of
the family did and going to Kansas for the express purpose of fighting in behalf of *others* as the first group did.[9]

From the same daughter of John Brown, Sanborn received a
statement in 1885 to the effect that "his first and main object in
going to Kansas was to find men, and an opening or base on which
to commence operations—or, as he said 'to see if something would
not turn up to his advantage.' "[10]

These reminiscences contrast rather sharply with the contemporary evidence on the points involved. The family correspondence
of 1854 recorded the unfavorable agricultural conditions in Ohio
and specifically the short crops of that year. The result was that
the Brown family was again on the move. John Brown, Sr., was

[8] AGES OF THE CHILDREN OF JOHN BROWN

	Born	Age in 1834	1839	May, 1856
John Brown, Jr.	July 25, 1821	13	18	35–
Jason	Jan. 19, 1823	12	17	33
Owen	Nov. 4, 1824	10	15	31
Ruth (Mrs. H. Thompson)	Feb. 18, 1829	5–	10–	27
Frederick	Dec. 21, 1830	4	9	25
Watson	Oct. 7, 1835		4	20
Salmon	Oct. 2, 1836		3	19
Oliver	Mar. 19, 1839		1–	17
Anne	Sept. 23, 1843			11–12

[9] *Kansas Daily State Journal*, September 18, 1886. This clipping is available also in the John Brown *Scrapbooks*, Volume I, Kansas State Historical
Society. The original is in the possession of the K. S. H. S.

[10] Sanborn, *Recollections* of Seventy Years. 2 volumes (1909) I, 152.

soon to move his family back to North Elba and five of the sons to move to Kansas. It was while these decisions were still to be made by some of the members of the group that the father wrote August 21, 1854 to his eldest son, John, Jr., as follows:

If you or any of my family are disposed to go to Kansas or Nebraska, with a view to help defeat *Satan* and his legions in that direction, I have not a word to say; *but I feel committed to operate in another part of the field.* If I were not so committed, I would be on my way this fall. Mr. Adair is fixing to go, and wants to find 'good men and true' to go along. I would be glad if Jason would give away his Rock and go. Owen is fixing for some move; I can hardly say what.[11]

By the late fall of 1854 the five brothers, John, Jr., Jason, Owen, Frederick and Salmon had decided and made preparations to move to Kansas, where Adair had settled. They transferred their live-stock, eleven cattle and three horses, to Meridosia, Illinois, where an uncle lived, and wintered them there. Three brothers drove the stock through to Kansas, while two brothers travelled the river route by way of St. Louis. In the meantime John Brown had changed his mind about where his obligations lay and on February 13, 1855 wrote an eastern correspondent:

Since I saw you I have undertaken to direct the operations of a Sur-veying, & Exploring party, to be employed in Kansas for a considerable time perhaps for some Two or Three years; & I lack for time to make all my arrangements, and get on to the ground in season.[12]

He was busy until June disposing of his stock preparatory to taking his family back to North Elba. During this period he had received a letter from his son John in Kansas dated May 24 in which he reported that the brothers were exceptionally well pleased with the country and the prospects of getting a new start. The principal object of the letter was, however, the opening of what appeared to be a subject new to the Browns. As a result of the aggression of the Missourians in the elections just held, the five had come to the decision that it would be necessary to fight and to do so would re-quire arms. The family had brought to Kansas only two rifles, of no special value, one revolver, one pocket pistol, a bowie knife, and two "slung shot." They wanted for each man, one large-sized Colt revolver, one Allen & Thurber rifle and a heavy bowie knife. There are four important implications in this letter; first, that the mission

11 Sanborn, *John Brown*, 191.
12 Villard, *John Brown*, 84.

of the Brown family already in Kansas, as well as of the father and other members making preparations for coming, was such that they had not thought previously of fire arms as equipment; second, that active resistance to slavery by force was proposed as a new program for the Brown family; third, the sole cause assigned for the new departure was the recent action of the Missourians; and lastly, that the proposal for "force and arms" originated with the sons in Kansas and not with the elder John Brown. The letter served a significant purpose. On his way east to North Elba, John Brown stopped at Syracuse, N. Y., on June 28 and, presenting the appeal of his sons before an anti-slavery meeting, collected sixty dollars. This was John Brown's first recorded public appearance at begging money for anti-slavery work and it was to arm his own family. He followed up his first public appeal for money by holding meetings in Ohio at which he received both arms and money. According to Villard's estimate one two-day campaign yielded nearly two hundred dollars' worth, mostly arms and ammunition.[13] Brown seems to have solicited money in Springfield, Massachusetts,[14] and also to have purchased arms or ammunition or both in addition to what he had collected, because on December 14, 1855, after his arrival in Kansas, he wrote to Orson Day at White Hall, N. Y., asking him to buy a draft for the sum of $146.38 payable to I. W. Carter, Agent of the Massachusetts Arms Company of Chicopee Falls. He explained to Day that this was "in payment for Fire arms sent me by him; & without which we might have been placed in very awkward circumstances." He promised also that "I will make the same all right with you."[15] It is of interest that the Browns either did not know about the famous Sharps rifle or did not appreciate its qualities. There is no clue to the price paid, but as the officers of the New England Aid Company had bought Sharps rifles some weeks earlier at a special price of $21.55 it is possible that Brown was paying about $20 to $25 each. At that rate, if all the sum to be paid Carter represented rifles, it would have paid for six or seven.

Several important questions arise out of these transactions. What had Brown done with the money he had raised at Syracuse and in Ohio, and in Massachusetts to expend for arms? Did he spend all of that money for arms and still have so large a balance to pay? What became of such a quantity of arms as could have

[13] Villard, *John Brown*, 85.

[14] Springfield *Republican*, quoted in the *Herald of Freedom*, March 1, 1856.

[15] A photostatic copy of this letter is in possession of the K. S. H. S.

been purchased by these sums plus the amount of aid collected in the form of arms and ammunition? Or had Brown diverted to his own use sums entrusted to him, as he had done in the case of the New England Woolen Company funds? Why did he write Day specifying particularly that it was the arms bought of Carter that had maybe saved them from "awkward circumstances," when he had collected other arms in Ohio in considerable quantities? There was never any accounting of the total collections either of cash, arms or ammunition, or of their disposition or use. Without more specific information, each reader of the record is left at liberty to draw his own conclusions.

While John Brown was making his preparations to go to Kansas, he was interested in such information as the sons already there could furnish regarding supplies and equipment which he could bring with him to advantage. Apparently two considerations were actuating this inquiry, to take certain things that would be of use to themselves and in addition to make some profit out of resale of articles in demand among the settlers. John, the son, replied on June 22 to his father's letter of May 24. He reviewed the prices of cattle and horses and pointed out that there was "no great demand for either." He gave prices for white beans, corn meal, flour, dried apples, bacon, fresh beef and enclosed a clipping from the Lawrence *Tribune* giving the markets at that place which differed from their locality. From the above group of commodities, he recommended three items: "Flour, white beans, and dried fruit will doubtless continue for some time to come to be high," while corn meal prices were "tending downward."

A second subject in the letter was the mode of travel and the route: "a good strong buggy would sell well,—probably a Lumberee best. Mr. Adair has had several chances to sell his." The son agreed that " 'a covered lumber buggy and one horse or mule,' " apparently quoting from his father's letter, would be both cheaper and healthier, "especially from St. Louis here" than to come by boat. "Besides," the son added, "such a conveyance is just what you want here to carry on the business of surveying." In another place he advised that "should you buy anything to send by water, you can send it either to Lawrence . . . or to Kansas City, Mo."

The third subject of the letter was the location of the Brown settlement, illustrated by a map, and a discussion of the land situation, all of which led to the conclusion that no money was to be made in that line: "owing to the rapid settlement of the country by squatters, it does not open a good field for speculation." [16]

The youngest son of the Kansas group, Salmon, aged nineteen, wrote at the same time as his elder brother. Obviously, he was not accustomed to letter writing. His was a short letter of a single paragraph, immature and disjointed in composition. It gives the impression that he had difficulty in filling space. The first three sentences came along fairly well, but the last four were short and choppy, each making a complete change of subject. He suggested the need of pork, meal and beans enough to last until the new crop was ready. He would have his house ready by the time his father arrived. He needed new boots, summer pants and a hat. He had an axe. The closing sentence was: "There are slaves owned within three miles of us." [17] Among other things this letter shows Salmon as a settler, Annie's letter to the contrary notwithstanding.

The second son, Jason, wrote the next day on the back of Salmon's letter expressing his satisfaction with the country, declaring that he could be "as well content here as anywhere else if it proves to be healthy." He thought best that his father "come by land from St. Louis." Jason's thoughts were not on speculation. He had spent all his money in making the move from Ohio to Kansas, they had no stoves, and his idea was that his father should buy him a middle size stove and some furniture, which he would manage somehow to pay for. These he should send to Kansas City, or bring with him.

It is particularly noteworthy that these letters, giving final instructions and requests before their father was expected to start, were just such letters as were written thousands of times from the frontier settlements in America to relatives and friends back home who were preparing to follow. They are properly supplemented by one written by another son, Oliver, to his mother from Rockford, Illinois, August 8, 1855, where he was working and awaiting the arrival of his father whom he was to join on his way to Kansas. It contained the following significant sentence, "I hope to see you all in Kansas in the course of a year or 2 two." [18] Clearly sixteen year

16 Sanborn, *John Brown*, 194–197. The original of the letter is in the possession of the Kansas State Historical Society, and the map is reproduced for the first time. Folder, between pp. 16 and 17.

17 Sanborn, *John Brown*, 197. The original is in the possession of the K. S. H. S.

18 Sanborn, *John Brown*, 198. The original is in the possession of the K. S. H. S.

old Oliver was not thinking of Kansas as a seat of war, but as a home where the whole Brown family soon would be united.

In placing emphasis on the typical character of this correspondence as representing the oft-repeated process by which the American people moved westward across the continent it is intended that it shall bring out the contrast between the contemporary record and the legend of the family pact sealed by solemn oath, the execution of which was said to have been "his first and main object in going to Kansas." The letter of August 21, 1854 spoke of defeating Satan and his legions in Kansas or Nebraska and that Adair was going, but that did not mean an attack by force on slavery because in Nebraska there was no particular contest and Adair was a man of peace and throughout the period of the civil war in Kansas deprecated violence and disapproved John Brown's methods. John Brown's obligation to operate in another part of the field, in the light of the Adair reference, could not have any violent implications unless he was misrepresenting to his son Adair's mission in Kansas. A more reasonable interpretation of the letter is the penchant of John Brown for grandiose statement. In truth he was under some obligation to Gerrit Smith in connection with the North Elba farm. In the absence of positive evidence to the contrary, there is no ground for any unusual reading of this figurative language. The letter of February 13, 1855 contains nothing on the face of it that indicates any ulterior motive, and no contemporary evidence has been presented to bear out any concealed meaning. Such contemporary evidence as might apply to the matter is rather on the opposite side. The first discussion of arms and fighting appeared in the appeal of the sons in Kansas to bring arms when he came, and John Brown's first attempt to collect arms and money for arms was in direct response to the plea of his sons in Kansas which he read at the Syracuse meeting. Annie Brown Adams's testimony to the "first and main object" was given in 1885 and was represented as the secret confidences of her father revealed to her as a little girl of eleven years (winter of 1854–1855) and she was repeating them from memory thirty years after. It is surprising any historian should take such testimony seriously, but it is curious to see how it has been used. Some supporters of the Brown Legend emphasize the first part of the statement as convincing proof that Brown had in mind his Virginia plan at that time and that the Kansas war was in the nature of an opportunity for preparation and training. Some opponents of Brown have emphasized the last part which was given as quoting the exact words of Brown (told to an eleven year old girl and repeated thirty years after) that he went to Kansas "to see if something would not turn up to his advantage." In the Wilson biography this phrase was given a sinister interpretation and in that application became a sort of refrain that pervaded the book. Nothing could be more unjustified. The same phrase could be applied to almost everyone who migrated to the frontier.

The nearest to a contemporary statement by John Brown that might be helpful in answering some of these questions appeared in a letter written in March 1859 to Teesdale, editor of the Des Moines *Register,* in justifying his Missouri raid of the previous December. He claimed then that "it has been my deliberate judgment since 1855 that the most ready and effectual way to retrieve Kansas would be to meddle directly with the peculiar institution." [19] While on the face of it this statement seems helpful, under analysis it proves to contribute little enlightenment. The difficulty lies in the fact that he did not indicate whether this conclusion had been arrived at prior to his decision to go to Kansas, or whether it was the product of experiences after his arrival, and that defect is nearly fatal. There is some significance, however, in the fact that he did not set some earlier date for his "deliberate judgment" that raids into the South were the most effective procedure for attacking slavery. After Harpers Ferry, in the Mason-Vallandigham interview, Brown was quoted as having said: "Four of my sons had gone there [Kansas] to settle, and they induced me to go. I did not go there to settle, but because of the difficulties." This also is not particularly helpful as he had committed himself to Kansas as early as February 1855, and at that time the Kansas troubles had not assumed a serious character.

There are certain principles of historical criticism which should be clearly understood in dealing with such a controversial problem as John Brown. A document should be taken at its face value so long as there is no positive evidence to the contrary. It must not be given a forced interpretation. An ulterior motive or a concealed meaning or double reading given to a document is justified only when supported by positive evidence. Such evidence should be contemporary or approximately so, and the more remote the greater the doubt of its authenticity. It is altogether unjustifiable to seize

[19] Quoted in Villard, *John Brown,* 386. The *John Brown Scrapbook* (K. S. H. S.) 14: 127 contains a clipping of the original publication of this letter, with photographic reproduction, in the *Evening Sun* [N. Y. ?] March 16, 1895.

upon a single phrase or sentence as a foundation for building a theory. The particular instance may be a chance combination of words, or a passing thought, or it may be a casual slip which would convey a meaning of which the author was unaware. The rule that more than one independent witness is required to establish an historical fact, applies to this case with particular force. To establish clearly so important a matter, there should be an unmistakable repetition of the idea or else, if the document must stand alone, it must represent an intentional and deliberate exposition of policy.[20]

In the present instance, the legendary stories do not meet, to a reasonable degree, any of these tests. Under such rules of historical evidence there was nothing unusual in the migration of the Brown family to the frontier. John Brown's preparations for the trip to join his sons were in keeping with his habits, except the procurement of arms which were unquestionably an afterthought inspired by the letters of his sons in Kansas. He was not accustomed to settle down to the routine and drudgery of farm life. He was almost continually on the move, on the lookout for a business deal, frequently something on a large scale. Wherever he went he inquired about prices of land, livestock, corn and other farm products.

[20] Annie Brown Adams is on record clearly as understanding the significance of the forced interpretation imposed on statements of the Brown family. In 1893 R. J. Hinton wrote asking her for a statement and she replied February 15, 1893 that she had written out a story for Sanborn several years before and that "If I should write out two statements so many years apart, I might vary a trifle without meaning to, and then some future historian would compare them, and claim that I had not told the truth, so I shall be obliged to beg you for an extension of time until I can procure those papers from him." The original of this letter is in the *R. J. Hinton Papers* in possession of the K. S. H. S.

Even though the various stories of different members of the Brown family did not agree, and the same members were not always consistent, only one instance has been found of outright dissent within the family circle. A long letter from Annie Brown Adams written to Hinton June 7, 1894 contains the following:

"If I survive John there are some things that I have kept back for fear of injuring his feelings (which I would not do willingly or intentionally) I may some day tell of, that would explain things that have puzzled a great many people. You know John's mind has always been more or less affected by the excitement and trouble in Kansas, and he has not always stated things exactly exact or as they were. These I should not think of correcting during his lifetime. I hope you will understand my motive in thus doing." *Hinton Papers.*

Apparently Mrs. Adams persisted in her determination, because there is no hint in the later correspondence that she revealed her version of the Brown story. Her testimony may have been of little or no value, but the fact that she challenged what she considered material parts of her brother's story and admitted his mental aberration leaves a question mark on these versions.

His letters illustrate this abundantly. Possibly every rural community had at least one such character, who lived by trading, by buying most anything he thought he could resell at a profit, moving restlessly from place to place engaging in petty business but always pursuing that illusive, spectacular big deal which would bring fame and fortune. In the early summer of 1855 it was these types of transactions, large and small, that were the theme of his correspondence with his sons in Kansas.

When the Brown boys arrived in Kansas the first major incident in the contest between North and South for political control of the territory had occurred,—the election of the first legislature, which was controlled by Missourians. Governor Reeder recognized and then repudiated it later in the summer. The more radical free-state men repudiated it at a convention held at Lawrence June 25, one of a series of conventions which led to one at Big Springs, September 5, where the free-state political party was organized. In simple terms this presents the background of Kansas affairs as the first contingent of the Brown family found them during the early months of their residence.

The three younger brothers, who drove the family livestock overland, arrived apparently during the last week of April 1855 and John, Jr., and Jason arrived about the first week of May. John, Jr., attended the first of the series of Lawrence conventions of August 14–15, and was at the Big Springs convention of September 5. At each of these he received some recognition in the form of office or committee assignment, although there is no record that he took any prominent part. Frederick Brown was in attendance also at one or more of these meetings. The only expression of John, Jr., which might have any significance, appeared in a letter to his step-mother, dated September 15 and 21, in which he boasted that he had denounced the slave code in the presence of a pro-slavery man and declared that he would kill any officer who attempted to arrest him for its violation. It was the next phase of the development of the free-state movement, the organization of the Topeka state government, which occupied the center of the political stage as the elder Brown found it.

John Brown had left North Elba on August 13, and Chicago, ten days later, the trip from the latter point being made with a one-horse wagon, well loaded. He arrived at the Brown settlement on October 7 in company with his sixteen year old son Oliver and his son-in-law Henry Thompson. He found the families of the two eldest sons living in unfinished houses and suffering from the elements. No satisfactory explanation has been advanced why after five month's residence, the five Brown brothers had not provided at least one decent shelter against the Kansas winter.

On the back of the letter of June 22, John, Jr., had drawn a map of the Brown settlement and its relation to the two principal streams of the community and to the new village of Osawatomie. From this the elder Brown had a general idea of the location of his sons. The claim locations showed that each of the brothers had chosen a half-section farm. Four were located on one branch on the east side of Middle creek and one, Salmon's, on a branch further south. In the letter on which this map was drawn, in fact at the end of the map itself, Brown had written the following: "But Missourians have illegally gone on these Peoria lands [north of the Browns], intending to combine and prevent their going higher than $1.25 per acre, and then claim, if they go higher, a large amount of improvements,—thus cheating the Indians." This is more interesting than the Browns realized as a commentary on both the American land system and on their own family, because the Brown claims as shown on this map were all half-sections and Salmon, the youngest was only nineteen years of age. Under the preemption law, the minimum age was twenty-one and the maximum size of a claim was a quarter-section. It was common for settlers to form claim associations, however, and by such organization to prevent competitive bidding on lands desired by its members making it possible for a preemptor to bid in a helf-section at the minimum price of $1.25 per acre. It was only by some such procedure that the Browns could have held their half-sections against other settlers, and that was exactly the procedure John, Jr., was branding as cheating when indulged in by Missourians.

The first few weeks after the arrival of John Brown were devoted to making the Brown cabins endurable in winter weather, but the Wakarusa war was soon to bring the Brown family into its first active "military" service. The murder of Dow, a free-state man, and the rescue of Branson, another free-state man, from the proslavery Sheriff Jones, brought about the crisis. The pro-slavery forces determined to punish the free-state town of Lawrence, concentrating on that place during the first week of December. In preparation for eventualities, Lawrence called upon other free-state communities for assistance. The character of the call is indicated in the following note from J. H. Lane to Charles A. Foster

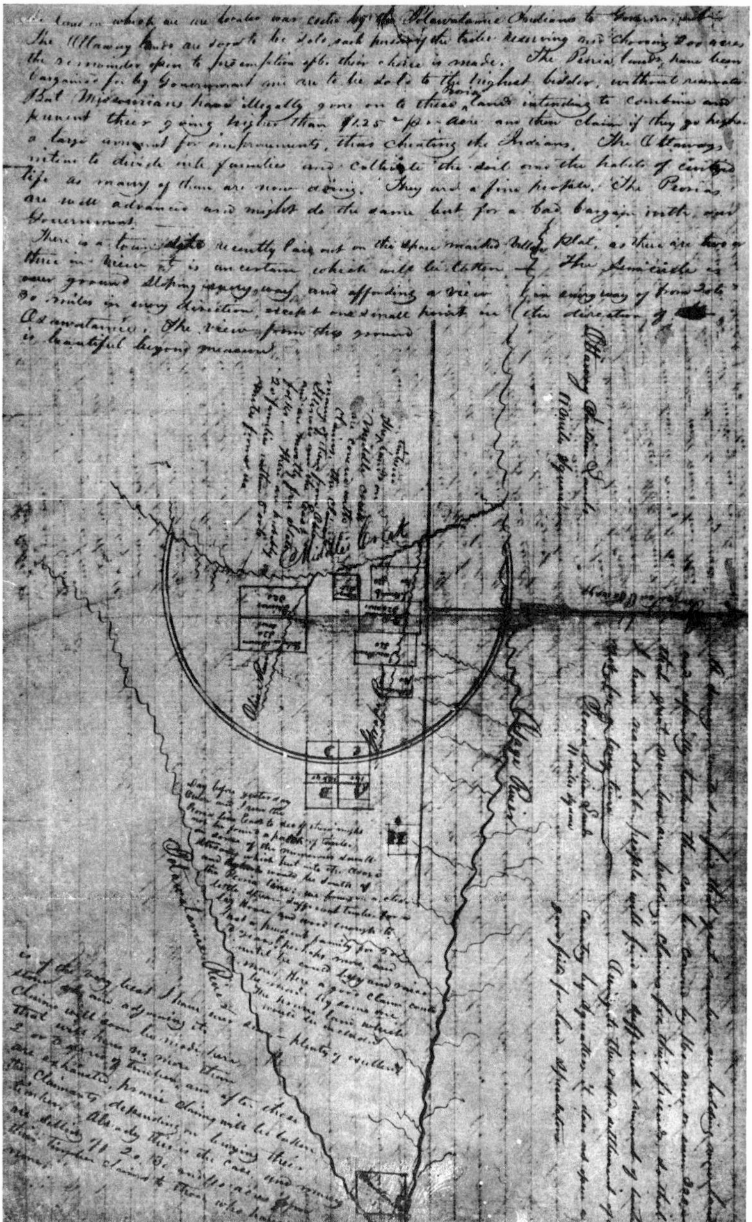

MAP BY JOHN BROWN, JR., ON REVERSE OF LETTER TO HIS FATHER, DATED 22 JUNE, 1855.

of the Osawatomie neighborhood, dated December 5, 1855: "We want every true Free State man in Kansas at Lawrence immediately." [21] The younger John Brown was on his way to Lawrence for news when he met a messenger with the call for aid. John Brown, Sr., and four of his sons set out about five o'clock that evening, December 6, for Lawrence, arriving during the forenoon of the next day, as he reported, "all of us more or less lamed by our tramp." [22] The treaty closing this war in which there were no military engagements was concluded December 8.

For purposes of defense the free-state forces under Charles Robinson and J. H. Lane had been organized into companies and regiments. In some cases military organizations existed already and where they did not, new temporary organizations were effected. The men from the southeast part of the territory fell into this latter group, twenty of them, with John Brown, Sr., as Captain, forming company K of the fifth regiment. A manuscript list of these companies has been preserved, giving the number of men in each, the number of Sharps rifles, other arms and cartridges, except for company K for which all items are blank. The paper bears no date, but apparently it was prepared before the Brown company was organized or about that time and the details were never filled in. From other sources it appears that there was at least one other organization, company L enrolled from Council City after the Brown company, but such a unit was not listed on this sheet. Without the companies K and L, the enrolled defenders of Lawrence totaled 349 men.[23]

The only contemporary account of the arrival of the Brown family in Lawrence is the following:

About noon [Friday, December 7] Mr. John Brown, an aged gentleman from Exeter county, N. Y., who had been a resident of the Territory for several months, arrived with four of his sons—leaving several others at home sick—bringing a quantity of arms with him, which were placed in his hands by eastern friends for the defense of the cause of freedom. Having more than he could well use to advantage, a portion were placed in

21 *Foster Papers*, K. S. H. S. This is the only original of such call that has been found, addressed to the southeast part of Kansas.

22 John Brown to his wife, December 16, 1856. Sanborn, *John Brown*. The original is in the possession of the K. S. H. S.

23 *W. I. R. Blackman Papers*. K. S. H. S. According to the *Herald of Freedom*, December 15, 1855, on Saturday, the day of the treaty "new parties were constantly arriving." The *Kansas Free State*, December 3–17, 1855 stated there were fifteen companies at Lawrence. John Brown in a letter to his wife dated December 16 said eleven.

the hands of those who were more destitute. A company was organized and the command given to Mr. B for the zeal he had exhibited in the cause of freedom both before and since his arrival in the Territory.[24]

This account was careless of certain facts because Brown had been in the territory only two months and had not yet established any record for zeal. It is possible that there was a confusion of father and son, both named John, as these remarks did apply to the Kansas record of the latter, and if so, it is only one of several cases of similar confusion within the next few months. The reason for giving the command to the elder Brown was indicated, but there were probably other contributory reasons. The muster roll of company K listed him and one other as fifty-five years of age. John, Jr., and one other were thirty-four. The remainder of the company were younger, ten of them being between nineteen and twenty-five. Seniority in years plus the fact that he headed a family group of five probably exercised some influence. The evidence is clear that the men in the company had not been organized previously, that they had gone to Lawrence either as individuals or as groups, and that in some cases they had little or no acquaintance with each other. John Brown's letter to his wife, December 16, made clear the fact that the company returned home, not as a company, but as independent groups, the Browns traveling alone as they had gone. Under the circumstances the choice of a commander of so casual and temporary a unit possessed little or no significance.

The muster roll has been printed by Villard, and two copies, differing somewhat, are preserved in the *Blackman Papers*. The period of service certified was sixteen days, from November 27 to December 12, 1855, "when discharged." Each man was assigned a mileage allowance for fifty miles traveled each way, as well as an allowance of twenty-four dollars for the use of a horse. Every point in this certification of service claim was false. The Browns were in Lawrence from the seventh to the twelfth inclusive, or six days, which was the maximum possible service.[25] As the war was over on December 9, any real services performed were limited to three days at most. The Browns were not responsible for the time

24 *Herald of Freedom*, December 15, 1855.
25 The discharge of William Partridge was dated December 11, effective December 13 and was signed by John Brown, Captain, also Lane and Robinson. This document used the name Liberty Guards to designate the company. *Brown Papers*, K. S. H. S. The name "Liberty Guards" was already in use, however, for the Wakarusa creek company. See a letter of introduction endorsing J. B. Abbott to eastern friends of Kansas, dated July 25, 1855. *J. B. Abbott Papers*, K. S. H. S.

count beyond the fact that they accepted the dating as arranged by the Lawrence committee which prepared printed service forms in which the date November 27 was printed in as the official opening of the war, the discharge date being filled in with a pen. The mileage allowance was excessive, because John Brown, Jr., had written his father during the summer that the distance from their claims to Lawrence was thirty miles, and the map shows thirty to thirty-five miles depending upon the angling of the road.[26] The allowance for one horse each was most remarkable, however, because the elder Brown gave his wife the impression in his letter of December 16 that they had walked.[27] In some of the reminiscences which circulated in 1859 and later, they rode in a one-horse wagon. The probabilitites are that the wagon was used to carry the luggage, but the men walked. Such fictitious monetary claims were more or less customary among the free-state men, and they hoped to collect such graft money after establishing themselves in control of the government. One other item in these papers calls for comment, the allowance for munitions. The *Herald of Freedom* story and the traditions credited Brown as taking to Lawrence more arms than needed by his family, the surplus being distributed for the use of others. Whatever the truth of this story, the only allowance for munitions was to William Partridge for a keg of powder and eight pounds of lead. The copies of muster rolls in the *Blackman Papers* presented the data in tabular form, one column being headed *enrolled* and the other *mustered in*. The date in both columns was November 27 and the place in the first column was given as Lawrence and in the second Osawatomie. When stated in sentence form this must mean that they were enrolled in Lawrence and mustered in as from Osawatomie.

Another crop of John Brown stories relates to alleged denunciation of the Wakarusa war treaty by the Old Hero. E. A. Coleman told Sanborn during the eighties how Brown entered the council rocm and denounced the treaty.[28] After sifting the evidence, Villard told a different story, that John Brown mounted the platform after Robinson spoke in justification of the treaty and attempted to denounce it and to propose an attack upon the pro-slavery men, but

[26] John Brown in his notes for speeches in England about 1857 said thirty-five miles. Sanborn, *John Brown*, p. 243.

[27] John Brown said in notes for speeches in the East, January–February 1857, that they walked most of the way. Sanborn, *John Brown*, pp. 243–46 at 243.

[28] Sanborn, *John Brown*, 219–220.

was pulled down.   Villard cited reminiscences exclusively, the earliest being one of James F. Legate dated 1879, but the most of them bearing the date 1908 or 1909, apparently not realizing how unreliable the notorious Legate was as a witness, and how uncertain the memories of his other witnesses after a lapse of fifty years.   Statements on the matter have been so loosely worded that it is important to distinguish three phases of the issue; proposals to attack the pro-slavery forces prior to the treaty, rejection or repudiation of the treaty, and proposals to attack the pro-slavery forces after the acceptance of the treaty.   There is ample evidence that there was difference of opinion in Lawrence before the treaty was drafted and accepted, whether the town should remain passive as Robinson advised, or take the aggressive and go out and fight as certain unnamed radicals advised.   Robinson won and was given the credit.[29]   No contemporary account of Brown's denunciation of the treaty has been found, and there is no contemporary record of opposition after the treaty was accepted.   The nearest reference to the matter is that contained in Augustus Wattles, "History of Kansas" published serially in the *Herald of Freedom*.   The incident was mentioned in the issue of October 10, 1857 as having occurred after the treaty was made: "Old Captain Brown made a short address, hoping the people would listen to no concessions to the bogus laws."   Robinson assured the people that no concessions had been made.

After Harpers Ferry the treaty story appeared, and so far as can be determined, for the first time in a communication to the New York *Herald* dated October 19.[30]   At that time there was little interest in his Wakarusa war record, however, as most of the controversy at that moment turned on other points.   In Kansas, G. W. Brown was reviewing John Brown's career in Kansas in his *Herald of Freedom*, the issue of October 29, 1859 containing the following:

When the Wakarusa war was impending the old man and four sons arrived in Lawrence, the balance he reported sick.   As they drove up in front of the Free State Hotel they were all standing in a small lumber wagon.   To each of their persons was strapped a short heavy broad sword. Each was supplied with a goodly number of fire arms, and navy revolvers, and poles were standing endwise around the wagon box with fixed bayonets pointing upwards.   They looked really formidable and were received with great eclat.   A small military company was organized at once, and the command was given to Old Brown.   From that hour he commenced

[29] *Liberator*, January 4, 1856, and Boston *Daily Evening Traveller*, January 9, 1856.   Clippings in the Webb, *Scrapbooks*, 8: 29, 80.
[30] Webb, *Scrapbooks*, 17: 7.

fomenting difficulties in camp, disregarding the commands of superior officers, and trying to induce the men to go down to Franklin and make an attack upon the Proslavery forces encamped there. The Committee of Public Safety were called upon several times to head off his wild projects [?], as the people of Lawrence had planted themselves on the law, claiming that they had not been guilty of its infraction, and that no armed body of men should enter the town for any purpose whatever, and that they would not go out of town to attack any such body. Peace was established, and 'Old Brown' *retired in disgust.*

At this time the *Herald of Freedom* was engaged in an exposure of Old Brown and in so doing was giving the worst possible interpretation to his record. G. W. Brown's reputation for veracity was much tarnished, but nevertheless the historian finds that on the main issues his position throughout that period was remarkably accurate. As regards both the manner of his arrival and his opposition to the peace policy, it may be pointed out that this was written within four years of the events when memories were relatively fresh. In this story, denunciation of the treaty was not listed as one of John Brown's offences, and the nearest to it was the last sentence. But did he retire ''in disgust''?

John Brown's own reports of the Wakarusa war differ from these stories as presented after Harpers Ferry by others. Writing to his brother-in-law, Orson Day of White Hall, New York, on December 14 just after his return from Lawrence, Brown said: ''I will only say at this time that the Territory is now entirely in the power of the Free State men . . . and I believe the Missourians will give up all further hope of making Kansas a slave state. . . . Indeed I consider it no longer a question whether this is to be a Free or a Slave state.'' The occasion for the writing of this letter was to discuss the house Brown was to build for Day on a claim selected for him in the Brown neighborhood, and to ask Day to pay Carter the $146.38 for arms. Brown wrote further: ''I am more & more pleased with this country : & with the prospects of my friends here; & think I may recommend it to you in good faith.''[31] A letter which Brown wrote to his wife two days later was in similar vein, but with more enthusiasm for the free-state victory.[32] Neither letter indicated any disagreement with free-state leadership and both asserted that the question of freedom in Kansas was settled.

The correspondence with Day regarding the house and giving instructions about details of the migration was continued in a letter

[31] A photostatic copy of this letter is in the possession of the K. S. H. S.
[32] Sanborn, *John Brown,* 217–221.

of January 23, 1856. John Brown, Sr., directed his letter to Day at Centreville, Pennsylvania, and John, Jr., wrote at his father's direction to Day at White Hall, New York. The son's letter has been preserved and extracts from it follow:

> In answer to Mrs. Day's questions "whether Mr. Thompson will settle there" (here) I will say he does intend to settle here and talks of moving his family to Kansas next Fall. He has chosen a prairie claim lying about ½ a mile from the one selected by Father for Mr. Day. . . .
> Right glad shall we be to see you and yours in this beautiful land, and enjoy your society as neighbors. Shall do all in our power to render your home among us a pleasant one.[33]

The last of the series of letters to Orson Day bears the date February 21, 1856 and was written by the elder John Brown. "We shall endeavor to be ready for you by the first of April;—I think you need not hesitate about starting with a view to reach [here] by that time. Such has been the state of the weather: that we could not undertake to set a time for you before." He pointed out that the distance from Lawrence was thirty-five miles and that there was no regular conveyance from that place and on that account he recommended that they take the stage at Kansas City to Osawatomie where they could stay with Adair temporarily. Regarding the possible dangers from Missourians he reported: "I think that Free State people who go quietly along their way will not now meet with any difficulty. I have been a number of times of late into the State [of Missouri] : & though *I always* (when asked) frankly avow myself a Free State man; have met with no trouble."[34]

If there is truth in the tradition as it has been handed down by the Brown family and its adherents that Brown went to Kansas to make war on slavery, either in Kansas itself or in Missouri, using the Kansas border as a base of operations, then this series of letters to Day makes of Brown a hypocritical fiend more vile than anything his worst enemies have pictured him. If Henry Thompson came to Kansas only to fight, then these letters lied. If Brown had a plan in mind at the time for precipitating a border war, then the assurances to Day were of the same brand, the pledge that we "shall do all in our power to render your home among us a pleasant one" was no less than a ghastly mockery. Within six or seven weeks of the arrival of Day and his family, Old John Brown plunged

---

[33] A photostatic copy of this letter is in the possession of the K. S. H. S.
[34] A photostatic copy of this letter is in the possession of the K. S. H. S.

the southeastern part of the territory into one of the bloodiest episodes of the whole period of Kansas border wars. Without more evidence than has become available such an interpretation of even Brown's devious career of falsehood and bloodshed hardly seems warranted. It would be more reasonable to discard the Brown tradition and give the two Johns the benefit of a more favorable interpretation of their relations with Day; credit them with sincerity in assurances of a peaceful future for Kansas. Nevertheless, in the weeks of terror following the Potawatomie massacre one cannot but wonder whether the Days reread these letters containing the cordial assurance that ''we shall do all in our power to render your home among us a pleasant one.''

CHAPTER II

JOHN BROWN IN 1856. A BRIEF FACTUAL SURVEY,
WITH QUESTIONS

The fateful year 1856 opened in Kansas with the most bitter winter weather, nevertheless the correspondence of the various members of the Brown family shows that Brown made several trips into Missouri for supplies. It was recorded also that in the particular part of the border state where he was visiting there was little feeling on the slavery question. The most complete record of these early weeks has been compiled by Villard, but possibly there was something in these expeditions which has been overlooked. John Brown, Oliver Brown and Henry Thompson had arrived in the territory during October with only sixty cents among them. The letters of the other sons indicated that during the early summer of 1855 they had little or no money. Early in December, according to Brown's letter of December 16 to his wife, he had received fifty dollars from his father. Was it this sum that financed the Brown tribe during the next two months, and was it from this sum that he made purchases in Missouri? A letter of February 1 reported that he had sold the horse and wagon, but the amount of cash raised in this manner was not indicated. On February 20, he had again returned from Missouri with corn purchased there. On April 7 he wrote that he had sent thirty dollars to the famliy at North Elba and would have sent more only money was scarce with him. Although the record must stand at its face value for the time being, there is much that needs explanation.

In spite of the struggle for subsistence, the Browns had time to participate in politics. John Brown the elder was chairman of a political convention January 5 held at Osawatomie for the purpose of nominating candidates for the Topeka state government. John Brown the younger was nominated for the state legislature, and in the subsequent election was successful. On January 24 the family participated in a settlers' meeting on the matter of a claim jumper, and in the eviction decided upon at that meeting. Henry Thompson voted in the election of January 15.[1] These incidents deserve

[1] James Hanway, "Reminiscences of Potawatomie township, Franklin County, Kansas," *The Kansas Monthly*, 3 (January 1880) 2.

more than the passing mention thus far given them by Brown biographers. The elder Brown was not supposed to be a resident of Kansas, and according to the family tradition, Henry Thompson and one or more of the Brown boys were placed in the same category. Yet these men were participating in settlers' meetings and Brown himself in acting as chairman of a nominating convention and Thompson in voting were exercising political privileges reserved exclusively to citizens. Here again, as regards right and wrong, if they were not citizens of the territory they had no more right to participate in political affairs than did the Missourians. It is the same code of ethics that appeared in the Brown preemption claims and in the Wakarusa war claims.

During these weeks the policy of the federal government was taking more definite shape. Governor Shannon was in Washington and on January 24, in a message to congress, the President recognized as legal the so-called "bogus legislature" dominated by the pro-slavery men, and on February 11, by proclamation ordered all organized bands to disperse. Also, in order to avoid difficulties with the local militia such as had occurred in the Wakarusa war, the President authorized the governor to call upon the federal troops if necessary to secure compliance. On February 20 John Brown wrote to Congressman Giddings of Ohio asking if congress free-state men to a position of resistance to the federal troops. In free-state men to a position of resistance to the federal troops. In reply, Giddings assured Brown on March 27 that he need have no fear of the troops and that the President would not dare to use them to shoot down citizens of Kansas.

In southeast Kansas some of the free-state people became concerned over the problem of law enforcement and a settlers' meeting was held at Osawatomie April 16 to consider the matter. A group of resolutions was adopted in which the authority of the territorial legislature was repudiated and mutual aid was pledged to resist by force any attempt to enforce its laws or to collect taxes. A few days later the federal district court met at Dutch Henry's Crossing and the free-state settlers made inquiry whether the court intended to enforce the territorial laws. Judge Cato declined to answer such questions, and in reply the settlers presented him with a copy of the Osawatomie resolutions. The incident passed off, apparently without any untoward results.

In northeast Kansas, in contrast to southeast Kansas, there were disturbances that resulted in loss of life. As a result of the elec-

tion of free-state officers set for January 15 a free-state man, R. P
Brown, was murdered near Leavenworth.   The Rev. Pardee Butler
was tarred and cottoned at Atchison on May 2.   But the principal
disturbances centered around Lawrence.   Sheriff Jones had tried
to serve warrants in Lawrence, especially to arrest S. N. Wood,
one of the Branson rescuers.   He had arrested Wood, who escaped,
and later Jones was roughly handled by Lawrence men who indulged in the amusement of sheriff-baiting.   Jones had appealed
for federal troops and on April 23 made some arrests with their
support.   At night in camp he was shot, but not killed, by an unknown person.   The responsibility rested heavily upon Lawrence,
however, and a public meeting was called which repudiated the
would-be assassin.   One incident led to another.   The federal court
met the first week in May and indicted the outstanding free-state
leaders for treason or for conspiracy or for usurpation of office.
The excitement culminated in the "sack" of Lawrence by a pro-
slavery mob under Jones on May 21.

During the growing tension at Lawrence, communications were
kept open with other parts of the territory.   In a letter to Charles
Foster, dated May 9, 1856, L. P. Hanscom, a clerk of the congressional committee investigating Kansas affairs wrote that "the Lawrence men are determined and resolute and will make no attack
themselves but will defend themselves." [2]   When the threat of attack was imminent, messengers were sent to different parts of the
territory calling for help.   In response to such calls, the free-state
men of Osawatomie, the Potawatomie creek and the Brown settlements on Middle creek set out toward Lawrence.   John Brown, Jr.,
was in command of the Potawatomie Rifles and was recognized,
formally or informally, as leader of all the forces converging on
Lawrence from that direction.   Near the crossing of the Marais
des Cygnes a messenger met them reporting the destruction of Lawrence, and near Prairie City another brought instructions not to
proceed further as the federal troops were in control at Lawrence
and food was scarce.   The men of Brown's command camped near
Prairie City and later at Palmyra, near by, during May 23, 24
and 25.

On Friday afternoon, May 23, John Brown, Sr., with five sons
and two other men, started back toward Potawatomie creek on an
unknown mission.   The remainder of the expedition did not start
until Sunday afternoon, when a federal army officer found them

2 *Charles Foster Papers*, K. S. H. S.

south of Palmyra and ordered them to disperse. Sunday night was spent at Ottawa Jones's on Ottawa creek, and during the night John Brown, Sr., and his party rejoined the expedition.

In the meantime, news came from the vicinity of Dutch Henry's Crossing on Potawatomie creek that five pro-slavery men had been called out of their cabins on Saturday night and murdered with swords; Doyle and two minor sons, Wilkinson and William Sherman. On Monday morning, after the arrival of the elder Brown, men in the camp recognized one or more horses belonging to the murdered pro-slavery men. There is a dispute concerning much of what happened in the camp that morning, but John Brown, Jr., resigned the command and H. H. Williams was chosen in his place.

After crossing Middle creek, the elder John Brown turned off from the main road toward the Brown claims, but the younger John and his brother Jason, to whom the claims and cabins belonged, went with the Osawatomie contingent as far as Adair's house just outside of the town. They found the country in turmoil as a result of the murders. The settlers in the vicinity of the murders held an indignation meeting and denounced the murderers, and pledged their united support, regardless of party, in bringing them to justice. Suspicion was directed at the Browns, and John and Jason, the innocent ones, were arrested, together with a number of other men, all of whom were soon released except the younger John Brown and H. H. Williams, who were held in the prison camp near Lecompton until September.

Captain Pate leading a pro-slavery band, crossed over from Missouri into Kansas in search of John Brown. They met at Black Jack on June 2 where Pate was captured by Brown and Captain Shore of Prairie City. At this time the federal troops intervened in the southeast, disbanded the armed forces ranging the country and restored a semblance of peace during June. The returning Missouri forces had taken the opportunity, however, to raid Osawatomie on June 7 and free-state forces raided the pro-slavery towns of Franklin, St. Bernard and other places.

Relative quiet reigned until August when the so-called Lane army of the north was about to enter Kansas. Whether this was a cause or just an excuse, it became a signal for renewal of warlike operations. The free-state men raided the camp of Georgians August 8, the house of Martin White August 13, Franklin again on August 12, Ft. Saunders August 15 and Ft. Titus August 16. Colonel Harvey raided the county west of Leavenworth, Lane threatened Lecompton, and finally Colonel Harvey captured the pro-slavery stronghold at Hickory Point and in turn his force was captured by the federal troops. The reentry of the federal troops in the territorial disturbances was occasioned by the arrival of Governor Geary early in September and he set about to restore order.

John Brown's whereabouts were unknown during much of the summer. He had been in the vicinity of Topeka when the free-state legislature had been dispersed by the federal troops July 4, but later had gone northward into Nebraska. He returned with Lane in August and toward the end of the month was in the vicinity of Osawatomie, where on August 30 he was one of the defenders of that town in the famous battle of Osawatomie. The free-state men were defeated and the town burned. He spent part of the second week of September in Lawrence being present during the third Missouri raid on that place September 14–15. By October 10 he was at Tabor, Iowa, his sojourn in Kansas being at an end for the year 1856.

The six months, April to September inclusive, cover the period of John Brown's activity around which most of the controversy centers. Was he present at the Potawatomie massacre? If not, did he command the expedition which did the killing? If in command, did Brown order others to do the killing? Did Brown participate with his own hand in the killing?

What motive lay behind the massacre? Was it retaliation against pro-slavery aggression in general, that is, Leavenworth, Lawrence and other places? Was it retaliation for particular outrages already committed in the Potawatomie creek district? Were there insults or threats made by pro-slavery men against free-state women? Was it a case of striking in anticipation of aggression known to have been planned, but not yet executed by pro-slavery men? Were the men killed agents or spies of the border ruffians? Was the killing a means of taking advantage of the disorders to cover up a horse and cattle theft ring? At one time or another all of these motives have been alleged, even though certain of them are clearly contradictory.

If any of these motives were correct, why did the expedition under John Brown, Jr., leave its own neighborhood for the assistance of Lawrence, or if it was thought necessary for some to go, why was no organized guard left to protect the communities. One line of defense was that John Brown knew of the danger before the expedition left and decided to strike first. The other view was that a messenger followed closely upon the departed expedition with news of danger and as a result the elder Brown decided to return. But if such news arrived, why did the main expedition go on and loiter around Palmyra for nearly three days after Lawrence requested them not to continue to that place, and why did the elder Brown rejoin the expedition leaving the country behind in commotion? If there was such a messenger, who was he and why did he not come forward to testify specifically to the startling information he carried which would justify the Potawatomie massacre? If a justification existed why was the mission of the elder Brown shrouded in such secrecy and why did Brown and most of his associates refuse to admit complicity until after full exposure compelled the surviving members of the party to confess to certain things? And why, even in the belated confessions, did they still evade everything except what exposure compelled them to admit, and even in that to try to shield themselves by shifting responsibility or by alleging motives that were false?

The controversy extended to the matter of results, because most of the allegations with regard to motives turned upon the principle that the end justified the means. Did the punishment of pro-slavery men on the Potawatomie put an end to outrages and war in southeast Kansas, either in the form of private action or in the form of organized invasion under the disguise of official action? There can be no question that the immediate effect was the over-running of southeast Kansas by pro-slavery forces, one of which was under Captain Pate, whose objective was the capture of John Brown, and which resulted in the battle of Black Jack. Who was the hero of Black Jack, Brown or Captain Shore, or were they entitled to share the honors equally? Were there any honors to be divided? Brown was a fugitive charged with murder and fought to escape capture and not to defend the Potawatomie or any other district from invasion. Captain Shore was on his home ground fighting the invader. Without the Potawatomie massacre would there have been any pro-slavery invasion, any Black Jack, and subsequently, any sacking of Osawatomie in June by returning Missourians dispersed by federal troops? Exactly where did John Brown's heroism enter, if at all?

It is quite certain that John Brown and his guerilla band spent most of the summer living off the country, but what Kansas outrages were chargeable to them? Exactly where and how did they operate? Why did Brown leave Kansas in July? Was he disposing of stolen property? Did he intend to leave Kansas? Why did he return in August? What did he intend to do with the livestock stolen in August and concentrated at Osawatomie and divided between himself and Cline the day before the battle of Osawatomie? When and why did he decide to leave Kansas and return East? How and when did the plan develop in his mind to solicit support there for his Kansas work? Is it possible there is significance to Ruth's letter of July 20 referring to Gerrit Smith's plan to finance a company of one thousand?

What did John Brown leave in Kansas? Did he leave an armed organization to carry on the "Kansas work"? In the hands of J. H. Holmes, or others? Were his organizations and methods continued by others on their own initiative, in the same and in other parts of the territory? Did he set precedents or follow precedents of others? Or are later developments and similarities of procedures during the winter of 1856–57 and in the southeast Kansas war of '57–'59 merely coincidence?

CHAPTER III

THE LOCAL PRO–SLAVERY PRESS; EARLY 1856

INTRODUCTION

The history of the Kansas question has been so completely over-laid with propaganda that it is only with great difficulty and at the expense of some tediousness that the historian can reconstruct even an approximate picture of the contemporary scene. If one were excavating the ruins of an unknown civilization, it would be necessary only to present the findings, but in this case the eradi-cation of misunderstanding, misrepresentation and falsehood must be done before reconstruction is possible, and even then the histor-ian is not always certain that he has accomplished his purpose. The period may be presented as a whole, weaving the national and local aspects together, but with the danger that the particular prob-lem of Brown will be lost in the process. On the other hand, the narrative may be focused on the man John Brown, but that leaves Brown not only unexplained, it renders the Brown problem unex-plainable. The setting must be presented in greater fullness than is usually considered desirable in biography, yet the details of the personal picture must be incorporated.

The particular plan of procedure adopted for this section of the book is to look first at John Brown and the Kansas Civil War of 1856 through the eyes of contemporaries. In historical work it is often essential to know as exactly as possible what certain people knew at any particular time, or to what information they had ac-cess in forming opinions and in making decisions. Most people read only one newspaper or group of papers, and presumably only those which reflected the view of the political party or faction to which they adhered. For convenience of treatment, the year 1856–1857, from spring to spring, is divided by the temporary summer peace into two parts. In each period each party to the conflict is permitted to tell its side of the story as it was made public through the press; the pro-slavery (law-and-order) party, the free-state party, the territorial officials,[1] and lastly a survey is made of por-

---

[1] The territorial officers saw fit to suppress documents, some of which are now available, and there are many other manuscript records accessible, but they

31

tions of the Eastern press. In the chapter on the Eastern press the New York *Tribune* is treated separately because it occupied so prominent a position in forming public opinion in a great portion of the Northern states, as well as in Kansas. The conservative *National Intelligencer* is handled separately also, as a contrast to the radical journalism of the *Tribune*. The final part of this chapter on Eastern opinion is drawn from miscellaneous papers both North and South. Fortunately for this method of procedure, Webb of the New England Emigrant Aid Company maintained an elaborate clipping bureau on the Kansas problem which covered the year 1856 as far as September. It is convenient for the present author, and it is significant from the standpoint of reconstructing 1856, to know that here is a body of information to which Webb and his associates had access continuously as the situation developed. Whether or not they used it, the New England Emigrant Aid group at Boston possessed an unusually wide range of information reflecting the views of all factions, politically and all sections, geographically.[2]

Although this handling of the materials entails some repetition, the advantages are unmistakable, because in so bitter a controversy as the Kansas troubles, there is no such thing as the ideal of abstract, absolute truth. Each faction, or even each individual, had a measure of truth on his side, because truth was relative and was conditioned by the interests and position each occupied in the world in which he lived.

Some attention must be given to the problem of the handling of the news in 1856. Partly the procedures were inherent in conditions of the time, but to some extent, not always determinable, they were an aspect of the technic of propaganda, which has been neglected almost altogether in dealing with the anti-slavery movement historically. Kansas had an unusually large number of newspapers, although only a limited number of them have been preserved in continuous files, if at all. The two leading free-state papers in 1856 were published at Lawrence until May when they were destroyed by a pro-slavery mob. A third, the *Kansas Tribune* was issued from Topeka. The *Herald of Freedom,* allied with the

are reserved from the treatment at this place because they did not represent contemporary public knowledge.

[2] The most serious defect in the plan outlined above is that continuous files of one or more national democratic administration papers have not been available for the present study.

New England Emigrant Aid Company in its early history resumed publication November 1, 1856, but the *Kansas Free State* was not revived until late the following year. This left the free-state movement at Lawrence without a satisfactory local press at the time most critical to the problem of John Brown in 1856. On the pro-slavery side, the Lecompton *Union*, established at the territorial capitol during the spring of 1856, is represented by incomplete files. The Leavenworth *Kansas Weekly Herald* has been preserved and occupied a position of importance among its contemporaries. The files of the Atchison *Squatter Sovereign*, a radical sheet, are available also. The conservative democratic Kansas City (Missouri) *Enterprise* presented the reaction to territorial problems of the pro-slavery commercial as distinguished from the agricultural interest. The papers published in Westport and Independence and in southeastern Kansas are all missing. That is particularly serious because those papers covered more specifically the area of Brown's activities. All the papers, whether free-state or pro-slavery, were strongly partisan, and their control from behind the scene is not always clear. There was a dearth of news in territorial Kansas, and no agencies existed by which news could be gathered regularly outside the local community. As a result, the editors frequently resorted to unusual means to fill up space. For news from outside their communities, they made liberal use of clippings from other papers. In this manner within about a month of the event many of the more important stories had made the rounds of the press of the territory. On the pro-slavery side, the Westport *Border Times* and the Lecompton *Union* were active news gatherers and were largely drawn upon by their contemporaries. The reader of the press of 1856 is impressed especially with the rapidity with which rumor seems to have spread by word of mouth, and the slowness with which events were recorded in print. By the time the facts arrived, if they came at all, the impression was already firmly fixed in the public mind by the rumor interpreted according to factional and individual prejudices. A specific point can be cited as an illustration. Writing from near Osawatomie June 27, 1856 a settler wrote his family in the East that "When Lawrence was sacked, we heard the same account as you first got, but the subsequent accounts came correctly. And when they came to be printed they seem like accounts of different events." [3]

[3] *Everett Papers.* K. S. H. S. *Kansas Historical Quarterly*, 8 (February 1939) 33.

The Eastern press gathered its news primarily by two methods, the special correspondent and clippings from other papers. The New York *Tribune* had the largest staff of special correspondents in Kansas and, most of them being actively engaged in the partisan strife, wrote accordingly. The *National Intelligencer* (Washington, D. C.,) on the other hand, had no correspondents, but depended altogether upon exchanges for Kansas news. In contrast with the twentieth century, there were no non-partisan press associations which gathered and verified news for news' sake. The telegraph was coming into use as an important medium for the transmission of news, but the chief reliance was still upon the mail. This had a far-reaching effect upon newspaper composition. Brief telegraphic notices of events arrived from Kansas within a few days, while the full accounts by mail did not arrive for two weeks to two months. This time lag was confusing and it is important to the interpretation of the press for historical purposes. Telegraphic reports might be published in the same column with mail correspondence as much as two months old. Before an old episode had been completed by mail reports, a wholly new situation was being reported by telegraph. A reader could not, if he would, preserve a clear-cut sense of continuity of developments. There is reason to believe also that editors sometimes did not wish to keep clear these time distinctions.

Before proceeding further with this chapter, one other matter should be considered. There is a tendency among historians as well as readers to feel an obligation to decide who was the aggressor in the slavery controversy. Much energy and good feeling have been dissipated in such efforts without arriving at any conclusions satisfying to any one else. In this study nothing of the sort is attempted. The conflict developed out of so complicated a course of events and over so long a period of time that it is futile to assume that there is such a thing as an initial aggressive act. In both North and South most all divergent points of view were represented and it is manifestly unhistorical to pit the two sections against each other as though they were units. The conflict involved so complex an interaction of personalities and forces within each so-called section, as well as between them, that there could be no such thing as an aggressor section.

The first part of the year 1856 ran through three phases. From mid-December of 1855, the Wakarusa war settlement, to April 19, 1856 peace predominated, although there were sporadic disorders.

The destruction of the free-state *Territorial Register* at Leavenworth in December and the seizure of arms at Lexington, Missouri
in May were both chargeable to the pro-slavery side. The murder
of R. P. Brown near Easton in connection with the election of January 17 was generally charged to the pro-slavery party, but whether
the responsibility properly rests on that side may be open to question. On the other side, in January near Lecompton, the free-
state party made attacks upon Clarke, who was accused of the
murder of Barber, and in February raided the country near Easton on the excuse of protecting free-state settlers from the border
ruffians who had murlered R. P. Brown. The second phase was
one of agitation and civil war opening with the steps taken by the
territorial government to enforce the laws, especially through judicial processes. The third phase was one of peace established and
maintained during June and July by force of the United States
regular army.

THE PRO-SLAVERY PRESS IN KANSAS

During the last part of December 1855 and a considerable part
of January 1856 the local pro-slavery press was occupied largely
with controversy over the Wakarusa peace. The Leavenworth
Herald was incensed over the claim of the *Herald of Freedom* that
the town of Lawrence had made the settlement in the interest of
peace, because their gallant soldiers could not longer be restrained.
The Leavenworth *Herald* version was that "while the trembling
traitors were cooped up in that hole of iniquity [Lawrence] . . .
supplicating committees were sent to the Governor's camp, stating
that the people in Lawrence were willing and ready to conform to
all reasonable requests of the Executive, promising to yield up all
offenders of the law who might be found in their midst, and hereafter to obey and respect the laws." Some thought they had repented, while others thought they were merely trying to save themselves, but the *Herald* concluded that "the credulity and kindly
feeling of the Governor prevailed, and these outlaws were spared."
The correspondent of the *Missouri Republican* (St. Louis), quoted
in the same issue, was somewhat more charitable, expressing the
opinion that there were some good citizens in Lawrence as well as
bad ones who were always agitating and keeping the place in commotion. He reported, however, that "they agreed and bound
themselves to abide by the laws, and assist in enforcing them, until

such time as the Supreme Court decided the legality of the Legislature. . . ."[4] The *Herald* explained the raid on the *Territorial
Register*, destroyed on December 22, as the result of several "in-
flammable and abusive articles" in its last issues, one of which
charged that the militia had gone to "raze Lawrence, *Ravish* the
women, and kill the children."[5] The charge was made further
that after this, and because of fear of the consequences, the ownership of the paper was transferred. The *Herald* of January 12 reviewed the rescue of Branson from Sheriff Jones and the killing of
Barber a few days later to prove that they were free-state outrages,
and reported a new attack of the Lawrence "outlaws" who had
turned to attempts at mid-night assassination of Major Clarke near
Lecompton. Sheriff Jones was reported also to have received an
anonymous note from Lawrence threatening to kill him if he undertook to arrest another man in Lawrence. The account of the letter concluded, however, that "such dastardly threats as this will
never intimidate Sheriff Jones. But it is characteristic of Yankee
Abolitionists." The same issue presented exchanges from the Boston *Post* and the New York *Journal of Commerce*, both national
democratic papers, defending the legality of the territorial legislature. They pointed out that in spite of irregularities in the election of some members, with few exceptions they had received their
certificates of election from Reeder who had given them official
recognition. If the legislature was once legal, they argued, it was
still legal.

An exchange from the *Georgia Southern* expressed the conviction that the subject of slavery would inevitably lead to civil war,
and that it had better come now in Kansas than fifty years later in
Virginia. A week later the *Herald* copied a paragraph from the
Lawrence *Herald of Freedom*: "Come one! come all! Slavocrats
and nullifiers; we have rifles enough, and bullets enough, to send
you all to your (and Judas's) 'own place.' " The *Herald* called
to the South, "Do you hear that Southern men? Can you resist
the invitation [and will you] quietly submit?" A report was
made at the same time of the escaped free-state murderer, Cole Mc-
Crea, who was lecturing in northern cities on the Kansas outrages.[6]
This was followed shortly afterwards with an item reporting that
the "Abolitionists" had sent a committee North to deal out lies and

[4] Leavenworth *Herald*, January 5, 1856.
[5] Leavenworth *Herald*.
[6] Leavenworth *Herald*, January 19, 1856.

slanders. Again it warned: "People of the South, do you hear that? The crisis is at hand . . . Kansas must, yea *shall* be a slave state."[7] The inconsistency of the free-state party was emphasized by pointing out that they denounced the Missourians for assisting the governor in suppressing revolution, and at the same time sent to Iowa and Illinois for fighting men. "But we are told," the *Herald* said, "that these men from Iowa and Illinois are to be immigrants . . . [but] it is reasonable to believe that the Missourians who live so convenient, will *emigrate* also, to prevent the scheme of the enemies of their institutions."[8] When Governor Chase addressed the Ohio legislature on the subject of Kansas the *Herald* announced it with the headline "War on Kansas by Ohio."[9] The problem of citizenship was made an issue again in comment on G. W. Brown's statement in his *Herald of Freedom* relative to the vote of Representative John Dick of Pennsylvania in the speakership contest, when Brown said, "He will accept our thanks, as one of his constituents, for that vote. . . ." In other words, the *Herald* argued, Brown admitted that he was still a citizen of Pennsylvania.[10]

The "correct history" of the death of R. P. Brown was related as the result of a fight treacherously forced upon the pro-slavery men.[11] Another free-state scandal was exposed in the *Herald* of February 2 in comment on a *Herald of Freedom* article on the Addis case. Two Lawrence men had a difficulty and one of them, Addis, resorted to the territorial court for redress. Addis was denounced by the *Herald of Freedom* as a recreant free-state man and that paper advised a complete social and economic boycott. The Leavenworth *Herald* stressed this procedure of the Lawrence "outlaws" in coercing all within their control into resistance to the laws. G. W. Brown, the editor of the *Herald of Freedom,* was condemned as one of the chief instigators of resistance, and "he had been shipped out to the territory by the Emigrant Aid Society, is supported and fed by that Society, and he is now doing their treasonable work." The charge was true that he had been financed by the Emigrant Aid Company.

The prolonged controversy over the Wakarusa war treaty was renewed again in the publication of letters of leading participants.

[7] *Leavenworth Herald,* February 9, 1856.
[8] *Leavenworth Herald,* February 23, 1856.
[9] *Leavenworth Herald,* March 1, 1856.
[10] *Leavenworth Herald,* March 1, 1856.
[11] *Leavenworth Herald,* January 26, 1856.

After the war was over the free-state men denied having agreed to submit to the laws. Jones questioned Robinson and Lane in a letter dated January 15, and in their reply the next day they had agreed to assist "any proper officer," and that they would cooperate in the arrest of one Branson rescuer as a means of securing a test of the legality of the legislature before the Supreme Court. Jones restated his inquiry on the same day, asking whether they recognized him as a "proper officer" and whether they would assist in the arrest of any process. Robinson and Lane made no second response, and Jones submitted the documents to the Leavenworth *Herald* together with a letter dated January 23, leaving the public to judge these "hired ruffians or pseudo gentlemen of the Emigrant Aid Society—men who deserve more the gallows or Penitentiary than the liberty of American citizens.[12] Governor Shannon felt he had been misrepresented by the free-state men in connection with the note given Robinson and Lane December 9, 1855, the day after the treaty, authorizing them to take necessary steps for the defense of Lawrence. His formal statement repudiating the free-state interpretation was given to the press. He insisted the note in question was secured under false pretenses, and that it had applied only to an attack on Lawrence which Robinson had misrepresented as threatening that night.[13]

The *Enterprise,* published at Kansas City, Missouri, had a perspective different from the other papers quoted. The town was situated on the south side of the Missouri river just below the elbow where Kansas river joined the larger stream. One of the border towns, it was actively contesting with its rivals, Independence, Westport, and Leavenworth, for the commerce of Kansas and of southwestern Missouri, northwestern Arkansas, the Cherokee country, Santa Fe and Utah. The town had been chartered in 1853 and the *Enterprise* was its aggressive promotion spokesman under the able editorship of R. T. Van Horn, for many years to be identified with the growth of Greater Kansas City and onetime congressman. Its theme song was law and order, rebuking the pro-slavery radicals in the Parkville, Missouri, disorders, and refusing to believe the first sensational news about the Wakarusa war in Kansas. When challenged as to what kind of a democrat it was, the reply was unequivocally that it was national, recognizing neither of the Missouri factions, Atchison or Benton, and that it endorsed the Kansas-Ne-

---

[12] Leavenworth *Herald*, January 26 and February 2, 1856.
[13] Leavenworth *Herald*, February 9, 1856.

braska act.[14]   The abolitionists were denounced as the party of disunion.[15]

The Wakarusa War was treated as a matter of law enforcement, not as a political party matter, and responsibility was placed primarily upon Lane and upon Delahay of the Leavenworth *Register*.[16] Refusing to discuss the merits of the question at issue between the parties, Van Horn declared that "there is but one way for every American citizen to pursue—appeal to law for vindication—always bearing in mind, that one wrong never was righted by the commission of another."[17]   That the paper seems to have been reflecting a substantial body of public opinion in the town is attested by the list of promient business men whose names were associated with public meetings held December 14 and 20 and seven resolutions adopted. They invited pro-slavery men to settle Kansas and to control her future by legitimate means, pledged protection to all law abiding citizens so long as they did not violate hospitality, and declared that all difficulties arising in the territories were exclusively the province of the authorities of the territories and of the general government.[18]

The only consolation the *Enterprise* was able to squeeze out of the Wakarusa war disturbance was that if such a resort to force was necessary it was fortunate that it had come during the season when river and plains trade had retired to winter quarters, and "we trust they will have done by the opening of spring business.   We want to commence work upon the railroads in the spring, and there are numerous improvements to be undertaken and prosecuted at the same time."[19]   Among these other projects were an extension of the wharf, grading of streets leading to the waterfront, a new hotel, a new road up the Kansas river cutting off six miles of distance from the Santa Fe trail.   Every issue of the paper during the winter and spring months gave additional news or restatement of the improvements which would make Kansas City the commercial center of the West.   As the time approached for the opening of both spring immigration and spring trade, a prominent place was given to the mass meeting and resolutions of the Kansas Pioneer Association of Jackson county which pledged financial support to pro-slavery settlers and repudiated any intent of armed resistance.   When Platte

[14] Kansas City *Enterprise*, January 5, 1856, February 2, 1856.
[15] Kansas City *Enterprise*, December 22, 1855, June 7, 1856.
[16] Kansas City *Enterprise*, December 15, 22, 1855.
[17] Kansas City *Enterprise*, December 22, 1855.
[18] Kansas City *Enterprise*, December 15, 22, 1855.
[19] Kansas City *Enterprise*, December 8, 1855.

county to the northward did likewise, the *Enterprise* joined the
Weston *Reporter* in emphatic approval.[20] The opening of navigation on the Missouri was recorded in the *Enterprise* of March 15,
and the arrival of the first Santa Fe train April 12. Kansas City
was prepared for what it hoped would be its biggest commercial
season and the establishment of supremacy over its nearby rivals.

As the date approached, the plan of launching the Topeka free-
state government on March 4 assumed importance as a topic of discussion. In commenting on the candidates for offices in that organization the *Herald* singled out P. E. Schuyler of New York for
special comment. He had gone on record as advocating negro suffrage and it was thought that other candidates held similar views.
The *Herald* exploded on the subject; "Talk about a Free State! It
is nonsense! The *true* question is a slave state, or an abolition
state."[21] The free-state plans in congress were reported according
to two letters from which excerpts were published.[22] A letter of
S. N. Wood discussing the possibility that neither Reeder nor Whitfield would be seated, but new elections would be ordered, protested
that such a course would plunge the territory into civil war. His
suggestion was for the lower house to pass a bill admitting Kansas,
a bill declaring the territorial laws illegal, and a refusal of all ap-
propriations to support the territorial government. This would
place the free-state party on an equality with the pro-slavery party.
Another letter, unsigned, stated that Kansas wanted martial law to
protect it from the "savages" across the river, and "then let congress wrangle for a year, if it choose." In the same issue the
Leavenworth *Herald* accused the free-state party of laboring to produce civil war in Kansas by violating both United States and territorial laws in setting up the state government:

One abolition humbug follows another so close, that we are led to
exclaim what next? We have witnessed the efforts of the abolitionists to
control this Territory first by fraud, and then by importing voters, and
then by resistance to the laws, but now they actually claim, that their State
Government will go into operation on the 4th of March.[23]

In the issue of the next week the *Herald of Freedom* was quoted
on war preparations to meet the attack planned by Missourians on
the Topeka government, commanders appointed, regiments organized, and forts built, and friends of Kansas in the East might

[20] Kansas City *Enterprise*, March 1, 22, 1856.
[21] Leavenworth *Herald*, January 12, 1856.
[22] Leavenworth *Herald*, February 2, 1856.
[23] Leavenworth *Herald*, February 2, 1856.

and denounced the murderers, and pledged their support, regardless of party, in bringing them to justice. Suspicion was directed at the Browns) and John (Jr) and Jason, the innocent ones were arrested, together with a number of other men, all of whom were soon released except the younger John Brown and H.H. Williams, who were held in the prison camp near Ⓣ Lecompton until September

1856 The six months, April to September, cover the period of John Brown's activity around which most of the controversy centers. Was he present at the Potawatomie massacre? If not, did he command the expedition which did the killing? What motive lay behind the massacre? Was it retaliation against pro-slavery ⚡

When challenged as to what kind of democrat it was, the reply was unequivocally that it was national, recognising fought with musket and ball.

In spite of the struggle for subsistence, the Brown family had time to participate in politics. John Brown, the elder, was chairman of a political convention held at Osawatomie for the purpose of nominating candidates for the Topeka State government. John Brown the younger was elected for the legislature.

On May 23, John Brown, with 5 sons and two other men, started back towards Potawatomie creek on an unknown mission. In the meantime, news came from the vicinity of Dutch Henry's crossing on Potawatomie creek that 5 pro-slavery men had been pulled out of their cabins and murdered. The country was in turmoil. The settlers in

neither of the Missouri factions, Atchison or Benton, and that it endorsed the Kansas-Nebraska act. The abolitionists were denounced as the party of disunion.

As the date approached, the plan of launching the Topeka free-state government on March 4 assumed importance as a topic of discussion. In commenting on the candidates for offices in that organization the "Herald" singled out P.E. Schuyler of New York for special comment. He had gone on record as advocating negro suffrage and it was thought that other candidates held similar views.

expect to hear of the blow being struck. The Leavenworth *Herald* denounced the charge of a Missouri invasion as humbug and as an excuse "for their revolutionary movements and preparations for war."

It was during this agitation that the President issued his proclamation warning all parties, either in or out of the territory, arraying themselves against the laws, preparing to invade the territory, or to ship arms into the territory, to desist. The Leavenworth *Herald* undertook to advise its friends: "In the meantime, we say to our citizens, keep quiet, and on the side of law and order, and we will have the Government on our side to crush out the revolutionary spirit in the Territory." [24]

In response to the President's special Kansas message, a meeting was called at Tecumseh February 13, which was reported to be the largest and most enthusiastic ever held in the territory.[25] Although the meeting was supposed to be irrespective of party, the list of officers and speakers, with one exception, were from the southern states. A committee of five drafted resolutions which were adopted and may be summarized as follows:

1. The tone and policy of the message was approved as affording a fair and honorable basis for quieting conditions in the territory.

2. The President's suggestion was approved that congress enact a resolution authorizing the people at the proper time to frame a state constitution, the meeting recommended that the resolution should be adopted immediately and that it is "most advisable that the preliminary arrangements for admission as a state should take place under the protection and sanction of the general government."

3. The meeting concurred with the President in his view that when a proposed movement, revolutionary in aim, reaches a point of organized resistance, that it is treasonable insurrection.

4. The meeting adhered to the constitutional guarantees of the right of peaceful assembly and petition, but everyone should be held responsible for abuse of that right, and the President was upheld in his determination to enforce the laws.

5. All "true patriots, bona fide settlers and conservative men of all classes" should unite on one platform; "The Supremacy of the Laws— Sovereignty of the people of the Territory and Non-intervention with or from the people of the States."

6. That the proceedings be published.

From the floor General Strickler offered an additional resolution which was adopted:

[24] Leavenworth *Herald*, February 23, 1856.
[25] The full report of the meeting is in the *Squatter Sovereign*, March 4, 1856.

7. An endorsement by the meeting of "the prudent and commendable efforts of Governor Shannon" to maintain peace in the territory.

As reported, the principal speech was made by Edward Hoogland of New York, who was a member of the resolutions committee as well as one of the secretaries of the meeting.   Special interest attaches to his theory of treasonable insurrection:

E. Hoogland being called for said that he considered the message itself a complete epitome of the history of Kansas, and that no speech from him could enforce or make stronger the position of the President. Mr. H. alluded to the anticipated assemblage of the so-called constitutional legislature and protested against it as a party movement, premature in its character and dangerous to the peace of the Territory. He went into a short but succinct argument as to the precise time when "treasonable insurrection and organized resistance by force" against the authority of the United States would begin; and was of the opinion that the taking of an oath to support a constitution and laws which virtually ignored the authority of the Territorial and General Government would be the first overt act, and he was assured that at the proper time the United States authorities would interfere and punish the offenders. Until called upon by the United States authorities it is unnecessary and unadvisable for any of the people of the Territory, or their sympathisers abroad to interfere and attempt any counter movement. Let everything be done coolly and according to law. Uncle Sam is strong and rich enough to protect himself. Mr. H. believed that the message would exert a beneficial influence, not only in the Territory but in the United States, and by the means of maintaining peace and order.

The prediction of the Leavenworth *Herald* was correct that there would be no Missouri invasion of Kansas on March 4, but the free-state agitation was kept up on one pretext or another.   At a free-state meeting in March, Lane presented a resolution that for every free-state man killed, a free-state man should kill the first pro-slavery man he should meet.   This resolution was adopted, and then on reconsideration voted down.   The Leavenworth *Herald* exclaimed March 22, "To what depths of *infamy* Lane and his party would resort to, may be seen from this resolution."   The responsibility for the disturbances was placed again upon the free-state party who was unwilling to see the territory settled by fair and legitimate means. It was pointed out that up to this time the South had remained quiet and only Missouri had taken an active part in resisting the torrent of Northern fanaticism, but now the South as a whole was active.

The *Squatter Sovereign* March 11 reprinted an article from the New York *Day Book* arguing that as the *Tribune* and the *Times* were appealing to the North for money and arms, why not the pro-slavery party,—"This fighting is a game that two can play at . . ." During the next two weeks it pointed to the volume of immigration pouring into the territory from Missouri and the South which would leave few good claims when the Yankees arrived. The recent seizure of one hundred Sharps rifles from New England at Lexington, Missouri was an early indication of what was to come. The *Missouri Democrat* (a republican paper) explained that the rifles belonged to the United States, not to the New England emigrants, but the Leavenworth *Herald* pointed out that Hoyt, the abolitionist, had applied to Governor Shannon for the recovery of the rifles as private property, and demanded who lied? [26]

The trade rivalries of the pro-slavery border towns became involved in the controversies between free-state and pro-slavery factions. Leavenworth was accused of issuing a circular prepared for the purpose of discrediting Kansas City, runners were supposed to be plying the steamboats spreading statements designed to divert trade and immigration from that point, but the climax was reached when representatives from Lexington and Independence ascended the river to Kansas City and there invaded the warehouse of a commission firm and opened a box which was found to contain a piano instead of arms. The papers of Leavenworth, Independence and Lexington were called upon to disavow the act, but they gave no answer.[27]

Another month further convinced the *Squatter Sovereign* that the future control of the territory was settled beyond a doubt [28] and another week brought the organization of the last contingent of South Carolina emigrants into the Palmetto Guards, who were soon to be called from their "claims" for service at Lawrence.

Other means of insuring Southern success were faithfully reported by an announcement that none but pro-slavery settlers were wanted in Atchison county, in fact, abolitionists would not be permitted to remain.[29] The next week an object lesson was given in the case of Pardee Butler. He had first been sent down the river on a raft, but returning he had just been tarred and cottoned, and if he came again, a hemp rope would be used, and it further warned that within six months the families of the recipients of Sharps rifles

[26] Leavenworth *Herald*, March 22, 1856.
[27] *Enterprise*, March 22, 29, April 12, 1856.
[28] *Squatter Sovereign*, April 22, 1856.
[29] *Squatter Sovereign*, April 29, 1856.

would be trading them off for coffins in which to bury those who used them.[30]

It was inevitable that the spring of 1856 should bring a crisis in the affairs of the territory. The legislature of 1856 had enacted a code of laws which the free-state party had declared "bogus" and which they had refused to obey. This situation would have brought the crisis sooner, the Wakarusa war was a forerunner, but the publication of the laws had been delayed until sometime in March 1856.[31] The territorial courts had met for the most part at the appointed times for their fall terms, but in absence of the statutes could perform only limited routine functions. In the meantime business had been accumulating. The holding of the courts for the first time really in the spring of 1856 would inevitably bring the issue of law enforcement to a test. The sessions of the courts as they moved from county to county were incompletely reported in the press. In Atchison county the petit jury was not required and the grand jury returned ten indictments, mostly against abolitionists who had been taking the law into their own hands, as the *Squatter Sovereign* put it. In Doniphan county there were about seventy indictments, mostly for lesser offences. In Atchison county there were no indictments for murder, burglary, arson nor assaults with intent to kill, and yet, the *Squatter Sovereign* remarked, that to read the Eastern papers murders were daily occurrences.[32] When the court sat in Jefferson county during the week ending March 29 "Startling Developments" were reported and testimony before the grand jury was thought to prove that the free-state party had placed itself in opposition to the laws, that the Emigrant Aid Societies gave encouragement, and that "daily" Sharps rifles and cannon were shipped into the territory to be used against the general government and the law-and-order citizens which justified Missouri in detaining all such arms. A free-state man, Dr. A. J. Francis, divulged that an armed organization of the party existed under the command of Lane, sworn to resist the laws, and that during the meeting of the Topeka legislature three military companies paraded daily.[33] The description of this organization was similar to that given by Pat Laughlin the previous October.[34] "The Grand Jury

[30] *Squatter Sovereign*, May 6, 1856.

[31] Leavenworth *K. W. Herald*, January 12 and March 22, 1856.

[32] *Squatter Sovereign*, March 18, 1856.

[33] *Squatter Sovereign*, April 1, 1856. The text of the Francis testimony is printed in *Collections*, K. S. H. S., 4: 411–412.

[34] Leavenworth *Herald*, April 5, 1856.

found sixty indictments,'' characterized by the *Squatter Sovereign*
as mostly against the abolitionists for hog-stealing, higher-law elections, treason, and other crimes.''

The most significant part of the account of the court at Ozawkie
was the following:

> During the sitting of the Court, there was a company mustering about
> four miles from Grashopper Falls, in a very secluded and remote hollow,
> by the euphonious title of 'Granny's Hollow.' The free soilers threatened
> hourly to break up the Court by violence, but the fine bearing and deter-
> mination of his Honor, Judge Lecompte, deterred the armed perjurors
> from carrying into effect their damnable designs. It was testified before
> the Court that the company then drilling, were, when fully organized, to
> take the vote whether they should resist all process issued against them.
> If so decided, each man was bound by oath to resist its execution to the
> bloody end, and to be always fully armed, and that the condition of getting
> Sharps rifles from the Emigrant Aid Societies, was in consideration of
> their using them against any execution of the laws.
>
> The late Grand-General of the rebels—Hutchinson—was sent for to
> defend one of his brother traitors, who was indicted. This man whom
> Beecher styles the "immaculate," added perjury to his other crimes. He
> was sworn as an Attorney to support the fugitive slave law, the Nebraska
> bill, and the laws of the Territory of Kansas, notwithstanding his former
> oath to disobey and resist them. The efficient Grand Jury required his at-
> tendance, and he refused to testify, because he would implicate himself by
> his testimony. The question was submitted to the Court, and the Court
> decided Hutchinson should answer. Seeing the gallows staring him in the
> face, he quietly, but very hastily, made tracks for part unknown, on a fleet
> horse—perhaps to join his confreres, Robinson and Lane. . . .[35]

These events formed the setting for the attempt of Sheriff Jones
to arrest S. N. Wood at Lawrence on April 19. Wood was the leader
of the Branson rescuers and had just returned from Ohio where he
had been lecturing and had brought with him a large party of immigrants. Jones made his appearance in Lawrence with a warrant
charging larceny as well as one based upon the Branson affair.
Wood resisted arrest, the mob intervened, and Jones left town without his prisoner. He summoned a civil posse of four men and returned the next morning, but again the mob intervened, individuals
refused to assist in the arrest when called upon, the mob refused to
recognize his office or the territorial laws, and he was threatened
with death if he arrested anyone in Lawrence. Jones then applied
to the governor for assistance and a detachment of United States
troops were detailed under command of Lieutenant McIntosh.

[35] *Squatter Sovereign*, April 1, 1856.

The issues involved, as seen by pro-slavery men at Lecompton, have been recorded by H. C. Pate on April 22:

There is much speculation what the Lawrence rebels will do: the writs of arrest will be in the hands of the Sheriff of Douglas county, who will be supported by the United States troops. The question is, will they resist? They have always been willing to submit to the authorities of the General Government, and if the writs were to be served by the Marshall of the U. S., there would of course be no resistance. But in submitting to arrest by Jones, they are submitting to the Territorial laws of Kansas passed by what is called the 'bogus legislature.' So that we just speculate, and then speculate again.[36]

Pate's story presents a nice historical question. Who was responsible for the decision that the issue of law enforcement in Lawrence would be joined at this particular time and on the Jones-Wood matter? It would seem to have been a decision deliberately adopted, as Pate stated clearly the alternative course which would have evaded the test, but which would have vindicated the law, in having the arrest made by the United States marshal.

Jones appeared at Lawrence April 23 escorted by the federal troops, according to schedule, and made six arrests, all without resistance but with demonstrations of open hostility toward the sheriff. S. N. Wood could not be found. Jones prepared to spend the night under the protection of the troops. During the early evening he and McIntosh went for a drink and were shot at, the bullet passing through Jones's trousers. Later the same night, while sitting in a tent, Jones was shot, the bullet lodging in his back. McIntosh sent a messenger for reinforcements. The next morning the citizens of Lawrence called a mass meeting, at which Robinson and Reeder spoke, and resolutions were passed denouncing the crime, declaring it to be an act of an individual, and pledging cooperation in bringing him to justice. At first, Jones was reported killed, but the wound did not prove serious. Writing on April 24, Pate reported:

There is profound excitement here. The occurrence has produced a deep feeling of antipathy to Lawrence, and nothing but the love of law and order, with which our party is imbued, will save the place from utter annihilation. If the prominent men of Lawrence promptly disavow the base deed, and the murderer is given up—for they know him—then the excitement may be stayed.

He indicated that Jones had a claim near Lecompton and had lived

[36] St. Louis *Republican,* April 30, 1856.

there for two years. Pate reported that he himself had taken a claim.[37]

A mass meeting assembled at Lecompton April 25, at which the pro-slavery view of the Jones affair was presented, and a committee was appointed to prepare and publish a statment of facts. The committee argued that the recent immigration, especially S. N. Wood's party, was really a paid army bound to obedience to the leaders, Robinson, Reeder & Company in the same manner as Kansas Regulators, recently exposed, and that during the period of absence of these leaders there had been peace and obedience. The speeches made at the Lawrence meeting had counseled continuance of resistance to the laws, and the resolutions adopted there were interpreted as not condemning the assassination of Jones, but denouncing only the manner in which it was done. The resolutions prepared by the Lecompton committee declared that the purpose of the Lawrence meeting had been to deceive the public regarding the midnight assassination of Sheriff Jones, that the committee recognized the right of citizens to test the validity of the law in the courts, but that law-abiding people would limit their resistance to the laws to peaceable methods.[38]

The *Squatter Sovereign* reported "the Abolitionists in open rebellion—Sheriff Jones murdered by the traitors . . . —shot down by the thieving-paupers . . . who are shipped to Kansas to infringe upon the rights of Southern settlers—murder them when opportunity offers—steal their property, and if possible, to raise a storm that will cease only with the Union itself. . . . We are not prepared to hear of such lamentable news—the death of the patriot Jones. HE MUST BE AVENGED. HIS MURDER SHALL BE AVENGED, if at the sacrifice of every abolitionist in the Territory." The editor asked if they should allow a northern governor to cheat them again; "We are now in favor of levelling Lawrence, and chastizing the Traitors there congregated, should it result in the total destruction of the Union." [39]

When the news arrived in Kansas City of the resistance of S. N. Wood, the *Enterprise* branded him as the chief instigator of the

[37] St. Louis *Republican*, April 30, 1856.

[38] Leavenworth *Herald*, May 3, 1856 from the Lecompton *Union*.

[39] *Squatter Sovereign*, April 29, 1856. Several articles in this issue were devoted to the Kansas troubles, as well as several in the issue of May 6, one of which advised: "When a pro-slavery man gets into a difficulty with an abolitionist, let him think of the murdered Jones and Clark, and govern himself accordingly—let not such cowardly murders go unavenged. . . ."

Wakarusa war, and maintained that free-state men dispised him, while many abolitionists disowned him. Authentic details were not at hand, but the editor hoped that Missouri would not be drawn in, the plan being, according to his interpretation, to exasperate pro-slavery men into some recrimination while the congressional committee was in the territory. When the later news of the shooting of Jones arrived the real responsibility was not placed upon the individual who had fired the shot, but upon those who for the past nine months had been preaching resistance to law; Lane, Robinson, Reeder, Delahay, the Topeka convention and legislature. The *Enterprise* felt that the pro-slavery cause was won, and appealed to Missouri and to pro-slavery men in Kansas to do nothing to alienate public opinion.[40]

Ominous warnings of resistance came to the capitol from the second judicial district (southern Kansas), Judge Cato, and were reported in the press as follows:

News has just been received, at this office, through a private letter, that Judge S. G. Cato, (an Associate Justice of the Supreme Court of Kansas, who is now canvassing his district) was threatened by an armed force of fifty men, *in full uniform*, provided he tried to enforce the laws.—The circumstances are these: Judge Cato, after empannelling his jury, proceeded to charge them, when a *notorious* scoundrel, who has figured largely in Lawrence and other places, presented himself and interrupted the Court with written interrogatories. The Judge immediately ordered him out for contempt of Court. He was absent about an hour, when he again entered in full uniform at the head of fifty others, armed with Sharps rifles. He emphatically told the Judge, if he attempted to enforce the laws, they would resist 'unto death.'

Every fair wind that sweeps over our prairie hills brings us similar news of these rebellious movements. What shall we do? . . .

Our rights are denied us,—our laws are treated with scornful contempt—our property at the mercy of base incendiaries—our lives balancing upon the pointed blade of midnight assassins. Must every man place a guard about his house to protect his distressed wife and sleeping babes, and dare not pass beyond the rounds of that guard or be shot down in cold blood. . . . We repeat, must we act, as become men, . . . or must we bow our heads and march in one body to the air of submission, up to the axeman's block? . . .

Methinks I hear some, too dilatory man, say beware! beware! Make no step in the dark—consequences are dreadful.—Hush that damnable sound, for it has already hissed too long in our ears. . . . We have submitted, we have compromised, till we have almost mortgaged every principle, every honor, every right. . . .

40 *Enterprise*, April 26, May 3, 1856.

It must come, and the sooner the better. Gentlemen need not try to deny it. *The blow must be struck.*[41]

The unnamed "notorious scoundrel" of the above letter was John Brown, Jr., and although there are differences in details and interpretations the story was based upon an episode which occurred at Dutch Henry's Crossing April 21, but it was pure coincidence that the "blade of the midnight assassin" in the hands of his father's gang struck on May 24, the day the Leavenworth *Herald* published the above report.

A few days later, May 5, the United States District Court, Judge Lecompte's division, met at Lecompton to hold the spring term of court for Douglas county. The judge's charge to the grand jury had been variously interpreted, but the pro-slavery view emphasized that it required no little nerve, under the circumstances, to impress the jury with its responsibilities, but that

Judge Lecompte knew his duty, and, as an able, fearless and resolute jurist, he discharged that duty. He called the attention of the Jury to the rebellious and treasonable spirit now prevalent in our Territory, and referred to the foul assassination of a public officer, while in the discharge of his official functions. He spoke of the attempt on the part of men here to establish an independent Government, in opposition to the present existing one—also to assume offices of public trust, without due authority, and many other criminal offences committed in our midst. . . . Judge Lecompte's manner during the charge was firm, dignified and impressive. Occasionally, whilst recurring to the many outrages upon life and law, he grew warm and eloquent. . . .

At the close of this account of the judge's charge, the editor promised "to keep our friends posted, as this is an important court, upon the present crisis of affairs." [42]

Among the witnesses summoned to testify before the grand jury was A. H. Reeder, and as he ignored the summons, an attachment was issued May 8 for contempt of court. Deputy Marshal W. P. Fain served it the same day, and Reeder, who was at Lawrence in the rooms where the congressional committee on Kansas troubles was sitting, refused to obey, claiming exemption from arrest on ground of his status as delegate to congress. The two Northern members of the congressional committee upheld Reeder, who warned Fain that if he made the arrest, he did so at his peril. The deputy

[41] Lecompton *Union*, May 3, quoted in the Leavenworth *Herald*, May 24, 1856.

[42] Lecompton *Union*, quoted in the New Orleans *Daily Picayune*, May 7, 1856. The clipping is in Webb, *Scrapbooks*, 12: 59.

marshal retired. The Lecompton *Union* reported the episode with sensational headlines: "Reeder threatens the Marshal's life." It should be noted that in this case the free-state leaders had taken a new step, according to the distinctions made in the Jones case, because Fain was not a territorial officer, he was an officer of the United States. The issue which developed between the marshal and the town of Lawrence and ended in the so-called "sack" on May 21 was joined, not on the question of the "bogus laws" but on the authority of a federal court created by congress.

The congressional committee mentioned in the above article was adding many complications to the already impossible situation. The anti-slavery majority in the federal house of representatives had voted an investigation into the Kansas troubles by a committee of three. They had arrived late in April, the two anti-slavery members, Howard of Michigan and Sherman of Ohio, cooperating with the local free-state leaders, and Oliver of Missouri with the pro-slavery men. Whitfield, the Kansas territorial delegate, had returned to observe the course of events. The Lecompton *Union* in reporting the Reeder affair, emphasized the agency of the committee:

> This uncalled for, unauthorized interference, on the part of the committee, will no doubt involve Kansas in war. . . . Messrs. Howard and Sherman, this day, we assert, that you have declared war in Kansas. . . . Sirs, you have disgraced your commission—you have sacrificed your honor, and stand accused of a foul crime before your country. *Let the nation pronounce your sentence.*[43]

Judge Lecompte's court proceeded with the program indicated in the charge to the grand jury, returning indictments for usurpation of office, and more important, on May 20 indictments for treason against Reeder, Robinson, Lane, G. W. Brown, Deitzler, G. W. Smith, Wood and Gais Jenkins. In order to serve the warrants United States Marshal Donalson issued a proclamation May 11 calling a posse. The reaction of the *Squatter Sovereign* was in the usual vein: "By the proclamation subjoined, it will be seen that the seditious fanatics of the cracked-brain town of Lawrence have offered resistance to the authorities of the United States." It reported that already the citizens had responded and there was anxiety about the result, as a fight was certain unless the "cowards succumb," but "even this should not save them. Hang the leaders and give their blind and bigotted followers a stated time to

[43] *Squatter Sovereign*, May 20, 1856, from the Lecompton *Union*, May 8.

leave, and then let the law and order men stay on the ground until the last hound is outside the bounds of Kansas."[44] In the same issue a paragraph announced that Robinson and Reeder "Took leg bail. . . . What a commentary upon the valor of the Free State army." Robinson was arrested in Missouri May 10, and in announcing it, the recommendation was made that "These amiable traitors . . . should now be punished to the full extent of the law; and as the price of hemp is down, it would perhaps conduce to the interests of the raisers of that article if some of it were used on them."[45] Under the conditions of public excitement, pro-slavery sympathizers from various parts of the territory and from western Missouri moved toward Lecompton to have a hand in the humbling of the "Abolition Hell-Hole." The Lawrence committee protested that the marshal had not been resisted at that place and appeals were made, without avail, to the marshal, to Governor Shannon, and to Colonel Sumner, the commander of the federal troops. On May 21 the marshal presented himself at Lawrence where his deputy made arrests and then, withdrawing his posse some distance from the town, disbanded them. The sequel was reported by the Lecompton *Union,* May 24. Jones then called the same men to act as his posse, as he had a great many writs in his hands, "but could find no one against whom he held them. He also had an order from the Court to demand the surrender of their arms, field and side, and a demolition of the two presses and the Free State hotel as nuisances." According to the *Union,* Jones's instructions to his men were definite, they were not to injure private property, and therefore regret was expressed that the house of Robinson was burned. Twice the fire was put out, it was claimed, but the third time the building was destroyed.[46]

The Weston, Missouri *Argus* emphasized that:

[44] *Squatter Sovereign,* May 13, 1856.

[45] *Squatter Sovereign,* May 13, 1856.

[46] The claim was false that Jones was acting under orders of the court in the destruction of the presses and hotel, and it was well known at the time, but the pro-slavery party needed some show of justification for the act of Jones's mob. Without realizing it, they played into the hands of the free-state party, which welcomed the opportunity to fasten the responsibility for the outrage upon the administration at Washington during a presidential campaign, and provided them with a pretense of right for claims against the United States for damages. Regardless of the lack of truth in the allegations, the propaganda value of both points was great, and so long as it was effective the ethics of the matter did not bother the consciences of these reformers.

all [was done] in a quiet and orderly way. Attempts were made to pull down some other houses, but Sheriff Jones would object, and the men then desisted. Jones's actions reflected great credit to himself, and the quiet and orderly disposition of his men, showed no higher object than forcing obedience to the law. There were no women or children insulted or injured in the least.[47]

If a prize had been offered for originality in description of the "sack of Lawrence" surely it would have been awarded to the *Squatter Sovereign's* claim that "we simply executed to the letter what the law decreed, and left as though we had been to church—by the way, there is *no church* in Lawrence, but several *free love associations*."[48]

A few days later, May 27, the Westport *Border Times* printed a sensational story under the headlines "WAR! WAR!, EIGHT PRO-SLAVERY MEN MURDERED BY THE ABOLITIONISTS IN FRANKLIN COUNTY, K. T."[49] The authority given for the story was a letter from Paola, dated May 26, and signed by Generals Heiskell and Barbee. The murdered men were announced as Wilkinson, the three Doyles, Sherman, Whitman and two others. The paper declared that the only reason that could be assigned for this inhuman butchery, was, that the abolitionists (the court being in session) were afraid that these men would be called upon to give evidence against them, as many of them were charged with treason. The *Border Times* stormed, where is Governor Shannon? Where are the government troops? No names were given, but for the first time in Kansas Old John Brown had made sensational front page news,—the Potawatomie Massacre.

This story of the *Border Times* was printed in the Leavenworth *Kansas Weekly Herald,* May 31, together with an article announcing that the report of the murder was confirmed, and added that several free-state men had been arrested and others had been warned to leave the territory. Concerning those who had been arrested it said:

They were charged with different offences; some for inciting rebellion, and treason, and some for trying to head a mob to cut off and murder those who had gone from this place as a Marshal's posse, to aid in sustaining the law, and others for different offences . . . It is hoped no violence will be committed, but that law and order will reign supreme.

[47] Quoted in the *Squatter Sovereign*, May 27, 1856.

[48] *Squatter Sovereign*, May 27, 1856.

[49] This article was reprinted in the Leavenworth *Kansas Weekly Herald,* May 31, and in the Atchison *Squatter Sovereign*, June 10. It is a good illustration of how slowly printed news circulated through the local press.

The record of outrage in this issue of the *Herald* included another story from the *Border Times*, "More outrages at Hickory Point." It was an account of the driving out of Jones and Fielding, pro-slavery settlers, from the Hickory Point neighborhood south of Lawrence on Sunday May 25. Two adult negroes were offered their freedom and accepted, while one negro girl refused to leave her mistress. Jones reported at Westport that he had gone only a short distance when he was overtaken and the negroes returned, "the scoundrels thinking, doubtless, that their lawless acts were premature." It was reported also that "all the pro-slavery families at Hickory Point, have been driven off at the point of bayonet—having only one half hour's notice to leave in. Their horses are pressed into abolition service, and their provisions stolen by the abolitionists." [50]

A later report stated that Lieutenant Church and thirteen federal soldiers had dispersed an armed band of about eighty men at Palmyra who "had frightened off a number of pro-slavery settlers, and actually driven off two families. These armed outlaws were from Osawatomie. This is the place where a public meeting pledged to one another mutual support and aid in a forcible resistance to the territorial laws. They should be dealt with as rebels and traitors." [51] In neither of these accounts were the names of free-state leaders used, but both refer to the expedition of John Brown, Jr., to aid Lawrence.

To Lecompton the news of the Potawatomie massacre was brought by Judge George Wilson and Thomas Totten of Shermansville. The Lecompton *Union* May 31, after reporting the details declared:

> This is a portion of the Kansas wing of the 'Northern Army' who say that their houses are plundered and burned; their lives threatened, their rights as free men and American citizens denied them, and that they are ground in the dust by the 'iron heel of despotic tyranny, sanctioned by the Administration.' These are the 'Free State men' who have been so deeply outraged by the law and order party, but have, like martyrs, passed through the fire, without the stain of blood upon their skirts or the mark of pillage upon their consciences. This is the party, so pure and untarnished with dishonor that their very natures revolt at and recoil from the countenancing of even a minor disgrace, *much less the foul assassination of Sheriff Jones*. . . . In the name of God and equal rights how long will this last?

[50] The Leavenworth *Herald*, May 31, 1856 printed approximately one and one-half pages of Kansas troubles but only these three articles related to southeast Kansas.

[51] *Squatter Sovereign*, June 17, 1856.

How long shall we stand up against this, waiting for the tardy process of law to redress our wrongs? [52]

In reporting the Hickory Point episode, the *Enterprise* alleged that Feelan and Jones were the last pro-slavery men left in that community, the others having been driven away earlier, and that 200 head of stock were taken in this clean-up raid. The Potawatomie massacre was reported in a letter of Samuel M. Robertson, Commissioner of Franklin county, not heretofore known to historians.

Franklin County, K. T.
Sunday morning, May 25, 1856
To the Honorable Governor of Kansas Territory, or the
    Honorable Daniel Woodson, Secretary of the Territory.
Gentlemen: I will inform your Honors that there is a mob of the Yankees in this part of this Territory, committing dreadful outrages—of the most savage character.

An Express arrived this morning at my place of residence, from Potawatomie Creek, with information that an organized band of Abolitionists, at a very late hour at night, attacked the house of the men and tore them from their families and murdered them in cold blood, in a most savage manner.

The informer states that he believes nearly all the pro-slavery men on Potawatomie Creek were murdered last night.

This is to inform you that it is high time to send troops without delay. Send immediate relief, until other arrangements can be had

Yours in haste,
SAMUEL M. ROBERTSON.

In the same issue, a private letter written by one Stotts who left the free-state town of Osawatomie May 28, stated that the citizens of that town were highly inflamed at the crime, had arrested one and perhaps three of the murderers, and were using every exertion to bring to justice the others, whose names were known,—the whole party numbering sixteen.[53]

Other free-state raids were reported. Major Buford recently from Alabama, wrote Governor Shannon, May 29, of the night attack upon Martin Bowen two miles south of McGee's crossing in which a band of free-state men robbed him of fifty dollars in money, a rifle, a revolver, three horses, five saddles, and ordered him to leave the country within twenty-four hours. Lehay and Saunders on Washington creek were threatened, possibly by the same band, about nine o'clock that morning. Another item reported that at

[52] This article was copied into the Leavenworth *Herald*, June 7, 1856.
[53] *Enterprise*, May 31, 1856.

the junction of the Lecompton and California roads, just south of
the town of Lecompton, a party of men who responded to the call
from Lehay were attacked and three horses killed, and shortly afterward two citizens were ambushed and taken to Sam Walker's house
where some eighty abolitionists were gathered, but were released
the next morning.

One of the most widely circulated accounts of the Potawatomie
massacre was that of H. C. Pate, who reported it to the St. Louis
Republican. Pate's letter was dated from Baptiste Paola, May 30,
1856:

Your correspondent is in the neighborhood of the massacre. There
are over one hundred Kansas militia here for the purpose of catching the
murderers, who are an organized band of Abolitionists, armed and equipped
to thieve, murder, and resist all law. Such is the Free-State party here.
The honest freesoilers, who are ashamed of their confreres, have slipped in
and joined the proslavery party in ferreting out the criminals. The facts
as related in my last letter regarding the slaughter are correct; the circumstances are more aggravated than was thought. No grudges existed between the parties personally; in fact no cause whatever can be or is attempted to be assigned for the savage barbarity, but that the deceased were
proslavery in their sentiments.

Thirteen prisoners supposed to be connected with the affair are here
under arrest. What will be done with them is not known. The witnesses
are scattered about, and Judge Cato's court, now in session at this place,
will perhaps adjourn before they can be brought in. If ever Lynch law
was or could be justified it is in these cases.

It is said that the murderers are fortified on the Marais des Cygnes, in
a cave, about twenty-five miles from here, and are receiving reinforcements
from Lawrence and elsewhere. The leader of this party showed the bloody
dagger and boasted that it did the bloody deed; his name is Brown, two of
whose sons are arrested. One of them, who feigns to be crazy, has just
left in charge of the dragoons. He is made to accompany them on foot at
a pretty rapid gait of course, as the troops are mounted. His day's march
will help the craziness, and perhaps cool down the fanaticism which has
laid five innocent men in their graves. . . . The destroyed hotel and presses
at Lawrence were nuisances, because a means of resisting law, and were
abated as such, according to law, and this the fanatics claim as an excuse
for cold-blooded slaughter and theft. How long will the honest people of
the North be deceived?

The Leavenworth *Herald* printed Pate's account on June 14, and
in the same issue, from the Lecompton *Union* the text of the proceedings of "a meeting of the citizens of Potawatomie Creek, without distinction of parties, held at the Branch between Messrs. Potter
and Partridges, on the 27th day of May, 1856, C. H. Price [pro-
slavery], was chosen chairman, and H. H. Williams [free-state],

Secretary.'' The meeting appointed a committee which drafted a preamble and resolutions, unanimously adopted and ordered to be printed. The resolutions gave a pledge to lay all sectional and political feeling and to act together; repudiated all organized bands designed to excite violence, advising all citizens to remain at home; and lastly, declared ''That we pledge ourselves individually and collectively to prevent a recurrance of a similar tragedy, and to ferret out and hand over to the criminal authorities the perpetrators for punishment.'' [54]

On both sides, it was found to be one thing to make pledges but quite another to control the more extreme elements. Along the border, both in Kansas and in Missouri, the pro-slavery men rallied, ostensibly to capture the Potawatomie murderers and enforce law and order. Such bands had captured part of the prisoners mentioned in Pate's account who were turned over to the commander of the federal troops stationed in the vicinity of Osawatomie. Pate's own expedition became historic. On June 2, John Brown and Captain Shore attacked Pate at Black Jack and captured him. The Leavenworth *Herald* reported that and other disorders in an extra June 4, reprinting the story in the regular weekly edition June 7, under the title ''More Abolition Outrages.'' Captain Pate and about forty men were reported taken by one hundred-fifty Abolitionists. The battle was said to have lasted four hours, the first attack having failed, the surrender occurred only after the abolitionists had been reinforced and Pate's band completely surrounded. Coleman, Long and three others cut their way through the enemy while arms were being stacked, and James McGee who was wounded and was probably left for dead, had arrived at Westport. Other outrages in the same story included a report that J. M. Bernard, who left St. Bernard Friday for Westport was supposed to have been murdered. Three men went in search of him and had not been heard from since, and fear was expressed that they were probably murdered. An attack on the marshal and his posse was reported as resulting in the wounding of several men and horses. A man named Slade had his horse shot from under him, and H. M. McCarty's company of eight were attacked without provocation and all wounded, abolitionists stole a negro at Liberty but he was recaptured, and having exhausted specific instances, the enumeration

---

[54] The statement has been made sometimes that this meeting was held at Osawatomie. The location cannot now be fixed exactly, but it was in the neighborhood of the killings, several miles from that town.

closed with rumors of murder in other parts of the territory. The *Herald* was in no mood to await confirmation of the reports:

The Abolitionists shoot down our men without provocation, wherever they meet them. Let us retaliate in the same manner—a free fight is all we desire! If murder and assassination is the programme of the day, we are in favor of filling the bill. Let not the knives of the proslavery men be sheathed while there is one Abolitionist in the Territory.[55]

To restore order, Governor Shannon called out the federal troops and on June 4 issued a proclamation ordering the dispersal of all armed bands. This was not printed in the Leavenworth *Herald* until June 14, along with Pate's St. Louis *Republican* story of the Potawatomie murders and a story of an attack by about eighty free-state men on the town of Franklin, in which one pro-slavery defender was killed and another probably would die of wounds.

The St. Louis *Democrat* correspondent justified the course of the free-state party by claiming they were acting in self-defense, that they were not assassins and whoever made such a charge was a "wilfull liar." This kind of talk infuriated the editor of the Leavenworth *Herald*, who demanded, if it was self-defense when Branson was rescued, when women and children were driven out of their homes in winter to seek shelter in Missouri, when free-state men banded together to resist the laws, when an attempt was made to assassinate Pat Laughlin, when Sheriff Jones was shot, when Wilkinson was murdered, when Doyle and his two sons were murdered, when Whitman and others were murdered the same night by the same party? On the other hand, he declared, the pro-slavery party had ever been on the side of law and order.[56]

It is difficult to determine with any exactness the extent of the excitement among the people as a whole, because the exaggeration of the newspaper accounts is too obvious to require further comment. There was sufficient, however, that a mass meeting was called in Leavenworth on May 31 to determine upon future action. The meeting formally placed the responsibility for the disorders throughout the territory and the midnight assassinations upon the town of Lawrence as the center and headquarters of an organized band. The action decided upon was recorded formally in two groups of resolutions. The first endorsed the establishment of a vigilance committee, and the second recommended that all other counties and towns who sympathized with the pro-slavery cause should do like-

55 This story was copied into the *Squatter Sovereign*, June 10.
56 Leavenworth *Herald*, June 14, 1856.

wise. In the same paper in which the action of Leavenworth was
reported, a joint circular call to the South for support was printed
by committees representing the three northeast border counties of
Doniphan, Atchison and Leavenworth.[57] Such proceedings are not
much more enlightening than the newspaper reports of outrages, as
there is no means of checking the extent to which other parts of the
territory responded, or the proportion of the population participating.

The *Squatter Sovereign*, June 10, kept up the agitation with
eleven outrage articles and editorials. An editorial compared the
two parties; "midnight murders, assassinations, burglarizing and
arson now seem to be watchwords of the so-called Free State party,"
while enforcement of law and support of the courts was the stand of
the pro-slavery party, "but there is an end for all things. . . . If
civil war is to be the result, in such a conflict, there cannot be and
there will not be, any neutrals recognized." Since May 21 a Mr.
Crockett was said to have been murdered and other outrages were
reported from the vicinity of Lawrence, committed supposedly by
Walker and his mounted men. Commenting on Brooks's attack on
Sumner for his violent speech in the United States Senate on Kansas, the *Squatter Sovereign* expressed the opinion that Sumner had
jumped on the wrong man and "we think Sumner will learn a lesson
by his rough treatment, and be more careful in the future when
speaking of Southerners." The Kansas investigating committee
was denounced as a fraud and an outrage created to manufacture
propaganda for the presidential campaign. Reeder, the cowardly
deserter of Lawrence, was reported as having turned up in Illinois.
Again, the congressional committee: "Howard and Sherman are
chargeable with all that the posse was compelled to do. Since then,
midnight assassinations have been the work of those deluded
wretches that have been sent here by the aid societies." "A new
game proposed by the abolitionists," was the theme of another denunciation; first fraud, unscrupulous census takers and abolition
election judges, then an attempt to swindle the pro-slavery party
out of their representatives after election, then attempting to defeat
legislation by defying officers of enforcement, and now—mid-night
assassinations. "There must be no *night work*, but in the face of
the day," demanded the editor, "we must hunt these banded outlaws to death, or out of the Territory." He claimed that there had
been more than a dozen murders in Douglas county alone since the

[57] Leavenworth *Herald*, June 7, 1856.

posse of the marshal and sheriff left. "The latest news" was that the free-state men had shot into the camp of the United States troops and killed one soldier and two horses. In addition to these original articles, the *Squatter Sovereign* published three borrowed stories; the "War! War!" and the Hickory Point articles from the *Border Times* of May 27, and the last "Outrage" from the Leavenworth *Herald*.

Although peace had been restored for the most part by the second week of June, the *Squatter Sovereign*, June 17, printed a column of clippings from other papers under the heading "A Chapter of Outrages." The earliest of these, a *Border Times* article which bore the date May 30, reported the Potawatomie killings, the arrest of thirteen prisoners, Captain Brown among them, "whose father is the Captain of the Potawatomie murderers," and the gathering of about three hundred abolitionists at Brown's Station; another was the Leavenworth *Herald's* story of May 31; and one from the Kickapoo *Pioneer* reporting the burning of pro-slavery cabins above Grasshopper Falls. One of the last acts of violence was a night attack upon Haney's house, June 14, near Lawrence in which one of the free-state assailants, Hopkins, was killed.[58]

Later in June details of two important episodes were available. Oliver, the Missouri member of the congressional committee insisted upon investigating the Potawatomie murders, even though his anti-slavery colleagues refused on the ground that those matters were outside the committee's jurisdiction. The testimony of Mahala Doyle, the wife of one of the victims, was communicated to the Leavenworth *Herald* and was published June 21, 1856. Pate gave an interview to the editor of the *Herald* in which he attempted to explain some of the misunderstandings about the battle of Black Jack. He claimed that he sent out a flag of truce in order to gain time for the arrival of recruits. He charged Brown with violating the flag of truce, Pate refused to surrender, and his men voluntarily laid down their arms to save their commander. The report of the interview concluded, "Thus the Abolitionists violated every principle of honor in taking men prisoners under false pretences."[59] Undoubtedly, this was a logical conclusion to be drawn from certain of the facts, but unfortunately for the editor's perspective, it was only a half-truth. The evidence is equally convincing that Pate "violated every principle of honor" in using a flag of truce for the

58 Leavenworth *Herald*, June 28, 1856.
59 Leavenworth *Herald*, June 21, 1856.

sole purpose of securing reinforcements. The historian finds here
that he is dealing, not with one, but with two scoundrels.

The editor of the Leavenworth *Herald* had his blind spot, but he
was not without better judgment on the broader question of policy
for the summer of 1856. In an editorial, one and a half columns
long, entitled "A word of caution to our friends" he urged that
"we must not lose, by any indiscretion, our present moral position;
above all we must not come into collision with the public authorities." He pointed out that the President's orders were for all to
disperse, therefore, "Let us not embarass the Governor, nor do anything to place him in a false position."

The crisis at Lawrence which resulted in the destruction of the
hotel of the New England Emigrant Aid Company May 21 led to
action at Kansas City designed to forestall possible similar disorder
there. Eldridge, Lyman & Company operating the American Hotel,
were asked by a committee to dispose of the business, which they did
promptly. The *Enterprise* thanked them publicly with the following explanation: "It was thought that the interests of the city
demanded a change in proprietorship in consequence of their supposed connection with the Emigrant Aid Society. . . . We recommend Messrs. E. L. & Co., as good hotel keepers, against whom no
personal objections can be urged." The Eldridge in question was
the same man to whom the hotel at Lawrence had been leased by the
Aid Company. In order to balance the scales, however, the *Enterprise* at the same time gave warning to pro-slavery radicals by saying that some individuals, non-residents, had been imposing upon
the hospitality of Kansas City, and had been abusing the city for
not destroying "the mute bricks and mortar in the American
Hotel," and closed the incident with the comment that abuse of
some men was a compliment to a city.[60]

The editor of the *Enterprise* had been in Cincinnati during the
Potawatomie excitement, but upon his return to duty he summed up
the situation as of June 21:

The roads are clear in all directions—wagons are arriving in numbers
from all parts of the Territory, and trade is again looking up and promises
to be bouyant as heretofore.

There is one thing in this connection we wish to suggest. That as it is
to the business man, the farmer, the mechanic, and the artisan, that this
great Western land is to look for its great development in wealth, population and resources, *they* should take the control of the political affairs, at
least for a time, into their own hands. The interests of all portions of the

60 Kansas City *Enterprise*, June 6, 1856.

country demand this, and we trust it will be done. Let all good men support the general and territorial government in their efforts to restore order —*for there is safety to no interest outside the law.*—The revolutionists of the Territory have learned this fact by dearly bought experience, but the sword is two edged, and should be wielded only by the prudent, skillful and impartial hand.

This survey of the pro-slavery press prepares the way for some conclusions on the Brown problem. Two different motives were assigned for the Potawatomie murders. The one suggested by the Heiskell-Barbee bulletin was that the men would be called as witnesses against free-state men on treason charges as the court was then in session, while the Pate account stated that there were no grudges between the parties involved and concluded that the motive was nothing more than that they held pro-slavery views. The Wilson-Totten story was similar to the latter. The reaction of the local pro-slavery press was that the killings were a part of the general disorders, emanating from Lawrence. The Leavenworth mass meeting, particularly, laid the responsibility upon Lawrence, and the meeting itself was not the result of the Potawatomie murders except as they and the following disorders served as a climax to the spring civil war. Ex-Senator Hannegan of Indiana, a National democrat, visited Kansas in June and summed up his findings in a letter June 27 that "the first cause of the trouble was the injustifiable attempt of Eastern capitalists through what is termed the Emigrant Aid Society to engross the most valuable lands in the Territory, solely for purposes of private speculation. . . . The present disturbed condition of affairs is attributed solely to the glaring misconduct of Reeder in resisting the mandate of the court."[61]

It is significant that the news stories gave no special prominence to the name of Brown, and the name of John Brown, Sr., did not appear. The Pate account of the Potawatomie murders mentioned two sons of Brown, the leader of the Potawatomie murderers, and the *Border Times* article made a similar designation. Even in the reports of Black Jack, the names of the free-state leaders did not appear, until the Pate interview in the Leavenworth *Herald,* June 21. The only indication that the Browns enjoyed any notoriety appeared in the Cato court story, where the principal actor was referred to as "a *notorious* scoundrel, who has figured largely in Lawrence and other places," but no name was stated. The man designated by that statement was John Brown, Jr., however, not the

[61] *Leavenworth Herald,* August 2, 1856.

elder John Brown. The conclusion is clear, that the pro-slavery press gives no ground for the assumption that either the Browns as a family, or John Brown, Sr., had been the objects of special pro-slavery attention prior to the killings on Potawatomie creek. Even when the name Brown appeared in that connection, the reference was vague. The title "Captain Brown" began to appear in the press in June but was used indiscriminately for both the father and son named John, and the first attempt to clothe this anonymous being with a definite personality was made by Pate in a vivid word portrait attached to his report of the affidavit of Mahala Doyle in the Leavenworth *Herald*, June 21, 1856:

Brown told me he would take the life of a man as quick as he would that of a dog, if he thought it was necessary. He said if a man stood between him and what he considered right, he would take his life as cooly as he would eat his breakfast. His actions show what he is. Always restless, he seems never to sleep. With an eye like a snake, he looks like a demon. Apparently a miserable outlaw, he prefers war to peace, that pillage and plunder may the more safely be carried on. And this is a leader of the Free State party in Kansas.

CHAPTER IV

THE LOCAL FREE–STATE PRESS; EARLY 1856

The interpretation of the free-state press in Kansas is facilitated to some degree by the preservation of at least a few scraps of confidential correspondence concerning editorial policy and propaganda of those associated with the *Herald of Freedom*. G. W. Brown's paper was assisted through a loan advanced by the trustees conducting the New England Emigrant Aid enterprise and when the Aid Company organization was completed under the charter of 1855, S. C. Pomeroy, the financial agent, was notified of the transfer of the title of the power press from the trustees to the company and was informed that "you are its keeper."[1] The reference is not to the original press, but to the steam press sent out in the spring of 1855. Nothing was said in this correspondence about editorial control. Pomeroy was the business agent, Robinson the general agent, and the latter conducted most of the political activities of the aid company group. Pomeroy and· Robinson were not on the best of terms and Robinson and G. W. Brown quarreled during the summer of 1856.

On August 8, 1855 G. W. Brown wrote a most interesting letter to Thayer concerning news policy and the status of the free-state cause:

There is much excitement, however, that it is not deemed advisable to publish. We absolutely suppress all that we think it will do to keep down, on account of the injurious effects on emigration. The articles of a warlike character we do give are designed to prevent *cowards* from coming here, as we prefer no emigration at all to the miserable paltroons who fly at the first approach of danger. We do not love to blush for New England, and yet we are often compelled to do so for her degenerate sons. It is a common subject of remark among Missourians that the New Englanders are mere

[1] A. A. Lawrence *Letterbooks* (typed copies K. S. H. S.). A. A. Lawrence to J. S. M. Williams, March 17, 1855 said that "the press now belongs to the company" (it had not yet reached Kansas.) The cost was about $2,000 but Lawrence was not certain. A. A. Lawrence to Pomeroy, March 23, 1855. By this letter the latter was notified that "the loan to G. W. Brown has been assumed by the company." Reference was made in this letter to someone who challenged G. W. Brown's integrity and inquiries were to be made. The letter quoted in the text stated that Brown's steam press "now belongs to the Company and you are its keeper."

63

Sunday School *Children,* and that they are not adapted to border life. In any other place than Kansas it would be a high compliment to them; but here we want sterner material.

Brown had praise for Robinson and Deitzler, but not for Pomeroy who "has too much confidence in humanity to believe that they (border ruffians) can kill and plunder in cold blood," but "if the issue shall be kept open till fall I shall be disappointed if blood is not shed in profusion," and if so he admitted that the odds were against free-state men; besides, they were deficient in weapons. He illustrated his point by the difficulties at Hickory Point where the free-state men were ready to defend themselves but, like their ancestors at Bunker Hill, were inadequately armed.

With respect to Kansas propaganda outside the territory he wrote:

The press of the east, particularly that portion of it which boasts of being ultra, talk as you well said Rev. Mr. Starr did in New York, 'like fools.' They know nothing about Kansas; and were it not for the purpose of getting up an excitement they care less. Why will they in the face of the fact that they are doing immense harm to the cause—why will they represent that the slave power has triumphed, that Kansas is *doomed* to Slavery! That further efforts are unavailing The Slave power *in* Kansas does not exist, it *cannot* exist only in particular sections, and then in isolated cases. Kansas is free! The God of Heaven has made it such! Nature everywhere proclaims it!

After rhapsodizing upon the manifold manifestations of nature in Kansas, he insisted that the East must give support, yet he maintained that "Kansas is and shall *remain* free. The few persons attempting to make laws for us are too insignificant to merit consideration. They are subjects of our mirth, and excite occasionally our sympathies for their folly and fanaticism, but nothing more."

The letter had opened with thanks for a favor received, but gave no clue to its nature (might it have been money?) but closed with the statement "I know there is money to be made from the *Herald of Freedom* establishment, but I fear my means will not allow me to pass it on to that period when it shall be able to pay expenses." [2]

There is no indication in this letter that Brown was taking instructions from the Company. On the contrary, it would appear that he was taking his own line, or pretending to do so, and telling Thayer about it afterwards.

[2] *Thayer Papers*, K. S. H. S.

During the early months of the year 1856 the *Herald of Freedom* was particularly aggressive in the free-state ranks. Using the caption "The Storm Rising" it declared that another invasion was coming, only the manner and time were unknown. Some said it would occur when the free-state legislature met March 4, while others thought Sheriff Jones was planning a new issue.[3] In the same number the editor discussed the case of Addis who had applied to the territorial courts for redress against another free-state man:

It is an outrage upon the Free State settlers of the Territory, which should not be submitted to. We had a thousand times rather see the bowie-knife and revolver called into requisition for the adjustment of differences than to see the Courts, imposed upon us by armed men from a foreign State, appealed to for redress. . . . If the public cannot be sufficiently enlisted in aiding to bring offenders to justice . . . , he should call to his assistance the artificial aid which Colt and other meritorious gentlemen have devised. . . .

We are without law, and something *must* be devised for the protection of society. . . . While we remain in our present condition every man should be a law unto himself, adopting as his guiding star the 'golden rule' as promulgated by the Redeemer. . . .

As a punishment for these Free State men who appeal to the legislation of a mob from Missouri for protection, we propose that every man withdraw his patronage and influence from him . . .; let those who desert us in this crisis feel the weight of public opinion in such a manner that it will be life-lasting.

As the vitality of the Kansas issue depended upon propaganda it was necessary to gather an adequate supply of material. The murders of Dow, Barber and R. P. Brown had possibilities too important to neglect. The *Herald of Freedom* published a call January 26 for biographical material on these men. In Preble county, Ohio an Ohio-Indiana mass meeting was held on the Barber murder, and the proceedings were published in the *Herald of Freedom*, February 2, and on April 5, a half column biography of Barber appeared.

An article of more than usual interest is "Notes of a Southern Tour" written by John Stewart.[4] The article carried the date January 15, 1856 and related the incidents of a tour by Abram Still, presiding elder of the southern district of the Methodist church and Stewart, a preacher of that faith. They started from Lawrence December 20, 1855, spent the first night in the vicinity of Ottawa Jones's place and set as the objective of their second day's

---

3 *Herald of Freedom*, January 19, 1856.
4 *Herald of Freedom*, February 2, 1856.

journey the house of a friend south of Potawatomie creek. A part
of the entry for that day, December 21, is as follows:

> During the morning we met delegates from the Potawatomie and Sugar
> Creeks, on their way to attend the delegate convention for the nomination
> of State officers. They had been informed that we had accepted peace on
> dishonorable terms. And I assure you, they were as happy to hear as we
> were to inform them that such a rumor was truthless. After giving them
> the leading facts in the case, including, of course, the humiliating retreat of
> our invaders, which made them laugh right out, we separated, feeling that
> we had a double mission to perform; not only to preach the Gospel, but to
> correct the errors about, and state the true position of the Free State party
> in Kansas.

During the morning in question they passed the cabins of the
Brown family, although no mention was made of them, and the
meeting with the delegates must have occurred in that vicinity.
Evidently the men who had been at Lawrence for the Wakarusa war
from Middle creek, Potawatomie creek and Osawatomie had not
spread the news either widely or accurately. Stewart made special
inquiry during this eighteen-day tour of southeast Kansas about the
political views of the settlers, and reported seven-eighths of the
"real" settlers to be free-state.

"What is in the wind?", was the title of G. W. Brown's editorial
of February 16, based on rumors of the gathering of pro-slavery
militia at Ft. Scott, and a report of a speech of Davy Atchison at
Platte City, Missouri, in preparation for another invasion of Kansas
when the Topeka legislature should meet March 4.

> The people of Kansas have been menaced for a long time; we have ob-
> served preparations for months to destroy us; they have invaded our Ter-
> ritory; robbed us of every legal right; and now they seek our utter extinc-
> tion.
> In law a person is not required to wait until he is knocked down before
> he is justified in resorting to force to disable his assailant.
> We go further, and will cheerfully exert all the influences which a wise
> Providence, assisted by inventive genius, have placed in our hands to rid
> the world of these monsters; or, in the graphic language of Mr. Stearns,
> these 'wild beasts.' . . .
> We know we express ourselves strongly. We feel as we write, and be-
> lieve the time is rapidly approaching for action. If others wish to remain

----

5 Still and Stewart carried with them the Wakarusa War issue of the
Herald of Freedom, December 15, 1856, from which they read extracts to support their version. Stewart stated also that on account of delays and bad
roads they did not reach their destination that day, so spent the night with a
pro-slavery family near Potawatomie creek and were hospitably entertained.

silent when threatened with extermination they may do so, but they shall not censure us for pursuing that policy which we believe the times demand.[6]

Another link in the same line of propaganda was the appeal to Governor Chase of Ohio by Lane, Robinson and Deitzler, dated January 21, and published February 23. "We have authentic information that an overwhelming force of the citizens of Missouri are organized upon our border, amply supplied with artillery, for the avowed purpose of invading our Territory—demolishing our towns, and butchering our unoffending Free State citizens." The desperateness of the situation was emphasized by asking aid, and coupling it with the expression of hope that they could hold out until it reached Kansas.[7]

The next week the R. P. Brown murder case bobbed up with interesting associations through a clipping from the Springfield, Massachusetts, *Republican* which identified him with the Brown of the firm of wool dealers, Perkins and Brown of that city. It volunteered the information also that "He visited Springfield last summer to procure contributions to assist the settlers in their work of defense." G. W. Brown of the *Herald of Freedom* evidently was not acquainted with the antecedents of the numerous other Browns in Kansas. Apparently someone with more accurate information corrected him and the next week it was stated that the Brown of Perkins and Brown was not the Brown murdered at Easton but "is living in this State, and an active Free State man."[8] The identification fell short of being complete, however, as neither his full name nor residence were mentioned.

The meeting of the free-state legislature at Topeka was attended by the most conflicting reports of facts as well as diverse opinions on policies. John Hutchinson arrived from Washington with the information that the administration threatened to arrest the state officers and the members of the legislature.[9] At a mass meeting called to consider policies, Robinson read a dispatch from Washington to the effect that the president had given orders to Shannon not to interfere with the meeting of the legislature.[10] The *Kansas Tribune* was frankly radical on matters of policy and argued that

[6] *Herald of Freedom*, February 16, 1856.
[7] *Herald of Freedom*, February 23, 1856. Lane signed the appeal as Chairman of the Executive committee, Robinson as Governor elect of the State of Kansas, and Deitzler as Secretary.
[8] *Herald of Freedom*, March 1 and 8, 1856.
[9] Topeka *Kansas Tribune*, March 10, 1856.
[10] Topeka *Kansas Tribune*, March 10, 1856.

to adjourn until congress had had time to act would be interpreted as backing down and recommended that the state organization be carried out and that "in our opinion arrests for Treason on account of the action of the State Organization, will only result in making still more apparent the imbecility of the present weak and wicked administration."[11] In other words, the *Tribune* hoped its fellow free-staters would be arrested for treason as a means of promoting the cause.

Before the day set for the meeting of the Topeka legislature it had become too evident for further concealment that there was no Missouri invasion in prospect. The *Herald of Freedom,* March 1, announced "Tactics Changed" and explained it as follows: "Until within the last few days we have been apprehensive of another armed invasion from Missouri. The tone of the President's late proclamation has evidently changed the tactics of our neighbors, and their policy now as shadowed in their late meeting at Independence, is to flood the Territory with mercenaries who are to appear to be actual settlers. . . ."

We look for no further invasions at present, and trust that peace and quiet will be restored to the community.

Speaking of "actual settlers" calls attention to a blunder made soon after, and exposes the pitfalls in the path of agencies of "propaganda." Announcement was made that the Reverend P. P. Fowler was about to take up his residence in Kansas, and something of his history was given which revealed that he was not quite, but almost, a stranger to the territory. He had been one of the free-state candidates for the territorial legislature at the election of March 30, 1855 and had received the unanimous support of "resident voters" in the Lawrence district. The election had been set aside and he had been re-elected in the special election of May, but private business had called him East on the eve of the election.[12]

Having carried for so long a heavy share of the literary burden of defense of the territory, Editor Brown went East on a vacation about the end of March leaving his paper in charge of the associate editor, J. H. Greene. The latter announced immediately his editorial policy; "We expect not to be ruffian beleaguered in the future and will therefore try to steer clear of a blood-and-thunder course."[13] The implication was too obvious to win for Greene any

11 Topeka *Kansas Tribune.*
12 *Herald of Freedom,* April 5, 1856.
13 *Herald of Freedom.*

prize for tact or strategy in art of propaganda, especially as this appeared in the same issue with the Fowler item.

Encouragement was given to the free-state cause by the announcement that the New England Emigrant Aid Company's hotel was completed April 12, 1856. A full description of the building was given and secrets were revealed about its structure and ulterior purposes:

It was into this structure the people intended to retreat, if driven from every other position, gather around them their household treasures, and make the last desperate effort in the defense of their lives and liberties. But fate ordered it otherwise [as it was not finished at the time of the Wakarusa war].

There are thirty or forty port-holes in the walls, which rise above the roof, plugged up with stones, which can be knocked out with the blow of a Sharp's rifle.[14]

The *Kansas Free State* also saw a change in policy on the part of the enemy, the abandonment of "the mob policy" and the adoption of the policy of executing the laws, now that they were passed. For one thing they proposed to indict for treason, it complained, and for another, it quoted from the letter of a free-state man who protested that he had been called to serve on the grand jury in order to prevent his attendance at the Topeka legislature on March 4.[15]

Southeastern Kansas received a substantial amount of space in the *Herald of Freedom* during the spring of 1856. An unsigned article in the issue of April 5 gave a description of the country, the extent of settlement, remarking that there was much interest in schools and temperance; and "we will add, that to those who prefer settling where they will be sure of assistance in maintaining and preserving their inalienable rights, we can recommend the region within twenty miles west and southwest of Osawatomie." Three weeks later the same paper published a letter from Abram Still, dated April 14 recommending this same country from Middle creek of the Marais des Cygnes south and east to Ft. Scott.

[14] *Herald of Freedom*, April 12, 1856. This article was copied into the Atchison *Squatter Sovereign*, May 27, the issue in which the destruction of the Free State Hotel by Sheriff Jones's mob was announced.

This was not the first time that a public statement had been made that the hotel was constructed with a view to using it as a fort. A correspondent "W" of the Boston *Daily Evening Traveller*, in a letter dated at Lawrence January 25, published in the *Traveller* February 13 explained that it was then being used as a garrison.

[15] *Kansas Free State*, April 14, 1856.

At Osawatomie a meeting had been called by twenty-three citizens to consider the problem presented by the proposal of the territorial authorities to enforce the laws and collect taxes to meet the expenses of government. A committee of five had been appointed to draft resolutions which were "unanimously adopted" and were sent by the secretary to the newspapers for publication.[16] The four whereases which introduced the resolutions cited invasions to subjugate, invasions which polluted the ballot box, invasions which imposed pretended legislators who attempted to impose laws and appoint officers contrary to the fundamental principles of government, and attempts made and continued to be made by these men to assess and collect taxes. The resolutions repudiated the legislature and officers, pledged mutual aid and support in forcible resistance to any attempt to compel obedience, provided that a committee of three was to present the resolutions to the territorial officers, and that a copy was to be furnished to the press.

An unusually full account of one phase of the movement which these resolutions represent was published over the initials "J. B., Jr.," obviously John Brown, Jr., the letter being dated Potawatomie April 29, 1856.[17] The editor gave the story his tacit endorsement by headlining the letter, "The Right Spirit." Apart from the portion that deals with the Osawatomie resolutions, however, the reader will recognize the principal part of the letter as a free-state version of the Cato court incident, reported quite differently in the proslavery press:

Some time in March last, a person calling himself an assessor, sent a verbal notice to the settlers of Osawatomie, that he would soon call upon them in that capacity, and would, before calling to assess their property under the enactments of the so-called Kansas Territorial Legislature, send them a written notice of the time he would meet them. Whether such written notice was ever sent or not I cannot say.

It was this crisis, according to John Brown, Jr., which led to the Osawatomie meeting and resolutions, although he pointed out one highly significant point, that "a meeting had previously been held in Potawatomie precinct, at which similar resolutions were adopted."

About the same time, I learned that an individual, purporting to be a stranger, making inquiry for claims, called on several settlers, and con-

[16] The *Kansas Free State* printed them May 5 and the *Herald of Freedom* May 17, 1856 as presented by the chairman, Richard Mendenhall and the secretary, Oscar V. Dayton. They were printed in the *Herald of Freedom* May 10 also, as a part of an article signed J. B. Jr.

[17] *Herald of Freedom*, May 10, 1856. It is peculiar that this letter has escaped the notice of writers on the Brown problem.

versing with them about their circumstances, drew from them such facts as
he could, and based his estimate of the value of their property on such
statements as he got in this round-about way. He, I learned, had been appointed assessor under the authority above named. Soon after this a man
calling himself a marshal, or deputy marshal, came into this neighborhood
and summoned persons to attend as jurors at a place known as Henry
Sherman's, or Dutch Henry's. Many of those who were summoned, appeared at the time and place—others, however, did not.

On the morning of the 21st inst., a court was there opened, Judge Cato
presiding. This Judge Cato takes the place of Judge Elmore, of Alabama, who was removed by the President on the same ostensible grounds
upon which Governor Reeder was removed. Prior to the opening of the
Court, Judge Cato was questioned in regard to his intentions to enforce the
enactments of said Legislature, or not; but gave an indefinite answer. On
the same day a volunteer company, known as 'Potawatomie Rifles,' met to
drill about one mile and a half from the place where Judge Cato was to
hold his Court, and this Company, composed of actual settlers in this region, feeling an interest in the proceedings of that Court, were dismissed
for a short time, and went to hear the charge of the Judge to the Grand
Jury.

The Marshal opened the Court, which he styled a 'United States District Court for the county of Franklin.' The Judge, in swearing in the
Jury, and in the charge which followed, did not at all inform them whether
they were to act under the laws of the United States or the acts passed at
the Shawnee Mission. He did not even name these acts, nor the body
which passed them, but spoke frequently of 'our laws,' at the same time
laying his hand upon a copy of those acts which was laying on the table.

Persons familiar with legal matters, could not for a moment doubt
what his design was, when he spoke of certain offenses and penalties not
named or provided for by the laws of the United States.

At the close, or near it, of the Judge's charge, one of the Rifle Company
rose and said: 'May it please of Court, I have a question in writing to propose to this Court, an answer to which, would enlighten the citizens, and
no doubt would be acceptable to the Grand Jury.'

The written question was this, and is a true copy:

To the Court. Does this Court intend to enforce the enactments of the
Territorial Legislature, so-called? 'MANY CITIZENS.'

The Judge replied that the Court could not then be interrupted, but
that when he had finished giving his charge, 'if the question was of any
consequence, he could answer it.' When he had done with the jury, he
took up the paper containing the question, and after looking at it, laid it
down near the clerk, in a rather contemptuous manner, without making any
reply what evere. The clerk then did the same thing, and also the marshal.
After waiting a while longer, the Captain of the Company left, and after
getting out of the door, called to the members of his Company to meet on
their parade ground, which they did immediately. I ought to have said
before that the military Company had all left their arms behind on the
ground where they were drilled. On their return, the preamble and reso-

lutions of the Osawatomie meeting were read and passed *unanimously,* taking the vote by 'shouldering arms.'

They also appointed a Committee of three of their number to wait immediately on Judge Cato, and place in his hands a copy of said preamble and resolutions. That Committee did so at once.

The next day, about noon—I am informed—the Petit Jury was dismissed before the Grand Jury had done reporting, and soon after, when the Grand Jury had brought in bills of indictment against three persons—one of them for shooting hogs—the Court adjourned until September next, not having, as I can learn, tried any cause or done any business, except to fine some who did not appear as jurors.

I attended the first day, and have my information from reliable sources as to what transpired on the second or last day. I also saw one copy of a subpoena that had been left with a person who was required to appear as a witness. But I am unable to learn of any attempt to arrest the persons who were indicted. Yours. J. B. Jr.

In the same issue reporting from Potawatomie, there appeared an article detailing new difficulties at Hickory Point. Coleman, the murderer of Dow at that place the previous November, was back and on the evening of May 6, visited a Mr. Ritch, destroyed his furniture and burned his house. The next day Coleman's supporters destroyed a tent belonging to another man, and it was reported that "they express their determination to stay in the neighborhood and regulate matters according to their notions of propriety." [18]

Lawrence was soon to have trouble enough of her own. One of the understandings in connection with the Wakarusa war settlement in December 1855 had been that the free-state party would permit arrest of Branson rescuers in order to provide a test case in the courts for determination of the validity of the territorial government. The Kansas *Tribune,* December 24, 1855, reported that

We understand that Messrs. Tappan and S. C. Smith, charged with rescuing Mr. Branson have voluntarily appeared before the United States Court for trial. Confident of the illegality of the Rump Parliament, they are anxious for a fair trial. It is reported that Sheriff Jones has arrested Mr. Hupp. Mr. H. Nichols was taken prisoner during the war, and detained as a rescuer.

In its issue of January 7, 1856, the New York *Tribune* reported that the court did not meet and that the trial would go over to the March term. These scanty news items give little clue to the intentions of the free-state party, and when the time approached for the spring term of court in Douglas county nothing more was said about test cases. The attempt of Jones to arrest Wood, one of the most prominent Branson rescuers, was represented as having been gotten up

[18] *Herald of Freedom,* May 10, 1856.

to put the free-state men in the wrong before the congressional committee. It was emphasized that Lawrence was determined not to resist the United States troops. The *Herald of Freedom* charged that Jones was deliberately offensive, exposed himself, and at night sat alone in a lighted tent, implying strongly that he invited or planned the attempt on his life and was therefore to blame, also it implied that it was the work of a personal enemy. The question was asked whether the border ruffian party had accomplished anything by this "last stroke of villany," or would it recoil upon them? The reader was assured that Lawrence unanimously condemned such crimes, and it was pointed out that the community could not be held responsible for the act of an unknown individual. In all, seven columns were devoted to the affair, much of it in a satirical vein, especially when referring to Jones, "a man styling himself 'Sheriff of Douglas County!'"

This man, dressed in a little brief usurped authority, has barely escaped a violent death from the hands of an unknown, unseen foe. Whether the man who sent the ball whizzing into Jones's body was a political friend or opponent, commiting the crime for political purposes or to gratify personal and private revenge, matters little. The consequences will be the same. The lesson it will teach the unfortunate tool of Oppression, will be valuable hereafter to him not only, but to all others who endeavor by fraud and violence to crush the aspirations of men for freedom.[19]

The *Kansas Free State* evidently felt that Lawrence was safe in this crisis. It noted that "the attempt to assassinate Jones on Wednesday night last, has aroused Missouri to the highest pitch of excitement." The Missouri border apparently was prepared for it, because the Westport *Border Times* issued an extra of incendiary character, but the situation was different, the editor pointed out, this time the United States troops would be pitted against them as already five companies were "stationed but a few miles distant, under orders to protect the citizens." [20]

Assassination seemed to be the order of the day, and on Wednesday night April 29, after testifying before the congressional investigating committee, Captain J. N. Mace a free-state man was shot in the dark near his house west of Lawrence and left for dead. Again a mass meeting was held in town, at which Robinson and others spoke and resolutions were adopted which denounced both the attempt on Mace as well as the one on Jones.[21]

19 *Herald of Freedom*, April 26, 1856.
20 The *Kansas Free State*, April 28, 1856.
21 *Herald of Freedom*, May 10, and *Kansas Free State*, May 5, 1856.

The Lawrence free-state press records end at this point, as the *Kansas Free State* had miscalculated the odds in the contest with Jones and both the Lawrence newspapers were destroyed May 21, the presses being broken and much of the printing material and equipment being thrown into the river. The court crisis which gave Jones his opportunity was the Reeder case, the defiance of a federal grand jury subpoena, not the Branson rescue cases. The Topeka *Kansas Tribune* was reputed to be the only free-state paper left in Kansas, and a Manhattan subscriber wrote, that in the absence of it, their only sources of news were travelers and a month-old New York *Tribune*.[22] The *Kansas Tribune* had been published in Lawrence during 1855, but being unsuccessful there moved to Topeka in December. The paper had difficulty in maintaining itself during the early months of 1856, but developed an aggressive and radical editorial and news policy in May and June. The difficulties of Sheriff Jones at Lawrence were summed up May 5 with more vigor than courtesy, and more imagination than truth, but at the end the truth did emerge that Kansas agitation was at the heart of the pending presidential campaign:

Great excitement has prevailed at Lawrence for the last week growing out of the assumption of one S. J. Jones, who has made several attempted assaults upon our citizens under the pretence of being "Sheriff of Douglas county," abetted by a degraded blackguard known as SAM SALTERS, who professes to act as "Deputy Sheriff," [Jones attempt at making arrests and the shooting—]. Such was the public indignation against Salters, that he dared not enter the town unsupported by the soldiers, to whom no insult or even the appearance of resistance was offered, although the exclamation was frequent, "No such brute as Salters can take a man here—it takes the United States and brass buttons to do that in this town. . . ." Resistance to all the [territorial] troops in the State would have been an easy matter, but our People are not disposed to resist legitimate authority, however tyranically and corrupt it may be used. The proper day of reckoning they hope to recognize at the ballot box next November, when the usurper and tool of the Slave Power who now occupies the Presidential chair shall be hurled from his present position.

The editor was clearly no respector of persons or of official dignity and June 6 denounced the policy of the territorial government; "the congressional commission, too, appointed to unveil the villanies of the Missouri usurpation, is to be broken up. . . . Why else the attempt to seize and imprison Reeder? Why the mad endeavor of that half-crazed Alabaman—Judge Lecompte—to put under arrest for treason every leader of the Free State men?" In the same issue the editor probably revealed more than he realized of the artificiality of the melodramatic propaganda he felt it necessary to print for party purposes. In paying his respects to the federal troops he admitted that "as men they are a first rate good hearted jolly set of fellows, under the command of kind and generous officers. But as U. S. troops we look upon them as our enemies —the emissaries of Frank Pierce sent here to enforce if possible a code of law the wickedness of which is surpassed by none since the rule of Jeffries."

But free-state exploits were treated in a different vein, as in the summary of "Our Troubles" published June 6, the only local free-state press version of the Potawatomie massacre and subsequent events including the battle of Black Jack. Only too obviously, the details of each of the episodes listed were largely the product of fertile imaginations:

We are enabled to lay before our readers the particulars of several skirmishes which have taken place between Free State Men and Border Ruffians within the past ten days. The dates of the several rencontres we may not give accurately, but the accounts are substantially correct, though entirely different from the statements laid before the world by the Lecompton Union, which every person familiar with the facts has pronounced a base fabrication and an unmitigated falsehood without the least shadow of truth or foundation.

On Saturday night the 24th ult., a party of ruffians, ten in number, went to the house of a Free State man residing on or near Pottawatomie Creek, dragged him out of bed, and took him to a grove near by, where they made the necessary preparations to hang him. A rope was put around his neck, and he was given time to say his prayers. Meantime, four or five of his neighbors, having received information of his abduction, armed themselves and went to his rescue reaching the grove just as he was being swung up. They poured a volley into the gang, killing five instantly; the other five fled. A Mr. Wilkerson a member of the Barrenial Legislature, was one of the killed.

A few days subsequently, a company of Buford's men were passing through the southern part of the State, driving men off of claims, stealing horses, &c; and fortune throwing them in the way of a company of Free State men, a sharp conflict ensued, in which seven of the former were killed. Their guns, horses, provisions, ammunition, &c., fell into the latter's hands.

A day or two afterwards a Mr. Bowen, who had command of a company of the Marshal's posse at Lawrence, and who had in his possession 10 Sharp's Rifles, which were stolen from individuals at the former place, was visited by some of the owners of the guns who demanded their property. He gave them up, protesting that he did not enter Lawrence willingly, but that he got upon his marrow bones when on the hill near Lawrence, and begged of them not to enter the town.

A few days after the affair with Bowen, some sixty or seventy of Buford's company were seen loafing around in the vicinity of Mr. Storr's house, near Washington Creek, and finally drove him and his family out and took possession. The neighbors soon rallied, and re-took his house, while a lady started for Lawrence in search of assistance, which she procured. Before their arrival the Buford company made several attacks upon the house but were repulsed with several serious wounds. The soldiers had in the meantime got wind that there was trouble brewing and a small detachment was despatched to ascertain the facts. Col. Topliff and Edwin Clark of Lawrence accompanying them. The men in Mr. Storr's house, who were much excited owing to the attacks that had been made upon them, and which they were momentarily expecting to have repeated, on seeing a company of horsemen riding towards them on a run, naturally supposing that they were their former foe, ordered them to halt; they did not obey the order, and the men fired, wounding one of the soldiers seriously but not dangerously, and two horses; on ascertaining their mistake they went out and rendered all the assistance in their power. One of them Mr. Bercaw, formerly of Ohio, being one of a party who fired from the house, accompanied the soldiers back to their superior officers, gave himself up and related the facts in the case. He was informed that they were not so much to blame after all, that the troops were very injudicious in going up in the manner they did. The Lawrence boys soon arrived took five prisoners, each with a Sharp's rifle, and dispersed the balance of the mob.

Last Sunday, June 1st., some half a dozen ruffians armed with rifles bowie knives and revolvers rode into Palmyra, some twelve miles south of Lawrence, plundered the houses and committeed various depredations, the inhabitants being away to church; they then passed on to Prairie city, a short distance from the former place, no doubt expecting to commit the same depredations there; but were foiled in their attempt. The people were at church, and it took but a moment for them to hear that the border ruffians were in town; a few men left church, gave them chase and succeeded in capturing five of them with their arms and took them back to town. During the evening, Mr. ᴾᵣown, of Ossawotamie, arrived with a few of his neighbors, and with the citizens prepared themselves for an attack. About nine o'clock, Monday morning, they made their appearance reconnoitering or skirmishing, till about 10 o'clock when a regular battle, the first and we hope it will be the last ever fought in Kansas. The battle only lasted a short time, when the Southerners surrendered, giving up themselves, their horses, guns, camp equipages, and everything, after having lost five men in killed and mortally wounded. Twenty-one prisoners were taken all having surrendered, except Coleman the murderer of Dow, who made his escape in the commencement of the fight.

It is rumored that a skirmish came off at Franklin on Tuesday which resulted in wounding a few pro-slavery men, the capture of some guns, powder, &c. by the Free State party.

On Thursday, June 5th, Col. Sumner hearing that armed forces were traversing the country, had started out with 40 men. In the neighborhood of Hickory Point, he met Gen. Whitfield who had under his command 250 men from the borders. Col. Sumner dispursed them, and started them back home. We have never before heard of a man claiming to be a Delegate in Congress, chosen by the people, and then raising an army in a foreign State and marching in with the avowed purpose of driving out, subjugating or murdering the very People he claims to represent.

A second thought or possibly fuller information sobered the editorial enthusiasm for the free-state executioners on the Potawatomie by the next week when the proceedings of the meeting near Dutch Henry's were published with vigorous editorial comment:

> We are glad that our Pottawatomie neighbors are making such earnest efforts to ferret out the perpetrators of the horrible massacre at that place. They are assisted by a number of Free State men from other places; such a cold-blooded, unprovoked assault in the stillness of the night hours, on sleeping, defenseless citizens, of whatever party, ought to meet with indignation from every lover of truth and right.

There was more cheering news for free-state readers in the same issue, however, as an attack on Captain Walker's house near Lawrence was reported. Walker had been warned and was ready, the marauders were repulsed and two of the number, Waufield and Roderick, were captured, also knives, rifles, hats, as well as "a bottle of whiskey which we believe is considered an actual necessity among our invaders to keep the courage up to the proper point." A more remarkable report was that of the Haney-Hopkins murder of June 15. Haney, a pro-slavery man had killed Hopkins a free-state man. At Lawrence a committee was appointed to investigate and a report was brought in, the contents of which was not stated. A substitute report was offered and adopted by the public meeting held June 18, which resolved cautiously that probably Haney was justified.[23]

In the way of conclusions drawn from the free-state press, the most significant one is that, except for the explanation of the mistake about R. P. Brown, the name of the John Brown family appeared but once during the period, and that only in a casual mention of "Mr. Brown of Osawatomie" in connection with the fight at Black Jack. The younger John Brown appeared by initials signed to his communication to the *Herald of Freedom*, and both Johns appeared anonymously in the reports of the disorders in southeastern Kansas, but no personalities emerged, even anonymously, around which to build a reputation. A second conclusion is outstanding, that John Brown's contemporaries in Kansas, publicly and without reservation, condemned the Potawatomie massacre; not only the local community, but also so radical an exponent of direct action as the *Kansas Tribune*.

[23] *Kansas Tribune*, June 23, 1856.

CHAPTER V

OFFICIAL TERRITORIAL DOCUMENTS

From the standpoint of the territorial officials, as well as the free-state party, the first test of the law enforcement issue was raised unexpectedly by the Dow murder and the Branson rescue in November 1855. Neither party appeared ready to carry the matter to a conclusion on that basis. The town of Lawrence repudiated all responsibility for the rescue of Branson, and the governor, after calling the territorial militia to assist in executing the warrants, realized the danger, attempted to secure United States troops instead, and having failed, compromised with Lawrence. The enrollment of unorganized bands, especially from Missouri, in the militia was not from choice but to bring them under a semblance of discipline and control. The governor understood the treaty to provide that the free-state party would recognize the validity of the laws, with the proviso they might carry a test case, based on an arrest of a Branson rescuer, to the Supreme Court. The governor reported the outcome to the President in a letter of December 11, 1855, accompanied by the documents. These the President submitted to congress in January and they were widely published in the press during the following weeks.[1]

In a letter of April 11, 1856, Governor Shannon summarized the events of about two months; the Easton difficulties in January had been exaggerated, the excitement attending the meeting of the Topeka legislature had subsided, the reports of armed organizations in Missouri designed to invade Kansas were without foundation, and the governor's course had been endorsed by the law-and-order party. Regarding the Topeka legislature which met March 4, and adjourned until July 4, he emphasized that its action was mainly prospective, and looked to admission of the state into the Union, or to future legislation before there should be any attempt to put the laws

[1] Shannon's *Executive Minutes* are reprinted in *Collections* of the Kansas State Historical Society, 3: 291–301. There is much confusion in the titles of the publications of the society, so for simplicity the title *Collections* is used uniformly for the series in this book.

The controversy over the meaning of the Lawrence treaty has been discussed in connection with the views of the pro-slavery press.

into force. The governor still had misgivings about the future, however, as arms were being brought secretly into the territory, and certain spirits seemed to want "a conflict of arms."

Shannon's next report to Washington was dated April 27, 1856, after the Wood affair at Lawrence and the attempted assassination of Jones. He reviewed that episode without adding any essential facts to those already brought out by the newspapers except that on this occasion Jones was vested with authority of a deputy United States marshal, as well as his office of sheriff, but he offered some comments about the situation which are significant. "There would seem to be at this time," he thought, "a more systematic and dangerous organization to defeat and baffle the due execution of the territorial laws, than at any former period." He was convinced that the plan was supported by an oath-bound military organization described before the grand jury at Ozawkie:

The plan is this: whenever an officer, whether United States Marshal, sheriff, or constable, shall attempt to execute a writ or process issued under any Territorial law, aided or assisted by a posse of United States troops, he is to be evaded, but not openly resisted. Should an attempt be made by any officer to execute any writ or process issued under the laws of this Territory, unaided by a posse of United States troops, he is to be resisted by force at all hazards. There is a determined purpose to carry out this programme, regardless of all consequences, and the country is filled with armed men, the greater portion of whom have already arrived in the Territory, ready to carry out this plan by force of arms. It will be obvious to the President that, if every officer of the Government charged with the execution of legal process, issued under, and to enforce the Territorial laws, is compelled to call on a military posse of the United States troops to aid in executing the law, that the Territorial government will be practically nullified. It will be impossible to collect the taxes assessed for county and Territorial purposes if this plan of resistance is successful.

He emphasized that many of the settlers who had supported Robinson the previous fall would not do so now, "but the recent emigrants from the East (with some exceptions, of course) seem determined to provoke a civil conflict. The law-and-order party of the Territory so far seem determined, on the other hand, to avoid this calamity." A great danger was that the friends of Jones on the Missouri border, where he was known, were excited over the attempt to assassinate him, but the governor reverted a third time to this letter to what he must have thought was the most dangerous factor: "Large parties, both from the North and South, are daily arriving with preexisting prejudices and hostile feelings, which will greatly increase the difficulty of preserving the peace of the Territory.''[2]

The multiplication of Shannon's troubles during May was reported to the President in a letter of May 31. He reviewed the Reeder matter bringing out new information on the conduct of the marshal:

Had the Marshal called on me for a posse, I should have felt myself bound to furnish him one composed entirely of United States troops. Knowing this to be the case, and feeling satisfied that with a posse composed of such troops, the parties to be arrested would evade the service of process, he determined, by virtue of the legal powers vested in him as Marshal, to summon his own posse from the citizens of the Territory.

On the events of May 21 at Lawrence his account followed approximately a moderate version of the pro-slavery view. As soon as he learned that the marshal had dismissed his posse, and without awaiting other news, he called upon Colonel Sumner for United States troops to take charge of the situation and maintain order in Lawrence and vicinity, Lecompton and Topeka.

The reports from Kansas to the war department supply some additional information concerning Shannon's correspondence with Colonel Sumner to whom he indicated his intention of calling troops. He insisted that it "cannot safely be done until the posse of the United States Marshal is dismissed." The difficulty was not explained so that it is clear to the modern reader, but it involved a conflict of authority as conferred by statute as between the governor and the marshal which the former felt was so serious as to require his delay.[3] Colonel Sumner received information concerning the situation from his subordinate, as well as from the governor. Lt. McIntosh reported May 21 the gathering of the marshal's posse, the stopping of free-state men by pro-slavery men, the stopping of pro-slavery men by free-state men, and concluded:

With such a class of men as there are in this Territory, excited as they are, and arrayed against each other, great excesses will be committed; and already persons who have taken no interest in the struggle, but quietly living on their claims, have been molested, and their personal property taken away and destroyed. . . . The last rumors from Lawrence were, that a great many persons had left, and that they did not intend to make any resistance. Even if they do not, I think probably that some portion of the town will suffer; for instance, the Free State Hotel and the printing

[2] Correspondence of Governor Geary, *Collections*, Kansas State Historical Society, 4: 404–408. This included a part of the Shannon Correspondence which was not transmitted to congress and published until 1857.

[3] *Collections*, Kansas State Historical Society, 4: 434.

office. It is very doubtful if such a body of excited men will go there and be governed and checked by the Marshall.[4]

In sending the troops to the aid of the governor, Sumner instructed Major Sedgwick to "use the utmost circumspection, and avoid, if possible, collisions with the people." [5]

In his letter of May 31 Shannon reported also on the treason cases, and replied to two sharp telegraphic dispatches from the President received at Lecompton that evening, dated May 23, inquiring concerning the action of the marshal at Lawrence, whether reliance was being made solely upon the United States troops, and if not why, as he could see no occasion for a posse reported to have been assembled at Lawrence.[6] Shannon's reply was explicit:

I have relied solely on the forces under the command of Colonel Sumner, in order to maintain peace and good order in the Territory and enforce the execution of the laws. I have furnished no posse to the Marshall, nor have I been called on by that officer to do so. The only posse I have furnished, or been desired to furnish, any officer of the Territory, since my return from Washington city, is the one furnished Sheriff Jones, on his written statement and request, dated April 20 last. . . .[7]

Attacks were made in the press and in congress upon Judge Lecompte, and in particular an attack was made by Schuyler Colfax in congress, to which reply was made by James A. Stewart of Maryland. On August 1, 1856 Lecompte wrote the latter a long letter in defense of his judicial career in Kansas and challenged the opposition to follow legal procedure and impeach him.[8] Among the many points in this lengthy document he summarized his ideas on the law of treason, his legal procedure in the Reeder contempt case, the action of the marshal, not of the court in calling the posse, and pointed out that the destruction of the hotel and the press was not an order of the court, because the court had taken no action whatever on such subjects and had no intention of doing so. When the Potawatomie massacre occurred, Lecompte stated that he had been at Leavenworth and described the tense excitement, insisting that he

[4] *Collections*, Kansas State Historical Society, 4: 435–436.

[5] *Collections*, Kansas State Historical Society, 4: 436.

[6] *Collections*, Kansas State Historical Society, 4: 414. The President commented with approval on a proposal Colonel Sumner had made to Shannon May 11, but the document has not been printed and has not been preserved among the manuscript papers of the territorial governors at Topeka.

[7] Having received no reply to his dispatches of May 23, the President wired again, June 6, demanding immediate acknowledgment, from either Shannon or Sumner. *Collections*, Kansas State Historical Society, 4: 421.

[8] Printed in several places, among them the St. Louis *Republican*, September 13, 1856, and the Leavenworth *Herald* September 27, 1856.

used his influence to prevent violence and at the request of the marshal he and General Richardson of the territorial militia had slept at the door of the room in which Governor Robinson was held a prisoner in order to insure his safety.

Whatever deficiencies may be charged to Lecompte, he cannot be accused of not appreciating the difficulties of dispensing justice in territorial Kansas. First was the problem of mixed jurisdiction which imposed upon a federal district court not only cases arising out of violations of federal laws, but also all infractions of local legislation, except petty actions before justices of the peace. The second point was the difficulties of administering justice in local circuits without any of the facilities necessary to the proper conduct of a court.

Following immediately upon the Lawrence crisis news arrived at the capital at Lecompton that a free-state band had been driving off pro-slavery settlers in the Hickory Point neighborhood. Lt. John R. Church was ordered to the scene, reporting the next day, May 26. At Palmyra he found this band, commanded by Captain Brown, from Osawatomie and the surrounding country.

They had been at Palmyra about two days, and had frightened off a number of Pro-Slavery settlers, and forced off, as far as I could learn, two families. I immediately stated to Captain Brown that the assembly of large parties of armed men, on either side, was illegal, and called upon him to disperse. After considerable talk, he consented to disband his party and return home. On yesterday evening he commenced moving. . . .[9]

The murders in Franklin county, the Potawatomie massacre, were disposed of in one brief paragraph in the governor's letter, although fortunately for the historian he enclosed the reports he had received and the correspondence covering his action on those reports. His conviction was that "Comment is unnecessary. The respectability of the parties and the crueltites attending these murders have produced an extraordinary state of excitement in that portion of the Territory, which has heretofore remained comparatively quiet . . . I hope the offenders may be brought to justice; if so, it may allay to a great extent the excitement; otherwise, I fear the consequences."[10]

The news had arrived at the governor's office about mid-night May 26–27. The notes from generals of the territorial militia, Barbee and Heiskell, dated from Paola, May 26 related the murder

[9] *Collections*, Kansas State Historical Society, 4: 441. This refers to John Brown, Jr.

[10] *Collections*, Kansas State Historical Society, 4: 414–418.

of six men. Barbee had interviewed the wife and family of one of the murdered men, and also McMinn, and declared that "all is excitement here; court cannot go on." He said he could not muster over 150 men, and had sent for 100 from Ft. Scott.[11] Immediately Shannon ordered Captain Woods and his company of regulars stationed at Lawrence, to go to Osawatomie, and asked Colonel Sumner, at Ft. Leavenworth, to send two companies to Lawrence to replace them. Commenting to Sumner on the affair, he said "it seemed to be a regular system of private assassination which the Free State party had adopted towards their opponents."[12] In reporting to his superiors on these troop movements, Sumner wrote May 28:

> From present appearances, it looks very much like running into a guerilla warfare. If the matter had been taken in hand at an earlier day, as I earnestly advised the Governor, the whole disturbance would have been suppressed without blood-shed.
> At that time we held a high moral position in the Territory that would have looked down all opposition from all parties. As the affair now stands, there is great danger of our being compelled to use force.

Sumner was concerned further on what should be done if General Haney should order his troops to Indian duty on the plains before Shannon was willing to have them moved.[13]

On the same day, Captain J. J. Woods, who had been sent from Lawrence to Osawatomie, was writing from Palmyra that he had started as ordered the previous day, but had found much to do at Palmyra. He had found several knots of free-state men, fifteen to twenty in number, and had visited two of their resorts. He had ordered them to disperse and while they agreed to comply, Woods remarked that they could reassemble. He suggested that a detachment of troops should be stationed at Palmyra as he was going on to Osawatomie in compliance with his orders.[14]

Meanwhile Judge Cato had written Shannon May 27 from Paola, Lykins county, where he was holding court, confirming the reports of the killing of five pro-slavery men in Franklin county, and that

> the community, as I understand, generally suspect the Browns and Partridges are the guilty parties. I shall do everything in my power to have the matter investigated, and there seems to be a disposition on the part of the Free State men in Franklin to aid in having the laws enforced. As soon as the proper evidence can be procured, warrants will be issued for the arrest of the parties suspected, and I have promised the officers to

11 *Collections*, Kansas State Historical Society, 4: 420–421.
12 *Collections*, Kansas State Historical Society, 4: 437.
13 *Collections*, Kansas State Historical Society, 4: 436–437.
14 *Collections*, Kansas State Historical Society, 4: 390.

whom these warrants will be entrusted all the aid necessary to execute the law. These murders were most foully committed in the night time by a gang of some twelve or fifteen persons, calling on, and dragging from their houses, defenseless citizens, and murdering, and, after murdering, mutilating their bodies in a very shocking manner.

As the murders were committed in the night, it has been difficult, so far, in identifying the perpetrators. I hope, however, that sufficient evidence may be procured.[15]

In closing his letter to the President, May 31, Shannon wrote:

At this time affairs seem to wear a favorable aspect, except in the Wakarusa valley and south of Lawrence, in the region of country where the recent murders were perpetrated. But there are so many disturbing causes that it is hard to tell whether we have passed the crisis or not.

On the same day Shannon was expressing these doubts about the future, Captain E. W. B. Newby, of the First Cavalry, was writing a report of a new incident. On receiving information that six families had been driven from their homes six miles west of Lecompton, a detachment had been sent to investigate and had been fired upon by free-state men, one man and two horses being wounded. Later one man involved in the affair had been arrested.[16]

On June 1 Major Sedgwick reported to his commander at Ft. Leavenworth on conditions in Shawnee and Douglas counties. Topeka was completely quiet, but as the court would meet in Tecumseh the next day, he said the governor had decided that the troops should be left there, a copy of Newby's dispatch was forwarded, but the matter of greatest concern was Franklin county and the country to the southward:

Captain Wood reports large armed bands prowling in his vicinity. He ordered them to disperse, which they did; but it is so easy for them to reassemble, he thinks they may have done so. The Governor says his information reports they are organized with cannon, etc., etc. There are so many rumors afloat, and so little truth in them, that it is difficult to separate them from falsehood. There are, undoubtedly, many outrages committed daily; some of them of the most atrocious character.[17]

On the same day Shannon asked Sumner for two more companies of troops and in view of Sedgwick's report, Sumner decided he must appear in person. He informed his superiors at St. Louis and Washington of this fact in dispatches dated June 2, and to Cooper at Washington he expressed himself rather freely: "If the armed

15 *Collections*, Kansas State Historical Society, 4: 419–420.
16 *Collections*, Kansas State Historical Society, 4: 390.
17 *Collections*, Kansas State Historical Society, 4: 438–439.

civil posse had not been allowed to act, as I earnestly advised the Governor, these disturbances would not have happened. As the matter now stands, no man can see the end of them. The firing upon the troops is a very serious affair." [18]

No further news from the southern part of the territory is on record until dispatches dated June 4. By that time matters there had reached a crisis, arrests had been made in the vicinity of Paola and Osawatomie, and Pate and the free-state men under Brown and Shore had met at Black Jack. On June 4 Shannon issued a proclamation demanding the dispersal of all armed forces in the territory. At the same time he communicated to Sumner copies of the proclamation with the information that "It is said there are about three-hundred Free-State men in Prairie City, fortified and prepared to fight. Captain Pate and some twenty or thirty prisoners are said to be confined at this place. This place is near Palmyra, and a little south of the Santa Fe road."

In another letter of the same date the governor reported to Sumner an attack upon the town of Franklin during the previous night, and threat of attack upon Lehay's house, southwest of Lawrence that night. To meet the disorders springing up almost simultaneously in several parts of the territory Shannon submitted to Sumner a plan for stationing troops immediately at five different centers of disturbance; Franklin, Lehay's, Hickory Point, St. Bernard and Palmyra. In still another communication of the same date Shannon, in the absence of a deputy marshal, designated Deputy Sheriff Preston to accompany Sumner "so as to be ready to act as circumstances may require." [19]

On June 5 Colonel Sumner moved on the Palmyra neighborhood with two companies, and coming upon Captain Brown's camp released the prisoners and dispersed the band. Within two miles of

[18] *Collections,* Kansas State Historical Society, 4: 437.

[19] All these dispatches are in *Collections,* Kansas State Historical Society, 3: 311–314.

N. B. All the places designated in the orders were located within Douglas county, and therefore were within the jurisdiction of the sheriff. The charges of cowardice against Preston in his failure to arrest John Brown are based on the assumption that Preston had federal warrants issued in Lykins or Franklin counties, or in both. The governor was not specific whether Preston was specially deputized on this mission as a United States Marshal. Two questions need to be cleared up, therefore, Preston's official status and the warrants he carried. Without authority as Deputy United States Marshal and without federal warrants issued for Brown in the counties mentioned, Preston possessed no authority to arrest John Brown, and the charge of cowardice would disappear automatically.

Brown's camp he was surprised to find Whitfield, delegate to congress, and General Coffee of the territorial militia in command of an armed band of some 250 men. He dispersed them and started them on the road toward Missouri, but he admitted that "whether this is a final dispersion of these lawless armed bodies, is very doubtful." [20] His scepticism was well founded. Lt. McIntosh was sent to disperse the Brown band a second time within three or four miles from the first camp.[21] The Whitfield-Coffee band, or irregulars attached to it, raided Osawatomie June 7.[22] Lt. McIntosh reported Buford's men committing depredations, and an attempt by an armed band to burn Palmyra. He pursued the latter, disarmed them, and sent a detail to see that they crossed the Missouri line. A second party near the first was disbanded, and the returning detail reported seven or eight companies between Westport and Palmyra. Another company was then, June 13, camped within three miles of the troops and they would be dispersed the next day, and McIntosh would set out to clear the road all the way to the Missouri line. These armed companies all insisted they were emigrants, but they were turned back anyway.[23] In connection with these proceedings, Sumner could not refrain from again expressing his views that "if the proclamation of the Governor had been issued six months earlier, and had been rigidly maintained, these difficulties would have been avoided." [24] After disbanding the maurauders in the vicinity of Palmyra, Sumner had returned to Ft. Leavenworth June 8 to prepare the last two companies in his command to take the field,[25] and five days later was again at Lawrence, leaving a force near Lecompton and between Franklin and Lawrence, he proceeded toward the Missouri border.[26] Shannon had called also upon Cook, the commandant at Ft. Riley for troops and they arrived at Lecompton June 15. In reporting on his activities, Cook declared that "the

[20] Shannon to the President, June 17, 1856, *Collections*, Kansas State Historical Society, 4: 386–389. Sumner to Adjutant General Cooper, June 8, 1856, *Collections*, K. S. H. S., 4: 439–440.

[21] Shannon to the President, *Ibid.*

[22] *Ibid.*

[23] McIntosh to Woodson, June 13, 1856. *Collections*, Kansas State Historical Society, 4: 391–392.

[24] Sumner to Cooper, June 8, 1856. *Collections*, Kansas State Historical Society, 4: 439–440.

Sumner's comment was too sweeping as the President's proclamation of February 11 was not yet six months old.

[25] *Ibid.*

[26] Shannon to the President, *Collections*, Kansas State Historical Society, 4: 386–389.

disorders in the Territory have, in fact, changed their character, and consist now of robberies and assassinations, by a set of bandits whom the excitement of the times has attracted hither.'' [27]   Sumner returned to his post June 22, reporting the next day that the only armed bands in the field were freebooters belonging to both parties, who were "taking advantage of the political excitement to commit their own rascally acts.'' [28]

The survey of the local sources leads to the conclusion that the central point in the free-state resistance to law enforcement was the courts upon whom devolved the responsibility for application of the laws, and especially any officer associated with the judiciary who was acting to enforce the territorial laws.   Although the free-state men abused the judges with the lowest forms of vituperative language, there was no record of violence to their persons, or authenticated threats of such violence.   Reeder's defiance of the marshal was the only specific instance of collision which might be termed resistance to him.   There was one instance of shooting at the federal troops, the incident at Storr's house, which may or may not have been adequately explained by the *Kansas Tribune*, (Cf. ante 76) but certainly Captain Newby did not view it in the same light when he wrote his report.   Clearly, the Reeder and Storr incidents were exceptions, which emphasize the prevailing situation.   The menace of armed free-state companies, which visited the courts or threatened to break them up, at Ozawkie in March and on the Potawatomie in April are suggestive of far-reaching possibilities, but the papers, pro-slavery or free-state, recorded no authenticated overt acts in this direction.

The situation seems too clear to admit of contradiction, that from the beginning the territorial government had reasonable grounds to believe that John Brown, Senior, and a band of men associated with him, were guilty of the Potawatomie massacre.   The inexplicable outcome, that John Brown was at one time actually detained peaceably by Colonel Sumner, that for some reason no warrants were available at that time, and that Sumner made no effort to hold him until the necessary papers arrived, creates one of the most portentous ''ifs'' in American history.   What if John Brown had been arrested, convicted of murder, and executed in Kansas in 1856?   Did Sumner singly, or in collusion with the territorial officials, de-

---

[27] Cook to Adj. Gen. Cooper, June 18, 1856. *Collections*, K. S. H. S., 4: 443–444.

[28] Sumner to Cooper, June 23, 1856. *Collections*, K. S. H. S., 4: 445.

liberately avoid making so important an arrest? Did he attach any particular importance to this unknown John Brown or is the perspective of the historian warped by a knowledge of subsequent events? It is clear that the chief objective of the federal troops was to disperse armed bands as the means of restoring peace, and furthermore, that Sumner was not in sympathy with Shannon's policies on all points. Did Sumner think of Brown's band as just one of a dozen or more similar thieving gangs of bandits, both pro-slavery and free-state, which he was engaged in dispersing, not arresting? Why did he not mention the incident in his report, unless he dismissed it as a matter of no importance?

The relatively successful pacification of June was threatened by the meeting of the Topeka legislature scheduled for July 4. Governor Shannon was leaving the territory for a brief period, but pointed out to Col. Sumner that in case that body should meet, enact laws and attempt to enforce them through courts, it would be a direct violation of law and would lead to conflict. Agreeing with the civil authorities on the necessity of action a program was worked out in conference. Dispersion of the legislature was accomplished without violence and Sumner reported the outcome to his superiors. Jefferson Davis, the Secretary of War, endorsed the report July 19 asking Sumner to explain more exactly what circumstances justified military intervention. He was exasperated particularly at Sumner's reference to the activities of the Missourians, holding that federal officers should not make distinctions between factions. Sumner's first reply was not considered adequate and he made his final statement August 31 interpreting the intent of his instructions as imposing upon him the duty of anticipating overt acts of treason by bringing to bear upon the situation the moral force of the military before it became uncontrollable.[29] The war department soon displaced him in Kansas and although no direct statement was forthcoming, the inference generally drawn was that the removal resulted from this affair. The petty partisanship and irritability displayed by Jefferson Davis emphasizes conspicuously a discord at Washington quite at variance with the ideal of a National Democracy and the paralyzing effect the knowledge of such differences imposed upon efficient action by subordinates who must deal with the local conflict in Kansas.

[29] Shannon to Marcy, June 23; Sumner to Cooper, July 7; Cooper to Sumner, July 21; Sumner to Cooper, August 11; endorsement by Jefferson Davis, August 27; Cooper to Sumner, August 28; Sumner to Cooper, August 31. *Coll.*, K. S. H. S., 4: 422–423, 429, 448–453.

CHAPTER VI

THE EASTERN PRESS; EARLY 1856

Any discussion of the New York *Tribune* and the Kansas question in 1856 should be introduced by reference to Horace Greeley's instructions written from Washington to Dana, his managing editor, on February 16, 1856: "We cannot (I fear) admit Reeder; we cannot admit Kansas as a State; we can only make issues on which to go to the people at the Presidential election." Shortly afterwards he added to the above: "Do not let your folks write more savagely than I do. I am fiery enough."[1] With Greeley as with most of the politically minded, the winning of the presidency was the prize and Kansas was the pawn. Anti-slavery people and abolitionists, who might not be republican or democratic, welcomed any agitation that would keep their issue alive. In its New Year's editorial, after referring to the most recent outrages following the Wakarusa war, the *Tribune* had declared that responsibility for further outrages rested, not on Shannon, Stringfellow or Atchison, or any other subordinate, but on Franklin Pierce and the democratic party. During January and February it rang all the changes on the Kansas disorders with predictions of renewal of civil war. Atchison's appeal to the South for emigrants was the signal for announcing "a new civil war in Kansas," and the next day's editorial explained "how to avert a Civil War." The solution was simple: "It is the immediate pouring into Kansas of a free population with the capital necessary to make its peculiar resources available for all the purposes of civilization."[2]

The keynote of the policy of the Pierce administration was to keep the Kansas question quiet in the hope of eliminating it from the campaign. The President's message insisted upon the enforcement of law and recommended organization of state government by

[1] Printed in the New York *Sun*, May 19, 1889 and cited in J. F. Rhodes, *History of the United States from the Compromise of 1850.* 2: 126.

[2] New York *Tribune*, January 21, 22, 1856.

The New York *Daily Tribune* was published in at least two editions, morning and 3 p.m., and as in the case of present day metropolitan papers, the contents and arrangement changed somewhat with each edition during the course of the day. The author has used the two editions indicated, one at the Kansas State Historical Society and the other at the University of Kansas.

duly elected and qualified voters. The *Tribune* said that he proposed a border ruffian convention to frame a state constitution and "finally, he winds up by calling for money to pay the expense of shooting down the Free State men. We shall see how much he gets."[3] When the President's proclamation was issued February 11, it was announced with the headlines "The Border-Ruffian Proclamation. Pro-Slavery War on Kansas Sustained."[4] This was followed the next day with a reprint of excerpts from the Kansas slave-property code, announcing that these were the laws the President was going to enforce.

In the absence of new outrages in Kansas during February and March Kansas news originated mostly in Washington. The lower house had before it the Whitfield-Reeder contest for the seat as delegate from Kansas, and the proposal, which was finally voted, setting up a committee to investigate the Kansas troubles. The senate received the Douglas and Collamer, majority and minority, reports on Kansas and in discussing the Kansas issue the *Tribune* attributed to Douglas the threat "We will subdue you." Douglas denied such a statement, but the damage was done and the phrase was to be repeated again and again in application to every new turn of the territorial disorders. When a Chicago minister, J. E. Roy, used it June 1 in a sermon dealing with the Brooks attack on Sumner, Douglas wrote him demanding that he make a retraction from the same pulpit.[5]

In spite of dire predictions of encouragement given the proslavery ruffians of Missouri by the President's actions, the *Tribune* reported news from the West that the border counties of Missouri would acquiesce in the existing state of affairs in Kansas and would make no aggressive movement, also, the Topeka state government would meet March 4 merely to organize and adjourn, so as to be prepared for other movements thereafter. "With these precautions on both sides," the article concluded, "no collision is now apprehended."[6] Some days later there was a return to the old form that there was "apprehension that a bloody collision is imminent." Encouraged by the President's message and proclamation the Missourians would make the meeting of the Topeka government "the

---

[3] *Tribune*, January 26, 1856.

[4] *Tribune*, February 13, 1856.

[5] Stephen D. Douglas to Rev. J. E. Roy, July 4, 1856. Cincinnati *Daily Enquirer*, July 19, 1856. Clipping in *Webb Scrapbooks* (K. S. H. S.), 15: 58.

[6] *Tribune*, February 23, 1856.

pretext for a raid, and if possible, a butchery. . . ." [7]   From Washington, Greeley announced that he had information that the arrest of the officers of the free-state government at Topeka was ordered and that Pierce believed they were already in prison.   He declared that this was Pierce's last bid against Douglas for renomination.[8] While Greeley was writing this from Washington, the *Tribune* published a five column report of the proceedings at Topeka in which part of the same theme was developed:

The immortal bogus Sheriff Jones, a tall, muscular, athletic loafer, with a cruel Mephisthophelean expression, clad in the Border Ruffian costume— blue military overcoat, large boots, skull cap and cigar in mouth—was present at the organization, and amused himself and the members both, by writing down the names of the Senators and Representatives as they took the oath of office.[9]

Later a report from the Boston *Traveller* was reprinted describing the enthusiasm of the members declaring that "every member but *one* readily and boldly took the solemn oath." Emphasis was placed upon the point that there would be no backing down and that a committee had been appointed to draft a code of laws.[10]

From Osawatomie came a letter dated March 5 stating that the community was free-state almost to a man, that the Missourians said the legislature should not meet, that they were encouraged by the President's message and proclamation "and if they do as they threaten now, you will hear of bloody work before summer opens." The writer admitted that the legislature had no right to enact laws, but also Missouri had no right to interfere, but hundreds of ruffians were said to be on the road toward Topeka.   In order to insure peace he said: "They have formed a volunteer company here, and have enrolled over sixty men.   Their rifles have not yet arrived, unfortunately.   If they come in season, you will hear from the Osawatomie Rangers.   If it gets hot, they will go in with pitchforks." [11]

The following day the *Tribune* published a letter from the Rev. S. L. Adair, a relative by marriage of John Brown, written from Osawatomie March 15:

Missourians are now and have been for about two weeks pouring into the Territory.   They come in Companies, take claims, squat, and claim to

7 *Tribune*, March 3, 1856.
8 *Tribune*, March 21, 1856.
9 *Tribune*, March 21, 1856.
10 New York *Tribune*, April 4, 1856.
11 *Tribune*, March 27, 1856.

be citizens. Missouri has somewhat changed her tactics. Emigrant Aid Societies have been formed, it is said, in various places, for the purpose of helping men to come to Kansas. The society at Westport, I am told, offers to give one year's provisions and money to enter one quarter section of land when it comes into the market to any man true to slavery, who will enter into the Territory and remain there. It is this effort that is now pouring them in upon us.

After expressing fears about the legislature at Topeka and the enforcement of the laws, he commented that northern immigrants were arriving, and concluded the letter in gloom; "Pro-Slavery men verily seem to be going mad. The grand struggle, to human appearance, rapidly approaches."

Agitation was kept up in New York by various means, one especially supported by the *Tribune* being mass meetings at the Tabernacle, where agitators returned from Kansas told their stories of the Kansas outrages, and incidentally money was raised to finance the cause.[12] On April 15 a change in Missouri policy was fully reported from the Weston *Reporter* which announced that the "day of folly" had passed and the self-defensive society was dead, and in its place was now the Pro-Slavery Emigrant Aid Society which was organized to promote immigration from the South into Kansas. The *Tribune* enjoyed the opportunity to point out the imitation of the New England Emigrant Aid Company which the pro-slavery men had been condemning as the cause of Kansas troubles. The southern efforts at emigration had been under way for several months and in the issue of May 13 the *Tribune* announced the arrival in Kansas April 31 of the most notorious of the southern parties under Buford.

If Kansas news had proved less sensational than the agitators had hoped during these early months of the year, the months of May and June turned out to be an agitator's paradise. William Walker's filibustering expedition in Nicaragua shared honors with Kansas, and for a time the Brooks attack on Sumner almost eclipsed both. Sheriff Jones's difficulties in Lawrence April 19–23 were announced in two five-line telegraphic items April 28, one by way of Chicago and the other from St. Louis. The former stated that Jones had been resisted in making arrests and the troops had been ordered out, but the public was warned that the story was doubtful. The second story stated that several arrests had been made by troops and Jones had been shot. By May 2 additional news began to ar-

12 For reports of these spring meetings, *Tribune*, March 26 and April 30, 1856.

rive and May 3 there were three columns. The issue of May 8 contained a letter of the *Tribune* correspondent "Potter," [Hugh Young] written April 25 including the proceedings of the public meeting at Lawrence repudiating the assassination. Potter said that it was generally believed that Jones was shot by a pro-slavery man with whom he had difficulties. On May 15, with the aid of some new developments letters from Lawrence made three columns, the one dated April 30 being devoted mostly to the Jones affair, in which he was blamed for getting himself shot because he spent the evening in a lighted tent instead of going to the Free State Hotel where he would have been safe.

The congressional committee had arrived in Kansas and was holding hearings during the last days of April and it became the central theme of much Kansas news. The subject of Potter's letter of May 2 was "subduing Kansas by assassination." Two instances were cited, an unsuccessful attempt on Captain Cracklin and the night attack on J. N. Mace because of his testimony before the committee. Potter declared: "The declaration of Douglas made with that cool affrontery which is one of the characteristics of Border Ruffianism, 'We intend to subdue you,' proves to be more than a mere threat. . . . Not content with enforcing the infamous laws . . . they now propose to subdue us by assassinating our most peaceful citizens. . . ." The issues of May 16 and 17 contained respectively seven and ten columns of Kansas material. On the latter date the Kansas editorial opened: "The Kansas letters which we give today, both from Lawrence and Lecompton, show the operation of 'We will subdue you' in full blast." Judge Lecompte's court and Pardee Butler's tar and cottoning stories introduced new themes to the narratives of outrages. On May 19 "Bostwick," another leading *Tribune* correspondent, reported in full on Lecompte's court and gave the text of his mythical charge to the grand jury on "constructive treason," and the subsequent indictments, an account of the Reeder affair, and arrived at this conclusion: "First, *they wish to shoot Gov. Reeder, and they will if they can;* second, they either wish to break up the investigation of the Commission, or by making these arrests, cause the Commission to report that we won't obey the law. . . . In the first they would delay a report until after the Presidential election, and, in the other, have a report in their favor."

The next day's headlines were "The Congressional Committee to be put down. Civil War close at Hand. The Missourians gather.

Lawrence armed and Fortified. God save the Right!'' These introduced two and a half columns of Kansas matter. On May 23 the headlines stated ''The War Actually Begun,'' but no news of hostilities was printed and no Kansas information later than May 15 was involved, but Kansas filled three and a half columns. The ''sack of Lawrence'' occurred on May 21, but the first news appeared in the Tribune May 26 headed ''Lawrence in Ruins.'' Only telegraphic news from St. Louis was available, but there was an accumulation of other Kansas correspondence bearing dates from May 10 and later sufficient to fill a whole page. The destruction of Lawrence was confirmed the next day, but the first particulars were printed May 28 from correspondence of St. Louis papers. Buried in this new sensation, however, was a brief paragraph of an incident over a month old, but without date: ''At the latter place [Osawatomie] Judge Cato of the District Court had been prevented from holding Court in consequence of threats of violence to the Grand Jury which had been made by Free State men.'' The following day, May 29, the Tribune could print for the first time an account of ''Lawrence in Ashes'' from one of its own Kansas correspondents, William Hutchinson. The fact that Jones led the mob confirmed the Tribune, May 31, in its conviction that ''We suggested at the first, that the alleged shooting of Jones was a sham and a trick.'' The same idea was repeated June 5 and the Tribune took Robinson's opinion that the ''pretended shooting was all a sham—a trick got up by the Border Ruffians to lay the foundation for a new Border Ruffian raid upon Lawrence.'' Jones's return to activity, it was argued, confirmed suspicion that the gun had no bullet in it and the wound was a pretense.

Although Lawrence continued to dominate Kansas news, it is time to introduce the disorders in the southeastern part of the territory. The first Tribune reference to the Potawatomie massacre was May 31 when a telegraphic dispatch was relayed from St. Louis, credited to the pro-slavery Republican, May 30 by way of Independence, May 26, but it was presented under the warning headline, ''Pro-Slavery Falsehoods.'' On June 3 it presented Kansas news from its own correspondent, by telegraph, dated Leavenworth, May 28, declaring ''events indicate that we have now reached a point when wholesale bloodshed is inevitable.'' He related that the Westport Border Times Extra headlined ''War! War!'' had been sent to all parts of the territory, a meeting was being held behind closed doors and a vigilance committee appointed at Leavenworth with instructions to let no free-state man pass, and a list had been prepared and arrests were in progress, one of the number being a clerk of the congressional committee:

> It is believed here that a bloody collision toward Pottawatomie is inevitable. The last serious difficulty occurred on the Pottawatomie Creek. A gang of Border Ruffians attempted to drive a Free-State man from his claim. He resisted, when they seized him and were about to hang him. But some of his neighbors came to his rescue, and in the fight that occurred some of the Border Ruffians were shot. · That a civil war is now begun is beyond all doubt.

The same issue published a St. Louis *Republican* story that the Leavenworth *Herald* had issued an extra confirming the murders, and reporting that all the pro-slavery families at Hickory Point had been driven off and their horses and provisions stolen by free-state men. The following day, a telegraphic story, after reviewing the activities of Buford's men and the Leavenworth men, drew a parallel: "The reported cold-blooded murder of eight Pro-Slavery men [near] Ossawatomie is altogether a different affair. Five Pro-Slavery men had got a Free State man, tied a rope around his neck, and were just about to swing him off, when a party of his friends came up and shot his persecutors dead." In the same issue of June 4 were two and a half columns of "Startling News from Kansas," devoted mostly to the Lawrence affair, but with one paragraph stating that Colonel Sumner had been removed because his activities were objectionable to the pro-slavery party and a Southerner, General Harney, placed in command of the federal troops in Kansas, and another as follows: "One hundred and fifty men from Osawatomie had started to Lawrence when the news of what had befallen it reached them; but the appearance of the United States troops showed them the rashness of commencing operations until the matter as it stands has been carefully weighed." "A Border Ruffian View" from the St. Louis *Republican* May 30 was thrown in for good measure, narrating the Lawrence law enforcement episode and one of the early reports of the Potawatomie massacre by a band of abolitionists who "have determined for some time past at the proper hour to wreak their vengence upon any opponents of their views. . . . What was the immediate exciting cause we have not learned." The *Republican* regretted the new outbreak of violence as it had hoped that after the necessary violence at Lawrence required in enforcement of the laws that the territory would remain

quiet. By telegraph from Chicago the same issue had still another
story, this time from the Chicago *Tribune's* correspondent:

> A gentleman, just arrived, reports that the difficulty mentioned as oc-
> curring at Potawatomie Creek took place at Osawatomie. The quarrel
> arose from depredations committed by the Pro-Slavery men on the cattle
> of the Free State men.
> On the 26th some Pro-Slavery men seized a Free-State man and pro-
> ceeded to hang him, when his wife fled and aroused the neighbors who
> came to his rescue. A fight ensued, and five Pro-Slavery men and two
> Free-State men were killed.

This account concluded with a report that "a force of sixty men
was organized at Westport, Missouri, on the 27th ult. and proceeded
to Osawatomie." On June 5 the *Tribune* had received a further
supply of stories. A letter from its correspondent dated at Leavenworth May 25 said that Governor Robinson had been indicted for
usurpation and for treason, and that in a conversation, Judge Lecompte had informed Robinson that the latter was based on the
events of November and December, 1855. The *Tribune* correspondent exclaimed: "Hear it, oh ye people of America! Gov. Robinson
stands indicted for high treason because he took a prominent part in
organizing resistance to an armed mob from Missouri. INDICTED
FOR THE DEFENSE OF LAWRENCE LAST FALL . . .!" [13]
Another letter from Leavenworth dated May 28 appeared in the
same issue with the above reporting as rumor, for what it might be
worth, that pro-slavery men took a free-state man from his house
and were about to hang him when his neighbors rescued him at the
cost of five pro-slavery lives. "If true," the correspondent pointed
out, "it is the first aggressive act of the Free State men, and is not
to be wondered at." Excerpts were printed from the Westport
Border Times reporting the Potawatomie massacre and the driving
of all pro-slavery settlers from Hickory Point. Another *Tribune*
correspondent in Kansas reported by telegraph the rescue story in
almost exactly the same words as it had been printed the day before.
And then, to clinch the Kansas horrors printed in the issue of June
5, the editor contributed a full column of comment. He argued that
the free-state men were not subdued, but were disposed to avoid
collisions, that they were widely dispersed over the territory and the
pro-slavery men found it a slow process to drive them all out:

> There are some outrages, however, to which they will not submit. A
> party of these Ruffians while engaged in hanging a Free-State man at

---

[13] It ought not to be necessary, but in order to keep the record straight,
the reader should be warned that the *Tribune* correspondent lied.

Osawatomie, were set upon by his neighbors, who shot five of them, with a loss of two of their number. This is the foundation of the story of the murder of eight Pro-Slavery men with circumstances of great atrocity, spread over the country by telegraph a day or two since.

Having given *Tribune* readers this practical demonstration in the relative veracity of free-state and pro-slavery news from Kansas, the editor returned to the task the following day. He charged that Judge Lecompte and Governor Shannon had never yet attempted to bring to justice a pro-slavery man who had murdered a free-state man, but, by contrast:

It appears that they are now determined to shoot or hang the Free State men at Osawatomie, who rescued one of their brethren whom a Pro-Slavery mob was attempting to hang, at the cost of five Pro-Slavery and two Free State mens lives lost in the fray. The Free State men are reported to bid defiance to those sent to arrest them.

On June 6 the *Tribune* published a letter "from a most respectable clergyman of the Methodist church," which had been communicated by the recipient for publication. The letter was concerned primarily with the Lawrence troubles, but toward the end there were a few lines dealing with local conditions at Osawatomie, from which place the letter was written May 23, the day before the Potawatomie massacre, in fact, on the afternoon of the day this letter was written John Brown and his seven companions set out on the expedition.

You may well suppose that many here are in a state of alarm. For my part I do not feel very much moved. I have been expecting this, and even worse than has yet happened. [He was still referring to Lawrence.] We have a company of Alabamans camped near us, some 60 or 70 in number. When sober they say that they came here to settle, and to make this a Slave State; are very sanguine that they will succeed; tell great stories of what the South are 'a-going to do.' But when they get drunk (and that is as often as they can get liquor to get drunk on) they are ready to fight, and threaten, and make a great noise. But they have a number of families with them, and although armed, are in no very safe situation to make an attack on any village or settlement.

In great haste I close. . . . I would, however, say further, that it is not yet known what Colonel Sumner and the United States troops will do under the present aspect of affairs. The Free-State men are rallying at Prairie City, some 15 miles south of Lawrence, to determine on means and measures for their own protection.

By the time of the June 9 issue the *Tribune* was receiving mail correspondence on the Potawatomie incident. A man traveling in Kansas wrote May 28 to Cincinnati, where the *Gazette* printed the story, and the *Tribune* was reprinting it:

I learned the following particulars of the Osawatomie affair from an eye-witness: a man was travelling alone, on foot, and was overtaken by a guerilla Pro-Slavery band of seven men. They asked him where he was from? He told them. 'Are you a Free-State man?' 'Yes, he replied.' They then robbed him, and after holding a consultation decided to hang him. A Free-State man, who happened to be hunting nearby, overheard and saw what was going on. He went off and raised twelve men, who came and concealed themselves in the brush near by, and when they were about to hang the traveler fired and killed five of the Pro-Slavery men. The other two fled, one of them being wounded.

The next day the *Tribune* made another original contribution, from another "eye-witness," a story related to a man in St. Louis, who wrote it to George Walter, General Superintendent of the New York State Kansas League. This story reported how a free-state man went to a store to buy lead, and on asking the price was informed, eighteen cents, but twenty-five cents to free-state men. On being asked what he wanted it for, he replied, "Wolves, if they come my way, or even a man, if attacked." He was then seized and hustled to the timber, but meanwhile another free-state man slipped out the back door and notified an armed free-state band. Just as the rope was being adjusted around the victim's neck, five shots were fired from the thicket and five pro-slavery men fell dead.

Events in Kansas were again outrunning the full details of the news. The same issue of the *Tribune* contained two brief notices of "A Field Fight in Kansas," being the story of a fight at Palmyra [Black Jack] between nearly equal parties with Pate the leader of the pro-slavery men captured. The federal troops were said to have known of the battle but did not interfere until the next day when they dispersed the free-state men and released their pro-slavery prisoners. The following day the spread of disorder was recorded from pro-slavery sources: The *Border Times* that the free-state men made an attack on Bernard June 3, and on Franklin June 4 where three pro-slavery men were reported killed; The St. Louis *Republican* that Marshal Donalson was killed by free-state men June 3 and after Pate's capture, the free-state men started driving out the settlers on Bull creek and Captain Reid had set out to aid the pro-slavery men. These stories were off-set by a report from the Chicago *Democratic Press* that a pro-slavery party which included the son of Governor Shannon, had attacked Captain Walker's house.

A mail version of the battle of Palmyra was printed on June 12, together with the exploits of free-state guerilla parties. The correspondent stated that he knew two such, and it was one of them that captured Pate, and six youths from one of these entered a camp of about eighty pro-slavery men and stole their best horses, and on another occasion some of these seized a large quantity of ammunition. Thus now that the war was on the free-state correspondents delighted to regale their readers with the superior qualities of their men in the arts of war. And still the stories from the Potawatomie came in, this time from the Chicago *Tribune's* meticulous correspondent who was so conscientious that he sent a special messenger to make a personal investigation, and the result was a highly dramatized version of the lead-purchase story, which demonstrates what a remarkable job of reporting could be done in Kansas if only the writer concentrated on his task:

Horrible stories are told in Missouri of the murder of five Pro-Slavery men at Osawatomie. It is said that their throats were cut, and their corpses mangled and chopped into inches. Of course the Free State party, as a party—every Northern man and every Southern man with Northern principles—in the Territory, is accused by the organs of the Ruffians with this imaginary and revolting atrocity.

It is stated that their houses were entered at midnight and the victims of this outrage murdered in their beds.

I remained a day at Prairie City, in order to find out the truth of this report. I sent a messenger to Osawatomie to investigate the circumstances.

The facts, of course, refute the Missouri version of the affair.

Five men were killed. There is no doubt of that fact.

Their names are William Sherman, better known as Dutch Henry; a father and two sons, named Doyle; and Mr. Wilkinson, a Member of the House of Representatives of the Bogus Kansas Legislature.

They were shot by a party of Free State boys—at least I infer so, from the cause of their summary execution.

These men have bullied and threatened the lives of the Northern Squatters in that section ever since the invasion of November last. Doyle and his sons have been particularly active in harrassing and assaulting the Free State men.

On the day on which these men were killed, a flag inscribed *"Head Quarters of the Pro-Slavery Army,"* was hoisted over Sherman's store. A Free State man went in and enquired the price of powder. The man told him he charged ten cents a pound to Pro-Slavery men, but as he was a d--d nigger thief he would have to pay twenty-five cents.

Some angry words passed between the parties. Wilkinson then seized on the squatter, and told him that, as he refused to acknowledge the Territorial laws as valid enactments, they would give him a lesson to teach him what his principles would lead to. They said he ought to have been hanged long ago; and now as they had him in their power, by G--d they would give him his due.

They kept him confined an hour or two. After dark they took him out, went down with him to the woods, put a rope around his neck, and an end of it over the limb of a tree, and were preparing to hoist him up.

"Fire!"

The report of five rifles were heard simultaneously with this unexpected command. Five corpses—the bodies of the Doyles, Sherman and Wilkinson were seen stretched on the grass as soon as the smoke cleared away.

"Fly!" cried the same voice who had given the order to fire.

The man whose life was so mysteriously and unexpectedly saved, as soon as he removed the rope from his neck, went into the woods and shouted for his friends.

But they had disappeared as suddenly and mysteriously as they came.

This act will be made the excuse for arresting every man in that section of the State, who has made himself obnoxious, or is likely to be a leader in defending the lives and property of Northern men.

A new horror story was ready June 13, the sack of Osawatomie on June 7 by the pro-slavery forces dispersed by the federal troops at Palmyra, twenty-five houses plundered, sixteen horses stolen, and printing materials destroyed and even the ear and finger-rings taken from the free-state women. Not satisfied with printing the story once, it was reprinted June 14 and again June 17. On the last date the correspondent added a personal comment that, "I could not learn whether this was done by virtue of a writ from the First District Court of the United States for Kansas Territory, or whether the Grand Jury had found a bill against Osawatomie and the earrings for a 'nuisance' that must be abated."

In the *Tribune* June 13, however, important news was printed without headlines or comment of any kind; buried in an account of the battle of Palmyra appeared a single casual mention of the name of a free-state leader, John Brown. Fate decreed, however, that it should be his erstwhile prisoner, Henry Clay Pate, who should really introduce him to nationwide notoriety. The line of argument given in an interview to the editor of the Leavenworth *Herald* was stated by Pate in a formal letter, first published in the St. Louis *Republican* and reprinted in the New York *Tribune* June 17. In this letter Pate had referred to Brown as the Potawatomie murderer, although he had not designated which Brown. The letter came to the attention of John Brown, Sr., who in a letter dated at Lawrence July 1 and published in the *Tribune* July 11, ignored the reference to Potawatomie but challenged Pate's account of the battle of Black Jack (Palmyra). This is only one of many controversies raised by that battle. Another Pate episode was a card to the *Tribune,* dated June 30, printed July 4, 1856 in answer to charges made by the

Tribune. First, the charge that he was not a citizen of Kansas was met by publishing a copy of his entry at the land office June 14, 1856 for the southeast fractional quarter (120 acres), section 1, T 12 s., R. 18 e., near Lecompton. Second, to the charge that Pate and his men had dodged behind logs and stumps, he answered there were none, and there was only one tree on the field, which was nearer Brown than himself. Third, to the charge of cowardice, he gave both his Lecompton and Washington addresses. Fourth, to the charge that he put prisoners in the front line, he stated they were in the rear under guard until both parties took to the ravines, and a guard was with them all the time. Fifth, to the charge that he was without authority, he cited T. W. Hays, United States Marshal to Judge Cato's court who had deputized him.

On July 16 Pate made an assault upon Hanscomb, formerly a clerk of the congressional committee investigating Kansas affairs and while in that capacity active in free-state politics in Kansas. Hanscomb had written an article published in the *Tribune* July 8 accusing Pate of showing the white feather at Black Jack. Pate challenged him, but failing to receive satisfaction, visited him at his lodgings and assaulted him.[14]

Whitfield, although territorial delegate to congress, had decided to take the field, and that needed explanation, which he took the precaution of making beforehand, or at least it was so dated. The *Tribune* printed it June 20 from the *Border Times.* His justification was that when the news arrived that Pate was attacked by Brown, the cowardly and fiendish manner of the Potawatomie assassination left little hope but that he would be annihilated, and so he raised a company of men to go to the rescue even though his act would be misrepresented. In the same issue was another story, this from another pro-slavery paper the St. Louis *Republican,* stating that Mrs. Doyle was then in Westport (June 9), confirmed the story of the massacre, and declared that the men who committed the murder were among those whom Colonel Sumner had dispersed the past week—

without an effort to arrest them—virtually turned them loose, that they may commit their fiendish acts again. Had the citizen soldiers been let alone, they would have secured them and brought them to trial; as it is, they are at large.

The excitement . . . is intense. The Abolitionists have driven nearly all the Pro-Slavery party from the Ossawatomie settlement. Several families from Hickory Point have been driven off from their homes. . . .

[14] New York *Tribune,* July 22, 1856.

P. S. Since writing the above, I have learned from Dr. Woods, who was present, that Colonel Sumner was not to blame for not arresting Brown. The Colonel thought Col. Preston, the Deputy Marshall, had writs for Brown and others, which turned out otherwise. Sumner detained Brown and his company, telling them Preston had writs for them, but when Preston came up he said he had no writs against them.

The arrest of the Browns supplied the theme of articles for some time. The *Tribune* correspondent, writing from Lawrence June 12, printed June 27, reported the arrest of Captain Abbott:

Peace reigns in Warsaw. I do not know a solitary Free-State camp in the field. Today Capt. Abbott was taken by the dragoons near his own house. They wanted to get John Brown, sen., Captain of another Free State company, and with a noble discrimination and delicate tact, they arrested Abbott, and insisted on his *telling them where Capt. Brown was.* That is, to secure his own safety, he must betray one who, whatever his faults, was a brother in arms.

The correspondent insisted that Captain Abbott probably knew no more about Brown than they did, but he made a damaging admission that Brown's "faults" were strongly disapproved by free-state leaders even though, out of loyalty to the cause, they would not betray him.

The excitement had quickly reached Ft. Scott, the most southerly outpost of settlement, a correspondent of the *Tribune* reporting June 4, printed June 30, that

The intelligence that Lawrence was burned was received at this 'rendezvous of Border Ruffianism' with general feelings of joy, but it was followed by the rumor that at Osawatomie five, and some said nine, Pro-Slavery men had been called up in the night and as soon as they made their appearance were shot by the Abolitionists. This caused a general feeling of alarm and indignation, and the young men of Fort Scott, on their own responsibility, organized themselves into a 'watch guard' to protect the Fort from invasion by the Abolitionists, as, to aid the excitement, it had been currently reported that Fort Scott was threatened to be burned, as a retaliation for the destruction of Lawrence.

The upshot was that Henry S. Clubb, of the Vegetarian Settlement, Neosho City, about forty miles west of Ft. Scott, arrived in town, and being a stranger to the vigilance committee, was seized although after some excitement released with apologies. The correspondent called attention to the strategic position of the town for the overland trade, Indian trade and other activities and urged that business should not be discouraged by disorders, adding that here was an opportunity for free-state capital to take possession and develop its trading possibilities.

The *Tribune* correspondent wrote from Lecompton, June 21 that there were no free-state bands in the field as the leaders had decided to comply with the governor's proclamation and give the troops a chance to redeem their promises, "but this course does not give peace; it does not give security, it does not give justice, or even hope of success to the Free State cause. The policy may be good, but all the Free State Settlers have to hope for must come from a different course." He insisted that pro-slavery bands were still roving. Many of the free-state young men had left, he said, as they could not live without money and could not take up claims without security. Referring to the past difficulties, he told of the Manhattan company that had started to the aid of Lawrence but had arrived too late, and of the Osawatomie company under Captain John Brown which arrived the day after the sack of Lawrence and camped some distance from the town. Of this latter company, many had since been indicted for treason and he reported eight were then prisoners. While in Lt. McIntosh's camp the correspondent asked about his promise that Osawatomie would not be sacked and about two particular prisoners, Captain John Brown [Jr.,] and his brother Jason:

Lieut. McIntosh accused them of being murderers, and said he *knew* that they were concerned in the killing at Pottawatomie Creek. I thought he was mistaken and told him so; but he was positive and said that was what they were kept for. There was no legal process against them. Now they are indicted with the others for High Treason, and this is the only charge against them. That TREASON being flying to the help of Lawrence, but all too late to save it. It is certain that these two Browns [15] were not engaged in the killing at the Pottawatomie. Let that killing have been in what manner it may, they at least were in Lawrence at the time. This can be sworn to by fifty witnesses, and I suppose their persecutors know it; and yet these brave men have been subjected to a cruel imprisonment, and are now in peril of their lives, for an act which there is not a generous mind in the country but will admire.

In addition, he reported that Pate, fresh from the sack of Lawrence, and before the return of the Browns to their home, burned their houses, Captain Brown losing a fine library. "So goes Dragoon Government in Kansas," exclaimed the correspondent. and when Pate was captured, the dragoons liberated him, restored his horses, and then he joined with Whitfield and sacked Osawatomie. In contrast, how were free-state men treated? "Captain

[15] Note the careful limitation of the statement to "these two Browns," which implied possibly that he knew that the other Browns were guilty.

Brown and his brother Jason, taken while returning home [from Lawrence] alone, by a band of Missouri Ruffians, and then transferred to the troops, ignominiously chained in the exposure of a soldiers camp, held without legal process, and then turned over to the Territorial Courts, where they were indicted for treason."[16]

The story of the march of the prisoners was told again with more lurid details in the *Tribune* July 7, and two days later an account of their examination before Commissioner Hoogland was summarized from the St. Louis *Democrat* of July 4. The accused were John Brown, Jr., Jason Brown, P. Maness, Samuel W. Kilborn, H. H. Williams, S. B. Morse, William Partridge, under arrest for treason on warrants issued by Judge Cato, and all were members of the military company which marched to the aid of Lawrence in May. The *Tribune* concluded:

The evidence established nothing against anybody but Brown, Jr., Williams, Partridge, and Morse, and of these it was deemed sufficient to hold only Williams and Morse to bail. The most serious aspect of the case, as the *Tribune* saw it, was the Osawatomie resolutions of April 16, 1856, which were reprinted in full.[17]

The next news from southeastern Kansas was the report of a tour of the Osawatomie region by the *Tribune* correspondent, dated from that town June 28, and printed July 11. He reported that the effects of the disorders were easily visible, and not a few of the deserted claims had been held by pro-slavery men:

In the neighborhood of Osawatomie lives Capt. Brown, and after the war had fairly broken out this spring, that gentleman went into it after a fashion not peculiarly suited to the views of the Border Ruffians and their confreres in the Territory. Those who had held a monopoly of infamous persecution, and who had been delighted to harass the Free State settlers, killing, burning, plundering, and driving off; learned to their astonishment that this was a game at which more than one can play, and terrified by the fearless energy of their opponent, quailed before it. Some of the more delicately scrupulous of the Free State settlers shrank from some of the acts of Brown, and when the account of his course reached them through Pro-Slavery channels, distorted by fear and bitter party prejudice, some of them did not hesitate to denounce those Free State men who

[16] New York *Tribune*, July 2, 1856.

[17] It is a matter of considerable importance that the *Democrat* had printed a stenographic report of the evidence taken at the hearing June 20. Some other papers did likewise, but not the *Tribune*.

It is remarkable that no historian of the Brown problem has used this important material. Cf., the present author's "The Hoogland Examination," *Kansas Historical Quarterly*, 7 (May 1938) 133–153, where the text of the hearing was reprinted.

thus stepped into the vortex of civil war in which others had plunged them, and anxious to eschew all imputation of such real or fancied guilt, freely condemned in others that which timidity, or a hope that there would be 'peace—peace when there was no peace,' had prevented themselves from doing. It is more than likely that some of the acts of these guerilla bands have been such as a peace-loving man would not admire, and perhaps the warfare may have been waged with a bitterness which every honorable man must deplore.

But as I stood on the ashes of the homes of the Free State men . . . [and reflected on their wrongs and on those in prison] then I comprehended the spirit and motives by which they might be impelled.[18]

"What is to be done for Kansas?" queried Horace Greeley from Washington, in the midst of the presidential campaign and the attempts of the administration to compromise the difficulties and bring peace to Kansas and, equally or more important, political peace to themselves. He was opposed to compromise: "What we must demand and must insist upon is" (1) admission as a state, (2) annulment of the bogus laws, (3) deliverance of the treason prisoners, (4) compensation of free-state settlers for losses incurred by pro-slavery plundering, (5) punishment of the devastators of Lawrence and the murders of Dow, Barber, Brown and others. As the first installment of this program, and during the current session of congress, they would accept the admission of Kansas under the Topeka constitution.[19]

But, in the meantime, devastated Lawrence was suffering from "outrages" other than those inflicted by whiskey-soaked border ruffians. Taking their cue from the free-state men who resisted the bogus laws they had not helped to enact early in July the women of Lawrence defied the government and with hatchets raided the liquor dealers' establishments.[20] Lawrence men must have been as persistent however because fifty Lawrence women were again in rebellion the following January and emptied into the streets seven barrels of whiskey and one of brandy.[21]

As the *National Intelligencer* was not particularly interested in Kansas as propaganda, its news policy was markedly different from that of the New York *Tribune*. It carried Kansas news only dur-

---

[18] In the above account and also in another in the same issue, the charge was again repeated that Pate had burned the Brown cabins. In the above account the statement was made specifically that it was done while Pate was travelling with the dragoons.

[19] New York *Tribune*, July 3, 1856.

[20] New York *Tribune*, July 11, 1856.

[21] Topeka *Tribune*, January 26, 1857.

ing periods of disturbances, and then only exchanges and telegraphic bulletins. The "sack" of Lawrence May 21 was first reported in the issue of May 29 in four telegraphic notices. The issue
of May 31 carried mail correspondence about Lawrence dated May
15 and other items by telegraph as late as May 30, the last mentioned being a report from St. Louis of the Potawatomie massacre.
On June 3, Lawrence news by mail bore a May 16 date line. On
June 7 there were two Potawatomie stories by telegraph, one of
which explained the affair as an attack on a camp of Georgians in
retaliation for depredations. On June 10 appeared the stock story
about hanging a free-state man, and another version of the Buford
depredations story. In a Leavenworth dispatch from the St. Louis
Democrat printed in the same issue, the writer complained of free-
state men leaving the territory and charged them with not having
sufficient nerve in the crisis, but in the southeastern part of the territory the free-state settlers were in arms. On June 12 pro-slavery
accounts were published of free-state depredations during the first
days of June, including a mention of the capture of Pate, but it was
not until June 19 that a free-state version appeared in which the
name of Captain Brown occurred. So far as the *Intelligencer* is
concerned Brown did not break into the news until the issue of August 26, and then, ironically enough, in connection with events in
which he was not a participant.

The Boston *Daily Evening Traveller,* during the first month of
1856, took much the same course as the New York *Tribune* on the
question of Kansas and maintained its connections through special
correspondents in Kansas. A letter signed "W" and dated at the
Free State Hotel, Headquarters, January 25, 1856, assumed the accustomed melodramatic war correspondent style:

> As I write, the heavy and measured tread of the sentinel, as he paces
> his beat on the roof above my head in the midst of a blinding snow storm,
> reminds me that I am at the very focus towards which all eyes are now
> turned. And well they may. This nation, at least the northern portion of
> it, are not aware that they are standing on the very brink of a volcano,
> just ready to belch forth its destructive torrents.

There was much of the same, the danger of a surprise attack at any
moment:

> Governor Robinson does not sleep at his own house, but takes his quar-
> ters here in this fortress, and sleeps sometimes in my room, while a com-
> pany of soldiers are quartered in another near by. The roof of the build-
> ing, three stories in height, has a parapet running all around it, pierced

with loop holes, from which in a street fight there could be poured a most destructive volley of rifle balls.[22]

The New York *Times* declared that "the proofs multiply that the question of Slavery domination must and will be fought out on the plains of Kansas," that the present peace was just a short armistice, and that the President's message was "in substance a declaration of war."[23] The Providence *Journal*, February 15, answered the *Post's* charge, that those who sent rifles to Kansas were responsible for disorders, by a comparison; "if a man anticipates a burglarous attack upon his house, the friend who lends him a rifle to defend himself," according to the *Post's* theory, "is just as bad as the robber who attempts to break in." The Cincinnati *Commercial* boasted that "there are thousands of young men in Ohio whose fingers itch for a trial with the Border Ruffians of Missouri," but the St. Louis *Evening News*, February 16, reproved its neighbor: "It is by such insane and senseless words as these that the warlike Ohioans and others are inflamed . . . , and by similar inflammatory appeals that the Border Ruffians, too, are made to 'itch.' . . . Let as many young men from Ohio as wish to, go to Kansas and buy farms, but let them behave themselves."

The Detroit *Advertiser*, February 18, denounced the President's proclamation as "a national insult," asked "at what point does forebearance cease to be a virtue," and implored its readers, "Has the blood of our fathers become rotten in the veins of their sons, that this infamous proclamation can be calmly pondered by them?" A New Hampshire paper argued that before a President enforced a law, his first duty was to determine its "wisdom and justice."[24] In Chicago a minister preached a sermon on meekness, saying that to furnish weapons with which to shoot down fellowmen was unbecoming a Christian. This sermon was intended as a criticism of Henry Ward Beecher, for taking subscriptions for Sharps rifles at North Church, New Haven. The Chicago *Tribune* was furious: "at such a time, it does not become ministers of the Gospel to revamp the doctrine of *passive obedience,* which has, in all ages, been the darling of tyrants."[25]

When the advertised Kansas outrages did not occur according to schedule on March 4, the New Haven *Register* asked why, and the

[22] *Daily Evening Traveller*, February 13, 1856.
[23] New York *Semi-Weekly Times*, February 15, 1856.
[24] Concord, New Hampshire *Independent Democrat*, February 21, 1856.
[25] Chicago *Daily Tribune*, April 1, 1856.

Springfield *Republican,* whose chief reason for existence was to look after the affairs of others, replied: "The outrages did not come off because the free-state men are well armed with those patent peace-compellers, Sharpe's rifles, and have the courage to use them." [26] A Boston paper was sure Providence had intervened with extremely cold weather. [27] The national democratic papers had their ideas why the Kansas agitation was being kept up in the face of generally peaceful conditions. First, to defray the expenses of itinerant agitators and further the interests of Seward for the presidency. [28] A second reason was to keep up a sham fight there as a means of raising money in the East for Kansas. [29] A third was by embittering the situation the republicans could keep Kansas out of the Union and make campaign issues. [30] A fourth was to elect Robinson governor of Kansas. [31] A fifth was to promote land speculation and sell land to the excited emigrants induced to go to Kansas. [32] A sixth applied to the New Hampshire election of March 11 in particular on which the republican party was concentrating in order to strengthen the general party position. [33] The New York *Journal of Commerce* thought the abolition republicans were hard to please as they had been denouncing the President for not using the federal troops, and now were condemning him for proposing to use them. [34] The Lowell (Massachusetts) *Evening Advertiser* argued that to set up a state government in Kansas and resist the federal government by force was treason, and likewise for people in the North to contribute money and arms to support such a movement was equally treason. [35] The interference of states, whether North or South in the affairs of the territory were denounced by the Governor of Indiana in answer to an appeal of the Kansas leaders, [36] and the same position was endorsed by a number of newspapers. [37]

The South had its full share of extremists, such as the Rich-

[26] Springfield *Republican,* March 10, 1856.
[27] Boston *Daily Courier,* March 11, 1856.
[28] New York *Herald,* February 3, 1856.
[29] *New Hampshire Patriot,* March 19, 1856.
[30] *Vermont Patriot,* February 15, 1856.
[31] St. Louis *Republican,* February 21, 1856.
[32] Providence (R. I.) *Post,* February 21, 1856, and Keokuk (Iowa) *Evening Times,* February 21, 1856.
[33] *New Hampshire Patriot,* March 6, 1856.
[34] *Journal of Commerce,* February 16, 1856.
[35] *Evening Advertiser,* February 20, 1856.
[36] *Daily Pennsylvanian,* February 21, 1856.
[37] Jackson (Michigan) *Patriot* quoted in Detroit *Evening Tribune,* February 25, 1856.

mond (Virginia) *Enquirer,* the Charleston (South Carolina) *Mercury* and the Mobile (Alabama) *Daily News.* The last named denounced the President's proclamation insisting that it was directed against the South to prevent southern emigrant aid societies carrying out their program.[38] Southern opinion was divided, however, on the emigration question.[39] The most moderate class of papers on the whole so far as the Kansas question was concerned were the Know Nothing papers.[40] As spring came the St. Louis *Evening News* was inspired to write: "It is refreshing to turn from the acrimonious wrangles and bitter disputes in Congress, where Kansas affairs are represented as they are *not,* to the peaceful, smiling Territory itself, where we can see things as they are. . . . By our files of western Missouri and Kansas exchanges, we see that the people of the Territory are over head and ears—not in fighting—but in farming. . . ."[41]

But such an idyllic picture of Kansas was not to be permitted to find lodgment in the public mind. The fact that the Topeka government had decided not to carry its laws into effect created a situation, as the Springfield *Republican* put it, where "the only thunder now left . . . is the enforcement of the bogus laws," and predicted that would be difficult.[42] The reports soon came out of Kansas that the law-and-order party was annoying free-state men in the weaker parts of the territory, Judge Lecompte bringing them into court for minor offences and fining them. Some were paying the fines, while others were leaving rather than submit. It was predicted that soon he would come to Lawrence "and bring us all to answer to the high crime of treason. I write you this timely account of this movement, that you may be prepared to hear the worst from us, if it come to a crisis; for Lawrence will not pay a fine to Wilson Shannon, or any of his fellows, unless they are first legally declared guilty. Guilty of what? Of protecting virtue and innocent life from the border ruffians."[43] The Milwaukee (Wisconsin) *Daily*

[38] *Daily News,* March 3, 1856.

[39] St. Louis *Daily Democrat,* March 8, 1856, reviewing a debate in the Georgia legislature. Augusta (Georgia) *Chronicle* quoted in the Boston *Post,* March 3, 1856.

[40] Louisville (Kentucky) *Journal,* March 15, 1856. Newark (New Jersey) *Mercury,* March 18, 1856. *Southern Watchman* (Athens, Georgia) March 27, 1856.

[41] *Evening News,* April 16, 1856.

[42] Springfield *Republican,* March 25, 1856.

[43] New York *Times,* April 22, 1856. This article was signed "Randolph" [William Hutchison].

Sentinel, April 30, regaled its readers with an elaborate and facetious account of sheriff baiting at Lawrence April 19. Practically the same story was published in several papers throughout the North. When the news came of the shooting of Jones, the Albany *Evening Journal,* May 7, 1856 declared approvingly "when assassins enter a house and burder its peaceable inhabitants, they only reap their just deserts if one of them gets a bullet-wound in return." To recount the various reactions to the events of May at Lawrence would be largely repetition of what appeared in the *Tribune* except that in June there began a succession of invented stories of outrages against women.[44] On the other hand, the Eastern press had much to contribute to a more intimate picture of the free-state settlements in the vicinity of Osawatomie.

Although the population of the southeastern part of the territory was relatively sparce the historian is gratified to find a few private letters written home to friends or families which bear the Osawatomie date line. Some have already been noticed from the *Tribune* and others have been found. Most of these were written, probably, without thought of publication and the picture they present is both more intimate and more accurate than the sensational stories of the professional newspaper letter-writers. Noah Barker wrote describing the country, January 25, 1856, and commented, of course, upon politics: "Kansas is a free State, and will remain so, unless all the free soilers in it are exterminated, which would not be an easy task for the ruffians at present, and they (the free-soilers) are growing stronger every day." Two things, he thought, ought to be done; put the state government into operation at Topeka, and enact laws prohibiting the immigration of all negroes. He was convinced that the majority of Missourians would prefer a free Kansas, provided all negroes were excluded. Barker had been a member of the free-state constitutional convention and consequently felt that he was in a position to know something of the prevailing sentiment.[45] A somewhat similar view appeared in the letter of an unnamed settler dated April 10:

Probably four-fifths of the actual settlers are in favor of a free State, but much to my surprise and more to my sorrow I found that a majority of these were governed more by self-interest than by principle. The term abolitionist is used here more than at home as a reproach. Then there are

44 Boston *Evening Traveller,* June 9, 1856 printed its own story and cited Cincinnati papers for corroboration.

45 Bangor, Maine, *Whig and Courier,* February 15, 1856. Webb, *Scrapbooks,* 9: 127.

too many seeking office; they have been growling together like dogs over a bone. A majority are in favor of 'the black law'—a law excluding free negroes from the Territory—one in my opinion degrading to men who have just been fighting, and yet will have to fight for their own liberties.[46]

Arriving at the Kansas border about the first of May, J. M. Anthony wrote a sort of diary letter home, the first entry in the installment published being written at Paola, K. T., May 2, the second next day at Osawatomie where he visited O. C. Brown, the founder of the town and the third May 5 when he selected a claim north of that place. Nothing was said in this journal of disorders, or political difficulties; it was just a detailed narrative of settlers in a new country making their first locations.[47]

Between Lawrence and Osawatomie, at Hickory Point, of Dow murder and Branson rescue notoriety, trouble was reported by a newspaper correspondent in March. Coleman, the murderer of Dow, was back in the community asserting his rights to two claims, on one of which a free-state man Ritch had squatted and on the other a free-state man named Gleason was accused of cutting timber. Warrants were out for Gleason and for Branson as a witness, the case was brought to trial in justice court and damages of $200 awarded to Coleman against Gleason, and Branson was fined $40 for contempt of court. Deputy Sheriff Salters seized two horses, harness and wagon from Gleason to satisfy the judgment and tried to take Branson's yoke of oxen to satisfy the fine against him. On March 8 Ritch was warned by Coleman to vacate.[48]

The next stories from the southeast were about the massacre. The Chicago *Tribune* and the *Daily Journal* June 3 carried the hanging and rescue story, attributing the incident to depredations on free-state crops by pro-slavery cattle. The Springfield *Republican,* June 4 assured its readers that the massacre story was invented by the pro-slavery party to inflame the rabble, the facts being, that pro-slavery men were trying to drive a free-state man from his claim, and with that introduction gave another version of the hanging and rescue story. The Chicago *Democratic Press,* June 5, was the first free-state paper found by the author to have associated Captain Brown with the affair. Its version was original in

[46] Cincinnati *Daily Enquirer,* May 8, 1856 quoting from the New York *Anti-Slavery Standard.* The *Enquirer* raised the question how many supporters of Robinson and Reeder knew that the Topeka free-state constitution had a supplementary act for excluding free negroes.

[47] Rochester (New York) *Daily Democrat,* May 15, 22, 1856.

[48] New York *Semi-Weekly Times,* April 15, 1856.

several respects, including the contribution made to the geography of Kansas:

Three days after the sack of Lawrence, Capt. Brown, at the head of a small party of Free State men from the Osawatomie, was passing through the neighborhood of Hickory Point, when they came upon a number of Pro-Slavery settlers of that locality who were engaged in executing a little 'law and order' on their private account, by hanging a Free State man to a tree. That spectacle did not strike Capt. Brown and his company as quite the thing, and they accordingly rushed upon the amateur execution-ers and rescued their intended victim. . . . Perhaps the vengence was too summary, but after what had happened at Lawrence, and was about to be consummated, greater forebearance could not have been anticipated.

After about a month of civil war, the letters of J. M. Anthony to his parents had changed tone completely. He reported that he might go to Topeka for the Fourth of July,

the probability is that there will be a battle at Topeka, or at Lecompton, or in the vicinity, as both parties are taking arms, ammunition and pro-visions.

Bogus law officers have been appointed in Osawatomie, but they had much rather appoint deputies than to act themselves. We shall now soon see whether we are to be haltered by bogus laws, or be governed by justice. There are secret things in preparation for the 4th, on both sides; what that day will bring forth, God only knows.[49]

A letter signed B. D. [Barlow Darrack] from a young man in Kansas to his father in New York was dated Osawatomie, July 2, and among other things he stated the free-state men were going to Topeka for the Fourth of July "not to celebrate their independence, but to win it." He explained that they were dependent upon Mis-souri for breadstuffs, but that they had plenty of meat, and that crop shortages would mean a continuance of dependence upon the out-side for food. But the most interesting part of the letter was his analysis of the settlement as matters stood in mid-summer:

This place and vicinity is almost entirely free-state, as shown at the polls. A number of these people are luke warm, keeping themselves in readiness to fall to the strongest side. Some, though they profess free-state principles, have made their submission to the bogus legislature. One of our representatives in the legislature, is believed to be of this number. These lead a small crowd, about thirty, and are in some favor with the ruffian party. They may fight with us, but it will depend much upon cir-cumstances; some would willingly act the spy. Of good staunch free-state men, ready to act their part in any emergency, and within four or five

[49] Rochester (New York) *Daily Democrat*, July 8, 1856. Extracts from the letters were published by permission of Anthony's parents.

miles, I count about seventy. Of these, about two-thirds live in town, or within a mile of it, and would rally at call, but they have not arms. I suppose there are not over twenty guns in town. The people in the country are better provided generally; scarce a house but has one, and sometimes more. . . .

Our greatest deficiency is that of arms and horses, and a fund sufficient to keep a small party in the field. Thirty or forty horsemen, well mounted and armed with Sharpe's rifles, Colt's revolvers, and a good sabre, could effectually scour this section of the country; cut off small parties and give us timely warning of larger ones. The men for such a company could be found had we the horses and arms. Such a method has been practiced with considerable success at Lawrence. At present we have but six or eight horses in town, and some of them miserable poor things. We have difficulty in finding enough to send out scouts.

Another difficulty is our vicinity to the border, with no friends between us and the enemy to give us warning. Eight miles north on Bull Creek are the Peoria Indians, under the control of the Missourians among them. On the east of us are the Miamies, also pro-slavery. Thus you see a considerable body of men might approach quite near us without discovery.[50]

As each writer saw things differently or chose to tell them differently another letter written by D. D. Fletcher about the same time in June is valuable for comparison. After describing the raid on Osawatomie early in the month and predicting difficulties on July 4, he gave his version of the community:

There are but a few real honest Free State men in this place who are willing to fight: those few are determined not to run, but to sell their lives as dear as possible. What few there are of us, twenty-six in all, are organized and well armed, all minute men, have our watchword and our *pass*. We keep a night watch, and scouts out all day, and have an ordinary log house (two stories) for a place of defence. Our men can all be raised in less than ten minutes and be at the rendevous. We are expecting to be attacked the 4th when the attention is generally called up to Topeka. . . . We are all tired out, and about half sick. Fare is hard—corn bread and bacon—out nights, either on the grass or in the saddle, constant excitement and in a climate hotter than that of Vermont. . . .[51]

On June 26 or earlier the elder John Brown wrote his notorious letter to his family at North Elba in which he misrepresented flagrantly the events of the preceding weeks.[52] His daughter Ruth, the wife of Henry Thompson, one of his followers, replied July 20:

[50] New York *Evening Post*, July 12, 1856. Webb, *Scrapbooks*, 12: 206. It is of interest to emphasize his comment on a guard of mounted troops in imitation of the Lawrence model.

[51] Burlington (Vermont) *Free Press*, July 18, 1856. Webb, *Scrapbooks*, 15: 32.

[52] Sanborn, *John Brown*, 236–241.

. . . The reception of your letters made us all both glad and sorrowful. Glad to hear that all were alive, but exceedingly sorry to hear that any of our friends were taken prisoners, or wounded, or sick. This was indeed sad intelligence, and we still live as we did for the last six weeks, in dreadful suspense. What the next news will be makes us almost sick at heart. But we hope for the best. We have seen for some time accounts of trouble in Kansas, that you were obliged to live in a cave to keep away from the ruffians, that two of your sons were taken prisoners, one of whom feigned insanity, (as they called it), and last that you had fallen into the hands of the border ruffians (or what might prove the same thing, the federal authority of Kansas). But last week's papers published the trial of John Brown Jun. by the bogus court, who had been called Captain Brown, which we all supposed to be you, not knowing that John was captain of a company. We here, and at ninety-five, take the New York Weekly Times, which gives us a great deal of Kansas news. It denounces in strong terms the conduct of the administration in reference to Kansas difficulties. Last week's paper gave a description. of the horrible treatment of John and Jason and the other prisoners who were taken to Tecumseh. It says that it was a scene which has no parallel in a republican government. You have no doubt heard all the particulars from Jason if you have seen him. We supposed that Frederick was the one the paper spoke of as feigning insanity. This was taken from a St. Louis paper; but the times said it was John, and was 'caused by his inhuman treatment.' Oh! my poor afflicted brother, what will become of him? Will it injure his reason for life? We hope not, but have great anxiety for him, and we sympathize most deeply with Wealthy. It is dreadful. I can hardly endure the thought. We felt afraid that if it was Frederick, it would kill him; but we pray he may escape any such trouble, and that John will entirely recover. I cannot be thankful enough that my dear husband so narrowly escaped being killed, and Salmon also. I cannot attribute it to anything but the merciful preservation of God, . . . I wish John and Jason had been in your company. You must have had very exciting times at the battle you fought, before it was over. I should hardly have thought twenty-three men would have laid down their arms to so small a company. But 'might was with the right' at that time. How mean it was in Colonel Sumner not to give up his prisoners after you gave up yours. . . . Gerrit Smith has had his name put down for ten thousand dollars toward starting a company of one thousand men to Kansas. We are constantly hearing of companies starting, but do not hear of their getting through without trouble. . . .[53]

This letter has historical significance for more than one reason. It indicates clearly how the Brown family were following the fortunes of the Kansas members. To them the name Brown possessed a particular meaning, but even with the advantage of that knowledge and family letters to supplement the newspapers, they were confused over which John was involved. This is particularly re-

[53] Webb, *John Brown*, 423–426. This letter seems never to have been reprinted elsewhere since Webb published it in 1861.

markable, because the younger John had been commander of the
Potawatomie Rifles since March or early April, and the elder John
had no military command except the few days at Lawrence the
preceding December.   The identity of the newspaper the family was
reading makes it possible to determine even more fully than the
letter just what the family knew about Kansas, and that leads to a
matter of particular importance to the history of the problem of
John Brown in 1856.   The report of "the trial of John Brown, Jr.,"
has been overlooked by every Brown biographer in spite of the fact
that attention was directed to it.   The New York *Times* published
the certified "full text" of all testimony taken at that hearing
June 20 before Commissioner Edward Hoogland.   The *Times* Kansas correspondent "Randolph" [William Hutchinson] sent the text
of the hearings and wrote his news letter June 23 but falsified the
whole matter by representing it as a trial and by saying three were
convicted.   The *Times* compounded the offense by publishing a
strong editorial introducing the letter and the hearings in which the
editor followed Randolph's copy instead of reading the text of the
hearings for himself.   In reality the proceeding was a preliminary
hearing to determine whether there was evidence sufficient to hold
the accused for the grand jury, and the outcome was that two, John
Brown, Jr., and H. H. Williams, were bound over on the charge of
treason to await the action of the grand jury at the September term
of court.   The editorial is worth reproducing as damning evidence
of what lengths the *Times* was willing to go in sensationalism and
falsification of news when the facts lay before them:

We publish this morning, together with some interesting Kansas letters,
a faithful report of the examination of the Free-State prisoners at Tecumseh, charged with the crime of treason against the United States.   The
proceedings in a case so novel—carried on in the name of justice and under
the formula of law—will be read with some curiosity and no little surprise.
At first sight the reader may imagine that the whole story is an absurd
farce; but a farce it is not.   The report of this examination, it will be observed, is authenticated and verified from beginning to end by the Clerk of
the Court.   All that is here recorded actually occurred.   The indictment
was originally laid against seven individuals conspicuous among those who
have endeavored to make Kansas a Free State.   For this crime they were
arrested near Osawatomie, and, like a gang of galley slaves, they were
chained two and two together and driven from thence to Tecumseh—a distance of sixty-five miles—where they have undergone a barbarous imprisonment and still more barbarous semblance of a trial for treason.
One of the prisoners, John Brown—unable to bear up against this misfortune—was driven mad by the treatment he received.   The reader will

perceive that the evidence adduced on this curious trial is precisely the same against all the prisoners; and yet, strange to say, three have been convicted while five have been unconditionally released.   What further proceedings will be taken in regard to those who have been sent back to prison remains to be seen, but the fact that this mock trial has actually taken place is of itself an outrage, under color of law, in the absence of the positive proof we now produce, few would believe.[54]

The evidence brought out at the hearing is of outstanding importance but as it has been ignored by the historians and has had no influence on the development of the Brown Legend it might as well not have been printed.   In view of these facts the detailed analysis of it is left to a later time when it is examined in connection with related manuscript materials, but there were a few points which came out clearly in the testimony as printed, that should have set the *Times* to thinking.   No indictment of a grand jury was involved. All the witnesses examined were free-state men.   Contrary to the editorial statement, the charges were not the result merely of the conspicuous position of the parties in the free-state movement.   The evidence made it clear moreover that John Brown, Jr., was insane before he was arrested and therefore that his treatment by the authorities after his arrest was not the cause of his mental derangement as charged by the *Times*.[55]

[54] New York *Semi-Weekly Times*, July 8, 1856.   The text of the hearings was printed by the St. Louis *Democrat*, July 4, 1856 also.

[55] James C. Malin, ''The Hoogland Examination,'' *Kansas Historical Quarterly*, 7 (May 1938) 133–153.

CHAPTER VII

THE LOCAL PRO–SLAVERY PRESS; LATE 1856 AND EARLY 1857

THE JUNE–JULY PEACE

Overlapping the last stages of the June clean-up campaign, new menaces to the peace of the territory appeared in the offing; the meeting of the free-state legislature on July 4, armed immigrants coming up the Missouri, and the gathering of armed northern emigrant companies on the Iowa and Nebraska borders, frequently referred to as Lane's Northern army.[1] In its leading editorial July 1, the *Squatter Sovereign* called attention to reports that large bodies of abolitionists were congregating in the upper part of the territory under Lane with a view to assisting in the establishment of the state government at Topeka. To meet this the editor urged that "We should have our horses saddled and bridled, our guns in good trim and ammunition in our cartridge boxes, and determination in our minds to SUBDUE THE FOE THAT THREATENS US, OR DIE IN THE ATTEMPT." The next week recorded further information about the armed companies arriving through Nebraska, and the editor shouted, where are Colonel Sumner and the troops, "are we to be disarmed and left in the power of fanatics, worse than savages?" Of course, he answered his own question in the negative. The papers recorded the disarming and turning back of organized companies from the North coming up the Missouri river on the *Star of the West*, the *Sultan* and the *Arabia*.[2] The *Herald* justified these measures on the ground that the men had been hired and armed by northern abolitionists to fight in Kansas, and especially that these particular parties were to be used at Topeka. It was determined to keep before the world that New England's "pious, just

[1] For the last half of 1856 and early 1857 the files of four territorial papers are available: The Leavenworth *Kansas Weekly Herald,* The Leavenworth *Journal,* The Lecompton *Union,* and The Atchison *Squatter Sovereign.* Although these papers were all weeklies in theory, they appeared somewhat irregularly, especially during periods of disturbances or paper shortages. The Kansas City, Mo., *Enterprise* file covers the period from the city commercial point of view.

[2] *Squatter Sovereign,* July 1, 8, and Leavenworth *Herald,* July 5, 1856.

117

and holy ministers'' denounced the last war with England, the war
with Mexico, and although they could not bear the shedding of blood
to defend the nation, they were raising men and money and arming
men to murder their fellow citizens for a difference of political opinion.[3] The Springfield (Illinois) *Register* described the Chicago
company which had been turned back on the *Star of the West;*
''Seventy-five drunken rowdies from the 'sands' of Chicago, passed
through our town accompanied with a quota of *nymph du pave* on
their way to Kansas. . . . A more ruffianly gang we have never
seen before. They favored Bloomington with their presence a day
or two, we are told being too much overcome with free rum to proceed further without resting.'' [4]

In spite of pro-slavery fears, the Topeka legislature was dispersed without disorder, a fact which was passed over lightly by the
party press. ''Their valor and patriotism quailed, and they quietly
gave up the ghost,'' declared the *Herald,* ''most of their leaders
were absent,'' Robinson, Smith, Deitzler in prison, Lane, as usual
in the hour of danger ''came up missing,'' and Reeder was in the
East making speeches instead of fighting. The *Herald* charged that
the whole affair was gotten up merely to promote strife and make
political capital for the campaign.[5] The *Squatter Sovereign* insisted that

> Since the departure of the Congressional Investigation Committee, af-
> fairs in Kansas have been comparatively quiet. We have no new 'out-
> rages' to chronicle and the abolitionists now act as if their advisers had
> deserted them. They are gradually yielding obedience to the Territorial
> Laws—pay their taxes as they should do, and as a consequence, there is
> not so much need for legal proceedings to force them into obedience.[6]

Another factor in the peace, according to the same paper was the
imprisonment for horse-stealing of Redpath ''the notorious liar, who
has manufactured in his fertile brain nine-tenths of the acts of violence said to have been perpetrated in Kansas.'' [7] To a newspaper
man in Kansas, however, peace was an inconvenience if not a minor
tragedy. One editor complained that although he had given more

[3] Leavenworth *Herald,* July 5, 1856.
[4] The Leavenworth *Herald* reprinted the *Register* article July 5, 1856, and
the *Squatter Sovereign,* July 22, 1856 reprinted it in part together with an editorial from the Chicago *Times* developing further the same theme.
[5] Leavenworth *Herald,* July 12, 1856.
[6] *Squatter Sovereign,* July 15, 1856.
[7] *Squatter Sovereign,* July 15, 1856. The editor was mistaken about the
imprisonment of Redpath.

than usual attention to the exchanges, he could find scarcely an item of interest in the whole batch.[8]

Not all free-state settlers were enthusiastic about their experiences in Kansas and some made reports or wrote letters to the northern papers. The Leavenworth *Herald* culled several such items from its exchanges. One gave a picture of Lawrence printed in the Hartford (Connecticut) *Times:*

Lawrence city presents an unfavorable appearance. There is no thrift, no prosperity, apparent; but whiskey—poor whiskey, too—is poured down on every hand. It is dealt out in almost every building.—Drinking is the principle business, and it is backed up by idlers, the people generally waiting for "aid" from the East.—Sharp's rifles were offered to him, he says, for ten dollars each. The price in Hartford, where they are made, is $25 and $28. Exaggerated stories are started in Lawrence city, and sent off to keep up the excitement at the East, and bring in more aid to support the idlers in doing nothing except drink whiskey, circulate false reports, and talk politics. Such is the state of things in Lawrence the result of unusual efforts to manufacture slavery agitation with reference to the coming Presidential election.[9]

Another from the Janesville (Wisconsin) *Standard* was dated August 5:

We all left here under good promises, and was to have our way paid through to that Territory with the understanding that we were to become actual settlers there. What did General or Colonel Lane want us to do when we got to Nebraska City? He would like to have had us all—about two hundred in number—fight against the government, and against the troops of the United States. What were the words we told him? The same as all the Free State men tell him in Kansas—"Before we will fight Uncle Sam's troops we will blow you through."

I can openly and boldly say that General Lane can never enter Kansas alive. His own party there say to him, why did you desert us in the hour of need? What do the Free State men want here? Lane, Robinson and others are a curse to honest and law abiding citizens. What company of young men are going there to back up such a man as J. H. Lane and his confederates? The young men who went from here are men, and Lane dresses in men's clothes, but he is far from being one. Before I close, I must say to the Kansas Aid Society to aid or send means to the company they have there, before they send any more men there in a helpless condition. . . .[10]

A third was from a Racine, Wisconsin, man who left his family in Missouri while he went into the territory to prepare a house for them. On his return he found his child seriously ill, and to his

[8] *Squatter Sovereign,* August 5, 1856.
[9] Leavenworth *Herald,* June 28, 1856.
[10] Leavenworth *Herald,* August 30, 1856.

surprise found the pro-slavery people there had been kind to his wife and child:

For many weary days I walked around, waiting for the returning strangth of my child, and during these days saw many things that would have been disbelieved by myself if stated to me before I left Racine, and while I was a reader of, and believer in the New York Tribune. I saw many, very many poor families, landed at Leavenworth—sent on by the New England Aid Societies who had not the means to bury the dead of their company. Men, women and children, were there, sent by these aid societies, without funds to purchase one meal of food after landing. They came there, expecting, no one knows what, but in as destitute a condition as ever emigrants landed at the docks of New York.

These men of Missouri, the "border ruffians," took them into their homes—they fed them—the living ones—and buried the dead—they gave them clothes, food and kind words; they acted, in short, the part of noble, generous Christian men, and their reward has been abuse, contumely and misrepresentation. . . . As I said before, I hate slavery, and never by act or word will give it aid or countenance, but, I hate it so much that I cannot bear even to see the mistaken (thought I believe honestly mistaken) supporters of it lied about and abused.[11]

The anti-slavery majority report of the congressional investigating committee was released in Washington in time to be summarized briefly in the Leavenworth *Herald*, July 12, Oliver's pro-slavery minority report July 26, and two weeks later five columns from the text of the latter were published. Among other things Oliver reviewed in this report the Potawatomie massacre committed by "Capt. John Brown, a well known character in the abolition party."[12]

The pro-slavery leaders issued an appeal for southern immigration, signed by David R. Atchison and five associates, dated June 21, 1856.[13] It reviewed Kansas troubles including the Potawatomie affair, without mention of John Brown, but most significant, it argued with respect to the Northern cause that

With them it is no mere local question of whether slavery shall exist in Kansas or not, but one of far wider significance; a question of whether it shall exist anywhere in the Union. Kansas they justly regard as the mere outpost in the war now being waged between the antagonistic civilizations of the North and the South; and winning this great outpost and standpoint they rightly think their march will be open to an easy conquest of the whole field. . . . These [outrages] are not as some pretend, the mere extravagances of a few irresponsible individuals, but on the contrary, are chargeable to the Abolition party. . . .

11 Leavenworth *Herald*, August 30, 1856.
12 Leavenworth *Herald*, August 9, 1856.
13 *Squatter Sovereign*, July 15, 1856.

The outrages above specified were preceded, and up to the present time have been followed by others of a like character and dictated by a like settled policy . . . to harass and frighten by their deeds of horror, our friends from their homes in the Territory.

A chronology of abolition outrages, 1854–1856, was prepared and published throughout the territory as well as in the East and South.[14] With the renewal of hostilities in August, Atchison and associates issued appeals for immediate assistance.[15] On July 15 the *Squatter Sovereign* claimed that the territory was fast filling with pro-slavery settlers and it was only necessary "to do as much as our enemies to *secure it.*"

The bravado of pro-slavery claims was not supported in all quarters. The election in Missouri was the occasion for pessimism for the Leavenworth *Journal*, which reviewed the situation under the title "Et tu Brute." Only incomplete returns were available, but the state vote split three ways, Benton's anti-slavery faction had probably won, and even if it had not won, he had piled up formidable numbers. The *Journal* admitted that it expected attacks upon the pro-slavery party in Kansas from other quarters, and was disappointed that the South had failed to give support, but for Missouri to strike also, that was too much.[16] With the editor of the *Journal* this issue of disloyalty of moderate southern leaders became a fixed idea, and later in the year was the subject of an editorial prolonged through three issues.[17] The Know Nothing party was conservative on the Kansas question and tended to divide pro-slavery sentiment, therefore, among the radical pro-slavery papers, it was denounced almost as bitterly as the abolitionists.[18]

The pro-slavery men set about during the summer peace to re-establish their settlements, to bring about the return of those driven out by free-state guerillas, to locate new comers and to insure their protection against the recurrence of similar outrages. A public meeting at Kansas City pledged support to city, state and federal officers in law enforcement, and in prevention of the landing of unlawful armed forces. The sixty-three signatures attached included the leading business men, and the *Enterprise* pointed out that as

[14] *Squatter Sovereign*, July 22, 1856 published it giving credit to the Lecompton *Union*, but it has not been possible to determine who compiled it originally.

[15] The appeal dated August 16 was published in the *Squatter Sovereign*, August 26, 1856.

[16] Leavenworth *Journal*, August 13, 1856.

[17] Leavenworth *Journal*, October 15, 22, 29, 1856.

[18] *Squatter Sovereign*, June 24, 1856.

Kansas City had been noted for order and quiet "her business interests require that this should be done."[19]   On the following day a meeting was held near Kansas City in the interests of Georgia colonization which endorsed a campaign for collection of money to finance those Georgia settlers whose funds had been exhausted.   The settlement was located under the leadership of Captain Cook, the *Squatter Sovereign* reporting on it July 22, 1856:

We are informed that a pro-slavery settlement has been made on Potawatomie creek, near Osawatomie, consisting of a large number of families, and at least one hundred and fifty Georgians. This will have its influence in restoring peace and quiet in that section of the Territory. Many of the Pro-Slavery settlers who were driven from their claims by the free-soilers have returned to their homes, and, with the reinforcements mentioned above, will be enabled to protect themselves from the depredations of the lawless traitors who infest that region of country. In other places, where the property of Pro-Slavery men is insecure, similar projects are being carried out, which cannot but result in much good.

Another attempt was reported by its leaders:

About a month since we formed ourselves into a company for the purpose of settling in Kansas Territory: Our company numbered about twenty-five men, under the direction of Col. Treadwell as the head of the Colony—the members of the company were all Southern men—and went to the Territory for the purpose of settling there permanently. We first went to Hickory Point, intending to build a town, but finding that we could not get possession of a eligible town site, removed to Washington Creek, at and near Capt. Saunders farm, each one taking a claim, and making Capt. Saunders' our head quarters. Capt. Saunders resides near the centre of Douglas county. . . . We went down to Washington Creek because we could get locations. We were warned by the Abolitionists that we must leave or they would kill us, and notified the neighbors that if they helped us they would murder them.[20]

A third project was reported by the Leavenworth *Journal*, August 13, under the leadership of Captain D. G. Fleming of Columbia, South Carolina, who with about thirty persons, had recently started for the interior to establish themselves on the Big Blue river.   The editor commented that "the company is composed of the right kind of material, and we may look for favorable accounts from them. . . . They will prove an invincible barrier to the assaults of the Land Pirate Brown, and his minions."[21]

[19] *Enterprise*, July 5, 1856.
[20] Leavenworth *Herald*, September 6, 1856.
[21] The reference to Brown must be to Brown of the *Herald of Freedom* who was financed by the Emigrant Aid Company.

The administration was determined to settle the Kansas question in order to remove it from the campaign. The republican party had pledged itself to the Topeka free-state constitution as the basis of admission. The Leavenworth *Herald* summarized and discussed the five leading propositions that had been presented in congress: by Douglas, Seward, Crittenden, Trumbull and Toombs. The Douglas bill postponed admission until the population had reached the number requisite for one representative under the congressional apportionment (93,000) provided for a census, and specified six months residence as a qualification for voting. Neither house had passed this measure. The Seward bill was the republican measure for admission under the Topeka constitution. It was rejected by the senate, but passed by the house. The Crittenden proposal was for General Scott to be sent to Kansas to pacify the territory, but it had been abandoned. The Trumbull bill proposed to abandon the whole Kansas government and extend the Nebraska government over Kansas. This was rejected. The fifth bill, that of Toombs, provided for a convention to decide whether a constitution should be framed, and if favorable, fixed the procedure. A commission was to take a census and make apportionment of delegates, and voting was limited to citizens of the United States with a minimum residence of three months in the territory. Important to the free-state contention it repealed the slave-property code, and test oaths and provided also for complete freedom of speech and press. The editor of the *Herald* gave it his full endorsement. The bill had passed the senate, and the responsibility lay with the republican-controlled house whether the Kansas question would be speedily settled or kept open for campaign purposes.[22] The republicans not only kept the controversy open, but aggravated it by attaching to the army appropriation bill a rider interfering with the President's use of troops in law enforcement in Kansas. The army bill was defeated and a special session required for its enactment.

There was a widespread conviction that the contest was a historic turning point in the struggle between abolitionism and slavery, with abolitionism determined to rule or ruin.[23] The Leavenworth *Journal* argued that this was different from any previous campaign, unlike those when Webster, Clay and Calhoun had led, and when "there were landmarks of reason and discretion to guide the politician in his course." It insisted that in two short years, fanaticism

22 Leavenworth *Herald*, July 26, 1856.
23 Leavenworth *Herald*, August 2, 16, 1856.

had driven the free-soil and national parties of the North to take refuge in the Democracy, and in the South had united all three. The purpose of the republican party, as the *Journal* saw it, was to deprive a portion of the states of their rights under the constitution by an uncompromising hostility to the South and her peculiar institution.[24]

Under these circumstances the gathering of the armed companies of northern immigrants in Iowa and Nebraska appeared as a menace. During mid-July rumor reported that large bodies of armed men were entering Kansas, but their object was a mystery.[25] In early August rumor credited Lane with entering the territory with six hundred men.[26] Some of these emigrants who were the subject of so much anxiety were independent groups such as the Wisconsin train. Some were organized in response to Lane's appeals. The most important agency immediately in charge was the National Kansas Committee recently organized at a convention in Buffalo under the presidency of Thaddeus Hyatt. As a matter of fact Lane did not have a great deal to do with this immigration, but was using the situation for his personal advancement. The immigrant trains did not begin to move into Kansas until the second week of August arriving at Topeka about August 13, but establishing three towns along the way; Plymouth, Lexington and Holton. The Leavenworth *Herald*, August 13, endorsed the views of the Kickapoo *Pioneer* that if they were a sovereign people, they should go to work and rid the territory of nigger thieves; but if they were not a sovereign people, they should go hide in the swamps of Mississippi, there was no middle ground.

As in all such cases, each side blamed the other for the first hostile act in the August civil war just opening. To free-state men the reestablishment of pro-slavery settlements were links in a well matured plot to exterminate or drive out all free-state settlers. To pro-slavery men, the armed emigrant trains entering the territory from the north meant the same thing for southern settlers. On August 8 an expedition led by Lawrence men attacked the pro-slavery Georgia settlement near Osawatomie, the whole settlement, men, women and children fleeing ahead of the raiding expedition. On August 13, a free-state band, probably Brown's men, but not John Brown himself, raided the Martin White neighborhood. This was

24 Leavenworth *Journal*, August 13, 1856.
25 *Squatter Sovereign*, July 15, 1856.
26 *Squatter Sovereign*, August 5, 1856.

accompanied and followed by a raid on Franklin August 12, Tread-well's settlement August 15, and Titus's house, just outside of the territorial capital, on August 16. Immediately the Kansas-Missouri border was a mingled panic and raging fury. The first reports attributed these outrages to John Brown, especially this was the burden of the Leavenworth *Journal Extra* which was widely copied in the other border papers and in the East. In this the *Journal's* informants were mistaken and the other papers quickly realized the error, so that after this first panic news, the responsibility for free-state action was placed upon Lane. By a selection of newspaper statements Sanborn and particularly Villard have made it appear that Brown was the one the pro-slavery people held responsible. If the files of the border papers are studied chronologically that contention proves untenable. Furthermore, geographical location played a part. Towns such as Westport, lying at a point where the roads from southeast Kansas converged, was more largely influenced by rumors of Brown, while towns lying further north, such as Leavenworth, Atchison and Lecompton, focused their attention upon the northern invasion.

The broadest perspective on the Kansas situation was pictured in the Kansas City *Enterprise.* Isolated acts of violence were reported, the murder of the Shawnee Indian agent Gay, late in June, the beating of a South Carolina man at Lawrence in the presence of his daughter and his subsequent death at Westport late in July, the seizure of the freight wagon of the firm of Northup and Chick on the Santa Fe trail just out of Westport July 29, the plundering of Lehay on the Wakarusa near Lawrence and of Crane near Franklin about the same time.[27] The seizure of the freight outfit touched a tender spot and affords the only instance to this point in the year's difficulties when the *Enterprise* was willing to endorse self-help, declaring that it was time to clean out the banditti by means of a vigilance committee in the San Francisco style. In the same issue it was reported that Brown, the Osawatomie murderer, was within a few hours march of the Georgia settlement and an attack was expected hourly.[28] Two weeks later the attack was recorded by Brown's "Northern Army," but the women, children and sick had been removed to a place of greater safety. The same issue recorded the attack on Martin White, a free-state man from Illinois, because he had denounced the Potawatomie massacre, a war of extermina-

[27] *Enterprise*, June 28 (Gay), July 26 (S. C. Man), August 2, 1856.
[28] *Enterprise*, August 2, 1856.

tion having been begun by the fanatics against all who did not join them:

It seems that this Brown is a power in the Territory—neither the Territorial or General Government having been able so far to stop his depredations. He is fast taking rank with guerilla chiefs of Mexico, and the robber bands of Cane Hill, Arkansas; and unless something is done to put a stop to his career, volunteer forces will be necessary to put him down.

The editorial in this issue of the *Enterprise* of August 16 pictured the territory as having three military centers each with different leaders; the Big Blue, Topeka, and Southern Kansas. In the last named district the forces were said to be "headed by a man named John Brown, who have been under arms more than two months. They were the party engaged in the horrible massacre at Potawatomie Creek, and the butchers at Hickory Point." He was erroniously credited with the attacks upon New Georgia, the post office at Franklin, and Martin White.

The first mention of Brown by name had been in the *Enterprise*, August 2, and the first identification as John Brown was in the editorial quoted above from the issue of August 16.

Kansas City took steps August 15, holding a meeting "to take measures for the protection of the trade from this city to the Territory." Resolutions were adopted and a second meeting was held August 16 to take further action.[29]

The next week another article was devoted to John Brown, by whose alleged specialization in horse stealing the Lane army from Nebraska was mounted. Now, instead of merely attacking travelers, emigrants and traders, they were charged with a new departure, the attacking of towns:

They have completed the sack of the Potawatomie settlement, not only driving off all pro-slavery settlers, but the Free-State men, who refused to join them. They have seized and fortified the fords and crossings of the Wakarusa, thrown up fortifications, and announce their purpose to keep out all persons from the Southern Valley of Kansas who do not subscribe to the Topeka constitution, and declare their purpose to be resistance to the general or territorial authorities indiscriminately.

The article closed with the declaration that unless the general or territorial government acted before the week passed, the people would, "and terrible will be the remedy."[30]

Reporting the attack on Franklin, the Leavenworth *Herald* declared that "The Abolitionists have thus rekindled a flame of excite-

[29] *Enterprise*, August 16, 1856.
[30] *Enterprise*, August 23, 1856.

ment in our Territory, which if not speedily checked, will deluge our land in carnage and blood." [31]   The excitement was not checked, however, and the list of free-state outrages lengthened, the raid on the second Georgia settlement near Osawatomie August 26, Lane's threat to Lecompton September 4–5, the looting of Tecumseh September 4, McKinney's Santa Fe train September 2, Indianola September 11 and Ozawkie September 8, Grasshopped Falls about the same time, the raid of "Colonel Harvey and his forty thieves" through the Stranger creek valley looting Easton, Summerville and Alexandria September 9–10,[32] Ozawkie by Lane September 14 and the attack on Hickory Point by Lane September 14 and by Harvey the following day. Day after day wagon trains loaded with loot and herds of horses and cattle were driven into Lawrence and Topeka.

The pro-slavery men issued an immediate call to arms and the gathering of the border ruffians began throughout the western counties of Missouri as well as in the territory.[33]   After about a week of war the Leavenworth *Herald* wrote:

Kansas is again invaded and the work of devastation again commenced. Armed bodies of men from the North are marching over the Territory ravaging peaceful settlements, destroying settlements, destroying crops, burning houses, driving off, imprisoning and murdering our citizens. Outrage follows outrage with fearful rapidity. ˙ Rebellion, violence, murder, houseburning, bloodshed and every crime that can disgrace humanity are being perpetrated in our Territory by Lane's armed band of marauders. . . .

The *Herald* insisted that it was not an alarmist, but was convinced that the time had come when the issue must be fought to a finish.[34] A correspondent wrote to the same paper proposing a call "for missionaries to go to New England to preach the Gospel to its benighted inhabitants." The *Squatter Sovereign* insisted that it had been slow to believe that serious fighting would occur, but was at last convinced. Although large forces were gathering, it warned that

[31] Leavenworth *Herald*, August 16, 1856.

[32] For a sketch of Harvey and the Chicago Company see the author's "Colonel Harvey and his forty thieves," *Mississippi Valley Historical Review*, 19 (June 1932), 57–76.

The Hickory Point involved in these September raids, was located some twenty miles north of Lawrence, near the present town of Oskaloosa and should not be confused with the Hickory Point south of Lawrence of Coleman-Dow notoriety.

[33] The Leavenworth *Herald's* first issue after hostilities began was August 16, the *Journal* published an Extra August 17 and left for the front not publishing again until September 24, the *Squatter Sovereign*, August 19.

[34] Leavenworth *Herald*, August 23, 1856.

no chances be taken: "Let it be the 'third and last time.' Let the watchword be 'extermination, total and complete.' " [35] "A crisis is at hand which involves the greatest question which can be addressed to any people," argued the *Herald*, "the right to enjoy the acquisitions of their common blood and treasure, and peaceably to spread their institutions and civilization.   Our Territory is invaded by a foreign foe . . . devoted to the one idea of crushing us of the South as a people, and extinguishing in Kansas the new born hope of Southern equality."   In another editorial of the same issue the editor stated that "the present state of affairs is to be attributed to the vile and unprincipled course of Reeder, Lane, Robinson and such like political demagogues.   Again in the next issue he pointed out there had been two months of peace before Lane and his banditte arrived.[36]

The Kansas City *Enterprise*, August 30, reported that

We have nothing reliable from the Territory. Lane with over one thousand men has cut off all communications. He has seized on all the crossings of the Wakarusa and Kansas Rivers and the roads will have to be opened by force. . . . We are in a state of seige. The Government of the Territory is subverted and the Revolution complete. A few more days and the "bloody issue," which Reeder threatened will be history.

In another article, after a denunciation of the abolitionists, only Lane being mentioned by name, the *Enterprise* concluded:

We speak now of its effects. The trade of our town (Kansas City) alone, since the opening of the Spring business, with the Territory, amounts to over $500,000. This has been almost entirely suspended—and entirely annihilated—and this is but the condition of all river towns and border trading posts.—Horses, mules, and beef cattle, have been stolen, provision trains, wagons, depots, have been robbed day after day, week after week, until everything was prostrated, and trade stopped. Then commenced the pillage of towns and settlements—for this army must be fed. Day after day there were arrivals in Missouri from the Territory, of families, . . . driven from their homes . . . destitute. . . .

After recounting the Potawatomie massacre and other outrages, the editor concluded:

We appeal to you to meet this crime at the threshold, and let this be the last as it is the only attempt at the destruction of those amicable relations which have made us so powerful and prosperous as a people. . . . The enemy is now before us—we must meet him. . . .

35 *Squatter Sovereign*, August 26, 1856.
36 Leavenworth *Herald*, August 30, 1856.

In response to news that a public meeting had been held in St. Louis to take active measures in the Kansas situation, the editor was gratified that "our commercial metropolis" was aroused. A private letter from Independence dated August 23 and printed in the St. Louis *Leader* described the prostration of trade in Kansas City, the pouring in of fugitives from the territory and the dangers of the roads, especially around Westport. The writer was convinced that besides the abolitionists and pro-slavery parties, there was a third and independent party,—

"a party of murderers, robbers, and horse stealers, who in the name of one or the other party, are interested only in the securing of plunder for themselves. They are robbing all parties. I believe the worst has not yet come. The two great parties are now about forty miles apart, industriously preparing to meet in battle. They are not only furious, but frenzied against each other. They are about equal in numbers, courage, abilities, hatred, fury, and longing for revenge. . . . Where will Lane's men find sustenance? Think you that desperate men, with arms in their hands, will permit themselves to starve whilst herds of fat cattle, grain, flour, bacon and stores of other necessaries superabound in the border counties of Missouri —an enemy's country? Think also of the danger of embroiling the whole nation in this quarrel, whilst fanatical preachers and midnight conspirators are running around the country, threatening and denouncing unoffending foreigners and Catholics—the most conservative and peaceful portion of the recognized citizens of the country.[37]

Meanwhile Acting-Governor Woodson had declared the territory in the state of insurrection and called out the militia. On August 26, Atchison, Treadwell and others issued an appeal to the people of the nation an explanation of reasons which drove them to an appeal to arms; the government had failed to preserve order, the old governor had failed, the new governor was unfamiliar with Kansas, and the people of Kansas could not hazard the uncertainty of imbecility or corruption.

We wage no war upon men for their opinions; have never attempted to exclude any from settling among us; we have demanded only that all should alike submit to the law. To all such we will afford protection, whatever be their political opinions.

* * * *

This is no mere local quarrel; no mere riot; but it is War! . . . a war on invasion— . . . properly named the "Army of the North."[38]

Pro-slavery armed bands acting as militia or independent guerillas roused the territory harrying independent settlers drifting to-

[37] *Enterprise*, September 13, 1856.
[38] *Enterprise*, August 30, 1856.

ward two objectives, Lawrence and Osawatomie. Reid struck the
first major blow at the latter place August 30. An impromptu defense was made by three leaders, John Brown, Cline and Updegraff,
the first two having recently arrived from marauding expeditions
and rich with stolen cattle, horses and other loot. After a short and
ineffective skirmish they gave way losing several men and inflict-
ing only a few wounds upon the invader. Reid's men then proceeded to burn the town. The leading reports of the raid on
Osawatomie emphasized, as in Reid's own communique the following day, that it was aimed at the headquarters of Old Brown, and
that a son and almost certainly Brown himself was killed.[39]   The
victory was not at all pleasing to the commanders, as the troops had
demonstrated that there was no discipline or organization worthy of
the name, especially among the horsemen, and but for the fact that
there was no effective opposition at Osawatomie they would have suffered a demoralizing defeat. Accordingly the troops were disbanded to be reorganized as infantry and mobilized for the principle objective, Lawrence, September 13. At Leavenworth the threat
of a free-state raid on that city created panic. It was claimed that
letters were intercepted which revealed a plot by which free-state
men within the city would rise as Lane attacked from without. Accordingly on September 2, Leavenworth underwent a purge by
which all suspected free-state sympathizers were driven out of the
town forthwith.[40]

The effect of the new war upon the national situation was appreciated fully by the Leavenworth *Herald* editor, who watched
with consuming fury its exploitation for political purposes:

The Abolition prints are holding high festival over Kansas affairs.
Our late disturbances have afforded them a fine opportunity to get out a
new edition of 'Border Ruffian outrages,' and renew their 'shrieks for
bleeding Kansas.' They would not have missed such an opportunity to
keep up the Kansas agitation for all the world. They have longed and
prayed for it for months past. Now that it has been given them, they
begin to shriek for Free Kansas and Fremont, and to draw upon their in-
ventive brains for more raw head and bloody bones stories.

With this as an introduction he reprinted a sample as follows:

[39] Leavenworth *Herald*, September 6, 1856.
A report by Captain D. Jernigan made almost the same statement relative
to the Browns. Leavenworth *Herald*, September 6 and *Squatter Sovereign*,
September 2.
[40] Leavenworth *Herald*, September 6, 1856.

The Free-State men discovered an organized plan to concentrate men, arms, and ammunition at different points in the Territory for the purpose of a sudden and general attack, immediately upon the adjournment of congress, to exterminate or expel all Free-State settlers. Twelve fortified block houses had been erected at different points—one at Shawnee, one at Osawatomie, one at Franklin, etc., supplied with cannon, rifles, and ammunition.

Of course the *Herald* denounced this story in the most emphatic terms:

This is a lie in the aggregate and in the detail—a lie from top to bottom—a lie from beginning to end. The capacity for lying of the Fremonters certainly exceeds that of any other class of persons in the universal world. Oh! those long-faced, sanctimonious, psalm-singing Yankees! [41]

According to the interpretation of the *Squatter Sovereign* the disbanding of pro-slavery forces for the purpose of reorganization had given courage to Lane's gang of marauders who were devoting themselves with renewed vigor to pillage during the early days of September. That spoils was the inducement that brought them to Kansas was its fixed opinion and the only way to restore peace was to fight the devil with fire: "Destroy their property, crops and every article that would conduce to the support of any or every person who is known or suspected of acting, cooperating or sympathizing with abolitionism." [42] From prisoners it was reported that Lane had agreed to pay his banditti eight dollars per month, and let them keep all they could steal. This is the way the *Squatter Sovereign* accounted for the number of plunderers who had gathered in the territory. [43]

THE GEARY PACIFICATION

In the midst of these disorders both Shannon and the President decided that a change of governors was necessary, although for different reasons. John W. Geary was appointed, arriving in the territory September 9, with instructions to pacify Kansas. In Kansas, both parties were always hopeful on the occasion of the designation of a new governor. The Leavenworth *Herald* was only cautiously hopeful this time, however, remarking that "It [Kansas] has been unfortunate in many respects, but peculiarly unfortunate in her

[41] Leavenworth *Herald*, September 13, 1856.
[42] *Squatter Sovereign*, September 9, 1856.
[43] *Squatter Sovereign*, September 23, 1856.

governors. . . . We think we see in the appointment of Col. Geary, an omen of better times in Kansas . . . The third time is the charm.''[44] Soon afterwards a Kansas bill was announced in the press as a Geary bill. The salient features emphasized were that,it did not impair vested rights, but suspended, not repealed, the territorial laws, saving the point of honor of the one side and remedying the alleged grievances of the other. The *Herald* approved this proposal under the administration of such a man as Geary. Immediately upon arrival the new governor issued a proclamation disbanding all the existing militia and ordering the enrollment of new militia subject to call, when they would be mustered into the service of the United States itself. Also he ordered the disbandment or departure of all organized bands of armed men.

Just as the new governor was executing this vigorous pacification policy, supported by federal troops, the reorganized pro-slavery forces were converging upon Lawrence to mete out summary punishment. Geary had an opportunity to strike in a spectacular manner in both directions at the same time. He ordered troops to pursue Lane's gang to the northward of Lecompton. Lane escaped, but the main body of troops of his subordinate Harvey was captured near Hickory Point, September 15. The governor was called to Lawrence to meet the advancing border ruffians and on the evening of September 14 rushed troops to Lawrence and the following morning met the Missouri leaders, arranging amicably for their return, without punishing the town.[45] The editor of the Leavenworth *Journal* returning from the war issued his first regular edition September 24. In his summary there was much of Jim Lane, but nothing of John Brown. He felt optimistic over the results as those of Lane's army not driven out by the border ruffians were being dealt with by the federal troops. As for the new governor, the *Journal* said, ''His course, thus far, fully sustains his promises.'' The *Squatter Sovereign* was more reserved, concluding that Geary gave Lane and his scoundrels the benefit of the law's delay and deferred if he did not prevent justice.[46] Two weeks later the paper was furious and condemning Geary declared that no northern man was fit to be governor of Kansas as he had'nt the nerve to do his duty. ''Geary is doing more mischief in Kansas than both his illustrious predecessors,'' the editor continued, ''If Geary has done

[44] Leavenworth *Herald*, August 30, 1856.

[45] The best pro-slavery summary of this expedition is that of the Platte *Argus* reprinted in the *Squatter Sovereign*, September 23, 1856.

[46] *Squatter Sovereign*, September 16, 1856.

what rumor charges, he is a perjured scamp, and should be booted
out of Kansas Territory instanter." After taking two weeks to get
out the next issue the editor decided he had been too hasty with the
governor. Although the episode has its humorous side, it is a significant illustration of the extreme uncertainty of public opinion in
which an official must perform his duties. The Leavenworth *Herald*
faced the facts squarely on the outcome of the war:

It seems to be now reduced to a certainty, and admitted on all sides,
that 'The Kansas War' is now over. The threats and thunders of war,
which, for more than four long weeks, have been going on . . . have
ended in nothing—save sound and fury. . . . There was no system, no
concert of action, no discipline—no nothing. . . .
We must confess that the past has been a sham, the present a masquer-
ade—and in the future we must encounter the sternly real. . . . The way
to arrest danger is to meet it half way. . . . T'is treason to cry 'Peace!
Peace! when there is no peace.' There can be no peace with Abolitionism
in Kansas. Either that political heresy must be, efectually and forever,
wiped out, or Kansas is forever lost to the South. . . . Give up Kansas to
it; give it all the territories. . . . Give it all the Territory north of 36 deg.
30 min. today, and tomorrow it will claim all south of it. Yield that, too,
and the next day it will invade the States, expel the slaves, and seize upon
our lands. . . . We agree with the N. Y. Tribune, that the sooner the issue
is tried and determined the better for all parties. . . . We have never been
of those who could see any good to be gained by postponing the struggle
which every reflecting man believes to be inevitable between the North and
the South.[47]

As usual the *Enterprise* viewed the situation somewhat differently from its neighbors, refused to publish news until substantiated,
insisted still that the issue in the Kansas question was not political,
but a matter of law enforcement, and with the McKinney wagon
train in mind declared that

Before this time [September] horse-stealing had become a business, and
wagons were pillaged everywhere upon the prairies; but now whole trains
were plundered and robbed, and business entirely destroyed.
It was to stop this that the people rose en masse, determined to rid the
Territory of a system of highway robbery, and midnight plunder, worse
than has ever been known in this country, and equalled only by the
Bedouin tribes of the desert.

The editor then paid his respects to both Brown and Lane, saying of the former that his career would have "immortalized an
Italian bandit," and that "there is not now a pro-slavery settlement
south of the Kansas river until you reach Ft. Scott; all have been

[47] Leavenworth *Herald*, September 20, 1856.

driven off or murdered.'' [48]   The editor stressed that upon the arrival of Geary, Lane broke camp and ran, while Reid remained until assured of the Governor's intention to maintain order.   The business men of Westport and Kansas City then called a mass meeting for September 23 ''to consult and decide upon some plan to give security to all peaceable inhabitants of both Missouri and Kansas, in the prosecution of their legitimate business, and to give greater security to both persons and property on all roads leading into Kansas Territory.'' [49]

During the following week one incident marred the record of Kansas City for law and order, the abduction of H. Miles Moore, a radical free-state man from the American Hotel.   The *Enterprise* warned that this did the cause no good and that the grand jury would take the matter seriously.   Later Moore's release was arranged without further unfortunate incident.   Except for this, it was claimed that the Westport meeting had had a salutary influence, and the roads were clear.   From Kansas ''a total quiet'' was reported, Geary was doing his duty and ''we are gratified to know that all men are satisfied.   Lane is still hanging in the outskirts of Nebraska and Iowa, coming out of his hole occasionally like an *old rat,* to see which way the wind blows. . . . Can't the Governor feign a nap long enough to entrap the traitor?'' [50]

The Boonville (Missouri) *Observer* was quoted favorably by the *Enterprise,* October 18, 1856 on the subject of nationalism and disunion:

It is patent to anyone . . . that the abolitionists of the North do not desire peace in Kansas, for they are brazen-mouthed disunionists, and traitors at heart. . . .

It is no less apparent that the disunionists of the South do not desire peace in Kansas, for their treasonable representatives in the territory . . . are chagrined . . . that Reid and the men under him, should have disbanded in patriotic obedience to the request of Gov. Geary.   Reid is now publicly ridiculed. . . .

This kind of talk may best suit palmetto politicians, and is very greatful to abolitionists, but it is not a fair reflex of Missouri sentiment, and is prejudicial to the pro-slavery cause in Kansas.   We are willing, now, and always have been, to tax ourselves in assisting pro-slavery emigrants in going to Kansas, that they may constitute a majority of actual residents, the only legitimate and practical mode of making Kansas a slave state, or of sustaining the institution, if established there. . . . But we have no

48 *Enterprise*, September 6, 13, 20, 1856.
49 *Enterprise*, September 20, Text of the resolutions, September 27.
50 *Enterprise*, October 4, 1856.   Four articles.

sympathy with disunionists be they from South Carolina or Massachusetts. . . .

The *Observer* charged that the *Squatter Sovereign* was edited by an avowed disunionist and "is odious among pro-slavery men here . . . on account of its treasonable sentiments" and other pro-slavery papers in Kansas should beware and not pattern after it.

It is high time for the press of Missouri to speak out, and let the puritanical traitors North, and their fire-eating co-laborers South, know that Missourians are ready to battle in defence of the Union, whenever and wherever assailed, and that we have no fondness for treason.

In the same paper in which the above was reprinted, it was reported that

Business is reviving rapidly, our streets are filled with wagons and teams, and the merchants all wear smiling faces.—This state of affairs we owe to the energetic policy of Gov. Geary. The change since his arrival in the Territory has been magical.

In spite of the past summer, it was claimed that more money had been spent for improvements in Kansas City than in all the other river towns below St. Joseph, either in Kansas or Missouri, and when the feud broke out between Geary and a faction of the pro-slavery party, the *Enterprise* expressed its loyalty by declaring that

Of one thing, however, we are confident—as long as the present Executive of the Territory preserves peace as it has been done for the past two months he will have the sympathy at least of all good men in Missouri.[51]

KANSAS AND THE ELECTION: LATER STAGES

The war was over, but the election was not. The Chicago *Democratic Press*, in discussing the canvass in Pennsylvania, expressed the hope that the treason prisoners in Kansas would be liberated in time to take the field as "the details of their treatment . . . would have a very salutary effect." This comment did not escape the eye of the editor of the Leavenworth *Herald* who pounced upon it with the exclamation "Here we have the plan of the Black Republicans exactly! The traitors, Robinson, Deitzler and Brown, are to be liberated to elect Fremont." The editor declared emphatically, they would NOT, and then, after the editorial had been set up in type, added a postscript; they had been.[52]

[51] *Enterprise*, November 8, 29, 1856.
[52] Leavenworth *Herald*, September 13, 1856. G. W. Brown was meant here.

The *Squatter Sovereign* reiterated the prevailing pro-slavery conviction regarding the Kansas troubles: "It is conceded that the beginning of the recent disturbances was with the free-dirt party of the North. To promote the cause of their Presidential nominee, they plunged this Territory into a short but disastrous civil war. . . . Such is the origin, but the end is not yet." [53] The *Herald* inquired why Nebraska was peaceful and Kansas in disorder, and answered the Emigrant Aid Company and the campaign to control its political destiny. The "Freedom shrieks" of the Chicago *Tribune* reported "eighty Free State men, women and children murdered at Stranger Creek" and "Five hundred Free State families sought refuge at Fort Leavenworth." All of this the Lecompton *Union* branded for what it was, "more Kansas lies." [54] The climax of campaign atrocities were the stories of outrages against women which were frequently told, especially by republican preachers. The Leavenworth *Herald* exposed these "Kansas lies" on more than one occasion, and pointed out that essentially the same story had appeared the previous winter, the location being southern Kansas, now it was being told as having happened near Leavenworth, near Lawrence, and near St. Joseph.[55] "The murder of Martin White, of Illinois, by the Border Ruffians of Kansas" was a shocking example of the work of those savages, as presented by northern papers. Seven balls were shot through his body and it was mutilated afterward. It was this same "poor Martin White" who some two weeks after his alleged death guided Reid's pro-slavery raiders to Osawatomie August 30 and shot with his own hand Frederick Brown. White prepared an affidavit on his murder in which he gave the details of the attack upon his family August 13 by Brown's gang of abolitionists who stole seven head of horses, and other property valued at one thousand dollars, all "because we took an active part in trying to arrest John Brown and his murdering clan." Later it was reported that his crop of corn was destroyed by abolitionists turning their cattle upon it. And then to cap the climax of pro-slavery outrages on "poor Martin White" his neighbors elected him to the territorial legislature.[56]

[53] *Squatter Sovereign*, September 23, 1856.

[54] Lecompton *Union*, October 2, 1856.

[55] Leavenworth *Herald*, September 6 and October 26, 1856.

It is not out of place to note that such outrage stories were to become an important part of the stock in trade for the purveyors of the John Brown Legend.

[56] Leavenworth *Herald*, September 20, November 8 and 22, 1856.

During November White visited his Illinois home and addressed his old friends on Kansas issues. Reports of this visit as recorded in the Illinois press found their way back to Kansas:

> We had a pleasure yesterday of greeting our old friend Martin White, in our sanctum. He was as 'live' and fresh as he ever was, notwithstanding the 'seven balls' with which he was killed by the Journal last summer to make votes for Fremont; and showed all the signs, physically and mentally of a long life of usefulness and good citizenship. In another column, we give a letter descriptive of a meeting which he addressed recently at Taylorville. He tells us he showed his seven wounds at Decatur, on Wednesday evening. We regret that he was not able to give us a discourse here, and show the true character of the wounds that [have] been inflicted on him, and by whom.[57]

The report of a speech delivered at Taylorville, Christian county, Illinois November 24 in which he reviewed the work of "Beecher's Christians," including the Potawatomie massacre was prefaced by a personal history of White:

> Col. Martin White, over whose dead body the Journal set up such wailing appeared at this place, and addressed a large number of our people, at the Court House, last night. There never was a more interesting time among the good people of Christian [county]. Col. White resided in this county for more than a quarter century immediately preceding his removal to Kansas. No man was ever more esteemed and beloved. He reared a respectable family of children among us.
>
> He once represented Christian and Logan counties in the Legislature, held many other respectable stations and resigned an office to go to Kansas. In every relation of life he sustained an unimpeachable character for truth, justice and unswerving integrity. During the late canvass no one in this country pretended to doubt the truth of any statement Col W. would make, but they disputed the fact of his having made the statement imputed to him.[58]

In the election of territorial legislature and congressional delegate held October 6, the *Enterprise*, October 4, hoped for a full vote as

> The whole country demands to know, and should know, whether a majority of the voters of Kansas are in favor of maintaining law in that Territory; and we ask that the ballot box be made the test. We have every assurance that the franchise will be protected. . . . We do not believe a solitary vote will be cast in the Territory by any pro-slavery resident of this state [Missouri]. . . . It is the intention of Missouri to make Kansas a slave state, but it will be done fairly, openly, and honorably. . . . If the pro-

---

[57] The Springfield (Illinois) *Register* quoted in the Bloomington (Illinois) *National Flag* and reprinted in Leavenworth *Herald*, January 3, 1857.

[58] Leavenworth *Herald*, January 3, 1857.

slavery party is in the minority, it should be known, and the sooner the
better, that the friends of southern institutions and equality may know
what they are required to do, to hold the equipoise with the North in the
American Senate.

The preliminary results were reported the following week; only a
small pro-slavery vote was cast because many had been driven out,
the "abolitionists" had no ticket and did not vote, and "as there
were no Missourians to vote this time, we are at a loss to know how a
contest is to be got up." Notice was taken by this paper also of the
election of "Poor Martin White."

CONTINUANCE OF OUTRAGES

Having recalled Martin White from the dead, the narrative now
returns to the days just following the election. Kansas was supposed to be at peace, but only in the sense that large armed bodies of
men were no longer in the field. Southeastern Kansas was agitated
and depredations of free-state men were reported. Dutch Henry's
house was reported burned, after being plundered, as well as the
property of four others.[59] Geary could no longer ignore the situation and went on a personal tour of that region, as the press put it,
"in search of the notorious Brown, and his band of thieves. One
report says that Old Brown has escaped from Nebraska, and another says he is still in the region of Osawatomie; we can't say
which is correct." [60]

The case of Jerome H. Glanville, while not of great importance
for itself, is of considerable interest for the Brown legend. He was
brought into Westport November 1, having been shot by abolitionists at Bull creek. On November 6 he made affidavit to the particulars of the attack. He was from Virginia and had settled on Ottawa creek. On October 30 he was on his way to Westport for flour
travelling on the Santa Fe trail east of Prairie City. Four horsemen, who had robbed a man named McCamish, rode on ahead and
waited for him about one hundred yards west of Bull creek. Two
rode up on each side of his wagon, demanding that he stop and deliver his money. The oxen did not respond quickly, and as Glanville snatched his rifle one man shot him and fled. Glanville said
"I think these four men who attacked me belonged to Captain John

[59] Leavenworth *Herald*, November 8, 1856.
[60] Leavenworth *Herald*, November 1, 1856. On December 6 the *Herald*
said that two of those who robbed Briscoe Davis's house in the rear of Geary's
tour were captured and hanged. There is no other evidence to support the
statement that they were hanged.

Brown's company, the notorious abolitionist of Osawatomie." He thought that a neighbor had betrayed him.[61] The report was circulated by free-state men that he was a free-state man who was shot by pro-slavery men and left for dead. The Leavenworth *Herald* attacked this story declaring that "This is the way that outrages of that party are covered up. Brown [of the *Herald of Freedom*] manufactured the lie, to do away with the effect of Glanville's affidavit." [62] The same paper that made this exposure carried the news that Kansas outlaws "after stealing everything they can in Kansas, . . . have extended their operations in the border counties of southwest Missouri." Two gangs were thought to be operating, and "Brown it is believed heads a party of these thieves." The first case related occurred November 13 in Jackson county, twelve miles south of Independence where eight horses were stolen. The thieves were pursued as far as Bull creek in the territory, and later one was recovered between Hickory Point and Lawrence in the hands of a free-state man. The second case was reported from the Osceola *Independent* which related that October 20 a man named Bernard near Pappinsville, living ten miles from the state line, was attacked by a band of twenty men who stole twenty head of horses, wearing apparel and destroyed other property.[63]

An unusual resignation from the postal service was published during this same period, dated at Council Grove October 3 and addressed to the assistant postmaster general: "Having been robbed and driven from my house on the 6th ult., by a band of highway robbers claiming to belong to 'General Lane's army of the North' and the postoffice having been robbed by the same band, and the mail key taken, I therefore beg to be released of the duties of postmaster at Allen, Kansas Territory." [64]

There is evidence that discipline within the free-state ranks was breaking down. A band of free-state "Regulators" made a night visit to Tuton, a free-state man and a leading member of the Topeka legislature, stripped him and beat him until the blood ran. Notice was reported to have been given another man, John Spicer, that he must leave the country in ten days. The Lecompton *Union*, which recorded these events demanded that the government suppress these outrages or another war would break out. In the Tuton case, the

[61] Leavenworth *Herald*, November 15, 1856 from the Westport *Star of Empire*, November 8.

[62] Leavenworth *Herald*, November 22, 1856.

[63] Leavenworth *Herald*, November 22, 1856.

[64] Leavenworth *Herald*, December 13, 1856.

Union said, "His offense was that he had served as one of the Grand Jury, during the session of the last court, and had faithfully, honestly and earnestly discharged his duty."[65]

Law Enforcement by the Courts

During the session of congress in 1856 authorization had been made for the Supreme Court of Kansas Territory to fix the times and places of holding sessions, providing that courts should not be held in more than three places. In so doing, the practice was abandoned of holding court in each county in circuit, and as the judge of the third district was not present the other two set their sessions for October, the first district court sitting at Lecompton, Judge Lecompte, and the second district court at Tecumseh, Judge Cato.[66] By the middle of November the first sitting of the court in the first district was summarized as resulting in about three hundred indictments, one hundred arrests, and twenty-two convicted and sentenced. The Leavenworth *Herald* predicted that "This will afford another pretext for freedom shriekers to raise the groan about the oppression of Free State men by the Kansas laws."[67]   Jim Lane had passed through Mt. Pleasant, Iowa, and the *Observer* of that place reported that he had said the prisoners would be executed unless rescued and he was on the way East to appeal to the northern governors to ask the President to intervene and release them.   The Leavenworth *Herald* wondered what the editor would say when he heard that four of them had been tried and acquitted.[68]   Some doubt was cast upon the value of these judicial deliberations as one paper reported that the twenty-two who were convicted had escaped, and another paper published a few days later stated that thirty-six prisoners had escaped.[69]

The court news for the second district was of particular interest:

There are two of the murderers of the Doyles and others of Osawatomie, now in confinement, and will be tried in a week or two at Tecumseh before Judge Cato. The evidence against them, it is said, is sufficient to convict them of murder in the first degree, beyond doubt. They will certainly hang. They committed the most fiendish and inhuman murder known in

65 Lecompton *Union*, December 18, 1856.
66 Leavenworth *Herald*, September 20, 1856.
67 Leavenworth *Herald*, December 2, 1856.
68 Leavenworth *Herald*, December 2, 1856.
69 *Squatter Sovereign*, December 2, 1856. Leavenworth *Journal*, December 4, 1856. Leavenworth *Herald*, December 6, 1856.

the annals of history, and yet there are free state men in the Territory, on
political grounds, who will deny in the face of facts that these men committed the murder.—Hanging is almost too good for such murderers.

A number of witnesses, having been summoned to appear before Judge
Cato's court, and refused to attend, the Judge issued writs of attachment,
and adjourned the court for a week, until these free soil witnesses can be
compelled to come into court and swear to the truth.

The free State men are beginning to denounce and abuse Judge Cato
for having the laws faithfully executed.   He will now be, in their estimation the second 'Jefferies' of Kansas.   Judge Lecompte was denounced by
the same party as the modern Jeffries. . . .

Free State men may committ all sort of depredations, plunder, steal and
murder, but if they are brought to trial before the courts of the Territory,
the officers of the law are denounced, vilified, and abused, while these outlaws have the sympathies, and the aid and comfort of these 'freedom
shriekers.'   A free State man in Lawrence, who had been plundered by a
band of outlaws, merely for appealing to the courts of the Territory for
redress, was denounced by the Herald of Freedom, and all free State men
cautioned against even trading with or patronizing him in any way.   Such
has been and is now the ostracising and arbitrary course of the leaders of
the free State party in Kansas to whip the refractory members in the
traces.   Many honest Free State men have left the party and joined the
proslavery ranks as the only law and order and conservative party in the
Territory.[70]

In spite of the extended interest seemingly taken in the Potawatomie prisoners nothing more has been found in the papers about
the outcome of the massacre trials.   Another prisoner from the same
region was reported upon: ''William Partridge, a notorious scoundrel, has been found guilty of burglary in the first degree, and sentenced to hard labor and imprisonment for ten years.''   The jury
was reported to have been made up of both pro-slavery and free-
state men and was out not over twenty minutes.[71]   At the close of
the six weeks term the *Union* gave a half column eulogy of Judge
Cato, expressing the opinion that ''his late term of court has done
more towards restoring peace in Kansas, than any move made since
the organization of our Territory.''   It had taught the people, declared the *Union*, that there was *law* in Kansas.   The mystery deep-
ens, however, with this article, because a summary was offered of
what were called the three leading cases disposed of, the Hickory
Point cases, the Partridge case, and a murder case involving one
John Cushion, but nothing was said of the Potawatomie massacre

---

[70] Leavenworth *Herald*, December 13, 1856.
[71] Lecompton *Union*, December 18, 1856.
[72] Lecompton *Union*, December 25, 1856.

case.[72] The only additional court news in the following weeks was
the arrival of Judge Cunningham in January, 1857.[73]

In this highly volatile Kansas atmosphere it would have been
impossible for a governor to have avoided some minor explosions.
The test of success lay in his ability to escape a serious one.
Whether it was his responsibility or not, Geary ran afoul of Judge
Lecompte.   Little appeared in the papers during the early stages of
the episode, but the storm broke publicly in November.   A free-state
man named Buffum had been killed during the disorders in September, supposedly by a pro-slavery man.   One Hays was arrested
and Lecompte released him on bail.   Geary ordered his arrest, the
marshal refused and then Geary ordered Titus, a commander of a
militia company, to make the arrest.   Hays was again released by
Lecompte, this time on writ of habeas corpus.[74]   If Lecompte was
upheld at Washington, it was felt that Geary would have to resign.
The Platte *Argus* suggested D. R. Atchison as the ideal man for the
new governor.[75]   The pro-slavery press was divided on the question
and the *Squatter Sovereign* hoped that those who had confidence in
Geary were right.   In an address at Leavenworth he had remarked
that he might commit errors, but if so they would be of the head and
not of the heart.   In recalling this remark the *Squatter Sovereign*
admitted that in social relations an error of the head might be
excused, but in politics *never:* "We want a Governor for Kansas
with a head on, no matter about his heart. . . . Hence we have no
mercy for Gov. Geary and his head."[76]

Another difficulty taken seriously by some pro-slavery men was
the governor's conduct with regard to the new militia companies

[73] Leavenworth *Journal*, December 4, 1856. He had not arrived. *Journal*,
January 15, 1857. He had arrived. This is the same Judge Cunningham who
was to figure in the apocryphal story of John Brown asking God what to do
with his prisoners, which was supposed to have occurred during an accidental
meeting of the two when Brown was leaving the territory in September or October and the Judge was supposed to be entering.

[74] *Squatter Sovereign*, November 22, December 2 and 16, 1856. Leavenworth *Herald*, November 15, December 16 and 20, 1856.

[75] *Squatter Sovereign*, December 2, 1856.

[76] *Squatter Sovereign*, December 16, 1856. The same issue contained a
bitter attack on the *Daily Jefferson Inquirer* and the Boonville *Observer*, in
Missouri for misstatements of facts. The former had said that the governor
had suspended Lecompte and Donelson. The *Squatter Sovereign's* major contention was that the statement was false on its face, as the governor and the
Judge both were appointed by the President and neither had power to remove
the other. In fact, the question was raised whether even the President had the
power to remove the Chief Justice of the Supreme Court of the Territory once
he had been appointed and qualified.

called into United States service. Titus had been one of the conspicuous pro-slavery leaders during the August war, and he was appointed to head one of the new companies. This caused no adverse
comment in the pro-slavery press. Sam Walker and James A.
Harvey were two free-state leaders and eminently efficient at fighting, horse stealing and house-burning as the record of the August
war illustrates. voluminously. The one-hundred-and-one Hickory
Point prisoners then standing trial were members of Harvey's raiding party. Walker and Harvey had been appointed to command in
the new militia, and this was more than the Leavenworth *Herald*
could understand: "Walker is captain of the company and Harvey,
Lieutenant. There is an indictment against Harvey for murder and
he cannot be found to be arrested. It is strange, passing strange,
that Gov. Geary should receive such notorious outlaws into the
service. But it is even so."[77] The *Squatter Sovereign* reiterated
that there was a plot to drive slavery and slaveholders out of Kansas. Every day there seemed to be new evidence, and Geary seemed
more and more to be implicated. An extract from a letter from the
East was printed in which the author reported a conversation with
Jim Lane to the effect that he was bringing twenty thousand men to
Kansas, that Geary was a friend and would not arrest him, and that
in September through an understanding with Geary the governor
did not offer a reward for him until he was out of reach. Vermont
had voted money for Kansas and was thanked by Greeley for
"pioneering in the path of duty." G. W. Brown, editor of the
Herald of Freedom was a friend of Geary. This alone was enough
to condemn him in the eyes of the *Squatter Sovereign*. But the
thing that caused that paper to doubt him most was his refusal to
arrest Walker and Harvey and his appointment of these murderers
and plunderers to place and distinction.[78]

LAND SALES AND BUSINESS PROSPERITY

The territory of Kansas had been open to settlement for two and
a half years before land was offered at public sale. The notices of
the offering of the Delaware Reserve lands were published late in
August, the sale to occur October 20, 1856. The disorders caused
postponement until November 17. Both parties to the contest for
control of Kansas looked forward to this event with misgiving. The
Leavenworth *Herald*, November 1, represented that northern men

[77] Leavenworth *Herald*, November 8, 1856.
[78] *Squatter Sovereign*, December 23, 1856.

were making efforts to introduce politics into the sales, that Robinson and others had written East appealing for money on the ground that pro-slavery men intended to buy up the claims of free-state settlers. It was feared that these representations would cause a great influx of northern capital for the purpose of speculation and furtherance of the cause of freedom. The Leavenworth *Herald*, November 15, addressed an editorial to all who were in any way interested in the land sales, saying that during the eighteen months' excitement all had complained more or less of the course of certain officials in relation to actual occupants, and that all felt that the Kansas pioneers had endured more than the ordinary privations. The squatters were warned to be calm, but firm, as a single rash act might involve all again in the troubles. To prospective settlers and to speculators it also addressed a word of advice, declaring that it could not credit rumors that either of these groups would try to revive the wars. There was land enough for all, outsiders should hold off awaiting the opportunity to purchase from squatters or else they could go into unoccupied lands. The squatters had a just right to believe that their rights would be respected, the editorial concluded, and they appealed to the outside groups that all evil consequences be avoided. In the next issue the *Herald* insisted that the squatters knew no other party than the squatter's party, that each *bona fide* occupant must respect the rights of every other one, that attempts to give a political coloring to the matter was the work of selfish, designing demagogues, the leading one of whom was Charles Robinson, and that "there is no danger of speculators bidding over the actual settlers." These lands were not open to pre-emption, but were being sold at auction at a minimum price determined by an appraisal of individual parcels. Under this procedure it was possible for competitors to outbid the squatter at the auction. A squatter's convention was held at which it was understood that there would be no competitive bidding on squatter's claims.[79]   Apparently there were some who argued that the Indians would be treated unfairly if the principle of competitive bidding was evaded, and replies were presented fully defending the squatters on the plea that the land had been appraised at fair value and the Indians could not justly expect more.[80]   A report was circulated that a Boston company intended bidding in city lots, and likewise reports were rife that citizens of Kentucky, Missouri and Alabama intended

[79] Leavenworth *Journal*, November 20, 1856.
[80] Leavenworth *Herald*, November 22, 1857.

to do the same. The *Herald* presumed, however, that they would respect the rights of settlers. Dr. Eddy, the commissioner in charge of the sale, was said to have the confidence of the settlers and would insist upon fair treatment.[81] The city of Leavenworth was crowded with three thousand to four thousand persons and an estimate was made that there was $5,000,000 in town.[82]

The first report published describing proceedings stated that the determination of the squatters prevailed. On the second day instructions were reported to have been given in favor of settlers and their lands were passed over until later in the sale, unoccupied lands being offered first. The competitive bidding was said to have been lively, most of this land going for $1.50 to $2.15 per acre.[83] At the end of the second week it was reported that there was no disposition on the part of the speculators to interfere with the settler, in fact they were ready to advance money at twenty-five to forty per cent interest in order to enable the squatters to make their purchases. As the payments must be made in gold or silver, there was a heavy drain on the hard money of the region. One of several interruptions occurred during this week when the discovery was made that one man had exercised squatter rights who was a non-resident. Eddy gained the confidence of everyone, apparently, by his insistence that all sales would be suspended from time to time until irregularities and disputes were satisfactorily settled.[84] The most serious interruption was on account of the Leavenworth city dispute so the sales were not completed until February, 1857. When it was all over a celebration was held, and honors were freely attributed to Eddy, W. H. Russell and Governor Geary.[85] That the land sales should have been carried out without any disorder and with general good feeling was one of the most remarkable things that had occurred in the history of the territory, and especially in view of the fact that within two months prior to the opening of the sales the free-state and pro-slavery parties had been arrayed against each other in open, organized warfare.

The orderly procedure at the sales did not mean that rivalry had disappeared, only that it had changed character. Charles Robinson was mentioned several times by name, as well as some others among

81 Leavenworth *Herald*, November 22, 1857.
82 Leavenworth *Herald*, November 15 and 22, 1856.
83 Leavenworth *Herald*, November 22, 1856.
84 Leavenworth *Herald*, November 29, December 6, 1856.
85 Leavenworth *Herald*, December 6, 1856. Leavenworth *Journal*, February 5, 1857, and *Herald*, February 21, 1857.

free-state leaders. He had established a new town project of Quindaro on the Missouri river three miles above the mouth of the Kansas river and the rival free-state town of Wyandotte.[86] It was said
that he had tried to buy Wyandotte, but failing in that had located
a rival at what the *Herald* called ''the most unsightly place for a
town above the Kansas river,'' and ''if Quindaro can succeed it will
only serve to show that capital *may* make a town where nature *never*
intended any.'' [87]   The next week Robinson's movements were again
the subject of comment, when he and two others passed through
Weston, Missouri, on their way up the river to Atchison with a view
to purchasing property for the Emigrant Aid Company, which ''is
very desirous of getting a foothold on the Missouri river.''   The
Herald admitted that Atchison had much better prospects than
Quindaro of becoming a rival for Leavenworth. Additional gossip
about Robinson and company, apparently meaning the Emigrant
Aid Company, was that he had bought a tract of about four sections
from the Muncie Indians three miles below Leavenworth, also that
the company had sold all its stock in the Quindaro town at a high
price and was devoting itself to Wyandotte:

This is sharp, though characteristic practice. They now very politely inform the present stockholders that it is not their fault if they do not make
a town there, and after pocketing the cash, leave their dupes to dig down
a bluff *two hundred feet,* in order to make a landing.

It is said that they now have the undivided possession of Wyandotte.
This place bids fair to become a town of some importance. We have been
informed that the same company has endeavored to obtain possession of
Atchison. We do not know how true this is, and only give it as a rumor.[88]

Wherever there was a town project during this period there was
almost sure to be a railroad speculation connected with it, and the
winter of peace and land sales opened the way to a new burst of activity. Wyandotte, Quindaro, Leavenworth, Atchison and other
places on the Missouri river were active in plans to procure railroads connecting with the East as well as railroads westward. The
Squatter Sovereign argued that heretofore it had said nothing about
railroads because it would be absurd to build them until they could

---

86 Leavenworth *Herald*, December 20, 1856.

87 Leavenworth *Herald*, January 3, 1857.

88 Leavenworth *Herald*, January 31, 1857. Robinson had resigned from
the Emigrant Aid Company late in 1856, but his relations with it during this
period are somewhat obscure. He was interested at this time primarily in his
personal speculations. There is no reason to believe that he had deserted
Quindaro.

connect with something, but now that the Hannibal-St. Joseph rail-road was assured the time had come to act.[89] Banking agitation became active for the first time and the legislature was induced to enact a banking law in February, 1857. The feeling of security manifested itself in other ways, the organization of a lyceum and a project for an historical and philosophical society. The opening of navigation and the spring immigration were discussed long in ad-vance, but as the presidential campaign was over no more scenes of bloodshed were expected, the *Herald* announced that ''we invite the emigrants from all parts to come along.'' [90]

In spite of the victory of the democratic party at the polls, the political outlook for the future was anything but satisfying. The *Squatter Sovereign* felt that a territorial convention ought to be called to discuss policies and suggested November 18. While await-ing reactions it discussed different phases of the situation. The Leavenworth *Herald* pointed out that the land sales began Novem-ber 17 and that people were interested mostly in land, although it might turn out that as lands in the immediate vicinity did not come up the first week that this date might be as good as another. It turned out that an informal meeting was held during the land sales although the formal meeting was postponed until January.[91]

The free-state party held a convention at Big Springs October 28 and nominated Reeder on first ballot as candidate for delegate to congress. Here again the party had refused to participate in the election for delegate, and the Leavenworth *Herald* inquired, would they again send Reeder to congress to contest Whitfield's seat? [92]

The *Herald of Freedom* had resumed publication November 1 and was greeted with the pronouncement by the *Squatter Sovereign* that it admired G. W. Brown's pluck, but damned his principles. Some doubt arose later, however, about what his principles were. He condemned free-state outrages, demanded peace, and offered co-operation with pro-slavery men in maintaining it. After pretend-ing to quarrel with Brown over a comparison between Garrison and Stringfellow, the *Squatter Sovereign's* senior editor, the latter got to his main point, asking what had happened to Brown since last spring when he was shouting from the famous heights of Lawrence about resistance to law at all hazards: ''Last spring we kindly,

---

[89] *Squatter Sovereign*, January 27, 1857.
[90] Leavenworth *Herald*, January 24, 1857.
[91] Leavenworth *Herald*, November 1, 22, 1857.
[92] Leavenworth *Herald*, November 8, 1856.

gently took you down from the lofty heights you had so impudently scaled.'' The suggestion was made, also gently, that next time the treatment might be rougher, and so beware ''for now we feel a sort of interest in you as you are going to assist us to prevent the commission of outrages. . . .'' But in closing, the habitual pro-slavery doubt of a free-state man in any circumstances emerged again; was Brown serious, or was this just some new abolition scheme?[93] Stringfellow's mind could not be set at rest, so a week later he reported four reasons he had thought of to account for Brown's change. First, Brown was gratified that the pro-slavery men had not hanged him. Second, the pro-slavery men had removed his financial difficulties by destroying his presses and enabled him to go East and raise enough money for a dozen such establishments. Third, the pro-slavery men had relieved him of the necessity of publishing his paper for six months which, according to *Squatter Sovereign* experience, would have resulted in a net loss of about two thousand dollars. Fourth, while safe in prison Brown had avoided all the dangers of civil war. But after exhausting all these reassuring possibilities of explanation for Brown's disconcerting conduct, Stringfellow still feared that he was trying a new game after finding that the fight game wouldn't win. Brown was given to understand, however, that just this sort of thing had been expected for some time and he would be checkmated.

Other dangers ahead were pointed out, one being indicated by the New York *Tribune*, November 15, which stated that now all northern states except Indiana had free-state governors and everywhere funds were being raised to pour fifty thousand men into Kansas between March 1 and June 1. This ought to be sufficient evidence that the pro-slavery work was not yet done, the *Squatter Sovereign* concluded, so don't listen to ''the siren song 'Peace, Peace,' for there is not even a truce in Kansas.''[94] Another danger was disunion, and on this theme, the editor pointed out that in both North and South the democratic party, the know-nothing party and even Fillmore himself had agreed that the election of a republican meant the dissolution of the Union. All of this led up to another editorial on the presidential election and its consequences. It was pointed out that the republicans themselves had not realized their strength, did not expect victory, and nominated Frémont just for a trial race. If it had not been for Fillmore they could have elected

93 *Squatter Sovereign,* December 2, 1856.
94 *Squatter Sovereign,* December 2, 1856.

him, and if the democrats had run anyone else than Buchanan they could have elected Frémont. With an experienced man like Judge McLean they could have won anyway. So much for what was just past. In the next race no Southerner could win. Only two Northern states could be considered to furnish a candidate, Pennsylvania and Indiana. The latter had no man of importance. By a process of elimination only Buchanan, who could carry Pennsylvania, had a chance. But how much chance did even Buchanan have? With the showing that the republicans had made in two years, what about the next four years? The conclusion of the whole analysis was a recommendation of the plan of the Charleston (South Carolina) *Mercury*, frankly to take up the problem of the division of the national property as a preparation for the inevitable separation of the states in event of a republican president in 1860.

The New York *Tribune,* November 22, provided the theme for editorials in the following week's issue of the *Squatter Sovereign.* That paper had stated the issue; that freedom and slavery were grappled in deadly conflict, with a single inevitable result, that one of them would lose all control over the federal government. Another editorial discussed why the constitution had been adopted, and after quoting the preamble pointed out that the constitution no longer fulfilled any purpose stated there as the reason for its adoption. The South was not permitted to hold either the office of President or Vice President, cabinet positions, important diplomatic posts, but, the editor asked, was there no means by which fraternal feeling might be restored?—"We had faint hopes that by the prompt reception of Kansas as a slave state into the Union, a kind of check may thus be formed, which may keep matters in statu quo till the people can have an opportunity of thinking soberly on the crisis which is impending. . . ."[95]

Toward the saving of Kansas the pro-slavery men were working. Several counties held conventions to discuss policy and elect delegates to a territorial convention. Resolutions adopted at Atchison and Tecumseh were printed in the papers during December.[96] The territorial convention met January 12, 1857 during the session of the legislature. The radical element seemed to dominate what appears to have been a turbulent meeting. Two of the resolutions indicate something of the contradiction and difficulty of the party;

[95] *Squatter Sovereign,* December 9, 1856.
[96] Both groups were in the *Squatter Sovereign,* December 16 and the Tecumseh resolutions in the Leavenworth *Journal,* December 4, 1856.

that it wished henceforth to be identified with the national democratic party and that it appealed to conservatives without distinction of party to support the law-and-order party of Kansas.[97]

The convention appointed a special committee to prepare an address to the people of the United States on the Kansas question. That document claimed for the law and order party the support of independent settlers from both sections. As an extreme brief for the cause, however, it did not set a high standard for either accuracy or fairness. All the disturbances were pictured as centering around three abolition strongholds, Lawrence, Topeka and Osawatomie, a thesis which was largely true, but nevertheless only part of the truth. The portion of the address dealing with the spring of 1856 related the determination of the free-state party to resist all execution of territorial law and to set up the Topeka government in its place. The punishment of Lawrence was represented as being under the direction of the courts, the marshal, the sheriff, and the grand jury:

It was everywhere anticipated that these events would put an end to violence, and restore the county to law, and order and quiet. But in a few weeks a man by the name of Brown, said to have been one of the leaders in the Massac difficulties in Illinois, made his appearance at the head of a band of some two or three hundred desperadoes, and commenced a series of the most atrocious acts ever committed in any country or age. He was a man of great energy and boldness; and though his black republican friends are now paying him every attention and respect, and endeavoring to make for him the character of a patriot, yet, when his house was examined, we are informed that all the instruments and dies for the manufacture of counterfeit coin were found on his premises. This was the man who committed the notorious murders on Potawatomie Creek, tearing men and children from their homes at night, and not merely murdering, but mutilating their bodies in the most savage manner. In the counties of Lykins, Franklin, and Douglas, the scene of his operations, murders, robberies, and expulsion of settlers from their homes were of daily occurance.[98]

THREATENED DISRUPTION OF THE PRO-SLAVERY PARTY

The seriousness of the difficulties with which the convention had to contend becomes apparent only with a survey of the dissentions which threatened to disrupt the party altogether. The Lecompton *Union*, bitterly anti-Geary, restated the whole case against him

---

[97] Leavenworth *Journal*, January 22, *Herald*, January 24, Lecompton *Union*, January 27, and *Squatter Sovereign*, January 27, 1857.

[98] Text published in Leavenworth *Journal*, February 19, and *Squatter Sovereign*, March 3, 1857.

January 8, 1857, in a series of articles aggregating six and a half columns. One article reviewed the Lecompte-Geary quarrel, while a second developed the thesis "the cry is peace, peace, when their is no peace." It covered the whole range of the outrages from August to date, pointing out that even the governor had kept himself surrounded by a guard. In connection with the whipping of Tuton, it gave information in addition to that previously available; three other members of the grand jury had been warned to leave the country, and every member had been publicly threatened. Other new matter was the revelation that "Dutch Henry" Sherman, who escaped old Brown in May last, when the Doyles, Wilkinson and his brother William were murdered, "has since fell a victim to their blades—this is another specimen of *permanent peace.*" [99] Governor Robinson had called the Topeka free-state legislature to meet January 6, 1857 and the *Herald of Freedom* had boasted that "there is no controversy between the Free State party of Kansas and Gov. Geary, neither will there be. Neither will there be one between Gov. Robinson and Gov. Geary." The *Union* wanted to know what this meant? A third article presented the peculiar case of Walker and Harvey being rewarded with commissions in Geary's militia instead of a rope, while the convicted Hickory Point criminals were permitted to run at large and live like aristocrats off the government. The fourth major article was a communication which discussed the case of the Doniphan *Constitution,* a pro-slavery paper defending Geary. Again the Walker-Harvey case was a grievance, and the escape of Lane, whom Geary permitted to escape although he traveled slowly on account of heavy wagons loaded with plunder. Had Geary redeemed his pledges?—"Did he catch Jim Lane, Harvey, Walker, Brown, and other notorious outlaws? Has he recognized us as the Law and Order party, maintained our laws and put down treason?" In his southern tour, did he arrest abolition thieves and midnight robbers?—"No, he travelled just slow enough and with sufficient pomp and parade, to alarm Brown and his gang of midnight murderers, and to permit them to get off." He took ex-parte statements of abolitionists against pro-slavery men, and while thus engaged, the free-state gang plundered the house of Captain Davis within ten miles of the governor's camp. Why were Lecompte and Clark dismissed? It was free-state influence, and in the case of Lecompte, the *Union* was sure that Geary was personally responsible.

[99] No verification of this has been found.

The *Union* declared January 27, that Geary put down his friends and raised up his enemies. If any one doubted that Geary had gone over to the free-state cause, the *Squatter Sovereign* called attention to the *Herald of Freedom* for unanswerable proof in the resolutions of a recent meeting soliciting congress for a land grant for a college, preferably at Lawrence, and Geary was nominated to head the board of trustees.[100] Also the *Herald of Freedom* was sure that there would be no interference with the free-state legislature. The interpretation given to this was that the free-state party wished to bring about a break between Geary and the pro-slavery party, and then they would throw Geary overboard, and thus Robinson would win out over him.[101] From the Cincinnati *Gazette* was reprinted an article stating that Geary had found that he could make nothing by being pro-slavery and therefore turned free-state.[102]

As against this radical pro-slavery position of the Lecompton *Union* and the *Squatter Sovereign*, the Leavenworth *Journal* assumed a more moderate attitude. The Lecompte-Geary quarrel was unfortunate, especially as it tended to divide the party, but the *Journal* thought conservatives should be willing to overlook minor difficulties in order to preserve harmony.[103] The Leavenworth *Herald* declared Geary's conduct "a high handed and arbitrary assumption of power," and took up the defense of Lecompte, but without taking an extremist view of Geary.[104]

The *Journal* and the *Herald* both approved the style and tone of Geary's message to the legislature, but felt they must take exception to certain things. The governor had recommended the repeal of laws designed to protect slave property and thus leave slavery where the constitution and the organic act placed it, permitting the courts to decide points that might arise during the territorial period. The *Journal* held that wherever slavery existed, patrols were necessary to preserve order among the slave population, and hoped that the legislature would not act upon this subject. The *Journal* was irked also by the way in which Geary had summed up the recent disturbances, making no distinctions between those who were upholding the law (pro-slavery) and those who were disturbers of the peace (free-state).[105] The *Squatter Sovereign* went further in criticizing the

100 *Squatter Sovereign*, January 6, 1857.
101 *Squatter Sovereign*, January 6, 1857.
102 *Squatter Sovereign*, January 13, 1857.
103 Leavenworth *Journal*, January 22, 1857.
104 Leavenworth *Herald*, December 20, 1856 and January 10, 1857.
105 Leavenworth *Journal*, January 27, 1857, *Herald*, January 24, 1857.

message while complimenting itself for refraining from attacking Geary until something tangible appeared: The governor objected to the appointment of local officers, recommending instead, their election by the voters, but if this arrangement had been in effect the law would have been completely nullified in certain counties. On the repeal of the test oath, it claimed that if that requirement was wrong then the constitution was wrong. The editor complained that Geary had taken up every free-state scheme that had been devised, and furthermore that Geary claimed he made peace in the territory, but he did not, it was the pro-slavery militia that ran Lane out of the territory.[106] Carr, a member of the legislature, in an attack in that body upon the governor, made essentially the same kind of a charge.[107]

The legislature had before it a bill directing the taking of a census and providing for a constitutional convention. The bill had been prepared by a joint committee.[108] In spite of this origin, the *Squatter Sovereign* suggested amendments, because the pro-slavery men must be sure that there would be no opportunity afforded the republicans to attack the procedure. Evidently success was not achieved, because Geary vetoed the bill, but the legislature defied the governor and passed it over his veto.[109] The Leavenworth *Herald* summed up the work of the legislature by saying they had banished party interest from their deliberations and "only an uncompromising enemy cannot approve."[110] The situation was imbittered by the delay in the Lecompte case and the senate debates at Washington which were discussed in the territorial press.[111] If the decision was against Lecompte, the Leavenworth *Journal* held that the responsibility lay with Geary.[112]

The climax of Geary's troubles came as a result of the Sherrard case. The origin of it was the resignation of Sheriff Jones of Douglas county and the appointment of Sherrard to the place. Immediately protests came to Geary that the new appointee was totally unfit and irresponsible and he refused to issue the necessary commission. Application was made to the court but Lecompte refused to

[106] *Squatter Sovereign*, January 27, 1857.
[107] *Squatter Sovereign*, February 3, 1857. The speech is printed at length.
[108] Leavenworth *Journal*, February 5, 1857.
[109] Leavenworth *Journal*, February 19, 1857.
[110] Leavenworth *Herald*, February 21, 1857.
[111] Leavenworth *Journal*, February 12, 1857 from St. Louis *Republican*. *Squatter Sovereign*, February 21, 1856.
[112] Leavenworth *Journal*, February 19, 1857.

issue a writ of mandamus. The legislature was more sympathetic and passed a resolution calling upon the governor to state his reasons. Sherrard publicly insulted Geary, an indignation meeting of Geary's supporters followed, and before that was over Sherrard had been shot and soon died. The Lecompton *Union*, February 25 denounced the "cowardly assassination" and insisted the governor was implicated. The *Squatter Sovereign* followed suit and reprinted the *Union's* article, February 21, 1857. The Leavenworth *Herald* declined to go into details at once because of the conflicting reports of the facts in the case. It did point out, however, that as the legislature had upheld the governor and disapproved Sherrard, the public meeting was unnecessary. Of course, the paper did not deny the legal right to assemble to discuss public questions, but it did hold that the meeting was ill-advised, and declared that the whole affair was deeply to be regretted.[113] Obviously, Geary's usefulness was about over, whatever the merits of the controversies involved. A breech in the party did materialize in May. Stringfellow, the editor of the *Squatter Sovereign*, came out as a candidate against Whitfield for delegate to congress.[114] Two tickets appeared in several places for the coming elections, but the Leavenworth *Herald* denounced emphatically any attempt to divide the national democratic party.[115]

Commerce, Land, Railroads and Immigration

In prospect of a big spring business, Kansas City devoted her attention to the promotion of railroads, east, west, north and south; to the extension of the wharf to thirty-five hundred feet covered with a "coating of stone eight inches in thickness," the best levee, save one, west of Cincinnati; to the opening of navigation on the Missouri, and to the arrival of the first wagon train of the season from Santa Fe, March 18.[116] It was estimated that the trade across the Plains the past season had meant eleven thousand wagons loaded out of Kansas City, with a prospect of twice that for 1857; the first train from the West had brought wool, which had been shipped experimentally in 1856 with such success that the volume of trade promised to be limited only by transportation facilities; and

[113] Leavenworth *Herald*, March 7, 1857.
[114] Leavenworth *Herald*, May 23, 1857.
[115] Leavenworth *Herald*, June 13, 1857.
[116] *Enterprise*, January 17, March 28, 1857. The railroad news and reports of meetings appeared in every issue during this period. Santa Fe train, March 21.

Kansas City is the great stock market for the territory west. There are more sold here than at any other point west of the Mississippi, and more work oxen than at any other single point in America.[117]

When the Westport *Star of Empire* attacked Kersey Coates, charged that he was in Washington retarding the opening of Shawnee Indian lands until he could bring out abolitionists, and threatened to fight for the lands, the *Enterprise,* February 2, explained that Coates had gone East to settle the estate of his father and that he had been appointed by Kansas City to urge in Washington liberal railroad land grants. Later, a mass meeting led by the business men of Westport and Kansas City met February 26, deplored the occurrences of the preceding year, blaming the abolitionists, but pledged that they would use every effort to prevent a recurrence. Only a few days later the news came of the murder of Henry Sherman:

The murderers are a portion of Brown's old band, who still infest that portion of the Territory. Sherman was a witness, with Martin White, against these men in the trial for the Potawatomie murders last spring, and was doubtless killed in revenge for his course in that affair. This is the first cold-blooded murder committed in the Territory since the restoration of peace.

The next week a correspondent specified that Holmes had killed and robbed Sherman, and the editor added that the death must be avenged—"but the spirit is law—the supremacy of law must be maintained." [118] A month later the *Enterprise* was still convinced that although there was much speculation on the subject, an outbreak of troubles was not expected:

The same elements are still there to some extent, the same differences are still there, but in a very modified form. . . .

The major differences in its opinion were Geary, the election, and the good sense of the people.[119]

After the opening of the Delaware trust land sales in November 1856, the next Indian lands to which interest was directed were the Shawnee lands south of the Kansas river, the Kaskaskia, Peoria and Piankashaw lands in Lykins county, the Iowa lands in the northeast corner. The Presidential proclamation ordering the sale of the last groups was published in May, 1857 and the Shawnee land offer-

117 *Enterprise,* March 7, 21, 28, 1857.
118 *Enterprise,* March 14, 21, 1857.
119 *Enterprise,* April 11, 1857.

ing awaited the selection of tracts by the Indians from their reserve.[120]   Other prospects of acquisition of lands were the Potawatomie, Kaw, and the western holdings of the Delawares on the Grasshopper river.[121]   The pro-slavery men had a grievance against
George W. Manypenny, the Commissioner of Indian Affairs and
were greatly pleased when the news arrived that he had been displaced.[122]   Land prices were booming as was indicated by the prices
at which sales were reported in the papers.   The prices ran so high
as to arouse some scepticism of the accuracy of the news, as in
Leavenworth lots supposedly changed hands at $250 to $300 per
foot, and land near the city at $125 to $500 per acre.[123]   Thus far
no lands had been opened for entry outside the Indian lands, but
the long awaited opening of the land office occurred on April 20 in
Lecompton and about the same time at Ft. Scott and Doniphan.[124]
Along with land speculation came a frenzied railroad promotion,
and if the papers are to be believed the spring immigration was of
such a volume as to give encouragement to the promoters of the
boom.[125]

With such prospects for easily acquired wealth, there was no
reason for either party to look with favor upon any act that might
reopen political disorders.   The rivalries for land and economic advantage were so intense, however, that they were a constant source
of suspicion.   During the late winter and spring the papers contained many stories of violence, mostly arising out of claim disputes,
but with few exceptions there was no attempt to lend them a political coloring.   Of the cases in the latter class, violence or discussion of violence mostly turned around events antecedant to this
particular period, harking back especially to the difficulties of the
preceding year.   On February 13, 1857, in the territorial house of
representatives, Martin White delivered a long address on the disorders of 1856.   He explained that it was in reply to the attempt of
the *Herald of Freedom* to vindicate the hero of the Potawatomie in

120 The Iowa, Kaskaskia, etc., groups were discussed in the Leavenworth
Herald, March 21 and the notices of sale appeared in the same paper May 9
and June 6.   The Shawnee lands were discussed in the Leavenworth *Herald*,
January 24, April 4, and Leavenworth *Journal*, February 12, 19, 1857.

121 Leavenworth *Herald*, December 20, 1856, *Squatter Sovereign*, February
10, 1857 and Leavenworth *Journal*, March 21, 1857 in the order named.

122 Leavenworth *Herald*, March 28 and May 2.

123 Leavenworth *Herald*, March 14, 1857.   Russell was reported to have
sold a ten acre tract at $390 per acre.   Leavenworth *Herald*, May 9, 1857.

124 Lecompton *Union*, April 25, 1857.

125 For examples see Leavenworth *Herald*, May 9 and 30.

which the accusation was made that White had murdered Frederick Brown. He branded this charge as "a slanderous lie." He said further that he had thought these difficulties would pass off, "but it seems that these Black Republicans prosper best in war and are not satisfied with peace." The article to which he referred must have been "Editorial Jottings" of a member of the staff of the *Herald of Freedom* made on a tour of Southern Kansas during December and January and printed in the issue of February 7. In the published summary of White's address he said:

I came as a free-State man, and remained so until I was pressed to leave the party. There are two kinds of free State men, one the Democratic free-State man, and the other, the Black Republican or negro-equal free State man, and their principles are as wide apart, and as different as black and white. I settled in Lykins county, near the town of Stanton, and there I found as clever free State men as ever lived in any country, and as fine pro-Slavery men as ever lived on this green earth, and we men got along very well together until last spring. In April last the free State men began to hold meetings and bid defiance to the laws of the Territory, defying the General Government, at the same time, to enforce them. This bold movement began to alarm me, and I went to one of their meetings and tried to reason with them for peace, but in so doing insulted the hero—the murderer of the three Doyles, Wilkerson and Sherman, who was an *'abolitionist of the old stock—was dyed in the wool,' and that negroes were his brothers and equals—that he would rather see this Union dissolved, and the country drenched in blood, than to pay taxes to the amount of one hundredth part of a mill.* This alarmed me still more, and previous notice having been given, we held a meeting at Stanton, and united all parties that were in favor of law and order to come and help us. At this meeting we passed resolutions declaring that we would submit to the laws, that we were in favor of the Constitution and the Union, of States Rights, the Fugitive Slave Law, the Kansas and Nebraska Bill, and the greatest peace prevailing among us, as in common with neighborhood meetings. But, sure enough, very soon we began to see the prospect of the shedding of blood.

He then related the story of the Potawatomie expedition for the aid of Lawrence in May under "Captain Wiggins" and the "Reverend John Brown," and the return from Hickory Point of fifteen men who murdered the Doyles, Wilkinson and Sherman:

They took all the saddles, horses and guns, that they could get, and then returned back, and upon meeting with his companions, this boasted hero displayed his sabre knife, which was yet stained with blood. Captain Wiggins who was in command of the Osawatomie company returned him with indignation at such cold-blooded murders, called a meeting of the citizens of Osawatomie, and they passed resolutions condemning such inhuman crimes, declaring that they would aid in bringing such cold-blooded murderers to justice.

The man to whom White attributed the name Captain Wiggins he said was a democrat from Indiana who, as did other free-state families, fled to Missouri for protection, and "in my neighborhood we turned out without distinction of party, and tried to take these murderers." [126]

White then reviewed the gathering of Lane's "Army of the North" in August a band of which he said drove out the Georgia settlement near Osawatomie, "and then commenced doing what Lane promised them on their way, taking all the Pro-Slavery men's horses they could get. They would ride up to a Pro-Slavery man's house in the night time, and make him saddle and surrender his horses." On the night of August 13 they attacked the houses of White's sons, Griffin and John W. and took seven horses. John W. White surrendered in order to save the women and children. The same band then attacked Martin White's house but was beaten off twice and then returned to Osawatomie. In the house at the time of the attack were eight men, six women and thirteen children, part of them White's grandchildren. White then wrote to the governor for militia and led in a movement upon Osawatomie and met Frederick Brown in the road. White said that Brown refused to halt and as he drew his revolver White shot him in self-defence. If White is to be believed Fred had on boots belonging to White's son, and as a result of the battle of Osawatomie two of his stolen horses were recovered and one belonging to a neighbor named Tooley: "Here is a specimen of the religion of the Browns, and the clergy of the North, who are engaged in preaching Sharpe's rifles, powder and lead, to send here to murder, not only men, but innocent women and children." The hostility to him he insisted was because he refused "to go heart and hand in stealing and murdering, and for that reason they desired that I should die. The freedom shriekers thought that a man dare not express himself in opposition to their politics." Of course, White did not let the opportunity pass to point out that the events of the night of August 13 provided the basis for the story in the Illinois *Sangamon Journal* reporting the murder of "poor Martin White," a free-state man by the pro-slavery men, at which time

[126] White said Wiggins was an Indiana democrat and that he fled to Missouri for protection, along with other free-state families. If H. H. Williams is the man meant, then the statement is wrong, because he was arrested and held in prison until September. A man by the name of Higgins was captain of an Osawatomie company prior to the Lawrence expedition. He was in Lecompton as a witness before the court June 20, but his whereabouts in the meantime is uncertain.

"the Editor spoke very highly of my character for truth and veracity." [127]

At the time of the Potawatomie massacre in May 1856 it was John Brown's intention to kill both William and Henry Sherman, but the latter was absent hunting cattle that fatal night. On March 2, 1857, approximately two weeks after White's speech in the legislature, Henry Sherman was killed by free-state men. The matter was referred to in three separate articles in the Leavenworth *Herald*, March 28. The more detailed statement among these originated with the Westport *Star of Empire* and attributed the murder to a remnant of Old Captain Brown's company who had murdered William, and stated that Henry was the chief witness against one of these assassins, who was charged with grand larceny. After following Henry into his house, the story went, they had abused him in the most brutal manner, rifled his house and left him to die. This was Monday, March 2. He had lived, however, until the following Thursday and had been buried Friday. The *Star of Empire* called upon the governor to pay his respects to this nest of cutthroats. But Geary had already departed and Kansas was enjoying one of those frequent interregnums, when the chief executive was either temporarily absent from the territory or when a change of occupant was taking place.

Geary's farewell address to Kansas, as well as an interview published in the St. Louis *Democrat*, convinced the pro-slavery men that he had been a partisan free-state man all the time, and these documents were linked in an editorial in the *Herald* with the murder of Dutch Henry. The *Herald* stated that it had had occasion to differ with Geary, but it had been done respectfully. In his farewell address, given out at St. Louis, Geary had not made a distinction as between parties in reviewing the disorders, but in the interview he had placed the responsibility upon the pro-slavery men. The *Herald* now joined the issue squarely, either Geary lied or the *Democrat* editor lied in reporting the interview. In regard to the controversy over the murder of the free-state man Buffum by pro-slavery men, the *Herald* agreed that it was an outrage and would not defend it, but what about Doyle and Wilkinson, the editor of

[127] The summary of White's speech was published in the Leavenworth *Journal*, March 12, and in the *Herald*, March 21, 1857. It was prepared for publication, it was said, at the instance of twenty-six citizens who signed the request.

the *Democrat* had nothing from Geary to report on that, and neither on the recent murder of Dutch Henry by abolition outlaws.[128]

The Potawatomie massacre simply would not down, and about six months later Mrs. Allen Wilkinson, widow of one of the victims, returned from exile in the hope of establishing her rights to the claim upon which she and her husband had settled and which they had improved. The story introduced the subject by reminding the reader that Wilkinson had been murdered "by Brown and his marauders" who pretended they wanted him as a witness and forced him out of bed.

In the morning, after that frightful night, Mrs. Wilkinson walked out of her house a few yards and found the body of her husband lying mutilated, headless and armless, and weltering in his own blood. This deed was done by abolitionists, and for no other reason than that he was a pro-slavery man. Mrs. Wilkinson was threatened by these fiends if she did not leave, they would treat her in the same way. This was done to keep her from appearing against them as a witness, as the murderers of her husband.

"In dread of losing her life, she left her claim, which was improved, and sought the protection of friends," and in her absence, according to this story, an abolitionist took possession:

Two weeks ago, Mrs. Wilkinson passed by her claim, on her way to Lecompton, for the purpose of entering it, when she stopped, and with slow tread and solemn heart sought the grave of her husband. While this poor woman was weeping over her husband's grave, the abolitionist living on the claim, hastened to the grave and then and there insulted this innocent woman, and told her that she would never have the land. Oh, what a fiend in human shape!

It was necessary for her to prove at the land office that she had been driven from her claim, and she was without sufficient money to pay the expenses of witnesses and to buy the land at the same time. The writer of the article said that the pro-slavery men at Lecompton learned of the situation and raised $150 dollars that he saw, and probably more, to aid the widow, and concluded, "Justice cries aloud for vengence to fall upon these traitorous villains. . . . But know ye that, ye villains, for all this will ye be brought to Judgment, at the last great day."[129]

128 Leavenworth *Herald*, March 28, 1857.
129 Leavenworth *Herald*, October 10, 1857, reprinted from the Doniphan *Constitutionalist*. The article was written by the editor of the latter paper who was in Lecompton at the time. No other mention of the episode has been found, although the following papers have been searched: The *Herald of Freedom*, The Lawrence *Republican*, the Topeka *Kansas Tribune*, The Quindaro *Chindowan*, all free-state, and The Lecompton *National Democrat* (broken file) and Leavenworth *Journal* (broken file).

Following closely upon the murder of Dutch Henry a convention
was called at Osawatomie March 31 to consider the matter of disci-
plining free-state men who refused to obey the dictation of the party
in repudiating the territorial laws. Four resolutions were adopted
in which the convention condemned the acceptance by free-state men
of offices under the territorial laws, demanded that those who had
accepted such offices resign immediately, and appointed a committee
of three to serve the notices upon these men, and the fourth resolved
"That in the event of their refusing, we *must* consider them as spies,
set over us by our oppressors and as dangerous to our cause; and
that we will avoid them in a social and political relation, and that
we discountenance in our community all men who acknowledge and
uphold the supremacy of the Border Ruffian power."

The president of the convention was Charles A. Foster and the
secretary was Leander Marting. The committee on enforcement included George O. English and Marting, the third member being unknown as he did not sign the written notice dated April 14 and
served upon Justice of the Peace L. D. Williams about April 20.
Williams refused to resign on the ground that although he disapproved the laws, still he felt that it was better to submit temporarily
in order to have order and government rather than to have anarchy.
His reply was dated May 5. The next day he went before Judge
Cato and make affidavit to the facts and submitted the documents.
The Lecompton *Union* published the documents May 9 with an editorial introduction "Here we have the practical working of the fanaticism which has been the curse of Kansas for the last three
years, the only threat made as yet by these abolitionists against
Squire Williams should he not comply, is that they would call him
a pro-slavery man." [130]

The entry of townsites offered difficulties to free-state men.
Some of them suspended their principles long enough to apply to
the bogus territorial legislature for town charters, but the ultra-
consistent men would make no such compromise. In either case,
the federal statute of 1844 governing townsite entries required that
the project whether incorporated or unincorporated must be regis-
tered with the probate judge of the county in which it was located.
In those places where the Osawatomie resolutions or similar ones
were enforced against free-state local officers or similar action was
taken against the pro-slavery occupants, free-state men now found

---

[130] The article and documents were reprinted by the Leavenworth *Herald*,
May 23, 1857.

themselves in difficulties. It was reported that in Franklin county
Probate Judge Wilson had been warned by free-state men to resign
or leave the country and he had chosen the latter. Since then some
free-state townsite promoters from that county had applied to the
Lecompton land office to enter their land and were reminded of the
terms of the federal statute applying to unincorporated towns.
They replied that they had no probate judge, only to receive the
disconcerting reply that in that case they had better hunt him up
and invite him back.[131]

Other echoes of the procedures of 1856 included an account of
horse thieves at Lecompton who attempted escape over the trail
made by Lane the preceding year. They were overtaken, the horses
recovered, and the thieves retired from business.[132] Marshal Fain
had occasion to visit Lawrence to make certain arrests during May,
when he was warned to leave within fifteen minutes. He refused
and was not molested, but this was said to have been the second
time such a warning had been served at Lawrence.[133] The trial of
Fugate, accused of the murder of Hoppe, the brother-in-law of the
Unitarian minister Nute of Lawrence in 1856, was held in June 1857
and he was acquitted. The reason given was that the evidence was
purely circumstantial. In proof that the trial was fair, it was
said that the prosecution included both free-state and pro-slavery
lawyers, the judge's instructions were strict, and the jury was
made up mostly of free-state men. The *Herald of Freedom* denounced the verdict and to this the Leavenworth *Herald* replied at
length, pointing out the above allegations and then pointing first to
the McCrea case, a free-state murderer who escaped jail and went
North electioneering during the preceding presidential campaign.
And further it referred again to the Potawatomie massacre cases:

We do not hear anything from the Herald of Freedom and kindred
prints, of the cold-blooded butchery and murders of the Doyles and Wilkinson. They were peaceable, law-abiding Pro-slavery men, who had never
done any man a wrong.—But they were likely to be called on as witnesses
in court to prove some of the damning acts of those who regarded no law
in Kansas. . . . These men [Brown's men] have never been arrested, and
yet we hear nothing of complaint. . . . No means is left untouched to
blacken the fair fame of the dead, as well as the living, if they be Pro-
Slavery men, in order to distort facts and pervert truth. The time has
passed for misrepresentations to have the desired effect—The great mass of

131 Leavenworth *Herald*, June 13, 1857.
132 Leavenworth *Herald*, May 16, 1857.
133 Leavenworth *Herald*, June 6, 1857.

the people are seeking for truth. They know that a set of hired letter writers have been sent to Kansas to manufacture something—anything to make political capital for the Black Republicans at the North.

We do not pretend to justify crime of any kind or from any Quarter. We want to see even and exact justice dealt out to all men, and none shielded by way of favor, fear or affectation. Many atrocious acts have been committed in Kansas under high political excitement, growing out of an almost civil war. A general amnesty seems to be desired for all political differences. We have no objection if carried out fairly and legitimately. We do object to making fish of one and fowl of another. We are not disposed to harrow up reminiscences of the past difficulties, but would rather bury them . . . , and direct our attention for the future to the encouragement of Peace, and the promotion of good order, obedience to law, the cultivation of all the enobling traits of human character, the proper development of which will make Kansas one of the most glorious States in the American constellation. Let us all argue questions of political differences in a dignified manner, and agree to unite on such measures in which there should be no dispute, that will develop the vast wealth and immense resources of our beautiful Territory.[134]

The spring of 1857 was a critical period for the free-state party as well as for the pro-slavery party, and the latter watched the developments with more than a little interest. Under the head of "coming over" the Leavenworth *Journal*, February 19 noted that Captain Walker, "the notorious abolitionist, murderer, robber and houseburner" had presented himself at court in Lecompton to answer three indictments, and had given bail on murder, arson and robbery charges,—so recently resisting the laws, he was now submitting! Jim Lane was reported upon as having turned to new, if not to more honest means of living:

Col Jim Lane we learn has stuck out his shingle at Lawrence to practice Law. He says his voice is for peace and no longer war. We presume he sees no further chance to 'feather his nest' by gulling the northern people with the tales and rumors of wars. Having made enough he is disposed to retire upon his ample means and live easy. We suppose he can *now* venture to practice law, as he will not be required to swear to support the fugitive slave law.[135]

The issue of submission to the territorial laws was presented more specifically by the census and constitutional convention law recently passed by the legislature. The Leavenworth *Herald* noted that both the Topeka *Tribune* and the Leavenworth *Times* advocated nonparticipation, the former on the principle of consistency and damage to free-state reputation in the North, and the latter empha-

---

[134] Leavenworth *Herald,* June 20 and 27. The quotation is from the latter.
[135] Leavenworth *Herald,* March 28, 1857.

sized that the legislature itself was not legally constituted. The
Herald charged that the real reason was to keep alive strife for political purposes.[136] Under the heading "in a dilemma" the Leavenworth *Journal* thought that the very fact that the free-state men
were discussing the subject of voting proved that they were uncertain of the correctness of their past position. It recalled that several had applied to the legislature for charters, and several others
had made bail bonds, both of which were a recognition of the territorial laws. Some were in favor of taking the final step and voting.
But however much it might enjoy their embarrassment, the *Journal*
had no sympathy for them in their time of trouble and was not
going to help extricate them.[137] The decision not to vote was
reached at a convention held at Topeka March 10 and at the same
time Robinson withdrew his resignation as governor under the
Topeka constitution. The Leavenworth *Herald* insisted that this
proposal was inconsistent with another party decision to run a
candidate for territorial delegate to congress. The only purpose it
could see in this procedure was to keep up agitation with a view to
the next presidential election and Kansas could go to perdition.[138]
Further opportunity to discredit the Topeka movement seemed to
be found in an exchange from the Madison (Wisconsin) *Argus and
Democrat* which stated that clothing sent to Kansas to relieve the
needy had been auctioned to redeem the scrip of the Topeka "state"
government, in other words, relief contributions were being diverted
for purely political purposes. Although the pro-slavery men always thought that the Topeka movement was being financed by eastern interests, the *Herald* had not suspected that the situation was as
bad as that.[139] The administration of the census law next came up
for criticism by the Leavenworth *Times,* which charged that many
free-state names were being omitted. The *Herald* replied that
many pro-slavery names were omitted also, and that the absence of
some from the territory as well as the roving, restless disposition of
the population made completeness an impossibility.[140]

Radicals in the republican and free-state parties gave pro-
slavery papers the opportunity to present "the reasons why Kansas
should bleed again," as it had the previous spring:

[136] Leavenworth *Herald,* March 14, 1857.
[137] Leavenworth *Journal,* March 12, 1857.
[138] Leavenworth *Herald,* March 21 and April 11, 1857.
[139] Leavenworth *Herald,* April 11, 1857.
[140] Leavenworth *Herald,* April 18, 1857.

Kansas was made to bleed for the benefit of Northern politicians in their pursuit of popular favor. It was distant from the ordinary travel of the country, and there was no small difficulty in ascertaining the truth. The Republicans had their agents in Kansas, who furnished accounts of horrible occurrances, as required, to meet the necessities of their employers. Many who had no such agents manufactured news to suit the occasion in their own offices. Poor Kansas was made to bleed to order. . . .

After the election, according to this story, they relaxed their efforts, support fell off and exposures of their methods developed. A rally of scattered forces was necessary and "nothing could be discovered holding out so much promise of favorable results as bleeding Kansas again. Hence it is resolved that she should bleed . . . and bleed she must." The resignation of Geary offered the opportunity to raise "the cry of blood in Kansas." Robinson had recalled his resignation as governor of the Topeka movement and the state government was to be put in motion [June 9] "with the hope of producing a collision, and shedding sufficient blood to answer the purpose of the distant leaders. The article closed with the plea, would the people be deceived again "by the hypocritical cry of those who bleed Kansas to order?"[141]

Acting Governor F. P. Stanton visited Lawrence late in April making a conciliatory address, but as a public official he insisted upon the enforcement of the laws. It was said that this pronouncement was met with groans and hisses. Robinson stated the free-state point of view at the same meeting.[142] The *Herald* thought that Stanton had gone as far as they could reasonably ask him to go, but if the free-state men refused absolutely to pay taxes and the governor insisted, the only outcome would be a collision. It asked also, whether the free-state men were the judges as to what constituted law.[143] Although Robinson was keeping up a strong show of loyalty to the Topeka state movement, he was influenced by practical considerations to join with a group of political friends in addressing Stanton on the possibility of changes in the administration of the census and constitutional convention law which might become the basis of free-state participation. Stanton replied that he had no authority to change a law enacted by the legislature. The *Herald* pointed out that the protest against the census was not altogether valid as many free-state men had refused to give their names to the enumerator or had given false names as a part of their program of

141 Lecompton *Union*, April 25, 1857, from the *Daily Pennsyivanian*.
142 Leavenworth *Herald*, May 2, 1857.
143 Leavenworth *Herald*, May 16, 1857.

non-participation and from this he drew the conclusion that Robinson's proposition was not sincere, but was designed to make political capital in the North.   In another editorial the editor pointed out that these Black Republicans at Lawrence and Osawatomie were also refusing to pay taxes even to the point of violent resistance, and except for these threats to peace the territory was quiet.[144]   Jim Lane made a speech in Leavenworth in which he refused to pay taxes, but in the same speech he declared he was for peace in Kansas.   Lane claimed also that at the Topeka convention investigation had demonstrated that the free-state men could win in an election, but that they had decided for other reasons to stay out.   Such reasoning the *Herald* could not understand, insisting that these statements did not make sense and that the reason the free-state men were not taking part in the election was because they knew they did not have the votes to win.[145]

It is uncertain to what extent Eastin of the *Herald* appreciated the seriousness of the rift within the free-state ranks.   The public exposure of the quarrel between Robinson and G. W. Brown in June should have been fully convincing that there was a serious difference of opinion regarding the wisdom of continuing the non-voting policy.   In this connection the *Herald* saw new light, interpreting the desire on the part of some free-state men to vote as a shrewd piece of strategy to take advantage of the split in the democratic ranks as exposed by the nomination of two democratic tickets. It was now a policy, he thought, of "divide and conquer." [146] Whether created by design or by accident, the situation presented interesting possibilities, but the Topeka state legislature and its accompanying convention met June 9 according to schedule and threw away any opportunity that might have developed by endorsing the March convention in the decision not to vote at all.

Peaceful Penetration by Free-state Interests

The pro-slavery party was becoming painfully aware that the future of Kansas was really settled, and the pro-slavery party was on the way out.   Following the Harvey raid of September 1856, the town of Alexandria, owned mostly by the freighting firm of Russell, Majors & Company, had not been rebuilt and in the spring the town was definitely abandoned by the company.   Atchison the

144 Leavenworth *Herald*, May 23, 1857.
145 Leavenworth *Herald*, May 30, 1857.
146 Leavenworth *Herald*, June 13 and June 27, 1857.

Squatter Sovereign surrendered a losing struggle for existence by
selling out to free-state men, R. McBratney and S. C. Pomeroy being
reported to be the new editors.[147] Pomeroy was then connected
with the New England Emigrant Aid Company. In answer to criticism for desertion of the pro-slavery cause for northern gold, one
of the editors, Josiah T. Hinton, explained in the Leavenworth
Journal that at best the South never contributed over a thousand
dollars per year toward the support of the *Squatter Sovereign* and
had not recently advanced that much. Without financial support
from pro-slavery people and without capital of their own to keep
the enterprise going, the proprietors followed the only course open
to them.[148] In Leavenworth, the free-state party had established
sufficient support to set up a paper, the *Times*. The *Journal* welcomed the new-comer with derision saying, "Give the *Times* rope
enough and it is quite apparent that it will soon hang itself." In
order to avoid doing that paper a gross injustice, however, it must
be recorded that the *Journal* was not without courtesy, because it
did acknowledge publicly at another place its obligation to both the
Herald and the *Times* for paper enough to get out this issue.[149]
With so clear a record in the pro-slavery press of the trend of history, why indeed should Kansas bleed again?

Profiting by the experiences of the previous year, Judge Lecompte took no chances in the spring term of 1857 with the im-
provisations of the free-state letter-writers. He wrote out his
charge to the grand jury and had it published, five columns in
length in the Leavenworth *Herald*, April 25. Not only did Walker
present himself before the court, but Clarke, the pro-slavery man
accused in the Buffum murder case, was reported to have surrendered voluntarily.[150] When the treason cases of the previous year
were called they were dismissed on motion of the prosecution. The
Leavenworth *Herald* took occasion March 7 to restate the old pro-
slavery charge that the Missouri invasions in the earlier stages of
the Kansas troubles were merely self-defense measures imposed
upon them by the action of the emigrant aid societies of the North
in importing hired voters to abolitionize Kansas. Apparently this

147 Leavenworth *Herald*, May 23, 1857. The file of the *Squatter Sovereign*
in the possession of the Kansas State Historical Society is broken at this point,
so the record of the change is used here as it appeared in the *Herald*. See also
Herald, April 18, and May 9, 1857.

148 Hinton's card was reprinted in the Leavenworth *Herald*, June 6, 1857.

149 Leavenworth *Journal*, March 12, 1857.

150 Leavenworth *Journal*, February 19, 1857. . .

was inspired by a report of a meeting held at Westport in which resolutions were adopted pledging resistance to any movement calculated to produce troubles, extending welcome and protection to all immigrants coming in through Missouri, and deploring the disturbances of the preceding summer, although going on record that "we declare that abolitionism was the first cause of them." The editor then concluded with the comment that "if our citizens live up to these resolutions we will have quiet in our midst."

The news of the appointment of Robert J. Walker as governor was greeted in pro-slavery quarters with cordial approval and his instructions were summarized as emphasizing recognition of the legality of the territorial government, freedom from outside interference, and free expression of opinion.[151]   Acting-Governor Stanton's address to the people April 17 brought out the comment that he recommended especially as a conciliatory measure the closing of the prosecutions instituted in the courts for crimes and misdemeanors committed during the past disturbances. The *Herald* was reluctant, "but if the step which is recommended will tend to any good result, then we heartily concur in the suggestion, and say 'let bygones be bygones!' " [152]

When Walker arrived, his inaugural of May 27 followed up in similar vein. The *Herald* again agreed with the governor, also it agreed that the constitution should be submitted to the people, that Indian titles should be extinguished, that congress should show Kansas the same liberality in railroad land grants that had been shown Minnesota, and that a tax should be placed upon unoccupied lands to relieve the settler and place the burden of taxation upon speculative holding of large tracts of land. In conclusion Eastin declared that the address was an able document and that harmony which would enable the state to secure admission seemed to be "the paramount object in view." [153]   The governor delivered another address in Topeka at the time of the free-state convention but the convention confirmed the previous decision not to participate in the constitutional movement under territorial authority. In comment upon this the *Herald* in disgust declared that this illustrated how the free-state leaders acted toward a governor whose every act showed his intention of fair treatment to free-state men.[154]

---

[151] Leavenworth *Herald*, April 11, 1857.
[152] Leavenworth *Herald*, April 25, 1857.
[153] Leavenworth *Herald*, June 6, 1857.
[154] Leavenworth *Herald*, June 27, 1857.

In concluding this survey of the pro-slavery press certain things stand out. The importance of land was stressed by the Leavenworth *Herald*, and for the early winter of 1856 was considered as decisive. Commerce was unquestionably the controlling element in the policy of the Kansas City *Enterprise*. In singling out free-state trouble-makers, the shifting emphasis relative to time is significant; the Emigrant Aid Company, Reeder, Delahay, Lane, Robinson, Brown, with Lane in first position in connection with the late summer war and associated especially with the northern part of the territory, Walker with the Kansas Valley, and Brown with southern Kansas. In emphasizing peace makers among the pro-slavery element, credit was assigned liberally to Geary, to W. H. Russell of the freighting firm, and in Kansas City the mass meeting leaders were the business men; Northup, Chick, Alexander Majors (partner of Russell of Leavenworth) and other substantial men whose names have been commemorated in the city's principal streets, parks and buildings; Scarritt, Gillis, Gilham, Lykins, Jarboe, Campbell, Van Horn, and Swope. The basic weakness of the pro-slavery party in the long run was not the outrages of the election of March 1855 and later border ruffian activities, but a lack of support in settlers from the South to maintain the original advantage. This is in contrast with the peaceful economic penetration of the free-state element which was dominant by the spring of 1857. Finally, internal dissention in both parties contributed to the maturing of natural forces.

CHAPTER VIII

THE LOCAL FREE-STATE PRESS; LATE 1856 AND EARLY 1857

In dealing with the latter part of 1856, a serious handicap must be clearly recognized in the fact that during much of the period there was only one free-state newspaper in the territory, and that one a radical, the *Kansas Tribune*. The *Herald of Freedom* resumed publication in November as a conservative free-state paper and was accused immediately of having sold out the cause to the pro-slavery administration for the public printing. Later G. W. Brown and Charles Robinson quarreled most bitterly and further weakened the conservative cause in the spring of 1857 when a strong, united moderating influence would seem to have had its great opportunity.

In June, 1856 the *Kansas Tribune* sounded the keynote of radicalism:

> Every resident of Kansas has become convinced ere this that something must be done immediately, some prompt and decided action taken for the protection of our lives and the defense of our homes, and stop if possible the effusion of so much innocent blood; or, if it must be spilled let it be upon the battlefield where each has an equal chance for his life, and not by the midnight assassin and the highway robber. It is useless for us to wait longer for the United States troops to do what we could have done two weeks ago, had we been left to ourselves—rid the country of a band of highway desperadoes whose only object is murder rapine and plunder.
>
> Scarcely a day passes but some of our citizens are murdered, or a town sacked, burned or otherwise destroyed. . . . Companies of armed men can come into our state marking their roads with the blood of our peaceful citizens, and not a reproachful word is uttered—all is well. But the moment that the residents of Kansas assert their rights, defend their lives and property, that moment the strong arm of the Republic is interposed. . . . Was ever such a farce made of Republicanism, or such a mockery of Justice?
>
> Such a course of procedure should not and must not be tolerated; we have waited in the vain hope that our grievances would be redressed, but it is useless to wait longer, our only hope is in our own prompt and decided action. It is an old but true saying that 'God helps those that help themselves.' In the Legislature which is to convene here on the fourth

of July next, is centered the hopes of Kansas. . . . We are capable of making our own laws, and those that come among us must abide by them.[1]

The Fourth of July at Topeka, the free-state legislature on which the hopes of free-state men centered, had three events on its schedule; a patriotic celebration which provided the excuse to have military companies assembled and on parade; a two-day mass meeting of the citizens of the territory for general discussion; and the more formal meeting of the state legislature under the Topeka constitution. Although each of these was technically a separate event, the circumstances of the occasion left no doubt of the intent of the planners. The mass meeting drew up resounding resolutions and created a central party committee to direct the interests of the cause. The troops made the necessary show of dispersing the legislature according to a pre-arranged plan,—thus the pro-slavery party secured its objective and the free-state party acquired a technical grievance. One of the free-state military companies, accidentally or otherwise, chose a particular time and place for a flag presentation ceremony by the women, which made it necessary for Colonel Sumner to march his troops into their midst in order to execute his formal dispersal of the legislature, and thereby they provided themselves with another precious grievance. As has been seen the pro-slavery interpretation of the dispersal of the legislature was that it marked the collapse of the State movement which had been manufactured in the East. In that they had not taken into consideration the subtle shrewdness of free-state tactics as directed by Robinson and his conservative advisers who had consented to the plan of being dispersed, but they had not agreed to abandon their movement and had made no promise not to meet again.[2] Also they had drawn up a new memorial to congress asking for admission under the Topeka constitution.[3]

Shortly after the Fourth of July episode Colonel Sumner was superseded in command of federal troops by General P. S. Smith of Louisiana. On the occasion of his arrival at Fort Leavenworth in July the *Kansas Tribune* gave him an interesting welcome, remarking that it remained to be seen what course he would pursue but by reputation, it will be "an upright course, such a one as had marked the steps of Col. Sumner." It was reported that the law and order men made the mistake of raiding the river boat on which

[1] *Kansas Tribune*, June 16, 1856.
[2] *Kansas Tribune*, July 28, 1856.
[3] *Kansas Tribune*, August 18, 1856.

the General was travelling, and that he ordered them off and after arriving at the fort sent troops to prevent a repetition of the outrage.[4]

The editor of the *Kansas Tribune* was not so constituted as to be consistent upon any particular occasion. In the same issue as the above he reminded his readers that the administration had been talking of subduing Kansas, "why don't they do it?" They say the whole army and navy will be brought against us:

We are satisfied with the display of the army in Topeka, on the 4th . . . but where is the navy that was to aid in this glorious work of subjugation, [are they laying up on some sand bar or obstruction not removed because Pierce vetoed the river and harbor bill?] Nothing would give us greater pleasure than to see the United States navy sailing up the Kansas river, plowing its way through the sand bars and snags, which he refuses to have taken out. . . . We would like to know where the fault is, whether in the weakness or direliction of duty in President Pierce, or whether the whole army and navy of this great Republic are not sufficient to enforce such a contemptible code. . . . The fault is either in the weakness of the President, or the weakness of the Republic.

LOCAL DISTURBANCES

Through July the *Tribune* kept hammering upon the outrages being committed against free-state men. Specific instances cited were the raiding of Barriclo's wagon loaded with supplies from Missouri and a little later the wagon of Fransworth.[5] A more conspicuous offence was a claim quarrel between Titus and a free-state man in which Titus with the support of ruffian friends was alleged to have beat his rival and then applied to the governor who sent troops to maintain him in possession. The *Tribune* complained of armed bands, numbering hundreds who were patroling the northern portion of the territory from Leavenworth and Iowa Point on the east as far west as Marysville, stopping immigrants entering the territory and plundering isolated settlers. The editor thought there was "no probability that they will ever leave as long as their masters are punctual in their payments, or until their supply of whiskey falls short," unless "they are driven out."

And who will do this? Will Gen. Smith? Or will it be done by a general crusade of the citizens? The Federal military officers have for a long time been promising to protect us and all peaceable emigrants— if we would only allow them to do so—that, if we would disperse and dis-

---

[4] *Kansas Tribune*, July 16, 1856.
[5] *Kansas Tribune*, July 28, and August 18, 1856.

band, they would drive out all armed bands from other States and prevent their returning. We have done as they wished; but hundreds of armed men from Missouri and South Carolina are still here. Shall we wait longer for them to be driven out by the authorities, or shall we do it ourselves? [6]

KANSAS AND FEDERAL RELATIONS

The reaction of the free-state party toward the conduct of the federal government showed little variety. The Toombs bill was just an indication of the extent of the alarm of the administration over the rising of the North, but friends of free Kansas would ever be on the alert to expose it as just another trick. The bill provided for the selection by the President of commissioners to administer it, and in view of other selections by that administration, possibly Jones and Donalson might be chosen to take the census.[7] There was a report in circulation that the order for land sales was to be issued earlier than had been expected, thereby giving the pro-slavery men an opportunity to purchase the lands ahead of the unprepared free-state men, still another trick.[8] And the news of the removal of Governor Shannon was announced charitably: "This miserable tool has at last been removed. Whether Geary will prove worthy of confidence remains to be seen.[9]

THE AUGUST WAR

During the early part of August the editor of the *Kansas Tribune* made a trip from Topeka along one-hundred-forty miles of the new emigrant route through Nebraska and gave it his approval.[10] He recorded also the arrival August 13 of the immigrant train over the route. The Wisconsin company had been on the road since May 20. Along the route in Kansas three towns had been established; Plymouth, three miles south of the Nebraska line on Pony creek, Lexington, fifteen miles further south, and Holton, about thirty miles further south, or half way between Lexington and Topeka.[11]

The August war was just beginning, Franklin had been captured the day before the immigration train arrived at Topeka, and

[6] *Kansas Tribune*, July 28, 1856.
[7] *Kansas Tribune*, July 16, 1856.
[8] *Kansas Tribune*, July 28, 1856.
[9] *Kansas Tribune*, August 18, 1856.
[10] *Kansas Tribune*, August 18, 1856.
[11] *Kansas Tribune*, August 18, 1856.

selected companies from the train, among them Captain Harvey's Chicago company was invited immediately to make a forced march to the scene of action. The *Tribune* introduced the new difficulties as follows:

> The pro-slavery men who infest our country, seem to be determined to give us no peace until they or we are exterminated or driven from the country. For some time past they have not only been harassing the settlers, stealing their horses, plundering their farms, and occasionally murdering one of our citizens, but have been allowed to go on and fortify themselves in their strongholds, and when complained of to the United States officers, the complaints have been met with 'they are settlers,' or some other equally absurd, or trifling excuse.[12]

A short time later the *Kansas Tribune,* upon reading the Leavenworth *Journal's* War Extra, announced that "for one, we are glad that the issue is thus finally reduced to one single, starting point, annihilation. . . . WE ARE READY."[13] The boast may have given the editor some satisfaction, but it in no way diminished his fury in denunciation of such atrocities as the shooting and scalping of a man near Leavenworth,[14] or the murder of Phillips in that city during the purge.[15] The editor thought that the Leavenworth outrages had gone so far that a reaction had set in even among pro-slavery supporters. He said that the St. Louis *Republican* failed to defend them, and that the St. Louis *Intelligencer* denounced them in the strongest terms.[16] In the midst of the war the *Tribune* reported the condition of the free-state cause as somewhat mixed, and could not predict whether to expect a general foray or a deliverance by diplomacy.[17] When Kansas was saved by the latter process after Geary's arrival in September, the editor expressed his appreciation of the new governor in a two column editorial.[18]

Geary and Factionalism

A record of events and opinions from the free-state point of view is deficient for the fall of 1856 as the *Kansas Tribune* issued

[12] *Kansas Tribune,* August 18, 1856.

[13] *Kansas Tribune,* August 25 and September 5. The paper carried the former date on the outside and the latter on the inside.

[14] *Kansas Tribune,* August 25 and September 5, 1856.

[15] *Kansas Tribune,* October 22, 1856. There had been no issue of the paper since September 5.

[16] *Kansas Tribune,* October 22, 1856.

[17] *Kansas Tribune,* August 25 and September 5, 1856.

[18] *Kansas Tribune,* October 22, 1856.

only one number between September 5 and December 1. The revival of the *Herald of Freedom* in November enlarged the record materially, and presented a conservative interpretation. Geary's course in the territory was given a qualified defense, recording that both parties had criticised him, but in spite of being bound down by tyrannical instructions "the MAN is seen through many of his acts." [19] Peace was restored for the most part although the editor stated some disturbances had been reported in the South and the governor was in that part of the territory to restore order.[20] The discontent within the free-state party was revealed by a convention at Big Springs where one of the resolutions presented denounced certain acts of Geary. Conservative counsels prevailed, however, and the resolution was defeated.[21] In defending Geary's course in connection with the rescue of Lawrence in September, it was pointed out that he had just arrived, was quite uninformed concerning the situation and under the circumstances "we cannot see how he could have acted differently." There was further reason for criticism on the occasion of Missouri voting in the election of October 6 and in the rumor of disbanding of a military company at Sugar Mound, but Geary's difficulties with the proslavery party were becoming even more serious.[22] The interpretation given the governor's relations with the opposing party was that he was proving too independent a man and that they were now determined to crush him.[23] When the Geary-Lecompte quarrel developed over the arrest of Hays, it was clear that the *Herald of Freedom* approved the attempt to bring a pro-slavery man to account, but it expressed apprehension over the assumption of excessive powers by the governor.[24] Whatever opinion might have been harbored in private about Geary, in public it was proclaimed that "he is not an efficient tool" of the pro-slavery party.[25] Whatever influence was at work, it became clear that the officialdom of 1856 was on the way out, Clarke, the Potawatomie Indian agent, was removed and so was Judge Lecompte.[26] Sheriff Jones of

[19] *Herald of Freedom*, November 1, 1856.
[20] *Herald of Freedom*, November 1, 1856.
[21] *Herald of Freedom*, November 1, 1856.
[22] *Herald of Freedom*, November 8, 1856.
[23] *Herald of Freedom*, November 15, 1856.
[24] *Herald of Freedom*, November 22, 1856.
[25] *Herald of Freedom*, November 29, 1856.
[26] *Herald of Freedom*, December 20, 27, 1856. Lecompte's successor was not confirmed by the senate and he continued as judge.

Douglas county resigned, apparently without regrets from either side. The Lecompton *Union* stated that "we have no eulogy to pronounce upon his character as an officer or as a man; we can only say that in our humble estimation, *God makes but few such.*" [27] The *Herald of Freedom* added the hope that "God will not make any more such during the present generation."

The arrival of the last of the contingents of organized immigration of 1856 was duly recorded, the Redpath company in September, and the disarmed Eldridge company in October. The latter consisted of one-hundred-fifty men arrived "in perfect order and discipline, marched down Massachusetts street, preceded by drum and fife." In the same number, however, the editor addressed a message "To our friends East" although he was conscious that he might give offence: A man who was worth nothing in the East was worth nothing in the West; it was not necessary to raise arms and ammunition; and lastly, send families with wagons, cattle and horses who were homemakers.[28] The devastation of the summer wars and the character of much of the immigration presented to the free-state party one of its most serious problems during the winter of 1856–1857. The National Kansas Committee and other eastern agencies sent relief funds and goods for distribution among the destitute, but in so doing aroused among free-state men the most bitter of quarrels. No one was satisfied and recrimination and quarreling went to such lengths as to threaten disruption of party councils. The *Herald of Freedom* tried to call a halt, warning that if Kansas was to be judged by what its people were saying of each other, there was not an honest man in the territory.[29]

TRADE, LAND AND RAILROADS

The relative peace in the more populous parts of the territory was accompanied by a revival of business activity. It was said that "one of the wonders of the age is Lawrence," which instead of being abandoned, was growing in spite of her troubles.[30] The *Herald of Freedom* refused to take seriously the disunion forebodings of either side, even those of the free-state leader Robinson, arguing that Kansas was not lost even if Buchanan won the

---

27 *Herald of Freedom*, December 27, 1856.
28 *Herald of Freedom*, November 1, 1856.
29 *Herald of Freedom*, December 20, 1856. Nearly every issue of the paper during the winter contained an installment of relief squabbles.
30 *Herald of Freedom*, November 1, 1856.

election, because the election in the states did not decide the issue of slavery in Kansas. Furthermore, the Union was a permanent institution.[31] A great deal of attention was given to shifts in trade which resulted from hostilities. Missouri had lost much of her trade to Iowa, when a policy of peaceful penetration would not only have developed her trade but would have given her control of Kansas.[32] Also it was said that the extreme scarcity of money in Western Missouri during the winter was attributed directly to the loss of trade; by impoverishing Kansas she ruined herself. Reports were circulated that the Pacific Railroad of Missouri had been refused loans in London on account of the Kansas troubles.[33] Attention was called to the loss of trade by the border ruffian towns of Westport and Kansas City, with a corresponding gain by Leavenworth.[34] Free-state activity at Leavenworth was one of the features of the winter developments.

Closely associated with this business revival was the imminence of the opening of the land office in Kansas and the advertisement of the Delaware trust land sales at Leavenworth. The *Herald of Freedom* was much concerned over the lack of capital on the part of free-state men in the territory to buy land. It issued a direct appeal for such money.[35] Except for one instance there was no reflection of hostility over the land question, and in that article a fear was expressed that the land sales would be used as an occasion for another edition of depredations.[36]

The third theme in the trilogy of trade and land was railroads. The subject moved Editor Brown to retrospective musings upon the origin of the Kansas question. He argued that when the Missouri question arose John C. Calhoun had determined to block the addition of free-states to the Union. His plan was to remove Indians from the East to reservations in the western territory to block expansion. The Indians were to be kept under pro-slavery influence as much as possible and as far north as the Delawares and Potawatomies the Indians themselves held slaves. Instead of the Indians increasing in numbers they diminished. And then "the agitation of the Pacific railroad again drew public attention to this vast territory," with the result that the Kansas-Nebraska

[31] *Herald of Freedom*, November 1, 8, 15, 1856.
[32] *Herald of Freedom*, November 22, 1856.
[33] *Herald of Freedom*, January 10, 1857.
[34] *Herald of Freedom*, December 6, 13, 1856.
[35] *Herald of Freedom*, November 1, 15, 29, 1856.
[36] *Herald of Freedom*, November 1, 1856.

act was passed with the clause repealing the slavery restriction.
Compromises with the North were broken like treaties with the
Indians, and Missouri held that Kansas had been delivered over to
slavery by that act and had been justifying her action on that
basis.[37] The editor called attention to the attempts of the administration at Washington to adapt camels to transcontinental transportation by the southern route, heaping ridicule upon the scheme.
He predicted a Pacific railroad by a northern route with trains
running one hundred miles per hour, as against southern drome-
daries and slaves.[38]

The yearnings released by this period of peace were not re-
stricted to sordid profits. Movements were started to establish
literary organizations and a university, the temperance question
was revived, and the editor thanked the women of Lawrence for
twice clearing the town of grog shops. The mission of Kansas, he
said, was "to plant . . . the institutions of Free Labor, Education
and Toleration, in such perfection as the world has never before
seen."[39]

Lawlessness and the Future

When the *Herald of Freedom* resumed publication November 1,
1856 the editor announced that it had been made possible by do-
nations from friends of freedom in the North. This was the effect
of the pro-slavery attempt to suppress the freedom of the press.
The Kansas City *Enterprise* took note of this rebirth and asked
its pro-slavery associations when the fact would be understood that
persecution is the life of fanaticism. They didn't understand it,
however, as the Westport *Star of Empire* observed that evidently
the *Herald of Freedom* wanted to be smashed up again. There
was a change in the paper, nevertheless, which the pro-slavery
papers refused to take seriously,—it was conservative. One of its
leading articles was an argument for peace, opening with a review
of the enormities of past Missouri outrages, maintaining that free-
state action was strictly in self-defense, and promising that in the
future if Missouri would leave Kansas alone, "Kansas will forgive
and forget." If the aggression was kept up, the editor warned, it
would induce into Kansas a type of free-state men who loved excitement and who would retaliate for every injury inflicted. In

[37] *Herald of Freedom*, November 29, 1856.
[38] *Herald of Freedom*, December 13, 1856.
[39] *Herald of Freedom*, November 1, 1856.

such operations Missouri would suffer more seriously than Kansas because she was an old state and would feel the shock more than new communities. He argued further that the decision about the future of Kansas had already been made by the actual settlers and agitation only prolonged the destructive forces. He claimed even that the majority of settlers from Missouri and other southern states favored a free state. In another line of argument developed in the same article he combatted the widely advertised view that Lawrence was a Yankee town. Its leading merchants were from Missouri, Virginia and Wisconsin, he said, with Missouri leading, and St. Louis merchants had stock of goods there, sons of Missouri people were there, and every blow at Lawrence meant Missouri whipping herself. Comparatively Missouri held ten times more trade in Lawrence than Massachusetts and in his opinion there was no reason why she could not occupy a similar position in the trade of all Kansas towns if only her respectable citizens desired it. From the standpoint of Kansas it was argued also that it was to her interest to buy cattle, horses and provisions in Missouri, and immigration to Kansas should pass through Missouri.

In another article headed "Guerilla Parties" reference was made to the alleged Southern plan to organize parties to harass and drive out free-state settlers and discourage immigration, but to the surpise of the Southerners they found that the Yankees could acquire these same habits, even though bad ones, and slave property suffered more than free property under that mode of warfare. But he closed, of course, with the justification that so far as the free-state men were concerned, they were acting solely in self-defense. Still another article commented that emigration was again coming in by way of the Missouri river and took the occasion to point out that immigration of families had been diminished by the excitement and that the East had "hurried forward the larger class of young men and adventurers." Again he warned that if Missouri wanted the latter class, all that was necessary was to keep up the outrages. The state of the territory at that moment was in good measure peaceful, although some disturbances were reported in the south and Governor Geary had gone down there in person.

In discussing difficulties in the south part of the territory the next week the *Herald of Freedom* charged pro-slavery men with attacking free-state men near Osawatomie, following closely upon

the governor's heels. A second outrage was charged against a
party of Georgians for attacking, robbing and shooting a man from
Ottawa creek who was on his way to Westport for provisions.[40]
Editor Brown may have been reporting these incidents in good
faith, but however that may be, he used them as a text upon which
to preach forbearance. Some free-state men believed that there
was afoot another organized campaign of harassment by Missouri,
but Brown declared ''Our reply is now, as it was before. Patience
friends. We strengthen our manhood, and gain our cause by forbearance.'' The next week he took a stronger tone in an article
on ''Lawlessness'':

> Two years of residence in Kansas without law, has begotten a spirit of
> disregard for the rights of others that needs restraining. . . . The time
> has come when this lawlessness should cease; when the right to personal
> property should be respected as it was formerly.

As another week passed the *Herald of Freedom* became more
specific, introducing the subject by explaining that his informant
was a man whose house had been burned by Missourians:

> He says that a small guerilla party of Free State men are committing
> outrages on pro-slavery men in Missouri for their past interference in
> Kansas affairs, whilst the latter are retaliating on honest settlers.
> We hope measures will be taken to break up these guerilla parties,
> else break the heads of those concerned in them. Any aid we can render
> either party against the opposite one, for future outrages, shall be cheer-
> fully furnished. The Free State party desires quiet, and should not be
> the aggressors.[41]

''Ruffianism'' formed the theme for further exposition in the
following issue:

> Disguise the fact as much as we will, there is a class of irresponsible
> persons, calling themselves Free State men, who are engaged in horse-
> stealing and other crimes against pro-slavery settlers, and excusing them-
> selves under the plea that they have sustained injuries at the hands of the
> party on which they commit depredations. . . . A vigilance committee,
> made up of the members of both parties, is needed to bring to justice those
> who are laboring night and day, to bring about another collision. . . .[42]

Concerning the situation in the vicinity of Lawrence a separate
article declared that some boys in and about the city had been

---

[40] *Herald of Freedom*, November 8, 1856. The man in question was later
identified as Glanville, whose story is of importance to the Brown Legend.
[41] *Herald of Freedom*, November 22, 1856.
[42] *Herald of Freedom*, November 29, 1856.

learning the art of border ruffianism and "a large number of such persons are collecting in Kansas, and must be reformed in due time, or serious consequences will follow." As regards the more conservative element among pro-slavery men he took an optimistic attitude:

It is evident to any observing person, that the pro-slavery party are desponding over their prospects in Kansas—They have seen that all their efforts are futile, and each effort has recoiled, with stunning effect on themselves. . . . There has been a heavy stampede of pro-slavery men from the Territory. . . . It is our firm conviction that the knowing ones have determined on abandoning the Territory, though they will keep up their bluster, and try and frighten Free State settlers back. . . . The political horizon of Kansas was never brighter than now. Courage, friends, and all is well.

The editor gave advice freely to the pro-slavery party as well, urging that "quiet is as necessary to the Pro-slavery party as to the Free State settlers. Sometimes we have thought it more important to the former." He suggested that the pro-slavery papers should try their hand at preaching peace: "Neither party can gain by war, but both can be injured." G. W. Brown's admonitions became a sort of continued story with another installment in the next issue. On December 6 the border papers were charged with making themselves ridiculous by asserting that every disturbance was the work of "Brown's outlaws." He explained that the reference was to John Brown, Sr., who had been gone from the territory two months and was more than one thousand miles way, "near enough, however, to be on hand, on short notice, in case of another invasion from Missouri. We trust the day has gone by, when fighting men, on either side, will be demanded in Kansas. Our opinion is, that all parties are weary of war, and hereafter will cultivate the spirit of peace." The name Brown was so common in Kansas that Editor Brown had been moved the week before to comment:

We occasionally see our name, G. W. Brown, in eastern journals as "the murdered Brown." The one to whom they allude was R. P. Brown, Esq. of Leavenworth. Frederick Brown, son of John Brown, Sen., was murdered at Osawatomie. The Browns have figured conspicuously thus far in the history of Kansas. None has fled from duty in the hour of danger, and none has proved false to his professions.

The *Herald of Freedom* recognized among pro-slavery men some "signs of returning reason" and said as much in commentary on

the views of the Kansas City *Enterprise* which had remarked that
so long as Geary maintained peace as he had done the past two
months good men in Missouri would sympathize with him.[43]   The
Herald of Freedom agreed with the Kansas *Tribune* that the emigrant aid companies, North and South, had been bringing into
Kansas "a great many specimens of humanity that the community
is better off without," especially the South Carolina and Georgia
contingents and isolated northern specimens.[44]

Editor Brown's professions were being put to a test, however,
in connection with the disorders in southern Kansas.   The governor
had made a tour of that region himself, with outlaw bands playing tag with his retinue.   Accordingly he had decided to send two
companies of troops to restore order and later sent Edward Hoogland, United States Commissioner for Kansas and J. A. W. Jones,
a Deputy United States Marshal to make investigations and arrests.

In the vicinity of Middle Creek and Potawatomie Creek, many com-
plaints were made before the Commissioner, seven arrests and the following individuals were committed for trial; viz: James Townsley, (for
participation in the murder of the Doyles, Wilkinson and Sherman) William Partridge, Henry Kilburn, William Kilburn and Samuel W. Kilburn
on other charges.   It is probable that more troops will be sent southward,
to remain during the winter, as the cavalry companies above mentioned
have returned to Ft. Leavenworth.

All Free State men of course

The above item was furnished us by the U. S. Commissioner Hoogland.

The Kilburns are peaceful farmers, living on the Potawatomie Creek,
twelve miles above Osawatomie.   Their buildings, and their hay and wheat
stacks were burnt by the Ruffians, now, they are suspicious persons, and
must be arrested.   We are disgusted with this one-sided business.   Is it
possible, that in all these excitements, no Pro-Slavery man has ever committed any crime worthy of arrest and trial?   Two or three hundred Free
State men have been arrested, most of them severely punished before
trial, whether guilty or not.   But one Pro-Slavery man has been arrested,
and he is out on bail.   If our opponents expect to make capital out of
such conduct they mistake the men they are dealing with.[45]

At the next session of congress the *Herald of Freedom* expected
that the bogus laws would be repealed, that congress itself would
enact some suitable legislation for the territory, that money would
be appropriated to pay for illegal destruction of property, and if
these things were done, it did not feel anxious to be admitted to

43 *Herald of Freedom*, December 6, 1856.
44 *Herald of Freedom*, December 6, 1856.
45 *Herald of Freedom*, December 6, 1856.

the Union until the population had increased to the congressional ratio.[46] At the same time it predicted the next pro-slavery move, saying: "We are satisfied from observation, *that the leaders of the pro-slavery party are intent upon another game besides Kansas.*" It was stated that although Atchison and some others may have not given up Kansas, many pro-slavery men, such as Titus, and Buford, had had their adventure and gone. Titus was in Nicaragua. Part of the program in the election of Buchanan, it was thought, was to acquire Cuba, Nicaragua would follow, and finally Central America, and if the North would consent to this course of external expansion the South would give up Kansas. An article in the Huntsville, Missouri, *Citizen* was cited as saying that a trip through Kansas had shown that the border towns were about evenly divided, but that the interior was overwhelmingly free-state in sentiment.[47]

Mob violence again became the issue late in December when free-state men made a nocturnal visit to Tuton, a free-state leader, and flogged him because he had served on the grand jury which had indicted free-state men for crimes. The Lecompton *Union* first printed the story, and then the *Herald of Freedom* joined in denunciation:

We have been cursed long enough with mob violence in Kansas. If Free State settlers, for real or imaginary cause, resort to such acts, the pro-slavery party can do the same, and the whole country will soon be in an uproar again.[48]

FREE-STATE PRISONERS

The free-state prisoners, most of whom had been captured in connection with the Hickory Point expedition, provided a theme for continuous agitation during the winter of 1856–1857. The trial began late in October at Lecompton in Judge Lecompte's court. Part of the prisoners escaped, others were acquitted, thirty secured a change of venue to Judge Cato's court at Tecumseh, and a few were convicted.[49] Late in November thirty-six of the forty-eight prisoners held at Tecumseh on various charges escaped.[50] The remaining twelve were acquitted.[51] As there was no proper place

46 *Herald of Freedom,* December 13, 1856.
47 *Herald of Freedom,* December 13, 1856.
48 *Herald of Freedom,* December 27, 1856.
49 *Herald of Freedom,* November 1, 15, and 22, 1856.
50 *Herald of Freedom,* November 29, and December 6, 1856.
51 *Herald of Freedom,* December 6, 1856.

to keep prisoners at Lecompton, the Master of Convicts, Captain Hampton, paroled them on honor.[52] The *Herald of Freedom* announced that the fifteen convicts would be pardoned cheerfully by Geary when asked.[53] On occasion the free-state men made merry over the embarrassment of officialdom as in the Ritchie escape:

> We forgot to mention in last week's paper, that John Ritchie, who was held in confinement at Lecompton a short time since, passed through here in route for Indiana, having become dissatisfied with his boarding place at Lecompton, he thought he would take a short pleasure trip, and being in somewhat of a hurry, he wished us to say to the Governor, Officers in command and friends in general, that he intends to return in the spring, and if it is their pleasure, he will then finish the term of boarding for which he first spoke.[54]

One of the correspondents of the *Kansas Tribune* reported regularly the news of the prison camp. He recounted in part the story of the man brought in from southern Kansas by Commissioner Hoogland:

> About two weeks ago, several prisoners were brought in from the vicinity of Osawatomie—some of them have since been discharged; not however, until the Marshal had taken care to rob them of their revolvers and other side arms. There now remains, Partridge, Townsley and Kilbourn. Kilbourn has been sentenced to twelve months confinement in the county jail, because he dared to take a horse or two from a band of Missourians, who had but a few days before burned his house and robbed him of all he possessed. Townsley is charged with being engaged in what have been known as the Potawatomie murders. I think he will hardly be able to get a trial at this term, and will consequently have to remain here until next April or May. There were three indictments against Partridge; one for buying a stolen wagon, another for grand larceny and a third for conspiracy against the territorial laws. He was yesterday tried on the second charge. He had engaged Johnson, of Leavenworth, commonly called "red-eyed Johnson," for his counsel.—Johnson is pro-slavery, and he and Judge Cato arranged the matter to suit themselves. Johnson told the Prosecuting Attorney—who of course is pro-slavery— all the points of Partridge's defense, and then left his client and the town, and Judge Cato forced Partridge to an immediate trial, giving him scarcely any time for the production of witnesses, or the procuring of counsel, Col. Johnson, of Kansas City, said to be the best pro-slavery lawyer in western Missouri or Kansas, and Mr. Parrott happened in. The Jury had already been packed to suit Judge Cato—just as many Free State men put on as could be thrown off by preemtory challenges on the part of the prosecutor, while several pro-slavery men were kept on, who

52 *Herald of Freedom*, December 6, 1856.
53 *Herald of Freedom*, December 6, 1856.
54 *Kansas Tribune*, December 8, 1856.

admitted in court, that they had already formed their opinion with regard to the guilt or innocence of the prisoner. Several witnesses were introduced, but none knew of Partridge ever committing any crime, except one, Mrs. Totten, who testified that he had once passed her house, stopping in the road to view it a moment then going on, and that another time he came into the house at night and inquired for Mr. Totten, and being informed that he was not at home, remarked that it was d—d strange. This was the sum total of the evidence adduced against him. Yet he was convicted by the jury of Grand larceny, and sentenced to imprisonment for ten years. So enraged at this result was Col. Johnson, that he commenced cursing the Court, Jury and all, declaring that all had been done through bribery from beginning to end. Even postcript Donaldson declared it a "damnable outrage and deserving of severe punishment." His deputy Fain, who was a partner of red-eyed Johnson, had selected the Jury.

This Mr. Partridge is a brother of the one killed at the battle of Osawatomie, and has been a warm personal and political friend of the immortal Capt. Brown's. This was his only crime—this and why he was condemned. Below I give a true copy of the indictment found against him for "conspiracy," in letter and punctuation. This was found against him while in prison with John Brown, Jr., at Tecumseh, last spring. He was out on bail during the summer. He will probably be tried on it next spring. It is a great document and shows what a man can do when he "combines, confederates and agrees together" and aids himself.[55]

This story of judicial manipulation, if true, was a most serious indictment. The Lecompton *Union* viewed it in a different light, praising Lecompte and especially Cato for their fairness and efficiency. This drew from the editor of the *Kansas Tribune* a sharp rebuke in which parallels were drawn between treatment in individual cases of free-state and pro-slavery prisoners.[56]

In the case of the Hickory Point prisoners who had been convicted, a petition to the governor was circulated asking for their pardon. The *Kansas Tribune* correspondent "K" stated that the plea was based upon the argument that the prisoners had been duped by Northern politicians, and charged that G. W. Brown was responsible for the petition and that the prisoners repudiated it.[57] Shortly afterward another petition was circulated in which the plea was based upon justice, not mercy.[58] At the same time

[55] *Kansas Tribune*, December 22, 1856. This correspondent signed himself "K," John H. Kagi, later at Harpers Ferry with John Brown.

[56] *Kansas Tribune*, January 5, 1857.

[57] *Kansas Tribune*, January 12, 1857. *Herald of Freedom*, February 21, May 16, 1857. Many years later G. W. Brown wrote a note on the margin of the bound file of the *Herald of Freedom* owned by the Kansas State Historical Society in which he claimed the authorship, and also that Geary used the idea in his farewell address.

[58] *Kansas Tribune*, January 26, 1857.

the escape of Partridge and Cushion was reported.[59] It was said that the governor had intended to pardon Partridge in a few days, but "K" thought that report was like an earlier one that he was to have been pardoned immediately after his conviction. The treatment of the prisoners was a theme of agitation, although Geary had remitted the ball and chain sentence and appointed Hampton, whom they credited with being a reasonable man, as master of convicts. In fact, Hampton was defended against pro-slavery attacks that he was too lenient with his charges, permitting them to run at large.[60] At last, however, among the final acts of Geary as governor, he pardoned those remaining.[61]

GEARY AND THE LEGISLATURE

By the time the territorial legislature opened January 12, 1857, the quarrels within the pro-slavery party had assumed serious proportions. Under a headline "the fight on the goose-roost" the *Kansas Tribune* January 5, described the newspaper war between the Lecompton *Union* and the Kickapoo *Pioneer* brought to a head by the Geary-Lecompte quarrel. The resignation of Sheriff Jones of Douglas county had led to the choice of Sherrard for the vacancy, but Geary was convinced by pro-slavery as well as free-state protests that he was unfit and refused to issue his commission. The course of events was keenly appreciated by free-state men and as the radical *Kansas Tribune* put it, although at first Geary had alienated free-state men, by his late acts he had redeemed himself.[62] Simultaneously with the meeting of the legislature occurred the meeting of the pro-slavery territorial party convention to discuss and determine political policies. The convention endorsed formally the national democratic party and its Cincinnati platform. Although approving the independent tone of the governor's message to the legislature, the *Kansas Tribune* objected to some points, but concluded that "as a whole, it is much like casting pearls before swine." The pro-slavery reaction to the Geary administration was reflected in the rumor that the legislature had acted in secret session demanding Geary's removal.[63]

[59] *Kansas Tribune,* January 26, 1857. *Herald of Freedom,* January 24, 1857. The latter paper stated that they were chained together and afterward the chains were displayed to arouse public sentiment.

[60] *Kansas Tribune,* February 2 and 23, 1857.

[61] *Kansas Tribune,* March 23, 1857. *Herald of Freedom,* April 25, 1857.

[62] *Kansas Tribune,* January 5, 1857.

[63] *Kansas Tribune,* January 26, 1857.

The legislative program at Lecompton was complicated apparently by advice from Washington. It was rumored at the national Capital that congress would be asked to enact bills providing for assessing damages suffered by citizens as a result of the disorders, for the establishment of two more land offices, and for repeal of the obnoxious sections of the bogus laws. In the same connection it was understood that free-state men must then consent to participate in the elections.[64] A story was given out at Lecompton that Stephen A. Douglas had written the democratic leaders that the legislature must repeal the obnoxious territorial laws, and that Delegate Whitfield had written also reinforcing the Douglas warning. The alternative threatened was that if the legislature did not do it then congress would.[65] This background was presented in order to explain the bills proposed in January and passed during February at Lecompton repealing part of the law restricting freedom of speech and press and repealing the test oath.[66] The *Herald of Freedom* marveled at such a reversal declaring that ''indeed the millenium spoken of in the scripture must be dawning, when fools and madmen can learn wisdom.''[67] Second thought brought moderation of sentiment, however, and it was pointed out that the repeal of restriction on freedom of speech and press extended only to section 11 and not to section 12 which contained everything included in section 11.[68] The free-state papers were agreed that the new legislation was more dangerous than that repealed. The *Kansas Tribune* warned, ''Let no true friend of Kansas be deceived.'' The line of argument was that the proslavery men had learned a lot during a year and a half of trying to enforce the bogus laws, and that the amendments were carefully considered for remedying the defects in tax laws, criminal procedure, redistricting the federal court in order to get safe pro-slavery juries, insuring that certain Douglas county cases would be tried in Cato's district rather than in that of the new judge whose appointment would soon be made, extending criminal jurisdiction to probate judges, extending jurisdiction of justices of the peace, and

[64] *Kansas Tribune*, January 5, 1857.

[65] *Kansas Tribune*, February 2, 1857 and *Herald of Freedom*, February 7, 1857.

[66] *Kansas Tribune*, January 26, February 2, 1857 and *Herald of Freedom*, January 31, February 2, 1857.

[67] *Herald of Freedom*, January 31, 1857.

[68] *Herald of Freedom*, February 7, 1857. *Kansas Tribune*, February 16, 1857.

providing for the new constitutional movement. This paper charged that certain free-state men had betrayed the cause, and Geary's vetoes of certain bills had failed.[69] The *Herald of Freedom* was of the opinion that "their entire code is an emanation better fitting a mad house than a sane body of men."[70]

The new rebellion law defined rebellion as consisting of two or more persons combining to usurp government or forcibly to interfere with the administration of government; of twelve or more persons conspiring to levy war against any part of the people of the territory; or of two or more persons conspiring to remove forcibly out of the territory or out of his habitation any portion of the people of the territory.[71] The *Kansas Tribune* pointed out the possibilities of the law in rendering settlers helpless to defend themselves against any kind of marauding or disorder. The *Herald of Freedom* approved it in one article and in another doubted whether Geary had signed it, and if he had, it was improper unless he felt confident of the removal of the whole herd of judges, marshals and district attorneys. If enforced properly, the editor thought it would be a two edged sword.[72]

The most serious aspect of difficulties developing within pro-slavery ranks was the Geary-Sherrard quarrel. The latter had strong support among the more extreme pro-slavery element, and wild rumors were circulated. One report said that Geary was besieged in his residence. Another that Judge Lecompte had issued a writ of mandamus to compel the governor to commission Sherrard.[73] The latter publicly insulted the governor and as a result of an affray at a meeting of citizens, both free-state and pro-slavery, called in support of Geary February 18, Sherrard was killed.[74] The *Herald of Freedom* characterized the attack on Geary as "the last expiring struggle of a few of the fire-eating, rabid ultra men."[75]

Rumors were rife that the pro-slavery men were trying to secure the removal of Geary, but the *Herald of Freedom* protested that no man of either party could desire his removal unless he wished

[69] *Kansas Tribune*, February 16, 1857.
[70] *Herald of Freedom*, February 21, 1857.
[71] *Kansas Tribune*, February 23, 1857.
[72] *Herald of Freedom*, April 11, 1857.
[73] *Kansas Tribune*, February 2, 1857.
[74] *Kansas Tribune*, February 23, 1857 and *Herald of Freedom*, February 28, 1857.
[75] *Herald of Freedom*, February 28, 1857.

to live by plunder made possible by another disturbance. The editor pointed out also that many papers in the North were doing Geary an injustice by impairing confidence in him and were thereby defeating the very object they had in view, by weakening his ability to protect actual settlers they discouraged immigration. Brown admitted that Geary had his faults, but emphasized that he had blocked the fire-eaters and had restored order.[76] The *Kansas Tribune* also took a fling at the ultras by praising Geary's master of convicts, Captain Hampton, a Kentuckian, for his kind treatment of the free-state prisoners.[77]

The census and constitutional convention bill offered another point of controversy between the governor and the pro-slavery party. The free-state papers objected to it and finally Geary vetoed it, giving much the same reasons as those offered by the free-state men.[78] He objected to giving the convention rather than the executive the administrative control and to lodging local management in the hands of political partisans. The bill became law, however, over the governor's veto, a fact which demonstrated that in spite of the differences within pro-slavery ranks the party could still unite on the major issue.

Whatever the merits of the work that Geary had accomplished during his brief sojourn in Kansas, it was clear that his usefulness was over, and besides, the new administration was inaugurated March 4. He gave the well-worn excuse about his health and resigned. The free-state men were in an anomalous position during these months of controversy, but they tried to keep the record straight. A. A. Lawrence had written warning free-state leaders that news from Kansas was too eulogistic of Geary and in order to avoid suspicion of his sympathy with the free-state cause to have him abused in the newspapers.[79] When they had called a mass convention February 19 to endorse Geary during the Sherrard affair, the *Kansas Tribune* had made it clear that the free state party considered the territorial government as bogus and in extending

---

[76] *Herald of Freedom*, February 7, 1857. The *Missouri Republican*, a radical pro-slavery paper at St. Louis doubted the sincerity of free-state papers and challenged them by name to announce that since Geary had restored order the Missouri river route was open to immigration. The *Herald of Freedom* accepted the challenge February 21.

[77] *Kansas Tribune*, February 23, 1857.

[78] *Kansas Tribune*, March 2, 1857. *Herald of Freedom*, February 7, 1857. The veto message was reported in the *Kansas Tribune*, March 23, 1857.

[79] A. A. Lawrence *Letters* (Typed Copies) K. S. H. S. A. A. Lawrence to Robinson, December 30, 1856 and to Schuyler, January 15, 1857.

to Geary their sympathy and support in the controversy by the formal resolutions adopted by the meeting, they specified that they could not be interpreted as giving party sanction to his attempts to enforce the bogus laws.[80]   When the governor's resignation was announced, they were again placed in a difficult position. As a matter of tactics they must denounce the forces which had driven him out of office for trying to enforce the laws impartially, but at the same time they must repudiate any implication of legality of his attempt to enforce the laws at all.   The *Kansas Tribune* regretted his resignation and expressed misgivings about the future.[81] The *Herald of Freedom* had been following a conciliatory policy since its resurrection and was not so much embarrassed by the necessities of consistency, and so Brown declared that "at no moment in the history of Kansas have we felt more oppressed than at that period." [82]   In the same issue, although requested by a free-state friend, he refused to denounce Geary on the rebellion law issue, but admitted Geary's mistakes and listed them; the arrest of the Hickory Point prisoners; his controversy with Judge Lecompte where, in spite of his good intentions, he did not have the law on his side; and his refusal to commission Sherrard.   The *Herald of Freedom,* on April 18 may be said to have had the last word when it declared that after six months of censure, now that Geary had resigned, every republican paper pronounced him an honest man trying to do justice regardless of consequences.

GEARY, TOPEKA LEGISLATURE AND THE FREE-STATE POLICY

According to previous arrangement the legislature of the Topeka state government was to meet on January 6, 1857 and the governor was under obligation to issue the call.   He did so and the discussion of the propriety of the meeting appeared in the press during the preceding December.   The *Kansas Tribune* admitted that "we are sorry to hear that some are arguing the impropriety of the Legislature meeting on that day, as Buchanan is elected and Ruffianism seems to hold the balance of power. . . . We have lived long enough without the benign influence of law," and believe the legislature should meet.   "We consider ourselves competent to choose who shall be rulers. . . . No man who is fit for a Freeman

80 *Kansas Tribune,* February 23, 1857.
81 *Kansas Tribune,* April 6, 1857.
82 *Herald of Freedom,* April 11, 1857.

will hesitate for an answer.'' [83]   The Lecompton *Union* took the ground that the Topeka government was going to defy the territorial government.   The *Herald of Freedom* answered the charge by denying it and went so far as to maintain that there existed no quarrel between the two governments, nor between the two governors, Geary and Robinson,—the Topeka government was simply awaiting the action of congress on its application for admission as a state.[84]   This explanation merely aroused the *Union* to further attack in the form of a demand to know who was governor of Kansas, Geary or Robinson?   As it was already suspicious of Geary on account of the Lecompte and other episodes, it was ready to believe the worst about Geary's loyalty in this matter, charging that he did nothing, he just sat at Lecompton awaiting the fourth of March and his inevitable removal.[85]   In spite of the *Kansas Tribune's* radicalism its confidence in Geary had risen to such a point that it expressed the view that if Kansas was admitted by the Buchanan administration free-state men must trust to the honesty of the governor and vote, test oath or no test oath.[86]

The Topeka legislature met as scheduled, prepared a memorial asking admission, professed continued loyalty, and adjourned until June 9.   So far as the free-state men were concerned the session passed off successfully, except for one serious failure, the absence of both the governor and lieutenant governor.[87]   The ultra proslavery faction was much concerned over the free-state legislature and Deputy United States Marshal Pardee attended the first sessions, followed the members to the Topeka House afterwards and read them a warrant placing them under arrest and then left.   The following day he returned and took them to Tecumseh where they gave bond on the charge of assuming office illegally March 4, 1856.[88]   The *Kansas Tribune* denounced the arrest as just another instance of the determination of the administration to crush free speech and the constitutional rights of free-state citizens.[89]   The Le-

[83] *Kansas Tribune*, December 8, 1856.   The call appeared in the *Tribune* December 15, 1856.

[84] *Herald of Freedom*, December 27, 1856.

[85] *Herald of Freedom*, January 3, 1857.   This paper presented the *Union's* views under the heading ''A choice document.''   *Kansas Tribune*, January 5, 1857.

[86] *Kansas Tribune*, January 5, 1857.

[87] *Kansas Tribune*, January 12, 1857.

[88] *Kansas Tribune*, January 12, 1857.   *Herald of Freedom*, January 17, 1857.

[89] *Kansas Tribune*, January 12, 1857.

compton correspondent "K" (Kagi) of the same paper reported that some said that the arrest was designed by the ultra pro-slavery men to embarass Geary as he had promised not to interfere with the legislature so long as it did not enact a code and attempt to enforce it through courts. The pro-slavery men were supposed also to expect that the free-state men would resist and then they planned to ask the governor for troops with which to make the arrests. This would place the governor in a position where he would be under the necessity of siding with one or the other party. Understanding this design on the part of the enemy, the free-state men were supposed to have decided to checkmate the plan by submitting to arrest, even though in so doing they must recognize the bogus laws and courts and give bail under them.[90] The story appears plausible, and if true, would explain the peculiar conduct of the deputy marshal in following the members to their hotel, reading his warrant and then leaving his prisoners to their own devices until the following day. It would explain why the technical prisoners consented to listen to the reading of the warrants in their own political stronghold, the Topeka House, and to remain until the marshal returned to escort them to court the day after. The *Herald of Freedom* complimented the legislature for its conduct saying that by so doing it had "added another leaf to the laurels of the Free State party in Kansas."[91] The correspondent "K" expressed a private opinion regarding the pro-slavery objective, holding that it was designed merely to maintain a record of consistency toward the Topeka legislature.[92] If this is the true explanation, however, it robs history of a very good story.

The one rift that marred the harmony of the free-state legislature did not have so happy an ending. The conduct of the two executive officers in not attending was the subject of an acrimonious debate in the mass meeting that accompanied the legislative session. The meeting was prevailed upon, however, to await a chance of explanation before condemning the accused.[93] Robinson's letter of explanation was not printed until February 23. It stated that he had resigned the governorship with the understanding that the way might be prepared for the admission of Kansas under the To-

---

[90] *Kansas Tribune*, January 12, 1857. Essentially the same story was published in the *Herald of Freedom*, January 17, 1857.
[91] *Herald of Freedom*, January 17, 1857.
[92] *Topeka Tribune*, January 12, 1857.
[93] *Kansas Tribune*, January 12, 1857.

peka consitution if that document was resubmitted to the people of the state and a new set of officers elected. The plan had not brought results, but it formed the background for the situation on January 6. Robinson understood that Lieutenant Governor Roberts would be present to meet the legislature and did not know until afterwards that he had not attended. Robinson's letter was plausible, but not altogether convincing and the incident left him with an impaired prestige in his party.[94]

The position of the free-state party became so favorable that it led to indiscreet boastfulness. The *Herald of Freedom* declared in answer to a Leavenworth *Herald* article on southern immigration that it could "bluster until doomsday" as these crusades "have lost their terror" because now the actual settler "has assurances that government intends to protect him. . . ."[95] The *Kansas Tribune* thought that prospects had never been so bright, the free-state party were almost victors, but a warning was given that the party should not lapse into inactivity.[96] Still another evidence of confidence in victory was the outbreak of quarrels over who should receive the credit for saving Kansas. The *Herald of Freedom* dismissed James Redpath's claim of credit for the National Kansas Committee, as well as Dr. Calvin Cutter's claim for himself and Martin Stowell. These men were on the wrong track, according to the *Herald of Freedom*, the honor was due Governor Geary:

On the arrival of Gov. Geary, Lane left the Territory, taking quite a number of persons with him. Dr. Cutter left about the same time in *disgust;* so did Capt. Brown and nearly all the other persons who distinguished themselves in Kansas history. Col. Harvey's command was taken prisoners. Gov. Geary disbanded the 2700 [invaders from Missouri]. . . . By his activity in less than two weeks from his arrival quiet was restored to Kansas.

General Lane, and all the other brave men in the late difficulties, contributed their share towards saving the settlers from annihilation or expulsion from the Territory until Gov. Geary came; and for this they should each have ample credit; but the kind of peace which followed in their train we hope never to witness again in Kansas. The peace which we had at the time was the *peace* seen in burning towns, desolated hearthstones and a depopulated country. A peace all men should pray heaven to avert till the latest period in our national history.[97]

94 *Kansas Tribune*, February 23, 1857.
95 *Kansas Tribune*, January 17, 1857.
96 *Kansas Tribune*, February 2, 1857.
97 *Herald of Freedom*, January 13, 1857. It should be noted that at this juncture Redpath was claiming the credit for the National Kansas Committee headed by Thaddeus Hyatt, and not for John Brown as he was to do after Harpers Ferry.

A short time later Redpath reported that in Boston it was thought that the chapter of Kansas history in the *Herald of Freedom* of February 28 had not done justice to Thayer, the originator of the New England Aid Company.[98] Still later a letter published over the name of Jeremiah Gage proposed G. W. Brown as the original promoter of organized emigration to Kansas and therefore deserving of the credit.[99]

The free-state leaders were keenly aware that the turn of affairs during the winter constituted a challenge for a redefinition of policy. A convention call was issued for discussion on March 10.[100] The *Kansas Tribune* admitted that the past four months presented an extraordinary situation, "a paradox in politics." This paper was impressed with the danger to the free-state party involved, called attention to the possibility that the release from outside pressure was liable to result in partially destroying unanimity, warned against any attempt to wheedle the party into a recognition of the legislature and the laws, insisted that the laws against free press and speech were still in force. It closed with the most solemn warning, not to permit the pro-slavery party to divide the free-state party on this issue.[101] The early date for the convention was not unanimously received and on request the *Herald of Freedom* offered the suggestion of some later time, on the ground that it would be better to wait until congress had taken definite action and also that a later meeting would draw a better attendance. Quoting political discussion which lay behind this proposal the editor said: "The object of calling the convention at so early a day, . . . was to forestall public opinion. Public opinion is independent of political conventions, and will not be governed by them unless they act wisely."[102] Two days later the *Kansas Tribune* took issue with the *Herald of Freedom* and thus revealed again the line of cleavage within the free-state party between conservatism and radicalism.

Regardless of other considerations of party strategy, the new law setting in motion the machinery for calling a constitutional convention provided as the first step the taking of a census, every free-state man must decide whether he would recognize the validity of the law and participate. The *Herald of Freedom* doubted whether

[98] *Herald of Freedom*, April 18, 1857.
[99] *Herald of Freedom*, December 12, 1857.
[100] *Herald of Freedom*, February 7, 1857.
[101] *Kansas Tribune*, February 16, 1857.
[102] *Herald of Freedom*, February 21, 1857.

free-state men would vote, but declared that if Kansas should be admitted into the Union under a pro-slavery constitution the first set of officers would be free-state men,—a declaration which turned out almost to be a prophecy.[103] As was to be expected the *Kansas Tribune* came out strongly against voting, holding that the paramount consideration was the maintenance of the integrity of the free-state organization.[104] This debate started before the bill had become law, but the free-state cause received reinforcement when Geary vetoed the bill and the legislature passed it over the veto. The veto message or extracts from it appeared in the free-state papers during the second and third weeks in March, along with the proceedings of the free-state convention on policy.[105]

The free-state party spent two days in debate and adopted a platform in which their old position was reaffirmed. The platform declared that the legislature possessed no authority to pass an enabling act, and condemned in detail the provisions of the act on the ground that the administration was placed in the convention instead of the governor, the control was thereby turned over to political party domination, and there was no provision for the submission of the constitution to a vote of the people.[106] The free-state settlers seemed to agree with the decision of the convention, or at least acquiesced in it. At Osawatomie positive action was taken by a public meeting held March 31 in which a "spirited" endorsement was given to the action of the party.[107] There were forces, nevertheless, which were working in the opposite direction as was recorded by the *Herald of Freedom*, March 14, in commenting upon the rejoicing among the pro-slavery men because the free-state men were recognizing the legality of the bogus legislature by applying for town charters. Here again the free-state men had been forced to meet realities because the land was being offered for sale and townsite rights could not be exercised except through the machinery of the territorial government. As between theoretical consistency and profits from land speculation, the latter consideration was undoubtedly the more powerful. Apparently the *Herald of Freedom* was considering the advisability of going a step further toward recognition, because it endorsed as "a suggestion worth consider-

[103] *Herald of Freedom*, February 28, 1857.
[104] *Kansas Tribune*, March 2, 1857.
[105] *Herald of Freedom*, March 14, 1857. *Kansas Tribune*, March 23, 1857.
[106] *Kansas Tribune*, March 23, 1857. *Herald of Freedom*, March 14, 1857.
[107] *Kansas Tribune*, April 13, 1857.

ing,'' the opinion of a friend in Manhattan who advised that the free-state men should register in the census, just in order to get on the books.[108]

SPRING DISTURBANCES

Although peace prevailed in the territory in general, the winter and spring of 1857 was not without its outrages. As in all frontier communities, there were frequent private brawls, especially associated with places selling intoxicating liquor, but there were a substantial number of acts of violence with a political significance, although the free-state papers scarcely recognized such irregularities. During the legislative session in January, ex-Judge Elmore attacked Kagi, a correspondent of the *Kansas Tribune* on account of an offensive newspaper article.[109]

As the spring immigration was soon to start, the *Herald of Freedom* sent staff members on exploration tours, one of the two special fields of interest being southeast Kansas as far as Fort Scott. In one of these reports the live embers of the last year's war on the Potawatomie were stirred:

> In passing south, before coming to the Pottawatomie Creek, we passed the ruins of several free state houses; amongst them the distinguished Capt. John Brown's and his sons', John Brown, Jr., and Jason Brown. These were all intelligent and enterprising men, and came to Kansas to build up homes for themselves, improve the country and save it to freedom.
>
> Old Capt. Brown has been a man of distinction, in the East. He was of the firm of Perkins & Brown, in Ohio, who took the premium at the World's Fair in London, and also in New York, on the finest and best wool. They were known through the country as importers of the best Spanish, French and Saxony sheep.
>
> Capt. Brown traveled over Europe, and examined the various woolen manufactories, for the purpose of benefiting the wool growers and manufacturers in America. In other branches of agriculture he also took leading premiums. His sons brought with them to Kansas imported stock of Devonshire and Durham cattle.
>
> One of them had established here a fine vineyard, and had in thrifty growth fine varieties of grapes. He also had a nursery of the most choice varieties of fruits.
>
> These were not the men to be intimidated or subdued; of course they must be destroyed.
>
> John Brown, Jr., was arrested by the U. S. Dragoons, for treason, for offering to defend the town of Lawrence on the 21st of May last, and was

108 *Herald of Freedom*, April 11, 1857.
109 *Kansas Tribune*, February 2, 1857.

marched in chains, with several others, for thirty miles, in one of the hottest days in June, without food or water. He was then confined in the U. S. Camp for nearly four months, without even an indictment against him.

Jason Brown was also arrested, but was afterwards set free.

When the ruffians thought the country was sufficiently safe, by the arrest or expulsion of the leading Free State men by the United States forces, they came in great numbers, and overran the country. They burned the houses of the Free State settlers, among other outrages.

Frederic Brown, a younger brother of John and Jason Brown, was shot in cold blood on the highway, by the Rev. Martin White, who acting as an advance guard to the main army, who were advancing stealthily to the destruction of Osawatomie.

Noble minded and generous men have ever been the mark of tyrants, and so here; this family of Browns, the most patriotic and enterprising of men, have been expelled from Kansas by the U. S. Government, set on by the brutality of pro-slavery officials.

John Brown, Sen., is a little past middle age, slightly gray—puritanic in his religion and habits, and whatever he does he does conscientiously, from a sense of duty, and as he expresses it, from a fear and love of God. He is mild and gentle in his manners, and fearless and uncompromising in the discharge of his duty. In losing these men, Kansas loses her most enterprising citizens, and morality her most devoted advocates.[110]

Unfortunately, it is only too clear that the Legend about the Brown family was already taking form, as scarcely any statement in the above account is true. The spirit of the description differs sharply from the editorial of January 31 already quoted concerning the assignment of credit for saving Kansas, as well as from other references to John Brown during the preceding months. It is reasonably certain that the writer was not the editor, G. W. Brown. It is possible, if not even probable, that the author was Augustus Wattles, the associate editor.[111]

Another part of the same narrative related the continuance of the tour: "After crossing the Pottawatomie Creek, the first object of interest is the ruins of the house owned and formerly occupied by the Kilburn family, who were recently arrested for some act of retaliation, and the youngest boy condemned to one year's imprisonment." The author went on to explain that the family was from Ohio, had been in the territory about two years, the father was dead, the eldest boy was twenty-two years of age, they had inherited recently from an uncle a plantation in Texas stocked with slaves, and "we hope they will be able to resist the temptation thus thrown in their path."

[110] *Herald of Freedom*, February 7, 1857.
[111] Wattles settled in Linn county during the spring of 1857.

The reference to the prosecution of the Kilburns, members of the John Brown gang, was typical of the free-state attitude toward the territorial judiciary when members of their party were captured and punished for depredations. Ridicule of the courts and judges was a method of bringing authority into disrepute. It was said that Judge Lecompte and his clerk knew no law and were able to proceed at all only with the constant aid of *Howe's Practice*. One day during the trial of the Hickory Point prisoners the counsel for the defendants wished an adjournment and the judge refused. Then it was discovered, according to the free-state story, that *Howe's Practice* had disappeared and the court was at a loss to know how to proceed. It became necessary to recess for a three-hour search, which was unsuccessful, and finally the court adjourned. The reporter testified that he saw the missing volume in the tent of the attorneys for the defense.[112] Another instance was reported from the spring session at Leavenworth when the case of H. Miles Moore was called, in which he was charged with usurpation of office. The indictments could not be found, "and what was still more wonderful, the Court is in the same perdicament in regard to all the prosecutions against the Free State prisoners during the last winter. The loss of the papers, however, if not found, will relieve the Court of much evident embarassment. It will have neither to convict, nor back down." Under these conditions, the story concluded, the Court adjourned to May 2.[113] The *Herald of Freedom* gave a different interpretation, charging that this was merely an illustration of arbitrary judicial abuse, using bench warrants instead of grand jury indictments as required by law.[114] These stories may or may not be true, but they illustrate what was circulated and believed among free-state people, and there can be little wonder that there was contempt of legal processes and frequent resort to self-help.

The warfare which had begun on the Potawatomie in May 1856 when John Brown had slaughtered the Doyles, Wilkinson, and William Sherman had persisted until many of the original participants were killed, imprisoned, or found safety in flight. The Browns were all gone, and the Partridges, the Kilburns, and Townsley had been arrested. Henry Sherman, known as Dutch Henry, had escaped in May 1856, but during the winter his house had been re-

---

112 *Herald of Freedom*, March 30, 1857.
113 *Kansas Tribune*, April 25, 1857.
114 *Herald of Freedom*, May 9, 1857.

ported burned, and on March 2, 1857 he was finally shot to death by free-state men.   Again it became necessary to manufacture alibis for the sake of the cause, even though the *Herald of Freedom* had pledged itself to its pro-slavery adversaries again and again to aid in the prosecution of all perpetrators of outrages, regardless of party.   On April 11, 1857 it informed its readers that "as various reports are in circulation, and innocent persons implicated, it may be proper to state what we know about it."   The *Herald of Freedom* had received a letter during February from a man boarding at Dutch Henry's, according to this story, who had lost $3,200 in Canadian bank bills which he had sewed into the lining of his overcoat.   He was offering a reward of half the sum for recovery and wished a notice to that effect published.

Suspicion rested upon Henry, and a few individuals determined to search him, and in the attempt, and his efforts to escape, he was shot.   Henry was a violent man, was at the head of most of the marauding parties in that neighborhood, and was the leader of the party which burnt and robbed Ottawa Jones' house last August, and attempted to murder him.   His antecedents were such as to direct suspicion towards him, and the circumstances confirmed the suspicion.

Sewanoe was the name of a new free-state town announced in the *Herald of Freedom* May 9, the name being borrowed from a Potawatomie chief who was buried on the brow of a hill on the townsite. It was near the junction of important roads and therefore occupied a strategic position in the probable future development of southeast Kansas, a significance that was indicated in the brief announcement: The road from Westport southwestward through Paola and Osawatomie, the road from Ft. Scott northwestward, and the road from Lawrence southeastward.   The approximate position was indicated further thus: "This town is located on Potawatomie Creek; at the crossing of the California road, at an old established point, known as 'Dutch Henry's Crossing,' eight miles from the town of Osawatomie."   What a coincidence!   Dutch Henry Sherman had been shot down by free-state men in this vicinity just two months earlier, and the postmaster at this point, Shermansville, had been Allen Wilkinson, one of John Brown's Potawatomie massacre victims of a year earlier.[115]   The description of the site was Dutch Henry's quarter.

[115] No other mention of this town has been found in the press.   The post-office at Shermanville had been established March 21, 1855, terminated August 28, 1856, reestablished March 14, 1857.   A town association was chartered by

Among the members of the Brown gang of 1856 was one James H. Holmes, sometimes called John Brown's "Little Hornet." Although his name did not appear in print in that connection, he was one of the men charged with the murder of Dutch Henry but he did break into print as a resident of the vicinity of Emporia. He and his friends had formed a settlers' claim association by which they expected to acquire a quarter-section timber claim under the preemption law and a second or upland quarter at the minimum price by means of elimination of competitive bidding through the agency of the association. The "Kaw Yankees" from Lawrence, as he called them, interfered and proposed to limit settlers to eighty acres, on the theory that closer settlement would produce more business. There was a test of strength, the nature of which was concealed by obscure language, but which he admitted convinced his association that it was good policy to compromise on the legal size farm of one hundred sixty acres.[116] This story is more than ordinarily interesting as illustrating a source of conflicts, and is instructive inasmuch as it constitutes a public admission of illegal intent and indicates what might have been the outcome had the rival association been pro-slavery in sentiment.

On May 9 the *Herald of Freedom* published a written notice from a pro-slavery source warning a free-state man named Sutton, living north of Willow Springs, to leave. The difficulty grew out of rights to a claim which Sutton had located prior to the war of 1856 and from which he had been driven during the troubles. In the spring of 1857 he had returned and reestablished himself, and hence the warning. The following week the same paper announced "the denouement." A pro-slavery man had appeared informing Sutton that the time allowed had expired, he opened fire but his revolver misfired and Sutton returned three shots, all taking effect.

In the same paper in which the Sutton killing was related there appeared a story of horse thieves who had stolen two horses at Lawrence and two at Lecompton, running them out of the territory over the trail which Lane had made notorious in the same business during the preceding summer. The thieves were pursued, overtaken and their activities brought to an abrupt close on

the free-state controlled territorial legislature February 9, 1858 under the name of Lane. The location was one adjoining Henry Sherman's quarter on the south. The name of the postoffice was changed to Lane on January 28, 1863. A later charter for the town of Lane was filed with the secretary of state at Topeka March 11, 1879.

116 *Herald of Freedom*, April 18, 1857.

the spot. The *Herald of Freedom* endorsed the procedure, it
"served them right," "the day of horse-stealing must end in Kansas *now*."[117]

THE TEST OF FREE-STATE POLICY

The news of the appointment of Robert J. Walker as governor
and F. P. Stanton as secretary of the territory was received with
optimism by the *Herald of Freedom* which assured its readers that
they would not find a word of censure in the paper so long as they
gave "equal and exact justice" to Kansas.[118] In comment upon
the address of Acting-Governor Stanton, it was stated that he indicated an honest desire to be just, he supported the laws, he
thought that the submission of the slavery question to a vote of the
people could be arranged, and suggested a general amnesty for
past offences. On this last issue the editor made the point that if
the judiciary were honest no general amnesty was necessary and
that it came too late.[119] Nevertheless when the New York *Times*
declared that the Topeka state movement was dead, Editor Brown
declared that it was "on the wrong track."[120]

The reception given the Walker appointment by the *Kansas
Tribune* April 25 was quite different. To this paper it was an
outrage, but the new governor's pledge was printed, promising
fair elections and submission of the slavery question to the decision
of the people. Following these events, the free-state men were
reminded that the Topeka legislature was due to meet June 9.
At the same time attention was called to army movements, alleging
that almost the entire United States army was concentrated in
Kansas, and asking "what does it mean?"[121] The next step was
to explain in an extended editorial why this paper would not cooperate with the governor in the constitutional movement, the editorial being headed, "Why we do not vote," and being directed
primarily at eastern critics. Those at a distance, it argued, could
not understand as well as those on the ground that a fair test of
strength was impossible under the existing territorial government,
especially when the law had been designed as a fraud on the free-
state settlers. The *Tribune* believed that free-state settlers were

---

[117] *Herald of Freedom*, May 16, 1857.
[118] *Herald of Freedom*, April 18, 1857.
[119] *Herald of Freedom*, April 25, 1857.
[120] *Herald of Freedom*, April 25, 1857.
[121] *Kansas Tribune*, May 2, 1857.

in a majority, and was anxious to submit the question to the people under proper safeguards authorized by federal law. And in any event, it contended, the situation would be an improvement over the existing one even if a pro-slavery constitution was adopted and the state admitted under it, because then slavery would be strictly a state affair and the constitution could be modified without federal interference.[122]

The problem of conflicting views in the East was more fully presented by the *Herald of Freedom* throughout the month of May. In the issue of May 2, note was made of the fact that the Washington *National Era* and the New York *Times* and other leading republican journals wanted free-state men to vote. Two weeks later the Quincy (Illinois) *Republican* received similar notice. Two important New York journals, the *Tribune* and the *Post,* were opposed, and the *Tribune* was bitter in its attack upon the *National Era* raising the cry that it had sold out to the enemy.[123]

The free-state cause seemed to be winning on count after count during this spring, and more than ordinary satisfaction was felt when the district court met under Judge Cato and on May 11 the treason cases were *nolle prossed*.[124] Unfavorable developments alternated, however, with favorable ones, and a serious rift within free-state ranks opened in May. Apparently there had been dissension for some time between G. W. Brown and Charles Robinson. Brown had made adverse comments upon Robinson's new Quindaro town promotion as early as February 7, 1857. When the free-state convention had met March 10 to discuss policy, Robinson indicated his willingness under the circumstances to withdraw his resignation as governor, thereby resuming his old place in leadership. The *Herald of Freedom* commented rather offensively that it was hardly possible for an officer to take off and put on official robes in that manner, and that they must be "a loose fit."[125] The violent quarrel burst into public prints in May. Robinson stated in a public speech May 15 that Brown had proposed to sell out the free-state cause the year before on condition of his liberation from prison. Brown denied the charge as basely false and called in Ex-Governor Shannon to testify that no such proposal

122 *Kansas Tribune,* May 9, 1857.
123 *Herald of Freedom,* May 16, 1857.
124 *Herald of Freedom,* May 16, 1857. For references to the course of the cases in the court see issues of April 18 and May 9.
125 *Herald of Freedom,* April 18, 1857.

had ever been made. Brown argued that this attack by Robinson, as well as an attack made by the *Kansas Tribune,* were acts of party tyranny similar to that of the New York *Tribune* when it attacked the *National Era* for daring to differ with party leaders. And in addition to this, it was alleged that Robinson was trying to divert public attention from his swindling of the stockholders of the Lawrence town company out of one-fourth of the town.[126] Through this same period the *Herald of Freedom* campaigned in article after article, in some issues two or more articles in a single issue, against the tyranny of party, the attempt of the eastern paid letter-writers to determine eastern opinion under the direction of their employers, and of men like Robinson and the editor of the *Kansas Tribune* to determine action in Kansas without full consultations. It went as far as to maintain that Kansas was more enslaved to party than to the unjust territorial laws, and doubted if one in a hundred would act as he then did but for the influence of neighbors or party leaders.[127] Although it agreed in general with the decision not to vote the *Herald of Freedom* admitted that the decision did not meet with the entire approval of the masses, and pointed out that it had counseled a delay in the calling of the convention to permit a fuller opportunity for development of opinion. Lawrence and Topeka were reported as of one mind on the issue, but correspondence from different outlying parts of the territory indicated division of opinion.[128]

The public Robinson-Brown quarrel was coincident with, if not related to a correspondence between Robinson and Acting-Governor Stanton on the subject of an agreement by which free-state men would vote providing certain concessions and guarantees were granted. Apparently this course had been decided upon at a meeting on April 29 of a small group of free-state leaders.[129] The *Herald of Freedom* denounced this attempt at dictation to the free-state party, and as the episode coincided in time with Robinson's accusation that Brown had offered to sell out the free-state party, the latter retaliated by telling the story of the Robinson-Stanton negotiations under the title "Selling out."[130]

The news of this move made its way east and was revealed there

126 *Herald of Freedom,* May 16.
127 *Herald of Freedom,* May 16, 1857.
128 *Herald of Freedom,* May 23, 1857.
129 *Herald of Freedom,* May 9, 1857. The correspondence was published in the *Herald of Freedom,* May 16.
130 *Herald of Freedom,* May 16, 1857.

by the administration, being given general publicity apparently by the New York *Times* from which several other eastern papers secured it. The Springfield *Republican,* a leading organ of the ultra-radicals, admitted that this decision must represent facts not yet known in the East, that the fact that it was revealed by the administration indicated that the government had been negotiating for the result, and that if the report proved to be true, the facts, when they became available, would vindicate the free-state men in their decision.[131]

In Kansas the voting faction was numerous enough to create uncertainty. In spite of a hostile press, record was made of one meeting held to denounce the do-nothing policy, and it was addressed to G. W. Smith and M. J. Parrott, both of whom wielded a substantial influence.[132] A subscriber divided the free-state party into three classes: those who wished to vote in June and demonstrate the superior numbers of the party, those who would vote if assurance was given of an honest election, and those who would not vote under any circumstances on the ground of consistency in attitude toward the bogus government. But the subscriber argued that a simple do-nothing policy would not achieve the free-state objective and recommended that the first necessary step was to get facts; how many voters there were in the territory, how many free-state and how many pro-slavery. With such facts in hand, a convention could be called and the party as a whole could arrive at a decision on policy. If the census should be completed prior to the election, he thought that this plan was the proper one, and stated that many concurred in the suggestion.[133]

The difficulty of making a decision was complicated by the conduct of some elements within the pro-slavery party. They had their ultras also, and they insisted that voting must be limited to the names on the census roll. Others insisted also on payment of taxes.[134] To these proposals the free-state ultras pointed in proof of their contention that no fair election was possible under the existing regime.

The *Lawrence Republican,* newly established radical free-state journal, endorsed the decision of the party not to vote in the June

131 *Herald of Freedom,* May 23, 1857 containing quotations from the Norwich (Connecticut) *Courier* and the Springfield (Massachusetts) *Republican.*
132 *Herald of Freedom,* May 23, 1857.
133 *Herald of Freedom,* May 16, 1857.
134 *Herald of Freedom,* May 23, 1857.

elections and called attention to Governor Walker's statement that he would use his influence to secure the submission of the constitution to popular vote. The argument was that he did not promise that it would be submitted,—merely that he would use his influence,—and the pro-slavery convention would do as it pleased.[135]

The Topeka legislature and a territorial convention met June 9–10 where the position of the party was confirmed, the latter body under the presiding genius of Jim Lane, who addressed the meeting in part as follows:

> Governor Walker I have great respect for as a man. I think his inaugural one of the finest, most flowery documents in the language. (Laughter.) He commences with telling us that we must obey the bogus laws. That's a bad introduction. Then he wants us to go into the bogus election; and if we only *will* go in, then what lots and lots of land he will give us for railroads and common schools! (Laughter.) That reminds me of the scene on the mount where the devil told our Savior that if he would fall down and worship him he would give him all the kingdoms of the earth, when all the while the old scoundrel hadn't a foot of land on the globe. (Great laughter and cheers.)[136]

The Independence (Missouri) *Messenger* hailed the approach of the millenium and gave as proof that Dr. Springfellow, senior editor of the *Squatter Sovereign*, had entertained Jim Lane at his residence, with a good dinner and good whiskey.[137] ''The Gibraltar of Slavery taken'' was the headline which announced the fall of the pro-slavery stronghold, both the Atchison townsite and the *Squatter Sovereign*, into hands of free-state proprietors.[138] The lamentations of the Leavenworth *Journal* were reprinted with exultation by the *Herald of Freedom*, May 23:

> If report be true, the *Sovereign* is to be no longer a staunch advocate of Southern rights in Kansas, but has gone over to the enemy, and will henceforth advocate the policy of Lane, Robinson & co., and in the whole Topeka faction in the Territory. "What a fall there was, my countrymen!" It is in reality true that some men would sell their souls for filthy lucre.
> The Donophan *Constitutionalist*, also heretofore claiming to be a national Democratic paper, we understand has been bought out by Jim Lane!

135 Lawrence *Republican*, June 4, 1857.
136 Lawrence *Republican*, June 11, 1857. One cannot avoid wondering whether Lane's reference to railroad land grants might have represented fact, or whether it may be only an evidence of wishful thinking,—a suggestion which he hoped might find lodgment in the minds of representatives of the administration at Washington.
137 *Herald of Freedom*, May 2, 1857.
138 *Herald of Freedom*, May 9, 1857.

—One after another of our presses fall and worship at the feet of MAM-MON.—Will not men of unswerving fidelity raise up other presses, that will not sacrifice principle to interest? [139]

The free-state cause was growing, not only at the expense of the pro-slavery interest, but its strength was represented also by the establishment of new presses. In all, there were twelve free-state papers, actually in publication or being launched within the month, as against three in May 1856.[140] The Kansas struggle has been variously interpreted; in terms of idealism, of politics, and of speculation. No doubt it involved a little of the first, but there is no question that it involved a great deal of the latter two. The St. Louis *Intelligencer's* view was stripped of every vestige of ideal-ism when it wrote the following in celebration of the coming of peace to Kansas:

> The Kansas troubles are over.—They were, from the beginning, nothing but a stock-jobbers war between Pro-Slavery and Free State speculators—some making "big strikes" for town sites, corner lots, and eligible quarter sections, and others "going it strong" for the offices of the future State. The question of slavery was simply a bugaboo, introduced to give character and acerbity to the contest.
>
> But all is peace now. Lane and Stringfellow have drowned their enmity in deluges of pacific liquor; Stringfellow has come out in favor of making Kansas only a Democratic Free State, and the Abolitionists are buying up all the Pro-Slavery towns and Pro-Slavery papers—actually seizing the guns of the bold "Border Ruffians," and turning them against their former owners. No doubt, there will be peace in Kansas, and Gov. Walker will have a pleasant time. Grim-visaged war hath smoothed its wrinkled front, and speculation is the order of the day.[141]

A most substantial source of support to the free-state cause was the spring immigration of 1857. The *Herald of Freedom* empha-sized the different types, ridiculing the "fancy emigrants," espe-cially those from Massachusetts, as well as the Hoosier who re-turned the next day after his arrival because he could not get cream for his coffee.[142] By the middle of April settlers were re-ported arriving at the rate of fifteen hundred to two thousand per day.[143] At the end of the month the two ferries across the Kansas river at Lawrence were kept busy continuously. The more

---

[139] *Herald of Freedom*, May 23, 1857.
[140] *Herald of Freedom*, May 9, 1857.
[141] *Herald of Freedom*, May 23, 1857.
[142] *Herald of Freedom*, April 11, 1857.
[143] *Herald of Freedom*, April 18, 1857. Probably the numbers were over-stated.

distant covered-wagon immigrants from such states as eastern Iowa, Wisconsin and Illinois were not expected to begin to arrive until the middle or end of May.[144] On Saturday, May 2, the streets of Lawrence were reported almost impassible on account of immigrant wagons, and the editor expressed himself as pleased with this type of settler.[145] The paper quoted from an eastern exchange which reported that "emigration to Kansas is immense; trains of wagons . . . pass through here daily. If politicians will only play 'hands off,' Kansas will soon be a free and flourishing state." [146] Near the end of the month, May 23, the *Herald of Freedom* reported that,

> The emigration of the "carpet-bag gentry," as they are popularly termed, has nearly closed for the season. Now comes the bones and sinew, "with their wives and little ones," not in a condition to return with the first wind storm. . . . They come overland, with teams, generally, with oxen and wagons. They are prepared to meet life as it is. . . . They are coming by hundreds, and the roads are white with the long lines of covered wagons. . . .

From the standpoint of the newcomers, one of the most serious difficulties was the scarcity of food and exorbitant prices. The letter of a correspondent published in the *Herald of Freedom* April 25 stated specifically that food scarcity was the real difficulty in making Kansas a free state. In the Neosho-Cottonwood country, the same letter reported that only one man within twenty miles had enough corn for seed, and even the border counties of Missouri suffered from shortage of supplies. The spring was abnormally dry, cold and backward. Nearly every issue of the *Herald of Freedom* through the latter part of April and May commented on cold, drouth, wind and dust, and even in the latter part of June it was maintained that the West would not suffer from the depression just closing in on the East, because of the high prices which the farmers would receive for their produce, and the immense amount of business created by the season's immigration. The drouth was broken partially during the last week of May, a local reporting "some fine showers during the forepart of the week has laid the dust, and given a new impetus to vegetation. Cattle and horses now subsist anywhere on the prairies without the aid of grain." The grass was slow to revive, however, compared with Kansas optimism after a

144 *Herald of Freedom*, May 2, 1857.
145 *Herald of Freedom*, May 9, 1857.
146 *Herald of Freedom*, May 16, 1857.

rain as is shown by the statement that the immigration had come a
month too early and instead of finding "verdure and beauty . . .
they found dust and blackened fields, and cold winds. . . . We regret that the thousands who came and have gone back disappointed
with Kansas, could not be here now. . . ."[147]   A month later the
weather report for northern Kansas was that severe drouth still
prevailed, although southern Kansas had received the usual spring
rains.   The slogan adopted was "Plant one more acre."[148]

If idealism, politics and speculation were not curses enough to be
heaped upon Kansas, the drought of 1857 certainly filled her cup of
woe to overflowing.   In this background the cry for peace takes on
a new significance.   G. W. Brown was particularly emphatic insisting that the day of disorder was over, and those who held that it
was not "have some past wrong they wish to redress, and they only
wish an opportunity to rush into Missouri and lay waste the planta-
tions there, and scatter death and desolation, just as the men did
from Missouri and the South in Kansas."   He referred to the suggestion of Acting-Governor Stanton proposing amnesty as a means
of preserving peace, and expressed himself as satisfied that the
United States troops would never again be used to enforce submission to the territorial laws.   The existence of the democratic party
depended upon peace and such being the case the renewal of disorder would not come from that direction, and therefore he admonished, let no free-state man do anything to disturb quiet.[149]
Lawrence had sufficient confidence in peace that they were engaged
in grading down the earthwork fortifications that had been erected
on Massachusetts street during the war of the preceding year.   The
stone breastwork on Mount Oread was not being dismantled, but its
preservation was advocated, not for purposes of war, but as an historical monument and a reminder of the heroic days that were
past.[150]

There was not as much unanimity in the East concerning peace
as in Kansas and the *Herald of Freedom* selected a headline from
an eastern newspaper "War is inevitable" as the text of an editorial
for the benefit of the East:

[147] *Herald of Freedom*, May 30, 1857.
[148] *Herald of Freedom*, June 27, 1857.   The slogan was attributed to the
New York *Tribune* but the Lawrence *Republican* used it in its second issue of
June 4, 1857.   The *Republican* also took up the slogan.
[149] *Herald of Freedom*, May 2, 1857.
[150] *Herald of Freedom*, May 9, 1857.

"This, we are sorry to say, is but a sample of the tone of many papers in the east. Now we who are on the ground . . . say that it is our firm belief that the days of bloodshed and strife are passed."

He then gave a statement of reasons; the pro-slavery party was tired of it, the western counties of Missouri were suffering as a result of past strife and were definitely opposed to a renewal, war had the effect of keeping peace-loving settlers away and of attracting adventurers, immigration was flowing in such volume during this season as to crush out all pro-slavery influence, and in conclusion, he reiterated the charge that war was the cry of "unscrupulous politicians." [151]

One more sample of this prolonged editorial campaign for peace:

The destruction of the printing offices, set free sixteen resolute courageous young men, who had lost their business, lost their clothing, lost their money, lost their homes and their all. Looking over the country, and seeing it, desolated by these Southern Guerilla parties, who were scouring it in every direction, they immediately formed themselves into a company to act on the defensive. They went out and in a day or two had armed, equipped and mounted themselves, and were in full tide of successful experiment.

They rode, they "pressed," they fought, they retaliated in every possible manner. They gave the first check to the pro-slavery ruffians and formed the nucleus around which the people finally rallied till the invaders were driven from the territory. We have no fault to find at anything that was done in defense of life, liberty and property, so long as the people were attacked and endangered by this roaming banditti.

But when peace came and the enemy were gone, and men returned again to reason, then we used our efforts to quiet the storm and bring back the agitated elements to repose. What in war phrase is called "pressing," and is justified by the circumstances; in peace, is stealing, and must be punished as crime. We are determined, so far as possible, to oppose every act and every measure calculated to again involve the country in another war. But if it is forced upon us by our enemies, we shall do as ever we have done, stand by the right.[152]

Although some details of this account of the opening of the war of 1856 need correction, G. W. Brown must be given the credit for throwing the influence of his paper on the side of peace throughout the following months.

The decision of the free-state party to continue the Topeka state movement met much opposition and from the Potawatomie creek country "An Old Squatter" of 1854 commended the stand taken by the *Herald of Freedom*. He reported that in his community about

151 *Herald of Freedom,* May 16, 1857.
152 *Herald of Freedom,* June 27, 1857.

one-fifth of the settlers had assumed the right to dictate to the other four-fifths whom they cut off and call "bogus."

As large majority here are newcomers, they would prefer to have this remain a Territorial government for some time to come, till they get their farms opened and became acquainted with each other. They have come out expecting peace, and they know this new measure now proposed by the leaders of the party is calculated to get up another disturbance for political effect.

I do not see why a few men who happened to be here first, and obtained a notoriety by being elected to office should in consequence of that fact, control all our affairs forever after, and also hold all the offices.

He attributed more than selfish motives to those behind the revival of the Topeka movement, listing speculation in Topeka state scrip of unknown amounts, back salaries claimed, and control of large amounts of eastern relief funds, mostly unaccounted for, and concluded: "In this region we go for new men, new measures, clean hands, and a new constitution, voted on by all the people, . . . Some think it not prudent to expose our friends. No dishonest man can be my friend; and besides, I am tired of being ruled by demagogues."[153]

With the developments of the summer the *Herald of Freedom* declared that the Topeka movement had served its purpose, that free-state men were in the majority and regretted that the party had declined to vote for delegates to the Lecompton constitutional convention; "the opportunity which, if improved, would have given us a controling influence in the constitutional convention, has been allowed to pass. . . ." Among the six points in its platform were defeat of the constitution, election of free-state officers under it if it was adopted, election of delegates to congress, election of the territorial legislature and prolongation of territorial status with federal financial support because of poverty of people asking admission as a state only in time to vote in the presidential election of 1860.[154]

These circumstances of the spring and early summer provide the Kansas setting for the activities of radical Eastern abolitionists who had fitted out John Brown and sent him to Kansas, as they thought, to carry on his Kansas work. For reasons that have never been explained satisfactorily, he delayed his start, finally stopped in Iowa, and Kansas was spared this additional complication to its troubles for yet another year.

[153] *Herald of Freedom*, July 18, 1857.
[154] *Herald of Freedom*, July 4, 1857.

CHAPTER IX

THE EASTERN PRESS; LATE 1856 AND EARLY 1857

Through exchanges the eastern press presented much the same materials that are found in the territorial papers, but through special correspondents, occasional letter writers and editorials much different material was offered.

The meeting and dispersal of the Topeka legislature July 4 was reported in the Eastern press, but the fact that it passed off without violence gave little new ground for agitation. In fact, for the latter part of June and for July the New York *Tribune* carried little Kansas news, although there was a great amount of Kansas material, sometimes from three to five columns in restatement of earlier events and issues which served to keep up the agitation. On July 21, the *Tribune's* theme was that "Kansas lies prostrate." The next day an account appeared of S. F. Tappan's appearance in Washington with one of the trace chains with which the Osawatomie prisoners had been shackled. Letters from the treason prisoners were featured in the issues of July 18 and 24. The release of the report of the congressional investigation afforded quantities of testimony on Kansas outrages. From the Lecompton prison camp, H. H. Williams wrote July 20 of the expedition from the southeastern part of the territory to the rescue of Lawrence in May and of the arrests, hearings and imprisonment of himself and John Brown, Jr.[1] The resident pro-slavery men were reported to be soliciting free-state men to unite with them in a band of secret regulators. Some free-state men were willing to engage in it but for the benefit of free-state men only. There was no possible apology for forming entangling alliances with the enemy, then the *Tribune's* special correspondent added in a sinister vein that some free-state men were too conscientious for the times.[2]

Kansas letters to the southern papers during the summer reflected conflicting currents. The agitation and organization for emigration from the northern states to Kansas was much more highly organized, the climax being reached at Buffalo early in July

[1] New York *Tribune*, August 20, 1856.
[2] New York *Tribune*, August 9, 1856.

in the organization of the National Kansas committee with its co-operating state committees and leagues. It was the emigrants directed by this committee who became the storm center during the August war and later.

For campaign purposes each side compiled a list of outrages against the other. The pro-slavery "chapter of outrages committed in Kansas by the Emigrant Aid Society" etc., comprised thirty-four incidents arranged chronologically from the fall of 1854 to date. It included three episodes in which the Browns were involved but did not mention their names.[3] The New York *Tribune* compiled a similar list of pro-slavery outrages, which was published from time to time with additions.[4]

With the coming of August the reports of outrages and threats became more numerous on both sides. Deputy Marshal Fain was reported to have been out collecting poll taxes at the rate of fifty cents to one dollar and also to have been assessing property taxes. The comment was offered that he had "doubtless, spent his share of the plunder taken on the 21st of May." When he went to Lawrence, it was said that he first visited a pro-slavery attorney and that before he did anything *officially* he was waited upon by a committee of three, "who, I rather think, represented an organization after the California plan of regulating." They advised him not to proceed and he took the advice. This episode was dated August 1, and in connection, the correspondent stated that the tax question was the subject of discussion at the Governor's office. The informant overheard and reported to the correspondent that the Governor opposed. At this point in the narrative there occurs one of those veiled references which are found rather frequently in free-state accounts and which indicate facts not put into print: "Shannon, who has not altogether forgotten how things are managed elsewhere, was at first anxious to persuade the leaders" to hold off, but pressure seemed to persuade him.[5]

Another episode from the same article related the capture of Cline and Randall, formerly of Milwaukee, Wisconsin, near Sugar

---

[3] The earliest printing of this list that has been found was the Cincinnati *Enquirer*, July 18, 1856.

[4] This was first printed September 11, 1856. It was later included in the *Tribune Almanac* for 1857.

[5] New York *Tribune*, August 11, 1856. This was one of several episodes related in an article by "Our Special Correspondent" bearing a Leavenworth date line of August 2.

creek in southeast Kansas on allegations of horse stealing.[6] The men were taken to Harrisonville, Cass County, Missouri upon recommendation of the justice of the peace until sufficient evidence could be accumulated. Additional information about this incident was printed in the *Tribune* August 14 in the form of a statement by G. B. Cline, himself. The people of Harrisonville, he said, objected to holding them there as it would bring trouble to the town, and, in the subsequent removal of the prisoners to Kansas, they had escaped.

The activity of free-state men is reflected in the preparations for the holding of federal court in the northeast part of the territory, when federal troops were assigned to accompany the judge on his circuit from county to county.[7] Intermingled free-state and pro-slavery outrages appeared in the press during August, usually without very exact dating. A letter by A. S. White, dated Osawatomie July 31 reported crops poor, but it did not matter as they would be destroyed anyway. He reported that Coleman was back in the Hickory Point neighborhood again with seventy Missourians committing depredations. After being watched for several days they were attacked by free-state men and they were taken prisoners, and one hundred fifty guns, provisions, ammunition and horses were recovered. Coleman was tarred and cottoned and released with the other prisoners. The same company of free-state men were expected to make an attack upon the pro-slavery posse at Franklin.[8] The *Tribune's* special correspondent reported from the same general vicinity under an August 7 date line that the summer's drouth was broken, that there were no open disorders, but that the community was unsettled. He stated that Southern bands ''are now engaged in land piracy.'' Three items were related in this connection; a murder on Rock creek by the Georgians who had settled on Washington creek, a warning to two free-state settlers from Masonic friends in Missouri that the Coal creek settlement (between Hickory Point and the Wakarusa) was to be broken up by a guerilla raid, and the story of the seizure by pro-slavery men of Preacher Stewart while on the way to Osawatomie and his escape. The correspondent believed a new guerilla war was imminent. He charged that General Smith was doing nothing to protect free-state settlers, that

---

[6] Cline was later associated with John Brown in marauding just prior to the battle of Osawatomie and shared in that engagement.

[7] *National Intelligencer*, August 19, 1856 from St. Louis *Republican*.

[8] Keene (New Hampshire) *Sentinel*, August 15, 1856. Webb, *Scrapbooks*, 16: 62–63. No confirmation of the Coleman story has been discovered.

Shannon had refused to permit the collection of taxes, and that now the pro-slavery men were going to make him the scapegoat for Kansas troubles. The appointment of Geary was merely for effect.[9]

A few days later the sequel to the above stories was reported in connection with an expedition which attacked three so-called Georgia camps, on Bull creek near Osawatomie, on the Marais des Cygnes below Osawatomie and on Sugar creek south of that place. The expedition was said to have been gotten up hurriedly, partly by persons who had suffered from depredations, and set out from near Lawrence with five wagons and a guide but lost their way. The Southerners learned of their coming, and, erroneously attributing the attack to John Brown, fled, so when the free-state men arrived at the first camp their prey was gone.[10]

In the last news letter already referred to under the Leavenworth date line of August 2, "Our Special Correspondent" reported the following incident as having occurred last week:

a settler had been to the post-office at Osawatomie to get his mail. On his return these [pro-slavery] gentry waylaid stopped and searched him. Besides the Topeka paper, and one or two eastern journals, he had the *Tribune*. He was at once accused of carrying incendiary documents, knocked down, beat and kicked. He contrived to get away from them. When they had him down they swore that any man who would take a paper that supported Fremont ought to be hung.[11]

The name of the settler was not given, but those familiar with the Brown Legend will recognize immediately that it is the Manes story, and that in the Legend it is assigned as one of the causes of the Potawatomie massacre.

Still another pro-slavery outrage was related in the same installment having to do with the fate of a storekeeper named Wines, who being absent from home was the recipient of a visit from the deputy sheriff, supported by dragoons, under orders to seize goods from the store to satisfy a debt. The friends of the absent storekeeper insisted upon a trial, and although the sum involved exceeded that subject to the jurisdiction of a justice of the peace, he assumed the authority. The story concluded that no plaintiff appeared, but that

[9] New York *Tribune*, August 16, 1856.
[10] New York *Tribune*, August 21, 1856. This attack is frequently dated August 7, but if the days of the week are correctly designated in this report the start was made Thursday August 7, and the attack Friday night, August 8.
[11] New York *Tribune*, August 11, 1856. James C. Malin, "John Brown and the Manes Incident," *Kansas Historical Quarterly*, 7 (November 1938) 376–78.

as the justice knew that the debt existed, he ordered the goods sold to satisfy it.[12] Wines was a free-state man and the episode was reported from Osawatomie. The identity of this storekeeper is a matter of interest, and possibly the name was Winer instead of Wines. In that form, if correct, it becomes a link in the Brown problem, because Theodore Wiener, often spelled Winer, was one of the John Brown party of eight who committed the Potawatomie massacre.[13]

How much of these stories was true? They might be only justifications invented by rumor, but, however that may be, they served as the preliminaries to the propaganda campaign associated with the August war opened by the free-state attack upon Franklin. Under the title of the "new outbreak," the New York *Tribune*, August 23, developed the thesis that the pro-slavery party in Missouri had matured a plan during the two months of seeming peace, that systematic fortifications had been built, and that action was beginning for sweeping the territory clean of free-state settlers, therefore the free-state campaign opened by the battle of Franklin was in the nature of a defense. The next few days the *Tribune* carried an average of about one full page of Kansas material each day. That a deliberate campaign of propaganda was launched in accordance with concerted action is given support by a passage in a letter of G. W. Brown from the Lecompton prison camp August 16: "Letter writers ought to be particular to show the *causes* of this uprising of the people. It was a defensive movement purely. The question was which should strike the first blow. We saw the preparation, fortifications were being erected and moved, and threats of extermination were heard on every hand."[14] The *National Intelligencer* followed a different policy and printed quantities of reports from both sides August 26 together with the comment that "even the most observant reader will find it difficult to comprehend the exact condition of affairs in this ill-fated Territory."

During the fury of the exaggerations induced by civil war an interesting letter appeared, written from Osawatomie August 23 and signed by Richard Mendenhall, a Quaker. He reported some twenty families of Friends in the territory, but that others were not

---

[12] New York *Tribune*, August 11, 1856.

[13] Theodore Wiener had a brother Herman who is less widely known to history. Together with Jacob Benjamin and August Bondi, the latter was one of the founders of the town of Greeley in Anderson county.

[14] G. W. Brown to William Hutchinson of Kansas State Central Committee. August 16, 1856. *William Hutchinson Papers*, K. S. H. S.

likely to join them on account of the excitement which imposed "close exercise of faith for a man of peace to maintain his principles," and, if defensive warfare could be justified, he thought it could be in these circumstances. But he closed with an important piece of information: "Some of our number have been threatened with violence, but, so far as we are certainly informed none has yet been offered. . . ." [15]

Not all the papers near the Missouri border were carried away by the extremes of the August excitement, although no systematic study has been practicable which would determine the exact number. The Jefferson (Missouri) *Inquirer*, August 22 explained that it had been warned by a man who came down by boat, and had refrained from publishing all the news received. It criticized the St. Louis papers for not using the same discretion with the result that they aided in keeping up the excitement, which had already transcended "the bounds of reason." [16]   A little later the St. Louis *Intelligencer* took the St. Joseph *Cycle* to task for its "raw head and bloody bones story" of the opening of the renewed hostilities, protesting that nearly every statement was untrue, and that such procedure only injured the cause:

We are forced to look upon this, as well as all the other highly colored accounts that have come to hand, as simply a device of one or the other party of agitators and factionists in the Territory to get up an excitement among their respective sympathizers, and induce prejudiced, misguided men to go into the Territory with a view of keeping alive the disturbances. The design of each is too apparent to deceive any man of ordinary sagacity.[17]

The *National Intelligencer*, at Washington, must be credited with reprinting a much wider selection of exchanges from the Kansas-Missouri frontier than was customary among the Eastern papers.

The pro-slavery forces in Missouri soon rallied to the support of their friends in Kansas. By August 24 they were organized on the border with Atchison elected Major General and Reid as Brigadier General. With additions bringing the total to over one thousand, they set out on the march, with Osawatomie as one

[15] *Friends Review*, August 23, 1856. Date of letter July 27.
   National Era (Washington, D. C.), September 4, 1856 from the *Friend's Review*. The poet Whittier was responsible for the printing of the letter. An editorial in the same issue stated that information had just come to hand reporting the breaking up of the Quaker Mission.
   [16] *National Intelligencer*, August 30, 1856.
   [17] *National Intelligencer* (Washington D. C.), September 2, 1856. The paper printed also a similar comment of the Columbia (Missouri) *Statesman*.

of the first objectives. Most pro-slavery accounts agree that it was looked upon as the headquarters of John Brown, the assassin. A portion of this force, variously estimated at 250 to 450 men, made the attack. Free-state firing began from the brush west of town at long range, one account saying as much as half a mile. The attacking force had one piece of artillery, but the mounted troops were undisciplined and after the opening of the engagement a small portion were dismounted and reformed as infantry for the real attack. The defending force was also variously estimated, from fifty to three hundred, although one pro-slavery account remarked that the numbers were unknown because they were concealed in the brush. When driven out of the brush, the free-state men crossed the river under fire, and twenty to thirty more, according to the pro-slavery account, were reported killed, including John Brown and a son. The pro-slavery men lost none, only five being wounded, and one account listed these by name. Prisoners were taken and the town burned. Also considerable herds of cattle, alleged to have been stolen from pro-slavery settlers, were recovered.[18]

Free-state accounts minimized the number of free-state defenders, the St. Louis *Democrat* story placing it at not over fifty and exaggerating the number of the attacking party. There was agreement, however, in this article with the pro-slavery accounts that the main attack was made by about eighty dismounted men.[19]   It is important also that this account credited the free-state command to two men, John Brown and Updegraff. The New York *Tribune* September 6 received its first news of the affair by telegraph through St. Louis from a pro-slavery source. By September 10 quantities of Osawatomie news was printed and September 13 and 15 Captain Shore was named as one of the leaders with whom Brown was associated in a punitive expedition on Middle creek where August 26 twenty-nine horses were recovered, and on Sugar creek where August 27 seventy cattle were captured from the enemy. The issue of September 15 named Captain Cline as associated with Brown in the defense of Osawatomie, Shore's men

---

[18] St. Louis *Democrat*, September 5, 1856 from *Western Dispatch*. St. Louis *Republican*, September 6, 1856. A pro-slavery chronology dated September 2. This was copied into the *National Intelligencer*, September 11, 1856 and New York *Tribune*, September 10, 1856.

National Era, September 18, 1856 from the Glasgow (Missouri?) *Times*, September 4.

[19] St. Louis *Democrat*, September 6, 1856.

having returned to the vicinity of Lawrence. The *Tribune* confused the Browns at Osawatomie, publishing a letter of O. C.
Brown, the original Osawatomie Brown and the founder of the
town, as coming from "Brown, the hero of Osawatomie" and as
proof that John Brown had not been killed.[20]   John Brown's own
account of the battle prepared for the press did not mention
Updegraff at all, and gave the impression that he was in command
with Cline taking orders from him.   John Brown claimed they had
killed thirty-one or thirty-two and wounded forty or fifty of the
enemy.   Cline was more modest, sharing the command with John
Brown and claiming only nine of the enemy killed and four
wounded.   Dr. Updegraff does not seem to have been a newspaper
letter-writer and his story remained untold, although he was the
only resident of Osawatomie among the three commanders.   "John
Smith's" free-state account explained that no defense of Osawatomie had been intended by free-state leaders who were certain
the attack was coming and that the women and children had been
removed to safety.   A second observer reported also that many
had left Osawatomie prior to the attack.

On the same night that Reid was marching on Osawatomie,
Hays took another band to Ottawa Jones's and burned the house,[21]
and the same party raided Prairie City.   The capture of the Mc-
Kinney Santa Fé train by free-state men on September 1 was reported in the New York *Tribune*, September 15, but with the warning that the news stories "coming, as they do, exclusively from
Border Ruffian sources, need confirmation."   The editor endeavored further to influence his readers by declaring that in all Missouri no newspapers, not even the St. Louis *Democrat*, "had dared
tell the truth with regard to the outrages and devastations to which
unhappy Kansas is subjected."   The next day the paper contained another account, stating that the capture was made by
Cutter, not by Brown.[22]   In contrast to this sensational handling
of Kansas news the *National Intelligencer*, September 13, labeled
a column of reports from exchanges covering the same events as
"*Rumors from Kansas.*"   The free-state plans for an expedition
against Leavenworth were reported in the *Tribune* September 9.
A few days later came the news of the drastic action of pro-slavery

[20] Correction was not made until September 19.

[21] New York *Tribune*, September 13 and 16, 1856.

[22] The *National Era*, September 18, 1856 carried a story similar to the
Tribune's story of September 16.

men at that place in expelling free-state men from the city in preparation for meeting the attack.[23]

The Lexington (Missouri) *Citizen* was quoted in the St. Louis *Evening News,* September 5, as saying:

> That abolitionists have been guilty of repeated acts of atrocity, murder, robbery, arson and horse-stealing in the Territory, none of their own villianous party will deny; but that they have done all that has been said against them is neither true nor probable. There are Southern men just as bad as the worst abolitionist. That some of these men have been guilty of horse-stealing and probably murder in the name and on the credit of the abolitionists—that their thefts have been perpetrated on Northern and Southern men without distinction—will hardly admit of a doubt.

The same Missouri paper was quoted in the *National Intelligencer,* September 16, saying that the free-state men had proved that they could fight and that it would be madness for the pro-slavery men to attempt to attack Lawrence without at least two thousand men, and it stated frankly that among the volunteers there had been no discipline or obedience and as a result it had been necessary to fall back upon Cedar creek in order to reorganize. The St. Lous *Republican* informed its readers also that after the "skirmish" at Osawatomie it was decided to delay the attack upon Lawrence in order to make adequate preparations for so extended a campaign. A similar comment appeared in the St. Louis *Evening News.*[24] The Boonville *Observer* reported the disbandment by Reid of pro-slavery troops with orders to reassemble them as infantry on September 13, because as mounted troops they had failed and at Osawatomie sixty dismounted men had done all the fighting. A similar story was reprinted from the Glasgow (Missouri) *Times* in the *National Era* September 18, with directions for reassembling in squads of ten men with a two-horse wagon for each squad. The *National Intelligencer,* September 13, reported in the same vein from the St. Louis papers, the *Republican* and the *Evening News.* The St. Louis *Democrat's* correspondent declared that "Lane was growing very bold and insulting, and had facetiously sent word to the people of Westport and Independence that in a few days he would be 'down and take breakfast with them.'"[25] The same paper reported that Leavenworth was deserted and business suspended. The Jefferson (Mis-

---

[23] *National Intelligencer,* September 16, 1856.
[24] Quoted in the *National Intelligencer,* September 13, 1856.
[25] *National Intelligencer,* September 16, 1856.

souri) *Inquirer* stated erroneously that Lane men under the "no-
torius Brown" had attacked Tecumseh and sacked it, and that
two hundred fifty women and children from the vicinity had fled
to Leavenworth for refuge. Tecumseh had been sacked, but by
Martin Stowell of Massachusetts, not by Brown. During this
period the free-state guerillas used Lawrence and Topeka as headquarters for raiding parties that scoured the country for twenty
to thirty miles in all directions. Whipple was credited with the
capture of eighty horses at one time in a raid on Ozawkie,[26] and
Colonel Harvey claimed one hundred on one expedition.

It was under these circumstances that Acting-Governor Woodson had proclaimed the territory in insurrection, and the Missouri
forces reorganized during the latter part of August, and again
about September 13 and set out toward Lawrence on their belated
mission to protect pro-slavery settlers and to destroy Lawrence
and Topeka. In the midst of this turmoil, Governor Geary arrived in the territory, the court was in session, but being unable
to perform its functions released prisoners on bail and adjourned.

The story of "Lawrence threatened by 2500 Border Ruffians"
was told in the New York *Tribune* September 22, 1856. "Randolph," related that the Missourians reached Franklin Sunday
and about five hundred defenders prepared to fight, when "our
advance guards came into collision and three of the enemy's men
are reported killed—none of ours injured. . . . Just then orders
came from the Governor, forbidding the approach of the Pro-
Slavery forces. They then fell back and camped at Franklin. . . .
Four hundred troops arrived here last night for protection."
"Potter's" letter, also written from Lawrence on September 15,
was printed September 27. He reported that the pro-slavery forces
were discovered when still fifteen miles from Lawrence, the governor called from Lecompton arriving Saturday morning with
troops. The advance guard of the pro-slavery force retired, he
said, and the governor assumed the danger was past and returned
to Lecompton. About five o'clock in the afternoon two companies
of pro-slavery horsemen one of about fifty and the other forty
men were seen advancing toward Lawrence in which were only
between two hundred and two hundred fifty defenders. A small
detachment of horsemen, part of the Wabaunsee boys, went out
to meet them, there was a brisk firing between them, the pro-

[26] *National Intelligencer,* September 18, 1856.

slavery men took refuge in a ravine and were followed by the Wabaunsee boys with Sharps rifles. At 9 P.M. two representatives of the governor arrived in Lawrence and at 11 P.M. the federal troops came and camped southeast of the city. The writer explained that the reason Lawrence was found so nearly defenseless was that Lane had called Colonel Harvey and about one hundred men to Hickory Point. "Potter" said Lane had received a copy of Geary's proclamation in the meantime and decided to retire to Nebraska, cancelled his call to Harvey but the latter disobeyed orders about his route and missed the messenger. Harvey's men were captured by the federal troops. It should be noted that in these accounts nothing was said about John Brown, and even more important they did make clear that there was no defense of Lawrence by anybody as the pro-slavery skirmishers made no attack.

Further light on the manner in which news from Kansas was inspired is found in a letter of instructions from J. P. Root, president, to his Kansas State Central Committee:

I wish every man who can wield a pen in Kansas would write a statement—*over his own signature in full* of the scenes that have occurred under his own eyes, and in which perhaps he may have taken a part, stating facts connected with murders, scalpings, burnings of houses & women and children being driven in the darkness of night from their homes &c. let nothing but the truth appear, and let these letters come from all parts of the territory, telling of the suffering occasioned by the recent and past lawlessness yet law supported invasions and have these letters sent to papers published in the immediate vicinity of the friends of the writer and the effect will be wonderful.[27]

The republicans took the utmost advantage of every aspect of the controversy that could be turned to their account. Kansas was their chief stock in trade for campaign purposes, and so far as the New York *Tribune* was the leading organ of political expression for the party, its news articles and editorials leave no room for contradiction. On September 15, the *Tribune* asked: "Now, is it likely, is it credible, that the little band of Free-State men in Kansas—whom their adversaries represent to be a minority . . .—have wantonly commenced a war, not only against their fellow settlers, but against Western Missouri and the whole power of the Federal Government."

The editor pleaded whether any sane man could believe that

[27] *William Hutchinson Papers*, K. S. H. S.

they would do such a thing to aid in the election of Frémont, but "It is wicked, it is atrocious, on the part of Pierce and Jeff Davis to uphold those Ruffian laws; but, when the Federal soldiery comes to enforce them, let the appeal from their injustice be made directly and solely to the American people. They can rescue the Free settlers of Kansas if they will; if they will not, no rescue is possible."

In another article in the same issue, the *Tribune* editorialized:

From what has happened at Leavenworth, we may plainly see what long before now would have happened at Lawrence, Topeka, and every other Free-State settlement in the Territory, but for those Sharp's rifles and that military organization for self-defense. . . .

We fear we went too far, on Saturday, in holding out any, even the least, encouragement that the arrival of Geary in the Territory will bring any relief to Free-State men. . . .

The next day the following editorial was printed:

It would be absurd to look to the drunkard Atchison, to the drunkard Shannon, or to the drunken rabble of Missouri, or even to the miserable President Pierce . . . as the really responsible parties for the atrocious crimes . . . of which Kansas is now the scene. . . . Pierce may be let off on the score of imbecility, natural or superinduced; but these four able men [Marcy, Cushing, Douglas and Buchanan] cannot set up the excuse of folly. They have gone into this Kansas business with their eyes open. . . .

Another day brought a slightly different tone:

If the news from Kansas received yesterday by telegraph prove true, Gov. Geary has made a good beginning, by releasing on bail Gov. Charles Robinson and his associates. . . . This is a wise and sensible step, in full accordance with the assurances from high quarters which secured the passage of the Army [appropriation] bill without the Kansas proviso [that no part of the money should be used to enforce the Kansas territorial laws].

This allusion to a bargain with the republicans in the house on the army bill is new to the whole discussion thus far and would be quite significant if it could be confirmed, but the other angle of the charge that the prisoners were released on orders from Washington has been noticed in other chapters.[28]

By September 22 the *Tribune* decided that there would "be no serious fighting in Kansas at present, but the subjugation of our people to the Border Ruffian code would seem to be nearly com-

[28] The *National Intelligencer* had noticed the rumor about the release of political prisoners as early as August 14.

plete. Happily, however, it is but temporary.'' The election of Frémont in November would change all that. By this time the text of Geary's inaugural message was available in New York and the *Tribune's* comment September 23 was that he said, let the past be buried ''in oblivion,'' but to him oblivion did not include the territorial laws which he declared he would enforce. On the same day the editor charged that Geary had been selected by Buchanan, the presidential nominee, and that the choice had been announced privately before President Pierce knew of it.

In commenting upon the report that the government had seized ninety free-state men at Hickory Point, the *Tribune* said: ''We are loth to believe that Gov. Geary has thus requited the confidence and trust reposed in him by the Free-State men,'' because they had just ''rid themselves of the responsibility and odium of holding Gen. Robinson and his fellow sufferers in durance, they are not likely to want another batch of political conscripts on their hands very soon.'' It was pointed out that the pro-slavery forces were allowed to escape, and so was Lane, because Geary had no desire to overtake him.[29] Later the editor declared:

Thus the Free State party in Kansas is temporarily crushed out by Presidential power, and Slavery is now established there by what passes for law. Titus, the leader of a band of robbers, Clark, the Indian agent who killed Barber, and Atchison, Reid & Co. are Geary's intimates and counsellors, and an election is this week to be held under the bogus ''laws'' for a new Legislative Assembly, which we hope to learn the Pro-Slavery party will have all to itself. They have Kansas now completely in their hands, and will keep it unless the People see fit to oust them in the Presidential Election. For Freedom in Kansas there is not another hope remaining.[30]

On September 16, 1856 the New York *Tribune* had published under the title ''subduing freedom in Kansas'' a chronology of pro-slavery outrages, and sufficient success had been achieved in the resistance to this subjugation for the free-state sympathizers to begin quarreling over who should have the credit. Thaddeus Hyatt wrote September 17 claiming for Martin F. Conway the credit for initiating the movement against the ''bogus'' legislature and expounding the argument for the first time in his letter of resignation June 30, 1855. Hyatt declared that with only two or three exceptions the free-state leaders at that time disapproved the

29 New York *Tribune*, September 27, 1856.
30 New York *Tribune*, September 29, 1856.

policy, but later accepted its wisdom.[31] From Osawatomie came another letter of protest written September 21 insisting that the first repudiation of the "bogus" legislature was the work of a free-state convention of June 25, 1855 and that the writer Charles A. Foster was one of the secretaries.[32] Thus opened one phase of the perennial controversy over who saved Kansas, and John Brown was not considered as a contender for honors.

On October 8, the *Tribune* published a letter over the name of "Worcester," the Reverend T. W. Higginson, a Unitarian minister of Worcester, Massachusetts, then touring Kansas, reporting on the action of the federal troops in stopping the Northern emigration at the Nebraska line. He declared that Geary was worse than Shannon in Kansas. The National Kansas Committee was active in keeping up the agitation by calling for well supplied men to go to Kansas even though the Missouri river route was closed. Frémont, the Pathfinder, would soon be the "Path-opener."[33]

The correspondent of the Boston *Traveller* expressed the opinion that Geary was "a pompous, self conceited personage" who "is a tool of nothing but his own vanity."[34] At Lawrence during the first week of October, "Worcester" picked up the news of the recent defense of Lawrence against the twenty-eight hundred. He reported enthusiastically that "ever since the rendition of Anthony Burns I have been looking for men. I have found them in Kansas." Only about one hundred defenders could be counted upon at first, but more than two hundred rallied to the fort, "the lame came on crutches, and the sick in blankets." It was two hundred, he said, against fourteen times that number:

And the fort a mere earthen redoubt, of no pretensions—for the only fort worth the name is on the hill behind the town, and was at this time useless. And yet (here comes the point) I was assured by Gov. Robinson and a dozen others that among this devoted handful the highest spirits prevailed; they were laughing and joking as usual, and only intent on selling their lives as dearly as possible.

They had no regular commander, any more than at Bunker Hill; but the famous "Old Captain Brown" moved among them, saying, "Fire low, boys; be sure to bring your eye to the hinder sight of your rifle, and aim at the feet rather than the head."

A few women were in the fort that day—all who could be armed.

31 New York *Tribune*, September 26, 1856. The protest was against the entry for July 2, 1855.
32 New York *Tribune*, October 7, 1856.
33 New York *Tribune*, October 11, 1856.
34 New York *Tribune*, October 16, 1856.

Others spent the whole day making cartridges. I asked one of these how she felt: "Well, I can't remember that I felt any way different from usual," answered the quiet housekeeper, after due reflection. . . .

The chief fighting was among skirmishers, and there was no actual attack on the fort.

In further comment upon the Kansas war he emphasized the shortage of ammunition and illustrated it by the defeat of the free-state men at the battle of Osawatomie. After retailing other particulars, much of which was untrue, he stated that on Sunday he had preached at Lawrence from the text: "Be ye not afraid of them . . ," the same text John Martin had used in preaching to the patriots after the Battle of Bunker Hill.[35] The bombast of the fourteen-to-one ratio in the early part of this account is offset somewhat by the admission at the end that there really was no attack upon Lawrence, and equally interesting is the admission that John Brown had no command.

Speaking of "Geary and his 'Peace' " the *Tribune* correspondent denounced "this delusive fallacy [as] an insult and another wrong to the unhappy free State people. Peace has been restored as it was in Hungary in '49, or, as Col. Sumner restored it last Summer, by disarming the Free State people, and leaving them at the mercy of their enemies. . . . God have mercy on them! I see no power here that can or will." He denounced the disarming of the emigrants on the Nebraska border, while Missouri kept the river closed and was permitted to come over into Kansas and elect the new legislature. He charged that Geary had boasted that he had a "Presidential candidate to carry on his shoulders":

Gov. Geary is either a very dignified man or a very pompous one— perhaps a little of both. He is a profound egotist, and talks about what he is and intends to be, in a somewhat ostentatious manner. Gov. Geary is a determined man, without the capacity to determine on any systematic course. He has an iron will without a purpose, his only aim being to carry the aforesaid Presidential candidate safely on his shoulders, and that is under instructions. He has made statements about having ten thousand dollars in secret service money. He also stated to a company of Free State gentlemen that 'there were not two men starting out over the prairie, but he knew where they were going.' 'You have not a secret meeting,' he said, 'but I know what takes place—I almost know your thoughts.' If this be all true, the conduct of his omniscient Excellency is still more culpable. . . . If Frémont is beaten, we tremble here to think of the consequences.

35 New York *Tribune*, October 17, 1856. The Anthony Burns case arose under the fugitive slave act, May 24–June 2, 1854.

We want money here to buy flour before the winter sets in, or before we are beleagured by another invasion.[36]

The same issue of the *Tribune* printed another in a series of letters from "Worcester" written from Worcester, Massachusetts, October 20, Higginson having just arrived from his visit to Kansas. The title was "An attempt at Prophecy." "I have observed for many years that the more thorough an Abolitionist any man is, the more correct are his prophecies as to American affairs; and in this respect, at least, the present writer is pretty well qualified."

With this introduction, he launched into his prophecy that: "The present comparative quiet of Kansas is only the prelude to a severer struggle than any she has yet seen; that this struggle will occur soon after the Presidential election; that it will be almost equally certain to occur, whether Frémont or Buchanan be elected."

Nine reasons for this prediction were stated at length:

1. The real question at issue is, not the invasions of Missourians nor the blockading of the river, but the enforcing of the bogus laws. The laws still exist, the courts are still controlled by Missouri, and this is the real root of the difficulty, over which neither Gov. Geary nor any one else (except Congress) has any legitimate control. The essential trouble, therefore, must remain unsettled till congress meets again, or be settled by force.

Reason 2 was increasing hostility. Reason 3 was actual preparations on both sides for renewal. Reason 4 was that neither side desired peace. In connection with reason 5 he stated: "War only educates men to itself, disciplines them, teaches them to bear its fatigues, anxiety and danger, and actually to enjoy them." This development he saw in evidence on both sides. Reason 6 was that Geary merely exasperated both sides. Reason 7 explained that the postponement of hostilities as the effect of the election; pro-slavery hope in Geary and free-state hope in the election of Frémont. Reason 8 was that the Lecompton prisoners would provide the basis of the new collision because "Pro-Slavery men will not submit to the liberation of all, nor the Anti-Slavery men to the execution of any." Reason 9 was that if Frémont was elected the Missourians would make a last desperate effort before inauguration, and if Buchanan was elected the free-state men would fight, the administration would be *"resisted as one.* If that is treason, make the most of it. Such treason as this is fast ripening in Kansas. Call it Revolution if you please. If the United States

---

[36] New York *Tribune,* October 23, 1856.

Government and Border Ruffians are to mean the same thing, the sooner the people of Kansas have revolution the better.'' Before the conflict was ended, he declared, the two Nations, North and South, would be separate.

The New York *Tribune* was a radical republican paper, but ''Worcester's'' prescription was too strong a medicine for the editors, even in the excitement of a final week of a presidential campaign. An editorial explained that ''Worcester's'' views were based upon personal observations, but that the *Tribune* had the impression that the people of Kansas would submit to the results of the election even if Buchanan was elected ''in the hope that an opportunity to throw off their chains will yet be accorded them.''

The next day the *Tribune's* leading editorial expounded ''the main question at issue in the election: That question is not, Shall Slavery be extended into Kansas? or, Shall she be left free and quiet, to decide for herself whether Slavery shall be introduced or not? *Slavery is already there!* . . . by *invasion,* and *violence,* and *fraud,* and *treachery.* . . . If Kansas *remains* as it is, it *remains* a Slave Territory, and becomes a SLAVE STATE, in violation of the ballot-box, of Free Speech, and of republican institutions—in virtual overthrow of the American constitution. . . . Nothing can now save Kansas or our republican institutions but some *revolution* of her affairs—some help for her from without—some overturning of the fraudulent legislation . . .—some restoration of her freedom. . . . THIS IS THE ONLY QUESTION IN THIS ELECTION. . . .'' The *Tribune* was using the same word, *revolution,* that ''Worcester'' had used the day before, but it was specifying that the revolution in question was at the ballot-box.

The news columns recounted a continuous stream of outrages during the next few days, culminating on Monday, November 3, in an appeal to the American people from the ''political prisoners'' at Lecompton, the signatures of all of them being arranged by states. The same issue contained an appeal to the President from O. C. Brown, the real Osawatomie Brown and founder of that town, in which he recounted its history and its peaceful existence until it was raided by the Border Ruffians on June 7.

On election day, Tuesday, November 4, the leading *Tribune* editorial admonished its readers: ''REPUBLICANS: the eventful day has dawned at last. Today gives a tremendous triumph to Freedom or Slavery. Resolve that no effort, no sacrifice on your part, shall be wanting to secure it to Freedom. . . . If we are baffled today, Kansas is temporarily enslaved; but we shall not give up the contest. . . .''

A reader must draw only one conclusion from this election editorial; that it conceded the election to slavery. On the day after, the returns were sufficiently complete to leave no hope, so the paper announced that the Bunker Hill of the war on slavery was lost, now the Saratoga and Yorktown must be won.

The *National Era* supported the republican ticket in the campaign but was not so sensational in its editorial treatment. After the news was received of the arrest of the Hickory Point prisoners, the editor confessed that he had little faith in Geary, and a week latter declared that:

> Governor Geary has secured what is called "peace in Kansas," in a way not at all unacceptable to the Border Ruffians. He has induced the Free State men to lay down their arms; arrested more than two hundred of them; called into the field eight hundred United States dragoons . . .; enrolled a large portion of the "Army of Law and Order," which came to destroy Lawrence. . . . This is Peace in Kansas.[37]

From the New York *Times* it copied an article denouncing Geary for his treatment of Lawrence and the invaders, charging the proslavery men with stealing cattle, recounting the murder of Buffum, the arrest of free-state men, and the distribution of sixty "free-state horses" to pro-slavery men on pretended claims of ownership.[38] Of course, neither the *Times* nor the *National Era* stopped to explain how the horses had happened to change their politics in the first instance. That might have spoiled the precious grievance.

From Lecompton J. H. Kagi wrote prison letters to the *National Era;* the one dated September 29 commented upon the coming of Geary as a promise of hope, as he had been on intimate terms with Lane during the past winter at Washington and was his friend in Lane's affair with Douglas. Lane made a speech at Topeka, September 11, in which he declared concerning Geary: "I know him well, and believe that he is true to us and to our cause."[39] The letter gave a lengthy description of Lane's activities, and his decision to retire from the territory after the Governor's proclamation was issued, the capture of the Hickory Point prisoners, the

---

[37] *National Era,* October 2, 9, 1856.

[38] *National Era,* October 9, 1856.

[39] *National Era,* October 16, 1856. The *Hinton Papers,* K. S. H. S., contain Kagi's correspondence. In a letter to his sister, dated November 30, 1856 he owned authorship of the letters to the *National Era.*

prison camp, Geary's visits to the prisoners and his expressions of sympathy, also Robinson's visits and the enthusiasm of the prisoners for him.   It related that troops had been sent to the north line to arrest Lane and predicted: "If they attempt it, he will give them battle.   He has been hunted, as a wild beast, as long as his spirit will bear."

The tone of the Kansas news was less favorable from other sources, and another dispatch in the same issue, dated Lawrence October 3, declared: "Only an armistice with the Border Ruffians" existed and that reliable information was at hand that a raid was scheduled for mid-November—"*Geary is a failure.*"   The Kagi prison letters continued to be printed through the winter, but otherwise the *National Era* did not make a specialty of Kansas as the *Tribune* did, either before or after the election of November 4.

The *National Intelligencer,* September 23, introduced the news of the release of the treason prisoners with the comment that "the strife in Kansas is about to be ended."   Talk of revolution and disunion, North and South, aroused the editors, September 30, to a four column rebuke on the theme of "The Union of the States":

The *Union,* then, is older than the formation of the Constitution in 1787, older than the articles of Confederation signed in 1778, older than the first Continental Congress of 1774, older than the Convention of the nine Colonies in 1765 to protest against the Stamp Act, older than 'the Albany Congress' of 1754; older than any or all of these, because in substance, underlying from the first the very existence of a people possessing a common lineage, speaking the same tongue, sharing in the same hopes, and encompassed by the same dangers.   The Union is an heirloom of the Anglo-American race, and as such worthy to be called a 'possession forever.'   It is native to our soil, older even than the evil freedom of which it now forms the surest pledge and guarantee.   It is not so much a part of our political life as the very seat and core of our national existence.

On October 14, they again expressed their loyalty to Union under the title "Submission or Resistance" to the results of the election. A week later in comment on "Party violence" they called attention to Washington's warning in his Farewell Address, pointing out the party leaders in the present campaign seemed to have as their object to intensify hate.   The *National Intelligencer* carried the slogan in 1856 "We join ourselves to no party that does not carry the flag and keep step to the music of the Union."   Just prior to the election this paper congratulated the country upon the relative calm which had followed the bitterness of a week or

so earlier. To the modern reader this comment is a reminder that
the New York *Tribune* in the last few days of the campaign had
impressed upon its readers that whatever the result of the election
it must be accepted in good faith. Did even the extremists come
to realize that passions had been whipped up to a point where
revolution was imminent? In this connection it is well to note a
comment in *Leslie's Illustrated Newspaper*, October 4, that "the
southwestern custom of stump speaking" had been introduced for
the first time in a large way into this campaign in the northern
states; it was more personal and effective, and brought facts to the
people that could not be transmitted to them otherwise because
of the partisan press. This is of particular significance to the historian inasmuch as it means that the newspaper record of this
campaign, more than preceding campaigns, is an inadequate medium from which to learn with exactness the material presented
to the public, and by which to gauge the intensity of the emotional
storm aroused by speakers who moved through every community
unshackled by such restraints as cold print would otherwise place
upon their harangues.

The present writer has arrived at the conclusion that it was
through the spoken word disseminated by the Kansas agitators
that the Eastern public learned first of the mythical exploits of the
leaders of the Kansas civil war, among them one Captain John
Brown, and in this manner the groundwork was unconsciously
laid for the later development of the Brown Legend. It is certain
that the press did not contain enough to account for the reception
which he was to receive in the East when he appeared there later
in the winter of 1856–1857.

After the election the agitation abated somewhat for a time,
but the new republican party had learned its lesson in campaign
technic, and during the next four years capitalized upon this new
found power to stir the emotions of the people. In 1856 neither
side was quite ready to force the issue of dissolution or to appeal
to arms in event of defeat, but another four years was another
matter entirely. As between the ultras of both sides, there is no
question of superior virtue or patriotism involved. The most extreme of them preached dissolution of the Union in 1856, and by
1860, if the trend of sentiment ran against either side, the one
finding itself in the minority after the votes were counted was
almost certain to make the attempt to force the issue. To be sure,
the ultras, both North and South, were in the minority, but an ag-

gressive, organized minority has ever been the active agent in revolutions. The stage was being set for a crisis, and had a democrat been elected in 1860, it is an open question whether the attempt would not have been made in the North to dissolve the Union, with the South in the role of defender of the National idea.

Events were taking shape meanwhile which precluded the civil war in Kansas anticipated by the extremists and deprived John Brown of his immediate opportunity to promote abolition and disunion there according to the tenets of his New England sponsors. First announced for October 20, but postponed to November 17, the Delaware land sales were the center of all hopes and fears. Charles Robinson wrote September 24 urging that Northern capital should be on hand, and particularly New York and Boston capital should have agents on the ground to checkmate pro-slavery advantage.[40] The control of a town fronting on the Missouri river was the chief objective of the free-state men, but in that the pro-slavery men had the principal sites. Robinson was reported to be negotiating with the Wyandot Indians for the site at the mouth of the Kansas river, which was recognized as even a greater prize than the Leavenworth site.[41] The *Tribune's* special correspondent in the territory added his voice to the call for eastern capital, a company or association, to make advances on mortgage security to free-state men to enable them to buy their claims.[42] When the sales were ready to open several correspondents reported on the number of purchasers and speculators on hand and attempted estimates of the amount of money in Leavenworth. One account placed it at three times the amount necessary. Squatters' associations were described, ''the settlers, without regard to their political opinions, are now united as one man, for the protection of each others' interests at the sales.''[43] The same reports stated that the sales began at the extreme northwest corner of the tract, some distance north of Topeka, where the settlers were fewest, and after the opening, the commissioner announced that instead of competitive bidding, the squatters might have their claims at the appraised price. The speculators either loaned money to the squatters at thirty or forty percent interest or bought from them,

[40] *National Intelligencer*, October 9, 1857.
[41] New York *Tribune*, October 16, 1857.
[42] New York *Tribune*, November 10, 1857.
[43] New York *Tribune*, November 29, 1857. Other accounts *Tribune*, November 27, December 15, and *National Intelligencer*, December 2, 1857.

rather than risk the vengence of the associations by competitive bidding, and probably at a greater profit.[44]

The correspondent of the Cincinnati *Gazette* reported that the pro-slavery men had overreached themselves in appealing to Pierce for protection against the influx of Northern capital, and that the recognition of squatter right had protected the free-state men. The stories of Northern capital were said to be myths; that Robinson had failed in his mission on that score, but instead had raised enough to finance the building of a town on the Missouri river above Wyandot,—Quindaro.[45] This was associated with railroad rivalries, one of which was the Kansas Valley Railway from Quindaro up the Kansas valley.[46] Except for the alleged settlement of disputed claims in favor of Missourians in certain cases, there was little criticism of the conduct of the sales until the Leavenworth city tract was about to be offered. Late in November new instructions were received requiring that actual competition in bidding must be insisted upon and that in case of combinations to prevent it the sales must be transferred to St. Louis. The commissioner knew a combination to evade competition on the town site did exist and decided to adjourn the sale without a day. Governor Geary and General Smith intervened on December 14, declaring that "they would regard such an adjournment as hazarding the peace of the Territory." While Commissioner Eddy did not share their apprehensions, he deferred to them on account of their responsibility and greater knowledge of the people and conditions and adjourned the sale from day to day awaiting further instructions. Eddy repaired to Washington where he stated that he thought the city lots would sell for two and a half times the appraised value. His suggestion was accepted and he returned to complete the sale.[47] In February the news was received that the land office in Lecompton would be opened soon to receive payments on preemption claims in other parts of the territory.[48] Good news usually alternated with bad and soon a sensational story was circulated that the Shawnee Indian agent had provided pro-slavery men with a map showing the selections made by the Indians and an association had been formed at Westport which had divided the

---

[44] New York *Tribune*, December 15, 1857 stated the interest rates charged.
[45] New York *Tribune*, December 10, 1857.
[46] New York *Tribune*, January 12, 1857.
[47] New York *Tribune*, January 10, 1857.
[48] New York *Tribune*, February 9, 1857.

surplus lands among some twenty-five hundred of their number.[48]
Similar proceedings were reported for the Miami lands. On the
authority of rumors of Indian treaties part of the Delaware Reserve was reported seized by another Association as well as the
Kaw Half-breed lands.[50]

The several controversies reviewed from the local press in previous chapters were canvassed also in the eastern press but occupied
much less space in proportion after the presidential election was
over. Also, there were fewer newspaper correspondents in the
field during the winter. Except for occasional articles or editorials
the *National Era* depended primarily for its Kansas news upon
Kagi who later became a follower of John Brown and was captured
at Harpers Ferry. He had entered Kansas during the late summer
of 1856 and allied himself with A. D. Stevens, who also later was to
follow Brown. Stevens was a murderer, army deserter and fugitive
from justice who went under the name of Whipple in Kansas and
operated as a guerilla leader from Topeka and was charged with
raiding such towns as Ozawkie on September 9, Indianola and other
places. As a result of his association with these operations Kagi
was arrested and held with the Hickory Point prisoners and others
brought in during the Geary pacification. At the time he was just
past twenty-one and Stevens was twenty-five. As would be expected, his letters reflected the radical tone, especially the earlier
ones, although he had his more conservative moments. The New
York *Tribune's* letters from Kansas were mostly those designated
as from "Our Own Correspondent," which, if the present author's
identification is correct, were always the product of William A.
Phillips. He was a radical but his views were usually tempered by
a practical trait of character which saved him from many of the
excesses of some of the Kansas letter-writers. Both men were severe
critics of Geary during the period of pacification, and Kagi in particular, as he was writing from prison and from a realistic experience in the results of Geary's domineering character. Kagi charged
Geary with duplicity in making arrests for offences committed prior
to his proclamation, apparently taking literally the latter's reference to "by-gones." [51]

It is not necessary to review the theme of the "political prisoners," as they were called, as little new light can be thrown upon

[49] New York *Tribune*, March 6, 12, and 17, 1857.
[50] New York *Tribune*, April 4, 1857.
[51] *National Era*, November 6, 1856.

the issues involved which would add to what has been presented from earlier chapters. There was one segment of the problem, however, the crisis developing in the southeastern part of the territory, which contributed substantially and directly to the John Brown theme. Geary's tour of the southern counties in October was the occasion for opening the subject. Kagi declared that "Geary is trying to find old Captain Brown; when he gets him, I will let you know." [52]   The *Tribune's* correspondent gave more detailed background for the Governor's expedition, declaring that for some time Law and Order bands had been harassing free-state settlers on the Potawatomie, Sugar creek in Linn county and as far to the southward as the Neosho settlements. The men especially charged with leadership in these forays were Martin White, Fox, and John E. Brown. Free-state settlers were said to have been forced to desert their claims which were immediately occupied by pro-slavery men associated with these organized bands of maurauders. When appealed to for redress, Geary informed them he could do nothing unless the free-state men would swear out formal warrants. That would mean a recognition by them of the legality of the territorial government, but it was reported that even that concession was made. It was charged that pro-slavery men followed in the wake of the Governor's party in Linn county and robbed and drove out free-state men; also that the governor had gone on the invitation of free-state men and while giving assurances to them, the marshal was engaged in making arrests of free-state men, and that the governor had not arrested the pro-slavery men but had chosen as his guides and advisers on the expedition none other than Martin White, Fox, and John E. Brown. Prior to this time the settlers had sent a delegation to Lecompton to offer a company of free-state militia for service in maintaining order, as was done in the case of the Titus and Walker companies, but they were not only refused but threatened with hanging if found under arms. The messenger was said to have been James H. Holmes. While the governor was on the tour the free-state men through different agents made a second proposition for defence and were refused. It was further charged that the arrests being made were without judicial process and the prisoners were held without charges against them, and to further illustrate the procedure a comparison was made with

[52] *National Era*, November 13, 1856.

the treatment of John Brown, Jr., and H. H. Williams during the preceding summer.[53]

The *Tribune's* correspondent made a personal tour of the area in dispute and wrote a long letter summarizing his findings under the date November 3. After the review of pro-slavery activities already summarized, he related the story of Redfield's Wisconsin company which had been delayed at the border by Geary's activities, had gone into camp in the vicinity of Osawatomie, preserved their identity as an organized company, and were engaged in securing claims. The manner of procedure in the search for claims was not detailed, but on two successive nights they were reported to have been attacked by pro-slavery forces who were equally determined that the region should be pro-slavery. The correspondent related also that the campaign against free-state settlers had been pushed as far south as the Neosho river and even while the governor was on his southern tour and within a few miles of him and the dragoons, the pro-slavery men raided free-state men on Sugar creek. A third phase of the disorders was related as an attack, by Georgians encamped near Bull creek, on an unnamed man en route to Westport for supplies. He was found by teamsters, shot by the Georgians and left for dead. He was taken to Westport and died there.[54] Two incidents in this account are important. The Governor's *Minutes* and the pro-slavery press attributed the attacks upon settlers in Linn county in the rear of Geary's party to free-state men who attacked and robbed Judge Briscoe Davis's house, and the pro-slavery press published the affidavit of one Glanville who was attacked by free-state men, left for dead, and picked up by teamsters who took him into Westport. Except for interchange of party labels, the accounts seem to describe identical incidents, the pro-slavery versions being correct.

The next outstanding news from the southeast was concerning a free-state raid into Missouri, and apparently the first such foray. The *Tribune's* correspondent explained that the remarkable aspect of the matter was that, after suffering outrages for so long, the free-state men had not retaliated earlier, but "a long series of outrages will work a change of sentiment, especially with those who have taken part in active engagements, and who, by the first touch of

[53] New York *Tribune*, October 31, November 7, 8, 13, 15, and December 15, 1856. *National Era*, November 13, 20, and December 18, 1856.
[54] New York *Tribune*, November 13, 1856.

human blood, have lost a little of that sensitive delicacy which makes men scrupulous.'' At Geary's suggestion, the correspondent's letter continued, the free-state men had sworn out warrants against White, Fox and J. E. Brown, but instead of serving them, the governor had consorted with these men on his tour. The free-state men then tried to seize the three offenders but were unsuccessful, and after that they decided to make reprisals by a raid into Missouri to revenge themselves at the expense of a Missouri leader who had been responsible for plundering the store of a free-state man named Dement and others. A party of six made the ride fifteen miles into Missouri, found their man, and plundered him, but it was pointed out, they did not burn his house as pro-slavery men had done. They were pursued into the territory, but on hearing that Captain Brown was near the pursuers fled back to the state.[55] It should be noticed that in the first letter the identity of the free-state men was carefully guarded, but the leader was none other than James H. Holmes, a young man who had been leading an independent command since mid-August and had been associated in guerilla warfare with John Brown.

In one of his long letters on the troubles in south Kansas, the *Tribune's* Kansas correspondent wrote in facetious style a detailed account of the arrest and escape of Holmes:

Col. Preston, with a party of these mounted militia, had undertaken the arrest of Mr. Holmes, formerly of New York City. This latter gentleman distinguished himself by his bravery at the battle of Osawatomie, and has been the hero of more than one daring affair since. As in all such cases, he has been credited with rather more than his share, and when anything in the shape of defensive warfare occurred in that quarter, Cap. Holmes was said to be at the bottom of it. The Pro-Slavery men have been anxious to get him arrested or into their hands in some shape. It has even been said that Governor Geary has offered a reward for his capture. Be that as it may, Mr. Preston, legally United States Deputy Marshal and Border Ruffian 'Colonel,' with the military force referred to, undertook his arrest. The gallant Marshal had a wearisome and profitless hunt on the Pottawatomie and among the thickets of Sugar Creek. No Captain Holmes was to be found, because that gentleman, who had been supposed to be prowling about with a band of armed men in that direction, was really in this vicinity [Lawrence], alone and peacefully engaged. As fortune would have it, Mr. Holmes started for Osawatomie just as Marshal Preston and his militia, fresh from their unsuccessful hunt, were returning. What happened was perfectly natural. Mr. Holmes was riding up the steep hill at Middle creek, a few miles on this

55 New York *Tribune*, November 28, 1856. The letter was dated November 14. Also cf., December 15, 1856; letter dated November 27.

side of Osawatomie, when he suddenly came upon Preston and his dragoon militia. Escape was just about out of the question, and as Mr. Holmes was not aware that anyone knew him, he attempted to pass. He was arrested by them, and as he, under the circumstances, made no resistance, he was disarmed and carried toward Lecompton. Here, by an unexpected piece of luck, the gallant Preston had succeeded in capturing the very man he was after; but 'there's many a slip 'twixt the cup and the lip.' The occurrence I narrate happened two days ago. That night they halted near Washington Creek, and Mr. Holmes, thinking that he had gone as far as it was desirable to go, took advantage of some slight inattention on the part of the guards, leaped a fence close by and started off. They shouted for him to stop, and several bullets whistled after him, but he escaped unhurt, and looked as composed as ever while he gave me the particulars of the adventure.[56]

Kagi reported that five prisoners from the Osawatomie region had been brought in to Tecumseh November 25; Sam, William and Henry Kilburn, James Townsley and William Partridge, and that "each of these men is charged with some eight or ten horrid crimes, which have never been committed by anybody." [57] He represented in a later letter that the grand jury was hastily discharged after indicting several free-state men. The reason for this he said was that a bargain had been struck with two free-state men on the jury that if they would consent to the indictments of the free-state men, the pro-slavery majority would open an investigation of the disorders in southern Kansas. The first witness was called in the investigation, according to the agreement, and on examination implicated all but four of the jury, and so Judge Cato agreed to relieve their embarassment by dismissing the grand jury before the matter became more complicated.[58] The Osawatomie prisoners were examined, and Sam and William Kilburn were discharged, but the correspondent stated that Henry Kilburn, a lad of fourteen, boldly announced that the Missourians had harassed them, burned their house, stolen their cattle and driven them into refuge in the timber along the Osage, so finally they had followed the Missourians home and compensated themselves for their losses; "all this the boy admitted and told them to do their worst." He was sentenced to twelve months' imprisonment.[59]

[56] New York *Tribune*, December 15, 1856. The letter is dated November 27.

[57] *National Era*, December 18, 1856. Also Cf. New York *Tribune*, December 15, 1856.

[58] *National Era*, January 1, 1857.

[59] *National Era*, January 1, 1857. The statement about the release of Sam and William Kilburn does not agree with the report of Hoogland. Cf. Chapter 29.

The trial of William Partridge was postponed December 2 on account of absence of witnesses for the defendant, and the marshal went in search of them, but found many "not at homes." One man was arrested but the prisoner decided that "evil communication corrupts good manners and decided to go no further." An attempt was made to take Silas Moore, but as the marshal had no United States troops with him, Moore decided not to go, as "Mr. Partridge had sent down intelligence to his neighbors of the extreme inhumanity and injustice with which Free State prisoners were treated, and recommended that no more of them allow themselves to be taken."[60] The first Partridge hearing was December 2, which allowed fourteen days before the trial proceeded December 16.[61] The *Tribune's* correspondent insisted that the court did not make the necessary effort to bring in Partridge's witnesses.[62]

Kagi reported that there was no free-state lawyer in town and no witness for the defendant within seventy miles. Partridge asked for a continuance, but was refused. Johnson of Kansas City, a proslavery lawyer, the best in western Missouri or Kansas, took his case and worked hard for his release, assisted by Parrott, a free-state lawyer who came in later, but failed to secure his acquittal. This is the story of the trial as told by Kagi who added that Partridge had been arrested along with John Brown, Jr., the previous summer, but had been released. Partridge was sentenced to ten years' imprisonment for burglary. The only evidence against him, according to Kagi, was that of Mrs. Totten, but the real reason he declared was that Partridge was a free-state man and a "friend of Captain Brown's."[63] The New York *Tribune's* correspondent reported the trial also and declared that "He was a most respectable citizen, and the charges against him are preposterous. His arrest arose out of the difficulties in that quarter. Those Pro-Slavery men who procured it were deserving of the fate they have planned, and, by legal fraud, secured for their enemies. His arrest was secured by the intervention of Gov. Geary. His brother was killed at the battle of Osawatomie, . . . One brother in his bloody grave; the other a convicted felon. So goes Freedom in Kansas."

The correspondents kept up the agitation reporting that all the prisoners at Tecumseh were ill with erysipelas, and attempts had

60 New York *Tribune*, December 24, 1856.
61 New York *Tribune*, December 13, 1856.
62 New York *Tribune*, January 12, 1857.
63 *National Era*, January 8, 1857.

been made to have Partridge moved, but without success. Geary
had promised relief, Kagi stated, but then it was said that Geary
had promised to reprieve him immediately and had not done so, and
"Now, Partridge lies at the point of death. Why does not Geary
carry out his promise?" [64]   Later it was reported that Partridge
had been transferred to Lecompton and held with the other convicted prisoners.[65] Neither the *Tribune* nor the *National Era* correspondents reported the specific charges against the other Osawatomie prisoners nor their fate. On April 2, however, the *National
Era* reprinted an unsigned article from the *Evening Post* [n. p.,
n. d.] regarding James Townsley. The letter itself was dated
March 16 and reported that only three prisoners remained at Tecumseh March 13 when news was received at Topeka that one of
them had been put in chains: "That night, a file was sent to him,
and yesterday morning he called at the Topeka Hotel, for lodgings.
He is almost totally deaf, in consequence of his long imprisonment.
His name is James Townsley. He was formerly from Maryland,
and was one of Capt. Brown's company. . . ." The other two prisoners escaped at the same time, one of them being "Henry Kil-
bourne, a boy of fifteen years, who had been sentenced to twelve
months confinement in the county jail by Judge Cato, without
trial." Even this account made no mention of the crime, the
Potawatomie murders, with which Townsley was charged.

FREE-STATE—GEARY RAPPROCHEMENT

In connection with the Geary pacification, the governor had arrested many free-state men, as has been recorded elsewhere, but he
arranged a suspension of actions against some of the leaders. The
Tribune's correspondent reported that when the deputy marshal attempted to arrest Captain Samuel Walker, the governor interfered,
and Kagi added further information to the effect that Titus intervened also because of Walker's generosity in August in saving his
life.[66] At about the same time Geary urged free-state men to participate in the October elections, and endure the pro-slavery domi-
nance a short time after which they could capture control.[67] The
free-state men did not trust him or the administration at Washington, so these overtures failed. The editorial policy of the *Tribune*

[64] *National Era*, January 8, 1857.
[65] *National Era*, January 29, 1857.
[66] New York *Tribune*, October 30, 1856 and *National Era*, October 30, 1856.
[67] *National Era*, October 30 and November 6, 1856.

seemed to reflect doubt about Kansas tactics, taking a moderate
stand even to the extent of urging that peace in Kansas must be preserved even at the cost of submission; anything except a permanent
surrender to slavery.[68] Shortly afterwards, however, it published
an extended article by that irresponsible sensationalist, James Redpath, which reflected an opposite spirit in maintaining that the Kansas leaders were not yet subdued:

> Messrs Hyatt and Arny, members of the Kansas National Committee,
> with Gov. Robinson and his accomplished wife, arrived in Chicago today,
> and will leave by the first train for St. Louis on their way to the 'outpost
> of Freedom.' Gen. Lane, Messrs. Deitzler, Jenkins, and John Brown, Jr.,
> are expected daily. It was their intention to return immediately after
> the result of the Presidential campaign was announced. Capt. John
> Brown, the elder, the heroic defender of Osawatomie, was in Chicago less
> than two weeks ago, and before this letter is received by you will be
> once more near the scene of his romantic and daring exploits. Col.
> Whipple has returned in company with Capt. Lenhart, the brave stripling
> who first taught the Missouri guerilla bands that a guerilla mode of war-
> fare could be urged by the friends as well as by the foes of the Northern
> settlers.[69]

That there was little in this paragraph that was true did not concern Redpath. A similar spirit was reflected in an article by another sensationalist, Richard Realf, who wrote: "I do not desire to
say much about Gov. Geary or I shall grow ill-tempered. He is as
many colors as a harlequin, though scarcely as dexterous; for his
feats of political legerdemain are beginning to be understood, because of which men despise the cheater. He has lately been amusing himself with arrests of Free State men in the region of Osawatomie and Fort Riley." He reported that the insults inflicted upon
the prisoners were devilish beyond description; that Judge Lecompte "appears like a human skin distended with whiskey"; and
that Titus was "a two-legged specimen of savage tigerhood." [70]
It would seem that the reader of the *Tribune* could find something to his taste in this Kansas material, ranging as it did from the
conservative editorial, through the relatively moderate reports of its
special correspondents, to the imaginative creations of Redpath and
Realf. The *Tribune* reader might be excused, also, if he failed to
understand accurately the conditions that prevailed in the territory.
Writing from Lawrence November 11, the *Tribune's* correspond-

68 New York *Tribune*, November 12, 1856.
69 New York *Tribune*, November 14, 1856.
70 New York *Tribune*, November 14, 1856.

ent felt that as the election was over, "Perhaps conscience may arise and assert its power over even a Governor. This would be rather romantic. . . . I have known instances, however, where politicians have had a conscience, and the thing is not improbable." [71] The *National Era's* correspondent, Kagi, thought that the trouble with Geary was pride more than wickedness.[72] When the break came between Geary and Lecompte, the *Tribune* declared editorially: "we do not mean to be betrayed into premature exultation; but it certainly does seem that Gov. Geary had halted in mid-career, and refused to be longer a mere tool of the Border Ruffians." [73] Next it appeared that there might be a rupture between Geary and the pro-slavery party.[74] The correspondent admitted, however, that "technically, the judge is right." Later the same writer expressed the conclusion that "Gov. Geary seems to have repented that he ever had the men arrested, and would have been glad if he could have found some plausible way of getting rid of them before now." [75] In the same issue another writer stated that, "The advent of Gov. Geary into Kansas was a hard blow to the Free State party. From his first appearance among us he has ever been blowing *hot* and *cold* with the same breath," but a little later so harsh a critic as Thaddeus Hyatt decided that, "It is but just to Governor Geary to say that he seems disposed to act fairly. No man ever had a more difficult part to perform." [76] These favorable expressions from Kansas must be balanced against the harsh ones already recorded in connection with affairs in southern Kansas. The net effect was such that a Kansas reader of the *Tribune* was moved to write that "I think your correspondent presents things in this Territory in too gloomy a light. I have no doubt that Gov. Geary intends to do justice by all parties." [77] Writing from Boston, "J. R.," probably James Redpath, reported that Charles Robinson was in that city and that "his views of Territorial affairs are very encouraging. He seems to be inclined to believe that Geary is disposed to act impartially as far as his oath of office will permit him to do so." [78]

[71] New York *Tribune*, November 22, 1856.

[72] *National Era*, November 20, 1856.

[73] New York *Tribune*, November 21, 1856.

[74] New York *Tribune*, December 1, 1856. Letter of "Our Special Correspondent." Cf., also *Tribune*, January 7, 1857.

[75] New York *Tribune*, December 10, 1856. "Edmund" in Cincinnati *Gazette*.

[76] New York *Tribune*, December 15, 1856.

[77] New York *Tribune*, January 8, 1857. Letter of John B. Wood, dated Lawrence, December 26, 1856.

[78] New York *Tribune*, January 12, 1857.

When the break did come between Geary and the pro-slavery party, however, the free-state men were not ready to give him full support. On Robinson's return to Kansas, strained relations developed with Geary on account of the incidents attending the meeting of the free-state legislature and the arrest of several of its members. Also Geary was charged with trying to break up the free-state party.[79] The *Tribune* editor predicted another civil war, however, on the ground that the spring emigration from the North promised to be so overwhelming that disorders were the only means by which the South could hope to discourage it.[80]

DISSENSION WITHIN FREE-STATE RANKS

The work of the territorial legislature drew out virtually a consistent condemnation from the correspondents of the eastern anti-slavery papers. The rebellion law was denounced,[81] the repeal of the test oaths was represented as a juggling of words,[82] the tax bill was considered particularly dangerous,[83] and the concentration of attention upon private bills for town companies, ferries, banks and such matters revealed how jealous the free-state men were of the advantages that were to be derived from the control of the government.[84] The outstanding measure of the session, however, was the census and constitutional convention bill. The fact that one faction of the pro-slavery element wished to divide with the free-state men the control of the machinery was scarcely alluded to, and then only to ridicule James Christian who urged the compromise in the council,[85] and predicted that "the People of Kansas are about to be subjected to the severest ordeal of their eventful struggle."[86] The resignation of Geary was exploited extensively. He was represented upon his arrival at Washington as much impaired in health as a result of his Kansas ordeal.[87] The *National Era* made the refusal of Buchanan to reappoint Geary a test of the position of his administration upon the Kansas question, while the *Tribune* argued that the circumstances surrounding the appointment of Walker

[79] New York *Tribune*, February 13, 1857, also March 17, 1857.
[80] New York *Tribune*, March 18, 1857.
[81] New York *Tribune*, March 2, 6, 1857.
[82] New York *Tribune*, March 4, 1857.
[83] New York *Tribune*, February 2, 1857.
[84] New York *Tribune*, February 2, 4, 1857.
[85] New York *Tribune*, March 9, 1857.
[86] New York *Tribune*, March 11, 1857.
[87] New York *Tribune*, March 21, 24, 25, 1857.

proved that he was a mere tool to be used by the Border Ruffians for the purpose "of cramming the bogus laws and bogus slaveholding constitution down the throats of the people." [88]

The *Tribune* contended that the policy of the national administration in Kansas was to divide the free-state vote as a means to accomplish its purposes, and accordingly advised its Kansas friends not to participate in the elections for the constitutional convention.[89] The *National Era* took the other side of the question maintaining that Kansas people must help themselves by voting.[90] It argued that the pro-slavery victories, Kansas, the election of Buchanan, and the Dred Scott decision, unduly depressed anti-slavery people, and pointed to two significant victories: the victory of anti-slavery in St. Louis, which indicated the trend among the border states, and the figures on the popular vote in the national election which showed that the North had three votes for every one cast by the South. The conclusion drawn was that "practically, our principles have become *aggressive*. We no longer stand upon the defensive. We have crossed the line, and are upon slaveholding ground." The *Ohio State Journal* took much the same line.[91] An occasional letter from the *National Era's* Kansas correspondent took the radical ground, but otherwise the paper was consistent in taking the moderate course during the early part of the year 1857.

The position of the New York *Tribune* was essentially radical, reporting some disorder, such as the rescue of a free-state man from a bogus sheriff in the style of 1856, and pro-slavery outrages on free-state men near Leavenworth and Lecompton.[92] There was not enough of such news, however, to prevent the reluctant admission that Kansas was generally quiet, although the readers were assured that the pro-slavery men had not changed.[93]

Lane reappeared in the territory during the spring, making a series of speeches at Lawrence, Topeka and Leavenworth.[94] The one at Lawrence was characterized as "Laneish" and demanded that the state government be put in readiness to function at a moment's notice, if admitted as a state, or if "*the Pro-Slavery State*

[88] *National Era*, April 2, 9, 1857. New York *Tribune*, Editorial, April 6, 23, 1857.
[89] New York *Tribune*, March 6, 31, 1857.
[90] *National Era*, April 9, May 14, 1857.
[91] Quoted in the *National Era*, May 14, 1857.
[92] New York *Tribune*, April 2, 23, 1857.
[93] New York *Tribune*, April 15, 1857.
[94] New York *Tribune*, April 8, 15, and *National Era*, June 11, 1857.

Government attempted to go in motion 'out of the Union.' " [95]   In
the same speech he defended his course the previous summer and
branded Geary's coming as a misfortune, because otherwise the territorial government would have been driven out in a few days more.
The *Tribune's* correspondent reported that "the gallant Colonel
Lane had again evaporated.   He made a speech in Topeka the day
after he got there and started for Nebraska in disguise"; the writer
thought that the officials and border ruffians were glad to get rid of
him rather than arrest him.[96]   At Leavenworth Lane spoke in the
presence of Governor Walker and declared that "the Constitutional
Convention would not meet in Kansas, for the reason *that it* would
endanger the peace of the country," and that it must meet in Missouri where it belonged.[97]

The conduct of the new territorial officials and their administration of the census law in preparation for the constitutional convention were the principal subjects of discussion through April, May
and June.   The *Tribune* protested the residence requirement for
voting, insisting that in view of the great spring immigration about
half of the white voters would have arrived after March 15 and
"not one of these new comers is allowed to vote at the Constitutional election which the bogus Legislature has ordered to take place
in June."[98]   This was strange doctrine indeed, as the absence of a
residence requirement, which would have excluded the Missouri invasions, had been a major grievance for the previous two years.

Acting-Governor Stanton landed from the river boat at Westport, thereby committing an error in etiquette which disqualified
him as an executive,—he had come in by the pro-slavery backdoor.[99]
He made himself still more unpopular in free-state circles by delivering an address at Lawrence on law enforcement.[100]   The
Tribune's correspondent reported from time to time on the progress of the census and the problem of posting the lists that they
might be scrutinized.   His letter of April 18 insisted that no lists
had been posted as yet and protested that a Kansas friend in the
East admonished them to be sure to have the lists carefully
purged.[101]   Of course, these comments were intended as a rebuke

95 New York *Tribune,* April 8, 1857.
96 New York *Tribune,* April 15, 1857.
97 *National Era,* June 11, 1857.
98 New York *Tribune,* April 13, 1857.
99 New York *Tribune,* April 27, 1857.
100 New York *Tribune,* May 5, 1857.
101 New York *Tribune,* April 22, 1857.

to those misguided persons, as he thought them, who were urging that free-state men vote in Kansas.

* * * *

The reader may ask,—what does all this have to do with John Brown and the legend of '56? Just this! A full analysis of the main stream of Kansas history reveals beyond question the fact that in the contemporary printed record John Brown did not appear to have had much influence either in making or marring Kansas history. In no place did he appear as a major factor. His exploits were sporadic eruptions of disorder which seem to have had no relation to free-state strategy, either radical or conservative. He and his followers brought tragedy to innocent settlers in the southeastern part of the territory, but at most that was only a subordinate factor in the stream of events when taken as a whole. Nevertheless in this limited respect, the systematic examination of the record reveals many ramifications of the Brown influence that have been missed completely by the historians and the Brown biographers, and emphasizes the degree to which a broad and critical analysis of the period has long been possible from the contemporary printed record, even without access to extensive manuscript sources.

PART II

THE GROWTH OF THE LEGEND

CHAPTER X

HARPERS FERRY AND THE MAKING OF A MARTYR; THE ACT OF CREATION

Leaving Kansas in October 1856, John Brown was in Boston during the most of January 1857, spent the remainder of the winter making friends in the East, soliciting money and finally May 13 after unexplained delays made a start, supposedly for Kansas. From August 7 to January 15, 1858 he was at Tabor and Springdale, Iowa, having made only a short, quiet visit to Kansas November 5–17. During the spring of 1858 the Virginia plan took definite shape, the Chatham, Canada, convention being held May 8 and 9, the constitution adopted, the plan exposed, and after consultation with fellow conspirators Brown was sent back to Kansas for a season. He arrived at Lawrence June 26 and then established himself in the southeastern part of the territory shortly after peace had been established in that region under the terms of the Denver-Montgomery treaty. He was active in the renewal of the war in the vicinity of Ft. Scott, and on December 20 after the second peace he made his first and only slave liberation raid into Missouri, his party killing one man, running off eleven negroes, who were hidden for a time and then conducted to Canada during late January and February 1859. By July he had established himself at the Kennedy Farm on the Maryland side of the Potomac river north of Harpers Ferry, from which point he made the raid on that place October 16, being captured at daybreak October 18. He was sentenced to death November 2 and executed December 2, 1859.

OPINION IN KANSAS

Kansas enjoyed a good crop in 1859 and entered the winter more hopefully, both economically and politically, than any previous year. Little did they suspect that the next few months were to plunge them into the most disastrous economic catastrophe in the history of the territory, the drouth of 1860, the climax of a long cycle of unseasonable weather, as well as the renewal of civil war in a form more bitter than ever before, but now on a national rather than a local scale. The territorial newspapers for the week of October 16–22 carried the first news of an insurrection in Virginia involving a number of men known to Kansas people either personally or by reputation. Reactions were mixed; it was an attack on slavery, it involved Kansas men, it would possibly furnish political explosives for the coming presidential campaign. Anti-slavery men would naturally be stirred with sympathy toward an attack on the peculiar institution, local pride was excited by the fact of some personal knowledge of the participants, but republican anti-slavery men were startled, realizing instantly that whatever their natural sympathies in the circumstances, any sign of approval would mean political disaster. Democrats were just as alert in sensing the potentialities of the unexpected issue. Elections were coming thick and fast under the new republican-democratic alignment; October 4, the adoption of the Wyandotte constitution; November 8, the election of a territorial legislature; December 6, the election of state officers under the new constitution, and in 1860 would come the presidential campaign.

At Atchison the republican *Champion* of October 22, edited by the twenty-year-old John A. Martin, took a strong ground:

This madman has met a tragic end at last. An insane effort to accomplish what none but a madman would attempt, has resulted as any one but a madman would have foreseen, in death to all who were engaged in it. The account of the wild foray in which he was engaged, we publish in another column.

Knowing the character of the man, and familiar with his course for the past two years [sic], as nearly all citizens of Kansas are, none here will be surprised at his attempted insurrection and its bloody termination. Of him, we might say with truth, his wrongs have made him mad. There was a time when John Brown, the Pennsylvania farmer, and his sons, were as peaceable and peace-loving citizens as could be found in our country. He came to Kansas early, and loving the cause of freedom, he was an earnest Free State man. For this he suffered. He saw his home invaded and destroyed; he mourned the death of a beloved son. And these great wrongs crazed the old man, and made him a fanatic, a monomaniac, with but one thought, one idea, one impulse—vengeance on the slave power, which had destroyed his peace, revenge on the men who had murdered his kindred and friends. It is said that he took an awful oath that while life remained his hand should be raised against this power, and he would wage war against it to the death.

No sane man, however strong in his convictions against slavery, will pretend to justify the mad course he pursued. All will unite in condemning it, and no Northern man but would use every effort to put down such an expedition as he undertook. The termination of his foray will be the termination of every such insane and murderous attempt to create a servile insurrection, as it ought to be.

Certainly Martin had had very little opportunity to consult on the issues, his reaction was almost inevitable, as was the reaction of the opposing paper, the *Union,* which replied the following week that "Of all the extraordinary articles which we meet with in Republican papers, the above is the cap sheaf." In civilized countries, the *Union* argued, insane men were not held accountable for their acts and hanged. The insanity issue was raised to save him from the consequences of his acts, but the *Union* editor insisted that Brown was not insane; his son was killed by one of his own men; he was never a peaceable Pennsylvania farmer, he was a horsethief in Illinois before he came to Kansas and here he was "a thief, traitor and murderer"; republicans such as Gerritt Smith befriended, supported him and sung his praises; now "they call him crazy—fling him a hangman's rope";—but Brown was no more guilty than the republican friends who supported him and supplied him with funds. The bitter controversy raged through November and December, and among other things, letters from James Redpath were printed by the *Champion* denying that either Brown or Redpath were republicans. In spite of its repudiation of Brown, on February 4, 1860, the *Champion* announced the receipt from Thomas H. Webb of Boston (Secretary of the New England Emigrant Aid Company) of a photograph with facsimile autograph:— "The photograph is at our office, and those who desire to see the Hero of Osawatomie, can have an opportunity of doing so."

At Leavenworth the same kind of a controversy was waged between the *Times,* republican, and the *Herald,* democratic, with the latter going into detail in reviewing the Kansas career of the different members of Brown's raiders, and of Brown himself it declared:

It was this miserable old wretch that committed the first murder, for *political,* offense, in Kansas Territory, and in atrocity it is unparalleled in the history of crime. We allude to the massacre of the Wilkinsons and Doyles in. '55. Brown, with five or six followers, dragged these persons, five in number, from their beds at night, split their heads open with sabres, in the presence of their wives, and then cut off their ears and fingers, and otherwise mutilated their bodies. The individuals had committed no offence—

the only *crime* charged, was that they differed politically from Brown. It was this same villain and his party who shot Little at Fort Scott, last winter; who killed an inoffensive old farmer, on the Missouri line, named Crews, and stole his negroes and oxen, and who afterwards boasted of his crime in a letter published in the *Lawrence Republican*.[1]

The exaggeration of the charges against Brown was characteristic of the opposition and entered into the pro-slavery and southern tradition or legend about Brown. The Potawatomie massacre was not the first murder for political reasons, there was only one Wilkinson, the date was 1856, and mutilation of the bodies was probably only the result of the killing by sabres rather than deliberate mangling after the crime.

At Fort Scott, the *Democrat*, although devoting most of its attention to Indian lands and railroad projects, turned aside from these objectives to express itself briefly but in no uncertain terms: Harpers Ferry revealed fully the motives in keeping up the Southern Kansas disturbances,—to incite a general civil war; either Jayhawking must have been a profitable profession or the republicans financed him for the Virginia raid; and "before either himself or his sons had been despoiled of the value of a pin, his hands were red with innocent blood."[2]   In connection with anniversaries the "singular coincidence" was emphasized that "On the 16th of December, 1857, the Jay-hawkers resisted the Deputy U. S. Marshal, at Bains Fort, on the Osage. December 16, 1858, Montgomery and his band invaded Fort Scott, murdered John Little, and robbed his store; and on the 16th of December 1859, three of their number will expiate their crimes on the gallows."[3]

In Topeka the *Kansas State Record,* republican, edited by the Ross brothers, took much the same course as the other republican papers but with some interesting variations:

Staring capitals announce that Brown has confessed, and again that he has not confessed, as though he were a thief upon the rack, from whom a bloody record of crimes were to be extracted, instead of a martyr to liberty and a victim of the bloody institution of slavery, which he is.

The raid at Harper's Ferry is, of course, a reprehensible affair, not to be justified upon any grounds whatever, but the advocates and apologists of American slavery should be slow to denounce John Brown as a murderer, traitor, etc., simply because he was unsuccessful in a daring project. He is simply what their pet institution has made him.

[1] Leavenworth *Herald*, October 29, 1859. The *Herald* was edited by William H. Gill and L. J. Eastin. The latter left the *Herald* during the excitement and Gill was new to the territory. This fact deprives the *Herald's* views of the significance that would attach to them under Eastin's editorship.

[2] Ft. Scott *Democrat*, November 10, 17, 24, December 1, 1859.

[3] Ft. Scott *Democrat*, December 1, 1859.

The paper attributed his frenzy to the wrongs he and his family had suffered. After the execution, the *Record* reported that "John Brown has paid with his life, the penalty of defeat in the illadvised project upon which he had entered, . . ." [4] Probably no other Kansas paper bungled so badly its task of dealing with Brown. Putting together the argument from different editorials it would run something like this:

"This martyr of liberty," who exemplified Christian and humane characteristics, in his "treasonable madness" was not guilty of any offense except that "he was unsuccessful in a daring" but "unjustifiable" project and must therefore suffer "the penalty of defeat" and "no member of the republican party, from one end of the Union to the other, has spoken a word of sympathy for his murderous designs," but "the premeditated killing of a brave man is well calculated to excite emotions of disgust for the executioner, and sympathy for the victim." [5]

And regarding Governor Wise of Virginia, the *Record* printed a pun that was going the rounds of republican papers, to the effect that "as Old John is called Ossawatomie Brown, a correspondent of the [New York] *Evening Post* suggests that old Wise should be called What-an-ass-am-ie Wise." [6]

The opposition Topeka *Tribune* declared that:

Nearly every paper we take up, contains a sketch of "Old Brown," nearly every man we meet tells us something about him, and from what we can learn, "Old Brown" will be used by mothers and nurses to frighten into subjection their unruly charges, while his example will be held up to youth forever, as one altogether wicked and unholy. Few apologize for him, none do so directly but only under the plea of insanity, and yet every editor tries his skill on the subject—comes out with a leading article on "Old Brown," and concludes with a homily on politics. Stump speakers cease to talk of the President, of his Administration or his faults, to tell us of this wonderful attack on old Virginia. Ministers of the gospel weave into their sermons a few mournful allusions to his career, and the cause of his conduct. And yet, who and what was John Brown?—A poor old man, a fanatical Abolitionist, one who out-Heroded Herod. In Kansas, he could not be called a leader; but fought on his own account, when, where and as he chose. No man respected his wisdom, none counseled with him in the hour of danger, no man called him brother. But now madder and more fool-hardy than while here, he has done what any mad man or fool might do—committed murder and treason. For this he is to be immortalized; for this, thirty millions of people turn pale, and a thousand editors write "Virginia Attacked," "Insurrection," and

[4] *Kansas State Record*, November 5, December 10, 1859.

[5] From three *Record* editorials November 5, 12 and December 10, 1859.

[6] *Kansas State Record*, December 24, 1859.

a thousand other things equally silly and uncalled for. Virginia attacked by a score of men! An insurrection on so small a scale! Ah! gentlemen, think you not old Brown and his foolish associates will thank you for the notice you have given them?—Think you not they have gained just what reckless, unprincipled men most desire—a notoriety that will live, be it ever so mean? But it is not their immortality we complain; but the influence the press is exerting for evil. . . . We are not the apologists of Brown; but we do most solemly protest against bosh and nonsense, the false conclusions and silly deductions of his thousand biographers.[7]

The *Tribune* returned to the task a week later:

There are two classes of men who apologize for "Old Brown." The one does so openly, boldly and without fear. These men, belonging to the Wendell Phillips school, call him patriot and christian. They class him with Tell, a Washington and a Bolivar, bestowing upon him all the praise due to a hero and a philanthropist. The other class, beneath a veil so thin that a fool can see the device, calling themselves law and order men, lovers of peace—Republicans, forsooth—apologize for Brown by publishing in their papers every word they can catch in his praise. . . .

These two classes are alike the friends and comfortors of Brown, one by open praise, and the other in a tacit endorsement by telling what somebody else has said, making themselves more than Phillips, the instruments in building up a reputation of *martyr* for Brown and his confederates.

The editor of the *Tribune* deprecated also what he called the spirit of proscription in the territory, taking as an example his experience with a subscriber who took exception to his remarks about Brown and ordered the paper stopped:

They . . . [seek] only to build up party, at whatever cost, even if bankruptcy follow in the wake. We, on the contrary, believe that our local interests are of far more importance than party—that the settlement of our country by honest and industrious citizens, the founding of schools, the building of railroads, for the purpose of connecting ourselves with the east, and inducing a lively trade to grow up between this part of the country and the Atlantic States, and the forwarding of many other improvements and institutions, we say, are of far more importance to us than the disgusting question of politics, and the fighting for personal preferences for office. . . .[8]

Along with the agitation of the Harpers Ferry raid was the record of various observers relative to the fate of slavery in Missouri. From St. Joseph came the estimate that twenty thousand slaves had been taken from Missouri during the year, and the Huntsville (Missouri) *Citizen* stated that some were selling, while

[7] Topeka *Tribune*, November 12, 1859.
[8] Topeka *Tribune*, November 12, 1859.

others were allowing slaves to run away. From Parkville came the report that about fifty slaves had been sold the past week and that "at the rate slaves have been sold South for the past six months, slavery in western Missouri will cease before the end of three years." [9]

The interest taken by Kansas in the Brown question found its fullest expression in the Lawrence papers. The *Republican,* radical republican in politics, was edited by T. Dwight and Solon O. Thacher. The *Herald of Freedom* was still in the hands of the irrepressible G. W. Brown, but although he was a conservative republican in party affiliation, he was charged by the radicals with having sold out to the Buchanan administration in exchange for the public printing. The *Republican* printed thirty-three different articles or paragraphs in the first six weekly issues after the raid as compared with its rival's sixty-nine, and fifty-two in the five December numbers as against nineteen in three numbers of the *Herald of Freedom* before the latter discontinued publication. The *Republican* tapered off in January to thirteen articles in four weeks.

The first issue of the Lawrence *Republican* after the raid was that of October 20. Telegraphic reports, relayed part way by special messenger, reported a servile insurrection led by John Brown:

It is doubted by some whether the report is correct—although we think it is quite likely, as ever since the old man's son was murdered by the Border Ruffians, he has been regarded here as a monomaniac upon the subject of the slave-power. His often expressed belief has been that he was a divinely commissioned instrument for the overthrow of the Slave-power in the South. If it indeed be true that the old man has engaged in the insane attempt of carrying out his wild scheme by the red right hand of revolution, it can only be regarded as the expiring effort of a brain maddened by repeated injuries and bereavements sustained at the hand of that remorseless power against which he has at last turned with such a recklessness and insane daring.

Another week confirmed the news and the editors took up the question of responsibility, declaring that

The slave-power itself commenced the desperate game of invading a Free Territory, and attempted by fire and sword, to establish slavery; old John Brown and his mad followers have matched them, but against ten thousand odds fold greater, by invading a slave state for the purpose of forcibly establishing Freedom.

[9] Topeka *Kansas State Record,* November 5, 1859.

The slave power failed; old John Brown has failed. The slave-power spilled the blood of innocent men and women in abundance, but could not establish slavery in Kansas. Old John Brown has spilled some blood—mainly his own and that of his followers, however,—but has not established Freedom in Virginia. It has been a draw game on both sides. But observe this marked difference . . . that in that Insurrection against Freedom, the whole power and influence of the General Government were on the side of the Insurrectionists . . . old John Brown has had to encounter the whole power of the nation. . . .

According to the *Republican*, the slave-power was not only first to set the example, but was directly responsible for Brown's action:

Old John Brown came to Kansas, some say a non-resident, at least a man who had lived a quiet, peaceful, God-fearing life. He came here to make a home for himself and family. The slave power met him here and attempted to drive him out. It burned his home and that of his sons. It took one of his sons and marched him in chains over the prairies and under a broiling sun until he was a raving maniac. It invaded the little town where the old man lived, pillaged and burned it, and murdered another of his sons in cold blood. From that hour old Brown vowed eternal vengance upon the slave-power. . . . Deeply pious, his monomaniacy assumed the type of religious fanaticism, and he became thoroughly possessed of the idea that he was God's chosen instrument. . . .

These editorials contain allegations as well as implications that would be most significant but for mixture with glaring errors. Possibly because of or in spite of the errors, they are still significant. The first point is that Brown's idea that he had a divine commission to overthrow slavery was treated as though it were a matter of common knowledge, and especially in the first, where the only element of surprise was that he may have attempted to put his ideas into execution. The second is the fixing of the date at which this became an obsession with him; after the killing of his son Frederick at Osawatomie, August 30, 1856. This was over three months after the Potawatomie massacre.

The *Republican* met the charge of republican party complicity by giving "the Leavenworth *Herald*, followed by the smaller curs in the Democratic kennel" an object lesson in their own line of argument. It had become known that Governor Willard of Indiana, one of the most prominent administration democrats, was the brother-in-law of John E. Cook, one of Brown's raiders; therefore, according to democratic logic the democratic party was responsible for the insurrection.[10] As did other republican papers, the *Re-*

[10] Lawrence *Republican*, November 10, 1859.

publican of Lawrence attempted to divert attention from the main issue by attacking the court in connection with the "so-called trial," declaring that "It is a horrible farce," and beyond all question he should be placed in an asylum—"The men who made John Brown crazy, who murdered his sons and outraged his family, are the men who ought to be tried for their lives." [11]

The theme was developed further at the time of the execution:

> The telegraph brings us the closing scenes of the judicial murder of John Brown. Heretofore we have called attention to the inhuman disregard of all forms of judicial proceedings, and the cruel violation of every sanctity which experience and wisdom has thrown around courts of justice, dealing with a human being for his life, in the so-called trial of the soldier of 1812.
>
> Wounded to death's door, unable from the loss of blood from haggard wounds made after his surrender, the old man, without one hour's delay, was hurried to a trial for his life. He was arraigned upon three distinct charges of as many distinct crimes, and forced to meet them *all* at the same time. Yet, notwithstanding all this, there was not a title of undisputed testimony to fasten the guilt of the alleged offences upon him. He neither committed treason, murder, nor incited slaves to rebellion. In all this, he himself insisted he was *guiltless,* and even Gov. Wise was forced to confess that Brown was a truthful, brave man.
>
> All that was necessary to complete the horror of the old man's conviction was the brutal way he was executed. Think of it. Two thousand armed men summoned from all parts of panic-stricken Virginia to attend at the execution. . . . No friend accompanies the heroic convict. . . . Virginia dreaded his magnanimous words, his living thoughts. That memorable courage of his when Virginia pronounced upon him the sentence of death, still rung in the ears of the Old Dominion. They wanted no more such as that. There was too much terrible truth.[12]

That every point made alleging irregularities in the trial has been demonstrated to have been false in no wise minimizes the importance of the charges, because falsehood believed is fact for the history of the building of a legend. As it happened Francis Lieber's book on *Civil Liberty* had only recently been published, and was used to add force to the criticism of the trial, because Lieber had said that *"the trial for treason is the gauge of Liberty."* [13] One of the important factors which aided the process of canonization was the remarkable rhetorical quality of Brown's speech before the court, which was recognized immediately by the

[11] Lawrence *Republican,* November 3, 1859.
[12] Lawrence *Republican,* December 8, 1859.
[13] Lawrence *Republican,* December 8, 1859.

comment that "for sublimity and solemn appeal, [it] has not been excelled since Paul spoke before King Agrippa." [14]

The first issue of the *Herald of Freedom* after the raid was that of October 22, in which was printed a telegraphic story borrowed from the Leavenworth *Herald*, together with G. W. Brown's own editorial comment that

Brown is crazy, but "he has method in his madness," and is a dangerous person to be at liberty. The idea of a successful negro insurrection, in the heart of Virginia, is just as impracticable as it is for a few crazy fanatics like Brown, Redpath and Lane, to overthrow the Federal Government by acts of theirs. Poor, silly fellows! A straight jacket should be their reward, for they lack moral responsibility because of lunacy.

It was not until the following week, however, that the *Herald of Freedom* opened its campaign to "ventilate" Kansas history. Taking as a text the Atchison *Champion's* editorial on the theme of the peaceful Pennsylvania farmer crazed by pro-slavery wrongs, G. W. Brown reviewed briefly, moderately, and with approximate accuracy the story of the Brown family in Kansas:

The first thing the people of Kansas heard of Old Brown was in the summer of 1855. A meeting of Ultra Abolitionists was held at Cazenovia,[15] N. Y., if we recollect rightly. While in session Brown, who is a native of Essex county, N. Y., appeared in that convention and made a very fiery speech, during which he said he had four sons in Kansas, and he had three others who were desirous of going there, and to aid in fighting the battles of freedom. He could not consent to go unless he could go *armed*, and he would like to arm his sons, but was not able to do so. Funds were contributed upon the spot, principally by Gerrit Smith.

Four sons had located on Pottawatomie creek, in Lykins county, and in the fall of 1855 were joined by the father and other brothers. When the Wakarusa war was pending the old man and four sons arrived in Lawrence, the balance reported sick. As they drove up in front of the Free State Hotel they were standing in a small lumber wagon. To each of their persons was strapped a short heavy broad sword. Each was supplied with a goodly number of fire arms, and navy revolvers, and poles were standing endwise around the wagon box with fixed bayonets pointing upwards. They looked really formidable and were received with great eclat. A small military company was organized at once and the command was given to Old Brown. From that hour he commenced fomenting difficulties in camp, disregarding the commands of superior officers, and trying to induce the men to go down to Franklin and make an attack upon the Pro-slavery forces encamped there. The Committee of Public Safety was called upon several times to head off his wild adventure, as the people of Lawrence had planted themselves on the law,

[14] Lawrence *Republican*, December 15, 1859. Editorial.
[15] Correction made November 26, naming Syracuse as place of meeting.

claiming that they had not been guilty of its infraction, and that no *armed* body of men should enter the town for any purpose whatever, and that they should not go out of town to attack any such body. Peace was established, and "Old Brown" *retired in disgust.*

When the news of the threatened siege of Lawrence reached John Brown, Jr., who was a member of the Topeka Legislature, he organized a company of about sixty men and marched towards Lawrence. Arriving at Palmyra he learned of the sacking of the town, and the position of the people. He reconnoitered for a time in the vicinity, but finally marched back towards Osawatomie. The night before reaching that place, when only a few miles away, they camped for the night. Old John Brown, who we believe was with the party, singled out, with himself, seven men. These he marched to a point eight miles above the mouth of Pottawatomie creek, and called from their beds at their several residences, at the hour of midnight, on the 24th of May, Allen Wilkinson, Wm. Sherman, Wm. P. Doyle, Wm. Doyle, and Drury Doyle. All were found the next morning, by the road side, or in the highway, some with a gash in their heads and sides, and their throats cut; others with their skulls split open in two places, with holes in their breasts, and hands cut off; and others had holes through their breasts with their fingers cut off. No man in Kansas has pretended to deny that Old John Brown led that murderous foray, which massacred those men. Up to that period not a hair of Old John Brown's head, or that of any of his sons, had been injured by the Pro-slavery party.

It was not until the 30th of August, three months after the Potawatomie massacre that the attack was made on Osawatomie by the Pro-slavery forces and FREDERICK BROWN, a son of Old John was killed.

The truth of history requires this statement. If Brown *was* a monomaniac, it dates back anterior to his first visit to Kansas.[16]

The Brown theme was developed further in another article in the same issue under the heading "The Harper's Ferry Tragedy —Originated in Kansas":

More than once during the summer of 1857, we asserted that the reason the "Do Nothings," as we called them, were opposed to engaging in the Territorial elections of that year, and competing with the Pro-Slavery party for the offices of the government, was found in the fact that they wished to prolong our Kansas difficulties; to keep the Territory in a constant ferment; that their design was revolution, and anything which looked like a peaceful solution of our troubles, had been and would be violently opposed by them. We stated that those who led off in the Do-Nothing policy had no material interest in Kansas in common with the settlers; that they were "birds of passage"; came here like buzzards to feed on dead carcasses; and as soon as the period should come when there was nothing left for them to feast upon they would leave the Territory. We charged them with subsisting almost wholly on funds sent here from the charitable in the East to supply the wants of the destitute and suffering.

16 *Herald of Freedom*, October 29, 1859.

He charged that most of them were newspaper correspondents; Walden, Thacher, Realf, John E. Cook, J. H. Lane, Kagi, Phillips, Redpath, Hinton and Company; and that such men as these attempted to prevent participation in the territorial election in October of 1857, and the election of state officers under the Lecompton constitution, and took steps to seize the persons implicated in the Oxford election frauds, which, if not prevented, would have brought on retaliation from Missouri:

The business men of Lawrence will remember the *insane* movement of James H. Lane and these anti-peace men, who projected the idea of murdering the delegates to the Lecompton Constitutional Convention, while on their way to resume their labors in October, and the *ordering* of the whole country to assemble at Lecompton with arms and four day's provisions, to take that town and *hang* the members of the Convention. They will call to mind the meeting in Duncan's building, followed by the one in front of the Morrow House, in Lawrence, when he was headed off in that demon work, and the contemplated sanguinary visit to Lecompton was changed into a peaceful one to protest against the Constitution then being framed.

In the list of offences included was the Fort Scott difficulties, backed up by Jim Lane, Old John Brown, Redpath, Phillips and that class of persons:

Then was organized the secret oath-bound league, the object of which was to *murder,* in cold blood, every officer elected under the Lecompton Constitution, be he a Free State man or otherwise. The pass-word to that secret organization was LANE. The whole plan of assassination, of relays of horses for the executioners, &c., are in the possession of good men in Lawrence, and have been for a long period.

But there was a peaceful adjustment of these matters, because Congress did not give legal sanction to the Lecompton Swindle. The southeastern border, however, was made the pretext for keeping alive this war movement. . . . Old John Brown, with his minions . . . appeared and took charge of the marauding forces. . . . When Montgomery discovered Brown & Co.'s plans of revolution, to his credit be it said, he protested, and in consequence of their quarrel, probably more than anything else, the latter made a brilliant *coup 'd etat* into Missouri, killed Crew, took his slaves, etc.

The *Herald of Freedom* insisted that Brown's plan was well known in Kansas, and earlier was to have been staged in Missouri, but, on being frustrated, Brown had turned to Virginia, and "since its failure, every one will deny being cognizant of it. . . ."

Persistence on the part of radical republican papers in harping on the theme of Brown's peaceful mission and the wrongs that made him mad led the *Herald of Freedom* to repetition of the opposite dogma, that he came armed, attempted to foment trouble at the time of the Wakarusa war and committed acts of violence repeatedly. Vallandigham's interview with Brown, published widely, was seized upon as complete proof. When Brown was asked how long he had been engaged in the business, he replied "From the breaking out of the difficulties in Kansas. Four of my sons had gone there to settle, and they induced me to go. I did not go there to settle, but because of the difficulties." [17]

G. W. Brown was one of those argumentative editors who flourished on the frontier, thrived on controversy, and lost all inhibitions in their desire to have the last word, even to the point of revealing their own deviations from truth:

> A gentleman remarked the other day, that the time had come when the history of Kansas should be thoroughly ventilated. During the disturbances of 1855–56, it was not to be expected that the politicians on either side would expose the wickedness of their own party. They could not do it, had they desired, from the fact that it was impossible, with the then state of the country, to understand the real facts transpiring around them. Their standpoint took in but a small portion of the then political horizon. Now, with a good *lens*, they can look out upon the whole field, on each side, and can understand not only the *action,* but the motives which led to such action.
>
> The Eastern presses at this time are attempting to recapitulate some of the incidents of 1856, and are offering them in mitigation of Old John Brown's recent outrages in Virginia; but, instead of giving the *facts* as they transpired, they are only giving exaggerated and partisan statements, made in self-exculpation at the time those "excesses"—as Mr. Buchanan had the modesty to call them—were committed.
>
> The New York *Tribune* and *Herald* each gave a sketch of Old John Brown. From a careful examination of them, we venture the assertion that no articles of similar length could have been published which would have embodied more statements at variance with the truth.

The *Herald* and *Tribune* articles were derived from a common source or one copied from the other, and to illustrate, a sample paragraph was quoted from each for comparison. The *Herald* said:

> One of his sons, who was elected to the Legislature, in February, 1856, was seized and taken from Osawatomie to Lecompton in chains, a distance of thirty miles. His feet and hands were chained together with a large heavy chain, the size of that used upon ox teams. He was compelled to walk the whole distance beneath a burning sun. The irons wore the

[17] *Herald of Freedom*, November 5, 1859.

flesh from his ankles; he was attacked with the brain fever, was neglected, and died in two or three days.

G. W. Brown replied to this by pointing out that John Brown, Jr., the son referred to, was a prisoner with himself until September, 1856, and was living in 1859 in Ohio. He then related the near true story of the insanity of this son of Old Brown:

As we stated last week, he raised a company of his neighbors and friends, and arrived at Palmyra on the 22 d of May, 1856, the day after the destruction of Lawrence. After looking about the vicinity for a day or so, on the 24th of May he marched towards Osawatomie, and arrived near the town, where they encamped for the night. Old John Brown, the father, stepped out in front of the company, and said: "If there are any *brave men* here, let them follow me." JOHN BROWN, Jr., replied: "I have the honor of commanding this company. Whoever leaves it does so at his peril." But Old Brown succeeded in getting seven men to join his company, one of whom was Frederick Brown, a son of the old man, who was subsequently shot while on his way to Osawatomie, on the morning of Aug. 30, '56, and not after he was taken prisoner, as has been alleged. Some of the surviving seven of Old John Brown's party still reside in Kansas. The curse of Almighty God rests on them, and we have no disposition to expose them at present to the public.

On the morning of May 25, one of the heavy broad-swords, alluded to by us last week, which Old John Brown brought to Kansas, was found leaning against a tent, wet with blood and covered with hair. It was pronounced dog's hair, but soon after intelligence was received in camp of the massacre of the Wilkinsons and Doyles, on Pottawatomie creek, John Brown, Jr., immediately mounted his horse, in the greatest possible excitement, ordered his company to disband, and rode towards Osawatomie. The news of the horrid murder alluded to had preceded him, and the people were so shocked on his arrival there, because of it, and supposing John Brown, Jr., guilty of the outrage, they turned on him. He went from there to the residence of his uncle, Rev. Mr. ADAIR, where he had sent his wife and boy. The reports of the awful murder of his neighbors, the consciousness that his father, brother and six other friends had been guilty of that terrible outrage, and the treatment he received at Osawatomie from his own political friends, crazed him. He sought the woods, and wandered about for days, with only an occasional gleam of recollection. He became tangled in the brushwood, waded streams, sometimes out upon the open prairie, and imagining crowds pursuing him. For days he suffered as only a sensitive and educated mind, wrecked by a great wrong like the one we have very briefly alluded to, could suffer. He remembers his little boy once, and kissing him, but cannot call to mind the mother. He learned by some means that a warrant was out for his arrest, charged with *murder*. Conscious of his own innocence, and still having a little spark of memory, he resolved to give himself up to the authorities, which he did. They, believing him guilty of one of the basest crimes recorded in American history, and hardly equalled in atrocity by the savages of the forest, when led on by revenge and madness, treated him in a very barbarous manner. It is true that he was chained and marched in a burning sun some twenty five or thirty miles, to what point we are not advised, probably Paola, but certainly not Lecompton. The fatigue, burning sun, excitement and chains did not, of course, improve his mental condition. He continued wild with delirium, and when brought into camp with the treason prisoners, he showed evidences of a wandering mind for many days afterwards. Yea, for months, whenever conversation turned, as it did sometimes did, upon the Pottawatomie murder, and we attempted to excuse his father for that act, giving the mitigating circumstances current among Free State men at the time, his eyes would sparkle with unwonted brilliancy, his manner would assume the wildest excitement; and in a loud and boisterous voice, which was uncommon to him on other occasions, he would exclaim: "Do not attempt to offer anything in palliation of such a crime! *Nothing* can excuse it! It was unequalled in atrocity, and displayed only *cowardice*. . . ." And thus he would run on for a long time, . . . until his attention was diverted by gradually introducing some other topic, when his excitement would quietly subside. . . .

When released from imprisonment, he expressed a determination to leave Kansas, and its excitements, that he might engage, in some peaceful locality, in tilling the soil, in the hope that he would forget the incidents through which he had passed while sojourning in the Territory, and that his brain might attain its equilibrium.

From this statement it will be seen that the insanity of John Brown, Jr., owed its first cause to other than the barbarity of the Border Ruffians, though their outrages upon him were enough to drive one mad.

We may also state, in this connection, correcting the many statements to the contrary which have appeared in the press, that the dwellings of the Browns, on Pottawatomie creek, were not burned until after the Pottawattomie murder alluded to, and then in retaliation for the damning crime of which John Brown, Senior, Frederick Brown, and their party, were guilty.

We sincerely hope that the future historians of Kansas will take pains to post themselves on these subjects, that they may not do injustice to innocent parties.

Old John Brown has figured as a hero in Kansas. The time will come when history will be *ventilated,* and instead of a hero, he will stand before the country in his true character. Under cover of night, and in the name of religion, he committed crimes too base "for common sinners to meddle with." Should his celebrated victory over Henry Clay Pate, at Black Jack, be properly inquired into, it would be found that Capt. Samuel Shore, now of Prairie City, was the real hero, though too modest and unassuming to even put in his claim, particularly after seeing the statements of the letter-writers, who gave all the glory to Brown.[18]

"The Key" to John Brown's conduct after the Potawatomie massacre was attributed by the *Herald of Freedom* to an attempt

[18] *Herald of Freedom*, November 5, 1859.

"to wipe out the Potawatomie massacre from his mind, appease his conscience, and reinstate himself, as far as possible, in the good opinion of Heaven. To do this he set about freeing the slaves of the South."[19] In the same issue G. W. Brown did a little more ventilating of Kansas history:

A correspondent of the N. Y. *Tribune,* over the signature of "Pennsylvania Republican," attempts to correct the misstatements of the press, relative to Old John Brown, and yet is guilty of as gross errors as were the papers which he pretends to correct. Old John Brown did not emigrate to Kansas from Pennsylvania. No son of his was driven all the way from Osawatomie to Tecumseh, where he died. On the contrary he was *carried* from Paoli in a Government baggage wagon, with several other prisoners, who had a hearing before Judge Hoogland, and all of them were discharged or held to bail, but John Brown, Jr., and H. H. Williams. Neither of these gentlemen died; on the contrary, Williams is now Sheriff of Lykins county, and John Brown, Jr., who is the one represented to have died, is now residing in Ohio, and figures occasionally in the Harpers Ferry correspondence of J. B. Jr., and West Andover, Ashtabula county, Ohio.

Old John Brown never had a house in Kansas, we presume, but lived with his sons. We never heard of any "insult" to any of the women of Brown's family, and doubt the correctness of that statement.

The 14th of September, 1856, the time when the army of 2700 men, under Reid, was marching into Lawrence, there were not to exceed 200 men, all told, in town. Old Brown did take partial command of the inside defenses, but he did not lead the Free State forces with Sharpe's rifles, against the advance forces of 300 of the enemy.

The representation that there were 500 men in town eager for the fray; that Old John Brown felt sanguine of our success, and all that sort of thing, is mere bosh.—Maj. Abbott was first in command. Capt. Walker, with 27 horsemen, and the Wabaunsee Rifles, numbering about 40 men, sallied out to meet the 300 horsemen, and their exhibition of a determination to resist the invasion, was all that saved us from a complete rout before Gov. Geary, with Col. Cooke's battery, arrived, which was at about 9 o'clock that evening.

To read the letters of Eastern correspondents, and editorials in leading journals, one would suppose there was no person else in Kansas during our difficulties, save Old John Brown and his sons.—While we are willing to do full justice to the bravery and honorable bearing of most of the sons, we must repeat that Kansas would have been infinitely better off if it had never been disgraced by the murders and violence of Old John Brown.[20]

[19] *Herald of Freedom,* November 12, 1859.

[20] *Herald of Freedom,* November 12, 1859. The editor attributed the *Tribune* article to his old friend G. B. Delamater, of Crawford county, Pa., and based probably on statements of Brown himself.

In the leading article for November 19, the *Herald of Freedom* again went over most of the ground covering Brown's career in Kansas, because the Lawrence *Republican* had printed a flat denial of the truth of the statements that the Brown murders had been committed prior to the "murder of members of his own family by the Border Ruffians, and the pillage and rapine of his own home and his neighbors." Although the text varied in detail, there was not enough material difference to warrant a summary of the body of the article, but in support of the *Herald of Freedom's* contention, the affidavits of Mrs. Doyle and sons, of Mrs. Wilkinson and of James Harris which had been made in 1856 for the congresisonal committee investigating the Kansas troubles were reprinted. The editor then concluded:

Since reading those affidavits we have heard the details from other living witnesses, some of them are now in Lawrence, but do not desire their names to be made public. . . . Suffice it to say, they agree substantially, and, in fact, in nearly every particular, with the affidavits which we have copied above.

These outrages led to retaliating ones on the part of the Pro-Slavery party. On the 28th of May, four days after, when the news reached Leavenworth, the Pro-Slavery party organized their Virginia Committee, and then commenced the days of terror in that ill-fated city. The renouned battle of Black Jack followed. A party of desperadoes marched against Osawatomie, and on the 8th of June entered the town without resistance, and "commenced a wholesale work of pillage." . . .

If the Republican press wish more facts on this subject, let them continue their villainous charges of *falsehood* against us, and we will continue the history. . . .

The editor, G. W. Brown, had been active in securing additional evidence, and in the same issue as the above printed an unusual story, which, among other things, seemed to implicate James Redpath. Although the part dealing with Redpath has never been substantiated, other aspects of the article are of particular interest:

A living witness, whose character for truth and veracity no man has ever called in question, so far as we know, will furnish us an affidavit stating that on the night of May 24, 1856, he was in camp with the company of John Brown, Jr., near Osawatomie, and only a few miles from the scene of the Potawatomie murders, which occurred a few hours after; that *Old John Brown* was there, as was James Redpath; that 'bad blood,' to use the narrator's term, seemed to exist between Old John Brown and the son, Capt. John Brown, Jr.; that he, our informant, left camp, and started for his residence, a few miles from Lawrence, travelling nearly all night; that two days after, a Free State neighbor, whom he left in Brown's camp, returned and informed him of the horrible murder, and of the mutilated bodies and he expressed regret that he had ever taken up arms in defense of the Free State cause, if it led to such awful results.

Old John Brown led that murderous foray, though he has frequently stated that *he* did not strike a blow. *Redpath* says he knows that Old Brown was sixty miles away from the scene of that outrage, on that fatal night. We are ready to prove, as stated above, that at *eight o'clock that night* Redpath was not eight miles away, and was then in company with Old John Brown. We leave it with the public to make their own deductions.[21]

As the *Herald of Freedom* saw it, the status of the Brown problem may be summarized as follows: Brown went to Kansas to fight and not for peaceful purposes, therefore the border ruffians could be held responsible for his career of violence; Brown had no wife and family in Kansas and would not have brought them on such a mission; Brown had no house in Kansas and therefore it could not have been burned by the border ruffians; Brown's sons' houses were not burned until after the massacre; Brown's sons were not killed prior to the Potawatomie massacre; free-state settlers were not threatened or molested prior to the massacre; the Brown women were not insulted by the border ruffians prior to the massacre; Brown was present at the Potawatomie massacre and was the leader of the foray; Brown was not a resident of Osawatomie; R. P. Brown was killed by border ruffians four months prior to the massacre but there was no family connection between him and John Brown; the Doyles and Wilkinson were not Buford men; and finally the reasons for the Potawatomie massacre were political and religious in the sense that the only offense of the victims was their political views and John Brown claimed a divine appointment to wage war against slavery. The paper insisted also that Frederick Brown was the only son implicated with his father in the massacre, and that the younger John Brown was not only innocent of the crime, but opposed it, and was driven insane by the horror of the crime of his father and brother. The defense of Lawrence in 1855, at the time of the Wakarusa war, was dealt with twice, and in both articles the same view was presented, that Brown advocated an attack on the pro-slavery forces gathered at Franklin, and one of the articles went further and charged

[21] There were two articles of the same tenor, the second of which argued from Redpath's own statements in the Boston *Atlas and Bee* and the N .Y. *Tribune* that Redpath was with the Brown party which committed the murders, or else he lied in claiming ''a knowledge of the fact, that Old John Brown was more than sixty miles distant. . . .''

him with attempting to prevent the popular endorsement of the peace treaty. In connection with the defense of Lawrence in September 1856, it was pointed out that Brown had a partial command within the town, but was not in command of the general defense, and did not even participate in the skirmishing outside the defenses on that occasion. On the other hand in correction of pro-slavery misrepresentations of John Brown, the same paper declared false the charge of the Atchison *Union* that he was an Illinois horsethief, as well as that of the Evansville (Indiana) *Enquirer* that he was for two years an inmate of the Kentucky penitentiary serving sentence for running off slaves from Morgansfield county, Kentucky, just prior to the presidential election of 1856. The editor claimed that the John Brown in question had been convicted in 1855, had served his term and been released in May 1857, had been a resident of Henderson county, Kentucky, and after his release had gone to Indianapolis, Indiana, where his family had moved while he was in prison.[22]

Attacks on G. W. Brown led to the explanation to the N. Y. *Tribune* that such procedure would not change the course of the *Herald of Freedom,* that nothing had been published in connection with the Brown question except with the intention of putting the facts on record. In reply to the inquiry why this had not been done sooner, it was pointed out that part of the story had been published in a series of articles under the title of "The Jayhawker" during the last spring and summer, but "if it had not been for the falsehoods of the New York journals, and some of our Territorial newspapers, edited by newcomers, we should not have spoken now. . . ."[23] The statement about newcomers is interesting. Only three of the important editors of 1859 had been active editors through the Civil War of 1856; G. W. Brown (Lawrence), W. W. Ross (Topeka), and L. J. Eastin (Leavenworth). No doubt that fact helps to explain many of the reactions of the press in 1859, and much the same would apply to the population in general. In Kansas the turnover of population had been so rapid that only a few knew anything of that year of disorder or of John Brown except from hearsay.[24]

22 *Herald of Freedom,* December 3, 1859.
23 *Herald of Freedom,* November 26, 1859.
24 On the general subject of the turnover of farm population in Kansas see the present author's article under that title in the *Kansas Historical Quarterly,* 4 (November 1935) 339-72.

Brown's own statements concerning his Kansas exploits aroused immediate discussion in connection with the *Herald of Freedom's* "ventilation" of Kansas history. The New York *Herald* reporter gave Brown's answer to the question whether he had killed Sherrard in Kansas. This was during the Mason-Vallandigham interview, and Brown replied: "I killed no man except in fair fight; I fought at Black Jack Point and Osawatomie, and if I killed anybody, it was at one of those places." This purported to be a verbatim report of the interview, and by enumeration it excluded any killing on his part at Potawatomie, although it was silent on the question of whether he had led the party of killers on that occasion. The interview occurred on October 19 and antedated the controversy precipitated by G. W. Brown. In the Lowry interview, Brown was reported as saying: "Time and the honest verdict of posterity will approve of every act of mine to prevent slavery from being established in Kansas. I never shed the blood of a fellow man except in self-defense or in promotion of a righteous cause." This was in direct reply to a query which involved the charges being made by the *Herald of Freedom* regarding the Potawatomie massacre. The declaration is not so specific as in the *Herald* report, but Lowry explained in his version that he took no notes at the time and reproduced the conversation from memory and wrote it out after his return to Erie, Pennsylvania. Editor Brown pointed out that in the Lowry version John Brown had not denied the Potawatomie killing, but had evaded the direct issue.[25] Brown's friends did not draw such nice distinctions, however, and in the creation of the Legend of John Brown interpreted both of these statements as denials. A more specific and much less widely quoted statement was printed over the name of "Milton" which alleged that John Brown told the writer "that he had no hand in it [Potawatomie massacre]," and that a man who was a participant informed him also that John Brown "had nothing to do with it."[26] John Brown left no statement on these matters in his own hand or over his own signature.

Members of the Brown family were drawn into the controversy, John Brown's brother, J. R. Brown, answering the *Herald of Freedom* charge in a letter to the Cleveland *Plaindealer* dated November 22, 1859:

[25] *Herald of Freedom,* December 17, 1859.
[26] Lawrence *Republican,* January 5, 1859.

My brother, at the time William Doyle and others were killed, was not present, did not assent to the act, nor had any knowledge of it, and was eighteen miles distant at the time of the occurrence.

My brother and his two sons were living in the same neighborhood, and a committee of five from the Border Ruffian camp called upon him, said that they were instructed to warn him that, if Free-State men were found there next Thursday night, they would be killed every one of them, and they could command force enough to carry the threat into execution. My brother replied to them that he should not be found there, as before this, he had made his arrangements to be in another part of the Territory. It was known to the Free-State men of that section that this threat to destroy them had been made, and, before Thursday night came, Doyle and others were destroyed—they being of the number of those who had been threatened the destruction of the Free-State settlers. The effect of this was, the Border Ruffians became terror-stricken, and left the Territory.

I have this account of this affair from my brother and his two sons; also from a sister and brother-in-law (now living in Kansas) who had personal knowledge of this transaction; and the statements of all of whom upon any subject were never yet questioned by anyone having anything like a perfect knowledge of their characters.[27]

Another family statement came from Salmon Brown December 27, 1859 in reply to a direct question from Rev. Joshua Young:

I was one of his company at the time of the *homicides* and was never away from him one hour at a time after we took up arms in Kansas. *Therefore I say positively that he was not a partcipator in the deed.* Although I should think none the less of him if he had been for it was the grandest thing that was ever done in Kansas. It was all that saved the territory from being over run with drunken land pirates from the Southern States. . . .[28]

The typical Brown Legend quibble is to be found in the use of the word "participator," a word which gave the impression unquestionably that John Brown was not present or even a member of the party of killers, but which Villard held was not an untruthful statement, because, although John Brown was the leader of the party, it was claimed that he did not kill, but left the killing to the men under him. In writing to R. J. Hinton January 10, 1860, Salmon said:

We received a letter from Mr. Redpath in which he says that Gov. Robinson said that he thought that Capt Brown confessed to him that he helped

[27] Clipping in Webb, *Scrapbooks*, 17: 127.

[28] This letter was first printed correctly in Villard, p. 612, note 90. It had been printed with an important error by Sanborn, pp. 261–62, which made Salmon say categorically that John Brown was not "there."

kill the Doyls. if Gov R said so he lies. In the first place Father never
put any confidence in *Robinson* after that Lawrence treaty in Dec. 55 or
56 and in the next place he would not lie to make him or any other skoun-
drel believe that he helped kill those spies for they believed it without.
I never knew him to try to steal any bodies thunder.   And surely the men
that struck the first blow with the sword against slavery in this country
had not ought to be called murderer in this case they were life preservers
and they saved Kansas.   I *think* now is the time to make another demonstration.   It will not do to have any reaction.[29]

The most complete and specific denial came from C. A. Foster,
a radical from Osawatomie, who was in Boston during the summer
of 1860.   He wrote out his statement for T. H. Webb, secretary
of the New England Emigrant Aid Company, dating it July 12,
1860:

Was John Brown present and participating in the massacre on Potawatomie Creek—John Brown has told S. L. Adair, Wm Hutchinson, Judge
Russell, & T. H. Webb that he was not present, but that he knew it was
going to be done, that he approved it, the men deserved it & the evidence
that they did was in his own possession.
    And T ——— y of Greely & W ——— r of St. Louis who were pres-
ent, and participating, also say he was not present.[30]

There was no quibble in Foster's statement, he used both words
"present and participating," and it is significant that he quoted
James Townsley and Theodore Wiener.   Under the circumstances
there can be little question that Foster's testimony was deliberately
false.

Had the accusations against John Brown been made only by
Southern or pro-slavery papers, they probably could have been
silenced by blanket denials, but when made by G. W. Brown in
his *Herald of Freedom,* it was a different matter.   He had been
not only the leading Kansas free-state editor, but he possessed an
innate capacity to create dissention.   For the most part, replies
took the form of personal attacks on G. W. Brown; some accused
him of selling out to the democrats in return for public printing;
Redpath ridiculed him as a coward; and all the opposition called
him liar and slanderer.   The *Herald of Freedom* discontinued
publication with the issue of December 17, 1859 and the editor
returned to the East, as he said, for supplies.   In January his wife
filed suit for divorce and the enemies exulted: "This slanderer of

---

[29] The original is in the *Hinton Papers,* Kansas State Historical Society.
[30] The original of this statement was deposited by Mrs. H. A. Webb with
the K. S. H. S., in 1878 as a part of the T. H. Webb *Collection.* The dis-
guised names were Townsley and Wiener.

the living and the dead is thus held up before the world by his own wife as an adulterer and an inhuman monster. The footsteps of justice are sometimes slow, but terribly sure at the last." [31] The divorce case was in the hands of General Smith and S. N. Wood, who carried the bill through the territorial legislature, receiving the approval of the Governor February 13, 1860.[32] Reports were relayed from Pennsylvania papers that G. W. Brown had called a public meeting to purge himself of the charge of treason and "to justify his cowardly and false attack upon John Brown. He made his speech but in the course of it, was confronted by John Brown, Jr., and branded as a liar and defamer of the dead. . . . Thus is it always with those who sell their principles for gain." [33] No doubt G. W. Brown was writing from the heart just after Thanksgiving day that "it is a good time to *wipe out* old partisan and individual feuds, and commence again. We need just such a day as often as once a year. . . . An *Amnesty Act* is needed in Kansas for other than political offenses, at least once a year, while occupying our chrysalis State." [34]

ANTI-SLAVERY SOCIETIES ORGANIZED

The *Herald of Freedom* declared that as a result of Old John Brown's raid real anti-slavery progress in that state "will be retarded half a century." [35] On the other hand, the correspondent of the Lawrence *Republican* wrote that "it is safe to say, that the death of no other man in America has ever produced so profound a sensation. . . . A feeling of deep and sorrowful indignation seems to possess the masses. The religious element is most profoundly stirred." [36] The anti-slavery forces in the East were determined to capitalize on every advantage, regardless of the politicians. The call for a mass meeting at Lawrence was as follows:

[31] Lawrence *Republican*, January 19, 1860.

[32] Private Laws of the Territory of Kansas, 1860, p. 234. S. N. Wood managed the bill in the House of Representatives. See *Journal*, Special Session, 1860, 217, 222–23.

[33] Atchison *Champion*, February 16, 1860. The present author has not found any confirmation of this particular episode, but local Pennsylvania papers may substantiate it. G. W. Brown did return to Kansas in 1860, sold his equipment, and entered upon a project to bore an oil well in Linn county. The venture was unsuccessful. Cf. Ch. 31.

[34] *Herald of Freedom*, November 26, 1859.

[35] *Herald of Freedom*, November 5, 26, 1859.

[36] Lawrence *Republican*, December 22, 1859.

It having been recommend by the Anti-Slavery friends at the East
that Friday, the 2ᵈ day of December, on which day John Brown is to be
hung, should be made "the occasion of a public moral demonstration against
the bloody and merciless slave system," we, the undersigned, therefore invite the citizens of Douglas county to assemble in mass meeting, in Lawrence, on that day—not to justify Capt. Brown in his raid into Virginia,
but to show sympathy for the disinterested nature of his motives, and our
admiration for his unflinching courage and manly bravery—eliciting, as
it does, the praise of the entire South, and to testify against that party
whose enormities in Kansas were the cause of John Brown's so-called
madness." [37]

The meeting was held under the auspices of the more radical
men in Douglas county; a committee was appointed to arrange for
the organization of county and township anti-slavery societies at
a meeting to be held December 16, the occasion of the hanging of
John Brown's associates; and eleven resolutions were adopted
unanimously the last three of which related to John Brown. Of
these three, one expressed confidence in his integrity and noble-
ness of motives; another although admitting differences of opinion
respecting the wisdom of his plans, declared that he had laid down
his life for the rights of man, and the third related to Kansas:

Resolved, That we especially declare our respect and esteem for John
Brown, in reference to his labors in Kansas, knowing him to have been
a true and disinterested friend of freedom here; and that he was among
the first to teach the Border-Ruffian invaders of our soil the wholesome
lesson, that oppressors of the poor might be made to "bite the dust," and
to flee from our soil, at a time when they imagined that their foulest dreams
were on the eve of being realized.[38]

It was announced that General Lane and Judge Conway were
to be among the speakers at the second meeting,[39] but in addition,
the reports of the meeting show that the conservative element was
represented in the person of Charles Robinson as well as others.
At the second, or evening session, on December 16, the climax was
reached in the debate on eight resolutions reported for adoption.
On this subject the secretary recorded in the official minutes only
that "The resolutions were at a late hour adopted unanimously,
save the last which was by a majority. In regard to the last reso-

[37] Lawrence *Republican,* December 1, 1859.

[38] Lawrence *Republican,* December 8, 1859. *Herald of Freedom,* December
10, 1859.

[39] Lawrence *Republican,* December 15, 1859.

lution there seemed to be a general unanimity of feeling of the justness of the executions referred to in the resolution.'' [40]

The resolution in question was:

> *Resolved,* That whereas the statements originated in the so called "Herald of Freedom," of this place, respecting the connection of John Brown with the execution of the Doyle family and others are calculated to lessen the sympathy in favor of the gallant hero, we the members of this convention do unhesitatingly affirm our belief in the fact that John Brown is not guilty of the charges of cruelty made against him, and that according to the ordinary rules of war said transaction was not unjustifiable, but that it was performed from the sad necessity which existed at that time to defend the lives and liberties of the settlers in that region.

The most significant aspect of this resolution is that it was an admission that John Brown was responsible for the Potawatomie massacre, the only issue being whether the act was justifiable. Of course the *Herald of Freedom* was exultant at this particular outcome of the meeting, and published five separate editorial articles on different phases of the subject.[41] The most important of the articles entitled ''The truth of history vindicated at last'' was devoted to a summary of the debate on the Potawatomie massacre resolution. Captain Samuel Walker declared that John Brown told him that he was present and approved, and admitted further that ''he [Walker] knew more about the matter than he thought it best to reveal, as there were persons then present in the room, who might be implicated.'' Charles Robinson was called upon and stated that it was best that the truth come out, that he believed that Brown had told him that he was connected with it, and that he understood that it was justified by circumstances. Robinson thought that the only difference between himself and G. W. Brown was on the issue, whether the massacre was justified, and the latter thought not. Robinson admitted that he cooperated with John Brown during the war of 1856, but when peace had been established he objected to Brown's interference and repudiated him. Allen and Deitzler sustained the views of Robinson. The Rev. S. L. Adair, the relative at whose home Brown often stayed near Osawatomie, admitted that John Brown had told him substantially the same story as related by Walker. Someone made the remark that although Brown was present, he did not act and

---

[40] *Herald of Freedom,* December 17, 1859. Lawrence *Republican,* December 29, 1859.
[41] *Herald of Freedom,* December 17, 1859.

therefore he was clear of blood.[42]   At that point, however, Robinson intervened with the cold logic that it made no difference, as
Brown was present, aiding and advising, and did not stop it, he
was responsible, though justifiable according to his understanding of affairs.[43]   On the main points in this report of debate the
Herald of Freedom was corroborated by the correspondent of the
Indianapolis *Journal* writing under a Lawrence date line December 17.[44]

Not only did published opinions of Brown vary, but private
letters reveal similar conflicts.   One case of particular interest is
that of the Everetts.   John Everett lived about two miles south of
Osawatomie in 1856 and took the non-resistant attitude in the
troubles, refusing to bear arms.[45]   After the execution of John
Brown, however, his wife wrote a fiery letter to a relative in the
East in defense of Brown: "If anybody knows of another way let
them attempt it and when they shall have succeeded I will submit
to hear the epithet misguided applied to that glorified Hero."[46]
In the same letter Mrs. Everett quoted Adair as describing John
Brown as "a man that had always been from his childhood impressed with the idea that God had raised him up on purpose to
break the jaws of the wicked."

On the other hand, Hugh M. Moore, a Pennsylvania whig, in
business at Topeka, held that the republican and democratic parties were equally corrupt and the only political hope lay in a new
third party independent of the slavery question: "You in the states
do not feel it as we do in Kansas.   Our people have got tired of
the question of Slavery.   That question has been happily settled
in our Territory & to the satisfaction of the majority."   He ab-

[42] The *Herald of Freedom* attributed the remark to Adair, but William
Hutchinson claimed in the *Republican*, December 29, 1859, that the remark was
his.

[43] The pronoun "his" occurs at both places in the article where Robinson spoke on the matter of justifiability, and is ambiguous.   The pronoun
might refer to either Brown's understanding of affairs or Robinson's understanding.   The point is particularly interesting because in later years Robinson was to take the ground that he (Robinson) did not understand the facts
at that time and on fuller information changed his mind on the matter of
justifiability.

[44] Undated clipping in Webb, *Scrapbooks*, 2: 1.

[45] Robert E. Everett to his son John in Kansas, dated Remsen, New York,
June 11, 1856.   John Everett to his father dated Osawatomie December 4,
1856.   *Everett Papers*, K. S. H. S.

[46] Sarah Everett to Jennie.   December 31, 1859.   *Everett Papers*, K. S.
H. S.

hored John Brown, ''a peculiar man and a blood thirsty villin
[sic] he was the Cause of a great deal of Blood shead in Kansas
he was a murderer & hanging was too good for him in my opinion
He Mr Brown Boasted in Kansas that he had a deadly Enmity
against all pro-slavery men & that he him self had killed 13 men
in cold blood.'' [47]

POLITICAL CONSEQUENCES IN KANSAS

The political consequences of Harpers Ferry were significant.
The first pointed example was M. F. Conway, candidate for congressman under the Wyandotte constitution. At first it was
thought that no member of the republican slate was tinctured with
John Brownism, but charges were made that Conway had acted
for Brown in taking custody of certain boxes of mysterious character, and a letter of Gerrit Smith's to John Brown was seized at
Harpers Ferry and published which mentioned Conway's contributions to the cause and his possession of certain papers. Strictly
speaking Conway's name was not used, but he was identified beneath the pseudonym. Of course he denied any knowledge of
Brown's plans. [48]   G. W. Brown sent John A. Halderman, Conway's democratic opponent, three hundred copies of the November
19 issue of the *Herald of Freedom,* the one which ventilated Kansas history, for use in the campaign. [49]   The election took place four
days after the execution of Brown, and whether it was John Brownism or the good reputation of his democratic opponent, John A.
Halderman, Conway ran about four per cent behind the ticket and
conservative Charles Robinson the candidate for governor, the loss
going for the most part to Halderman.

It happened that Abraham Lincoln was scheduled to make a
tour of Kansas during the early winter, and for such a delicate
mission, Brownism was most embarrassing. Apparently he made
six speeches, only two of which were reported, the Elwood and
Leavenworth speeches. [50]   In both he condemned the Harpers
Ferry raid, and in the second he warned that, if as a result of the

[47] H. M. Moore to William Moore, an uncle, Perry County, Pennsylvania.
January 9, 1860. Kansas State Historical Society. Typed copies.

[48] The principal documents and editorials on this controversy are to be
found in the two Lawrence newspapers for November and December.

[49] G. W. Brown to Halderman, November 19, 1859. *John A. Halderman
Papers,* K. S. H. S.

[50] The most convenient place to find them is Paul M. Angle (Compiler)
New letters and papers of Lincoln. (Boston: Houghton, 1930) 227–36.

election of a republican president, the South should attempt to break the Union, it would be the President's duty to deal with them as John Brown had been dealt with. The conservative *Herald of Freedom* was supporting Chase and Bates for the republican nomination, the radical republican journals supported Seward. It was pointed out that Seward with his "irrepressible conflict" and John Brown at Harpers Ferry were the same thing.[51] Kansas was not a Lincoln territory that year. The republican convention of April 11, 1860 instructed its delegation to vote for Seward. It is just one indication of how the tide had set in by the spring of 1860.[52]

The most bitter political fruit of the Brown controversy was its contribution to the feud between Lane and Robinson, leaders respectively of radicalism and conservatism in the republican party. On December 14, 1859, the United States ordered an investigation of the Harpers Ferry invasion, and on February 10, 1860 Charles Robinson testified before the commission. So far as publicly recorded, there are two parts to his testimony, that printed in the official report of the committee, and that excluded on the ground that it was hearsay but which was summarized in the newspapers. As printed officially Robinson declared that John Brown told him he did not come to settle, or establish a free-state government but to create difficulties; that Brown expected the Kansas troubles to spread into a general abolition war; that Geary's peace prevented the consummation of such plans in 1856; that in the later difficulties in southeast Kansas, Montgomery was the principal actor; that James Redpath in particular avowed the purpose of keeping up the difficulties in Kansas; that Redpath quarreled with Lane in 1858, called on Robinson in Lawrence and revealed the whole plot; that there was a plan for a general massacre of pro-slavery men announced at Lawrence in Robinson's presence, which would have extended to Missouri, but the opposition was so decisive it was dropped; the only connection with Brown was that Redpath declared that he expected his participation; and that only a limited number were in the secret, mostly

---

[51] *Herald of Freedom*, November 26, 1859.

[52] In the territorial house of representatives, January 31, 1860, a bill was under consideration for the abolition of slavery in Kansas, when W. L. McMath, moved a substitute declaring that John Brownism was the result of the Seward doctrine. The boys had their fun and laid the substitute on the table. *Journal*, Special session, 1860, p. 159–60.

the newspaper letter-writters for Eastern papers the majority of whom were foreigners.[53]

The newspaper report of Robinson's testimony which did duty particularly in Kansas was that of the Worcester (Massachusetts) *Spy*, reprinted in the Lawrence (Kansas) *Republican*, March 1, 1860, and elsewhere. The witness stated that the one attempt to set on foot a revolution was led by Lane; that after the creation of the Military Board Robinson heard Lane give orders to the Brigadier Generals to strike at several points in the territory, to slaughter pro-slavery men; that on information from Leonhardt, he learned that Lane had gone into southeastern Kansas with the purpose of attacking Ft. Scott, but the presence of federal troops prevented, and Robinson now understood that it was a part of a concerted plan of revolution.

The testimony of another Kansas man, Augustus Wattles, a radical abolitionist, is of interest by way of contrast. He emphasized that John Brown and sons came to Kansas to settle, taking with them blooded cattle and selected nursery stock; that "Captain Brown told me that he had no idea of fighting until he heard the Missourians, during the winter he was there, make arrangements to come over into the Territory to vote;" that his operations were only defensive and his military activities and abolition talk was only such as was common at the time.[54]   Of course Wattles's friendly intention was to protect John Brown's reputation and possibly his own person.   So far as his testimony can be verified, nearly every statement was false or misleading, partly probably through faults of a memory that seemed incapable of being exact, and there is a strong suspicion that in part the errors were deliberate.

The Robinson-Lane feud was of long standing and regardless of whether or not Robinson's statements were substantially true, there can be little question that he made the most of his opportunity to place Lane in as bad a light as possible.   Robinson knew that the republican party was condemning the John Brown raid and, assuming that the public would follow this lead, he could scarcely be suspected of not realizing that as Lane was already

[53] *Report* of Mason's committee on Harpers Ferry, S. rpt, 278, 36 Congress, 1 session (Public document no. 1040) pp. 196–200.   Other Kansas men called before the committee were W. F. N. Arny, Martin F. Conway and Augustus Wattles.

[54] *Report* of Mason's Committee on Harpers Ferry, 213–29.

somewhat under a cloud on account of the murder of Gaius Jenkins, the fastening of the stigma of revolution and John Brownism upon him would drive him out of public life. But by the time Robinson returned to Kansas he found himself the object of furious attack. In politics a single issue is seldom argued to a conclusion with a view to establishing facts. In this case the controversy over Robinson's testimony was confused by linking it with a local political issue, the alleged territorial bond swindle. The matter had reached the stage where the correspondence between a committee of the legislature and the secretary of the territory over the bonds was read in the house of representatives February 23.[55] The legislature had authorized, under certain contingencies, the issuance of bonds in satisfaction of warrants representing certain audited claims for damages on account of the political troubles. Different interpretations were placed upon the statutes, but under them in exchange for warrants Charles Robinson, S. W. Eldridge, Mrs. Gaius Jenkins and G. W. Brown had received $95,000 of the authorized total of $100,000 of bonds. Obviously, the great mass of the other warrant holders would get nothing. Lane took up the cause of the other claimants, but was accused of having acquired as a speculation a quantity of claims for himself. In either case, Lane had been outwitted and Robinson must be punished. In this manner the radical republicans linked the John Brown issue and the bond question in an effort to mobilize the masses against the conservative republicans and democrats. The nature of the appeal was politically perfect, idealism and humanity against alleged political ambition and corruption, and no demagogue knew better than Lane how to create and to use such an opportunity.

Lane, Phillips, and Redpath immediately made blanket denials of Robinson's charges.[56] Lane branded Robinson as a "corrupt defamer and cowardly assassin of his old friends." Redpath took particular offence at the statement that most of the letter-writers in Kansas were foreigners, declaring that only Realf fell in that class. As an index of Redpath's reliability, it is only fair to point

[55] Lawrence *Republican*, February 23, 1860.

[56] Lane's letter, dated February 28, was printed first in the Leavenworth *Register*, then the Leavenworth *Herald*, and finally in the Atchison *Union*, March 10, 1860. Phillip's letter was first printed in the Lawrence *Republican*, March 1, 1860. Redpath's letter was first printed in the Boston *Traveller*, and was reprinted in the Lawrence *Republican*, February 23, 1860. Robinson promised a reply to Lane at some future time. Leavenworth *Register*, reprinted in the Atchison *Union*, March 10, 1860. His letter was dated March 3, 1860.

out that of those mentioned only Kagi was native born; Redpath himself and Phillips being Scotch, and Hinton, English. In defense of the letter-writers the Lawrence *Republican*, March 1, 1860, stated that the charge of conspiracy among them had first been made by G. W. Brown early in 1857, but it maintained that the free-state cause would have been overwhelmed without the work of these men and especially of the New York *Tribune,* which did more to arouse the nation to the true character of the Kansas question than any other agency.

Lane and Phillips called a meeting at Lawrence February 25, where Robinson was called "traitor, liar, perjurer, villain, and many other names in common use among republicans," or at least that is the way the meeting was reported by a democratic paper.[57] Robinson had been invited to attend and replied by restating his charges. Reports differ regarding his success in meeting his accusers, but it was said to have been "the most lively meeting ever held at Lawrence." The bond question was aired and it was reported that Robinson did not deny that he held the bonds.[58] A similar meeting was held at Palmyra, March 5. Lane and Phillips restated the charges against Robinson; that the bonds were fraudulent; that Governor Medary had been coerced into signing the bonds; that the territorial seal had been stolen to seal the bonds; that Robinson's testimony before the Harpers Ferry committee was false. Robinson reminded them that he had been absent from the territory during the session of the legislature which enacted the laws on awards, warrants and bonds, and on his return had merely filed claims under the law and they had been granted; that the legislature and the commission on claims were controlled by republicans; and that Lane had been in the territory during the whole proceeding. On the second point Robinson called attention to the fact that Medary was no longer in the territory and was free to expose any coercion. The secretary of the territory furnished a letter stating that the seal had never been taken from the office. Finally Robinson reminded them that if there was any fraud, the courts were open and would obviate the stumping tour then in progress. Robinson was charged also with consulting a pro-slavery lawyer in New York regarding his Mason committee testimony before it was given, and to this he replied that

[57] Topeka *Tribune*, March 3, 1860.
[58] Topeka *Kansas State Record*, March 3, 1860. Topeka *Tribune*, March 3, April 21, 1860.

he had seen Stevens in New York, that he was a free-state man, and that a republican member of the Mason committee had joined in asking Robinson to testify. Reports of the Palmyra meeting differed as to which side made the best plea, but resolutions were adopted condemning the bonds as illegal. Robinson offered in a published letter to surrender his bonds if Lane and others would give up theirs.[59] In the same letter on the Palmyra meeting Robinson elaborated on Lane's hand in the claim awards, charging that he had boasted of securing the allowance of $200,000 worth of claims on a commission of 25 to 50 per cent, which meant that over $50,000 of claims warrants were in Lane's pocket. He charged also that Lane had made the ''consequential damage'' argument before the claims commission and had prosecuted more fraudulent claims before that body than all other attorneys together.[60]

The hostile press comment placed most of its emphasis on Robinson's alleged betrayal of the republican party and of former free-state associates; in fact, this matter of loyalty rather than the truth of the charges seemed uppermost in the minds of radical republican editors.[61] On the other hand the Robinson supporters insisted that his testimony was not only essentially true, but that by exposing the revolutionary character of the radicals implicated, he had vindicated the honor of the old free-state party. The *Kansas Press* expressed surprise at attempts to deny a fact so generally known as Lane's plot to assassinate pro-slavery men.[62]

The most elaborate review of the whole controversy was presented to the public in a series of letters written by the principals.[63] They are altogether too long to summarize in detail, but in closing the argument each took a parting shot which revealed the ulterior purpose behind the whole controversy. Robinson in-

[59] Topeka *Kansas State Record*, March 17, 1860, and Robinson's letter in the same paper March 31, 1860.

[60] Many other meetings were held over the territory in connection with this campaign to discredit Robinson; Blue Mound, March 6; Anderson county, March 10; Franklin county, March 15; Wyandotte, March 21; Leavenworth and Brooklyn (dates not exactly determined). Also both the republican and democratic county conventions in Douglas county, March 19 and 22, repudiated the legality of the territorial bonds.

[61] Topeka *Kansas State Record*, March 3, 10, 1860.

[62] White Cloud *Chief*, March 8, 15, 1860. Sol Miller, Editor. Council Grove *Kansas Press*, March 19, 1860.   S. N. Wood, Editor.

[63] Robinson's letter, Topeka *Kansas State Record*, March 24, 1860. Redpath's letter to Lane, dated March 8. Lawrence *Republican*, March 22. Phillips's letter, dated March 26. Topeka *Kansas State Record*, March 31. Lane's letter, dated March 11, *Kansas State Record*, April 7, 1860.

sisted that his testimony vindicated the old free-state party, and separated clearly the republican party from the Harpers Ferry men. Redpath assured Lane that "My opinion is, that his [Robinson's] road to the United States Senate does not lie in that direction; and that your chances . . . will not be greatly injured by his too transparent and unparalleled malignant perjury." Phillips averred that the old settlers would understand, but the new settlers might not, and so he was restating Robinson's record for their information; that the true author of the free-state policy of repudiation of the bogus territorial government was Conway, that Robinson had misled him and others in taking that credit for himself, and that Robinson's desertion of the Topeka State government had prevented Kansas from being a state in the Union long since. Lane declared that he had denounced the bond fraud as soon as he heard of it, that the issuance of the territorial bonds prejudiced the payment of claims by the federal government of the whole amount of claims amounting to a million dollars. It was a part of the contention of the Lane group that the federal government must pay Kansas for the losses during the territorial troubles, and Lane made it clear that as Kansas senator he would secure payment.

The democratic papers were delighted with this republican family quarrel and the revelations regarding the last six years of free-state and republican intrigue. The *Weekly Leavenworth Herald* handled the Robinson testimony and the Lawrence meeting under three indictments: that Lane's purpose was to incite revolution against the federal government; that Robinson's charges and Lane's denials and countercharges proved that both had been privy to the plan to slaughter the Lecompton convention; and that the charges and countercharges of the same men proved that both had been involved in the orders supposedly given to the free-state brigadier generals for general slaughter of pro-slavery men at several points in the territory.[64] The *Herald* editor was not concerned over why such massacres did not take place, but was intent upon fixing the responsibility for the six year campaign by "a partisan press and suborned correspondents" to place the blame upon the democratic party for "all the outrages which have been committed in Kansas." They claimed that it confirmed what

[64] Leavenworth *Herald*, March 3, 10, 1860.

they had argued at that time.[65]   The Topeka *Kansas State Record*
decided it was time to call a halt and with the publication of Lane's
letter announced that it was the last that would be printed from
anyone on the subject.   Of course the war between Lane and
Robinson did not end here.   Robinson took office as Governor in
January 1861 on the admission of Kansas as a state, while Lane
received the long coveted senatorship.   Lane contributed his best
efforts to prevent Robinson from receiving federal political pre-
ferment, intrigued to deprive him of military powers due him as
governor during the Civil War, drove him out of the directorship
of the Leavenworth, Pawnee and Western railroad, forced him to
sacrifice his interests in Indian land speculations, and finally induced the legislature to impeach him in 1862 in connection with
another bond controversy.   Robinson was acquitted, but Lane
permitted it only when he had accomplished his objective in railroad land speculation, and when, regardless of the outcome of the
impeachment trial, Robinson's political career was ruined.   After
1862 Lane was dictator in Kansas until 1866 when he sought escape
from his own misdeeds by suicide.

OPINION IN THE EAST

Immediately after the startling events in Virginia, the leading
newspapers felt obliged to print biographical sketches of the man
in the news.   The most accurate of these originated with the Akron
(Ohio) *Beacon* and was reprinted with the comment that it had
evidently been prepared by someone who knew Brown.[66]   It gave
his birthplace correctly and traced his changes of residence, his
tanning business, land speculations, wool venture, and the North
Elba removal, the emigration of his sons to Kansas with Devon
cattle, the sons' appeal for arms, John Brown's own emigration in
October, 1855 and the Battle of Black Jack.   It contained errors,
however, in attributing the sons' appeal for arms to pro-slavery
outrages actually inflicted upon the sons, and in having Brown and
sons remain in Kansas until the spring of 1859.   Nothing was said
about the controversial questions of the Wakarusa war, the Potawatomie massacre, the battle of Osawatomie, the defense of Lawrence

---

[65] The Boston *Herald* in the Lawrence *Republican*, March 1.   The Hartford (Connecticut) *Times* in the Lawrence *Republican*, March 8.   Topeka
Tribune, March 3, 10, 15, 24, 31, 1860.

[66] Pittsburgh (Pennsylvania) *Daily Journal*.   November 1, 1859, quoting
from the Akron *Beacon*.   Webb, *Scrapbooks*, 17: 5.

in September 1856, or of Brown's activities during the summer of 1858. Of course, such a sketch closed with an interpretation of Brown, he was more than a fanatic, he was insane at Harpers Ferry; but "no braver or truer spirit lives . . . ; to him, more than to any one hundred men in the country, is the fact to be attributed, that Kansas is a Free State today; let not that be forgotten in our estimate of the man, his motives and his life."

The Chicago *Press-Tribune* did not know Brown's birthplace but stated that he had lived in Ohio and as a tenant of Gerrit Smith in New York. It was erroneously claimed that in Kansas he offered to take command of the defense of Lawrence during the Wakarusa war and when Robinson and Pomeroy refused to defend the town, retired in disgust; he was thought to have been in the secret of the Potawatomie massacre; he was mistakenly credited with killing two wagon loads of pro-slavery men at the defense of Osawatomie; in the defense of Lawrence in September 1856, he was credited with taking out a small party of his own men, routing the vanguard of the pro-slavery forces, killing half a dozen, and, to make it more sensational, this last episode was offered as an hitherto unpublished story; he was credited with riding for two days with the federal troops who were seeking his arrest at the time he was on the way out of Kansas in 1856. The sketch indicated that Brown believed himself the chosen of God, pointing out that he denied acting in personal vengeance for the killing of his son, and the author insisted that the Harpers Ferry raid was in itself adequate proof that he was insane, and made the interesting comparison that the slave insurrection on the Cumberland river of Kentucky and Tennessee in 1856 was "a well matured conspiracy compared with this." [67]

The New York *Herald* did not know Brown's birthplace, but it was reported to be Kentucky; he emigrated with seven sons from New York to Osawatomie township in the fall of 1855; at the Wakarusa war he spoke against the peace treaty; was arrested by the committee of safety, but released with the admonition that as he was a stranger to Lawrence he should not compromise its people; a son was elected to the legislature, arrested on account of political opinions, driven across the prairie in chains and died of the resulting brain fever; in consequence John Brown took an oath of vengeance; a second son was killed at Osawatomie; free-state men considered him insane and did not consult with him; he was

[67] Chicago *Press-Tribune* quoted in the New York *Tribune,* October 24, 1859.

charged with the Potawatomie murders, but free-state men asserted they could prove he was in Lawrence at the time; Robinson
repudiated him as a result of activities in the war in southeastern
Kansas in 1858; Brown then proposed an expedition into Kentucky and Tennessee; and his wounds at Harpers Ferry were inflicted by "mercenary cowards after his surrender." [68]

The preeminent position in either ignorance, or falsehood, or
both, was earned easily by the New York *Tribune* in an editorial
correcting the democratic New York *Journal of Commerce:*

> John Brown, then a peaceful and quiet citizen, went to Kansas with no
> intention to do anything against slavery excepting so far as his vote and
> influence might go to keep it out of the Territory. He settled himself at
> Osawatomie, built a steam saw mill there, gathering quite a settlement
> about him, and devoted himself with energy to the business in which he
> was engaged.

According to the *Tribune,* it was when the Missourians invaded
Kansas, with the support of the federal government, that he joined
with the free-state men in forming the Topeka constitution. Under
this document a son was elected to the legislature, arrested, driven
in chains until insane and died. The chronology was reversed, the
Tribune having the sack of Lawrence follow, and then Buford's
men were imported from South Carolina "for the express purpose
of driving the free-labor settlers out of the Territory. . . ." It was
then that John Brown was converted into a captain of rangers,
and the remainder of the recital was in similar vein.[69] In the first
part of this editorial John Brown was confused with O. C. Brown,
the original Osawatomie Brown, and in the reference to the Topeka
constitution, with his eldest son, John Brown, Jr.[70]

The Harpers Ferry problem in the East is much more complicated than in Kansas. Most reactions toward Brown are suscep-
tible of classification into three types: that he was criminal, insane
or a hero. Those who branded him as a criminal were mostly from
the South and from certain democratic ranks in the North. In
the South particularly, many paid Brown the honor of elevating

[68] New York *Herald*, October 19, 1859. Webb, *Scrapbooks,* 17: 6–7.
[69] New York *Tribune,* October 21, 1859. In the issue of October 25
another biographical sketch was printed alleging gross insults to women of
the Brown family as a cause of the Potawatomie murders.
[70] Other notable cases of mistaken identity were in the New York *Times,*
October 24, 1859, and the Hartford (Connecticut) *Evening Press,* October 21,
1859, where R. P. Brown of Easton, Kansas, killed in January, 1856 in an election brawl, was said to be John Brown's son.

him to the position of arch-criminal or villain, engaged in executing the plot of a highly developed conspiracy, or as a criminal
adventurer using the slavery agitation as a cloak for an extensive
plan for personal plunder.[71]   It is evident that the South did not
know enough about Brown to realize that he was incompetent to
manage anything.   The anti-slavery element in the North, and
especially the republican party, seized upon the insanity issue as
in Kansas.   The greatest historical interest in the development of
the Northern legend centers, however, around the abolitionists,
both those who were courageous enough to speak out immediately,
as well as those who acquired boldness after the danger was passed;
they made the most direct contribution to Hero-making.

The news of the Virginia raid put John Brown's friends to a
test which most of them were unprepared to meet.   Of the so-
called "secret committee of six" (Higginson, Howe, Parker, Sanborn, Smith and Stearns) who had been more intimately responsible for his foray, most fled to safety: Parker out of the country
on account of his health was dying in Italy; Higginson alone of
the remaining group stood fast; Smith found refuge in insanity;
Howe, Sanborn and Stearns fled to Canada.   Of others associated
with Brown, Frederick Douglass fled to Canada, and Edwin Mor-
ton, Smith's secretary, to England.   Thaddeus Hyatt stood his
ground, refusing to testify before the Mason committee and was
imprisoned for contempt.

Redpath and Hinton, especially the former, came out among
the leaders in outright defense.   Redpath printed his "Reminis-

[71] As examples, may be cited the letter of a returned South Carolinian,
dated October 29, printed in the Charleston *Courier*, and reprinted in the
Buffalo (New York) *Daily Republic*, November 10, 1859, wherein it was stated
that in Kansas John Brown was merely a horse-thief using abolitionism to
cloak his crimes.   Incidentally, he pointed out that Frederick Brown had been
killed at Osawatomie by a free-state man, Martin White of Illinois.   It is
this classification of Martin White which accounts for the Southern theory
about that event, and in one sense it was true.   A statement of J. D. Penny-
backer, senator elect in Virginia, a returned Kansas man, contained essentially
the same thing, and in addition, stated that he was among the members of
Pate's company captured "by artifice at Black Jack" and was an eye-witness to the preparations for the raid by Brown's men on Bernard's store and
the return of the band loaded down with the stolen goods.   (Undated clipping in Webb, *Scrapbooks*, 17: 126.   K. S. H. S.)

H. C. Pate published a pamphlet (1859) in which John Brown was designated as "the senior partner" in a combination with A. A. Lawrence, Seward,
Greeley, Chase and Giddings.   Pate identified John Brown of Harpers Ferry
with the John Brown mentioned by the Evansville (Indiana) *Enquirer* as
having spent two years in jail for slave running in Kentucky.

cences of the Insurrectionists'' in the Boston *Atlas and Daily Bee*
in eight installments beginning October 21 and ending October 29,
and a second series in the form of "Notes on the insurrection"
beginning October 24, 1859. Redpath claimed intimate acquaintance with five of the Harpers Ferry men, opening the first series
defiantly:

> It is premature to write justly of their recent failure. It is easy
> enough to call it the insane attempt of a madman; to argue that old Brown
> was solely influenced by revenge; to invent ingenious theories of the lim-
> ited extent of the rebellion—easy enough, in other words, to utter false-
> hood. The truth of the recent outbreak has not been found out yet, and
> it would not be expedient to state it here. The prisoners are not yet
> tried. Let it pass, therefore—for the present; let curses increase—for
> *they* will pass too; and old Brown and his memory be duly vindicated
> when the right time comes.

The first three numbers were devoted to Brown and his Kansas
career, scarcely a true statement appearing in the whole lot. Redpath was constituted as most professional agitators in that he was
so emotionally unstable that he could not make a straightforward
statement of fact eevn when it would have been to his advantage
to do so. In addition to the above series, Redpath contributed
letters or articles to the New York *Tribune* and apparently most
any other medium that would publish them.

Hinton was less voluminous in his writing, but fully as inaccurate. His most important contribution was a letter to the Boston *Daily Traveller*, December 5, the letter being dated two days
earlier, in which he claimed the right to be heard, on the basis of
four years' service as correspondent for that journal, in refutation
of the affidavits made by Mrs. Doyle, Mrs. Wilkinson and others
relative to the Potawatomie murders. He claimed that the statements made therein were different from statements first made by
the same women, and that there was no real evidence that John
Brown had anything to do with the murders; that he had the
true story of that affair from one of the actors, then dead, who
gave not only the facts but the motives; that the massacre was a
righteous act; that the men were of bad character, "Doyle was
engaged with others in a fiendish attempt to outrage the persons
of Capt. Brown's daughter (the wife of Thompson . . .), and of
his daughter-in-law, . . ."; that Wilkinson was a renegade free-
state man and, along with Sherman, a pro-slavery tool who had
stolen the Brown cattle and outraged free-state men in other ways.

In amendment of other parts of the *Traveller* article, he correctly stated that this was not the first act of violence, but was not on quite so firm ground when he argued that Brown did not lose the confidence of free-state men as a result of the massacres, pointing to Robinson's letter of September, 1856, and offering himself as a witness that Brown was invited to a council of war at Lawrence on the first Sunday in September, 1856, declined, but was present a short time; that on September 13, he was solicited by all prominent men of Lawrence to take charge of the defense of the town; "In closing let me say that John Brown told me he was not a participator in the Potawatomie homicides. John Brown was incapable of uttering a falsehood. I would take *his word* against the oaths of a million Doyles." Hinton defied the world as Redpath had done in declaring that "I . . . dare to honor and vindicate John Brown, a man whom I love and reverance beyond all others who labored for the cause of Freedom in Kansas."

Among the most remarkable of the manifestations of the period were sermons and addresses of Beecher, Thoreau and Belcher. Although Beecher was a notorious trimmer, his sermon of October 30, 1859, declared: "Let no man pray that Brown be spared. Let Virginia make him a martyr. Now he has only blundered. His soul was noble; his work miserable. But a cord and a gibbet would redeem all that, and round up Brown's failure with a heroic success." [72] As printed in the contemporary press, it was shown to John Brown in his prison and he wrote his comment upon the margin. Opposite the above quotation he wrote the word "Good." [73]

Thoreau and Emerson met John Brown in March 1857 and apparently were much attracted by him. Thoreau had long advocated resistance to a government which is disapproved, holding that "any man more right than his neighbors constitutes a majority of one already." The resistance he proposed was non-participation even to the point of refusal to pay taxes, and he had been imprisoned for the practice of his theory. After Harpers Ferry he admitted that he knew little of John Brown, and the sketch of Brown in his address of October 30 at Concord proved it amply, but he declared that "it was through his agency, far

[72] Howard, John R. (Editor), Henry Ward Beecher, *Patriotic Addresses.* (Boston, 1887).

[73] R. J. Hinton, *John Brown and his men.* (New York 1894) 433–36.

more than any others, that Kansas was made free." With reference to the Harpers Ferry raid, Thoreau declared boldly:

> I am here to plead his cause with you. I plead not for his life, but for his character,—his immortal life; and so it becomes your cause wholly, and is not his in the least. . . . He is not Old Brown any longer; he is an angel of light.
>
> I see now that it was necessary that the bravest and the humanest man in all the country should be hung. Perhaps he saw it himself. I *almost fear* that I may yet hear of his deliverance, doubting if a prolonged life, if any life, can do as much as his death.[74]

The Reverend Mr. Belcher struck the same note in saying:

> John Brown will undoubtedly be hung. 'Tis well. He headed insurrection and became accountable for bloodshed, and must be hung. 'Tis well, I repeat. 'Tis better than that he should live. . . . On the day that that man is hung, the whole system of Slavery—that sum of human villainy will receive so fatal a stab, that it will never recover. . . . For this reason I shall thank God for the hanging of John Brown. There must be a martyr to truth, and each one that falls is a bountiful spring shower upon the buried seed.[75]

These quotations are from public utterances made prior to John Brown's own statement from his prison cell November 12 in a letter to his brother: "I am *quite cheerful* in view of my approaching end, being fully persuaded that I am worth inconceivably more to *hang* than for any other purpose." [76] The similarity of sentiment is remarkable and suggestive. Brown had been encouraged in building up this idea since early 1857 when he wrote Sanborn: "I expect nothing but to endure hardness; but I expect to effect a mighty conquest, even though it be like the last victory of Samson." This was followed by preparations to care for his family should he be killed. By the end of October 1859 the martyr ecstasy was "in the air," and in his prison cell, faced with the inevitable, Brown answered the call of the hour. Undoubtedly John Brown possessed a capacity for self-justification for his failures which amounted almost to genius, and on his final rôle he staked his claims to immortality and worked himself up to a state of religious immolation. Thaddeus Hyatt wrote John Brown November 14: "Your courage, my brother, challenges the admiration of men! Your faith, the admiration of angels! Be steadfast to

---

[74] Thoreau, "A plea for Captain John Brown" in his *Works* (New Riverside Edition, Boston, 1893). Miscellaneous, pp. 197–236.

[75] James Redpath, *Echoes of Harpers Ferry*, 176.

[76] Lawrence *Republican*, December 8, 1859.

the end!'' [77]   One wonders if these Hero-makers were worried
lest their mere man should not live up to his rôle and discredit
them.   They need not have been distressed on that score; it was
John Brown, not themselves, who was to be hanged by the neck
until dead on December 2.   If it is insanity that makes men martyrs, then Brown was insane enough to throw himself so completely
into the character designated for him that he met his doom with
''good cheer.''

The kind of man John Brown was, matters little.   There were
few who knew much in particular about him, or who cared sufficiently to know, to make the effort necessary to find out.   They
wished to see him hanged, and feared that he would not be.   They
were absorbed only in the coming of the Martyr,—their Martyr.
As men create God in their own image, so also do they evoke Heroes
and Martyrs.   Indeed, Thoreau spoke more prophetically than he
knew: ''He is not Old Brown any longer; he is an angel of light.''
Each created a John Brown to suit the occasion and therefore the
characteristics of this image depended upon the cause to which
the creator was pledged.   The South made of him a Villain, a
Devil, and demanded that, in fulfillment of their idea of a moral
world, he should be destroyed, and any defender was summarily
silenced.   In the North, he was dramatized in the rôle of Liberator, as they thought he ought to appear, to illustrate their ideal
of how right and freedom should triumph in their moral world.
John Brown seemed to appear in answer to their wish, and they
substituted his name, a homely, almost universal name, to their
idealization.   It is clear from their expressions, repeated again
and again, that they had no interest in the man, the human being,
—he interested them only as the fulfillment of their imaginary
drama.   Upon the occasions when such sacred rites of creation are
being consummated, it would be sacrilege for a realist to profane
the holy act by citing facts.   And if by accident or intention he
should do so, the unfortunate victim's reputation would be forfeit.
G. W. Brown had found this out during the early winter of 1859,
and many others were to pay a similar penalty.   It may be that
G. W. Brown was a scoundrel, but proof on that point, however
conclusive, did not cleanse John Brown of the blood of his Potawatomie victims.

All over the North meetings were held on the day of his execution, and through the period of November and December espe-

[77] *Hinton Papers*, K. S. H. S.

cially preachers delivered sermons on the hero. Many of these
were printed in the newspapers or in pamphlet form. His portrait was distributed far and wide. There was a veritable flood
of poetry. All kinds of anecdotes were circulated, some having
a grain of truth, mostly apocryphal. Songs sprang up from no-
where. "Illustrating the growth of public sentiment" the Lawrence, Kansas *Republican* November 10, 1859 printed "A new
version of an old song" to the air "Old John Brown had a little
injun."

> Old John Brown had a little nigger (three times)
> One little nigger boy

District Attorney Ould	—	One little, two little,
Secretary Floyd	—	Three little nigger,
Messrs. Mason and Vallandigham	—	Four little, five little,
Mr. Buchanan	—	Six little nigger,
Governor Wise	—	Seven little, eight little,
Washington Constitution	—	Nine little nigger,
New York Herald	—	Ten little nigger boy.

Democratic press throughout the country — (In recitative)—
> Ten *thousand* little nigger boys all armed with pitchforks
> eighteen feet long, and commanded by twenty *thousand* abolitionists.
> [Interval in which the election is supposed to have taken place]

Herald and Constitution	—	Ten little, nine little, eight little nigger,
Authorities of Virginia	—	Seven little, six little, five little nigger,
Authorities at Washington	—	Four little, three little, two little nigger,

People of the country (In accents of surprise at
> the upshot of the whole) — *One little nigger boy.*

The public took it as a matter of course that the name John
Brown should already be a part of the folklore heritage of the people.
Although the song armed the ten thousand nigger boys with pitchforks, the public was avid for more typical relics of the Old Hero.
Speculators manufactured bogus Brown "pikes" to sell on the
passenger trains until the railroad company at Harpers Ferry
interfered to prevent such selling and drove the venders off the
platform.[78] The Old Bowery theater in New York opened a play,
"Osawatomie Brown," on December 16, 1859, written by Mrs. J.
C. Swayze,[79] and two other theaters presented plays using the negro
theme. Even Garrison's non-resistant *Liberator* joined in the
pean after the accomplished fact:

[78] Topeka *State Record*, December 24, 1859.

[79] John Swinton in Lawrence (Kansas) *Republican* January 5, 1860. This
play has been reprinted in the *Kansas Historical Quarterly*, with an introduction by Kirke Mechem, 6 (February 1937) 34–59.

O, reader! turn from romance pages!
O, Nations! pause in your disputes!
Lo! this *sublime* deed of the ages!
One man against a million brutes.

The political theory of Brown's friends deserves some attention as a means of gaining perspective on Brown. Thoreau declared that "any man more right than his neighbors constitutes a majority of one already." It was the same idea which Wendell Phillips worded only slightly differently when he said "one, on God's side, is a majority." Emerson declared in 1851 that "an immoral law makes it a man's duty to break it, at every hazard," and four years later insisted that "the first duty of a judge was to read the law in accordance with equity, and, if it jarred with equity, to disown the law." Richard Cordley, the Congregational minister in Lawrence, Kansas, and leading exponent of transcendentalism in the territory maintained in his Thanksgiving sermon November 24, 1859, "that popular majorities are not the criterion of justice. Let us dare to be singular" as John Brown "has dared to stand up, unprotected and alone."

Gerrit Smith spoke vigorously during 1856 of armed rather than political action and argued that "peoples may break up and unite politically at their pleasure."[80] The Reverend George B. Cheever, of the Church of the Puritans, New York, preached that it was the duty of citizens to resist laws which opposed their ideas of right and that the right of revolution was as applicable in a democracy as under an absolute monarchy. This view was challenged vigorously in more conservative quarters on the ground that universal suffrage in a democracy provided government by a majority and that minorities must submit until change came about through majority action.[81] Cheever's Thanksgiving Day sermon during the Harpers Ferry period declared that "God . . . shot John Brown out of the cannon of his Providence right into the bosom of that vested interest [slavery]. . . . It looks, indeed, as if God had begun his work of judgment."

Theodore Parker recognized a defect which others did not in the theory of revolution as applied to John Brown and made an attempt to correct it. The rationalizations of the others had been based upon the assumption of individuals acting in defense of their

[80] R. V. Harlow, *Gerrit Smith*, 351–55, 357.

[81] *Herald of Freedom*, May 9, 1857. Quoting the controversy from the Philadelphia *Ledger*. New York *Tribune*, October 18, 21, 28, 1856 gives additional Cheever material.

own rights and the precedents of Bunker Hill and the American Revolution were called upon to do overtime duty. The slaves at Harpers Ferry did not rise in revolt either on their own initiative or under the influence of John Brown's incitement. It is at this point that Parker offered his doctrine not only of the natural right but of the natural duty of a freeman to intervene to aid slaves in enjoyment of liberty "and as a means to that end, to aid them in killing all such as oppose their natural freedom. The performance of this duty is to be controlled by the freeman's power and opportunity to help the slaves. . . . Hence comes Capt. Brown's Expedition—an attempt to help his countrymen enjoy their natural right to life, liberty, and the pursuit of happiness." Parker did not confine his doctrine to internal action but used the Greek and Polish revolutions as illustrations which extended his doctrine to include the natural right of individuals to aid revolution in other countries.[82]

Among radicals these ideas were looked upon as high thinking and fitted into another prevalent doctrine of the time; the Hour and the Man theory of history. Whittier's poem, Sierra, written for the Frémont campaign closed with the lines:

> Rise up, Frémont! and go before;
> The Hour must have its Man,
> Put on the hunting-shirt once more;
> And lead in Freedom's van!

Frémont had failed to fulfill the ideal, but not so John Brown. William A. Phillips declared in a lecture in Lawrence, Kansas, January 20, 1860, that:

Mediocrity has no immortality. . . . I have shown that history of the ages was but the history of a few men. Each recorded age has its man. He is the lesson of its history. This age has had its man. . . .

Neither you nor I mean to excite servile insurrections. Both you and I would prevent another Harper's Ferry, if we could. Yet shall the timid and soulless age get up 'union' meetings to denounce the old Puritan?— to persuade the South that they are not John Browns. . . . Thank God, Kansas has not been guilty of such nonsense. . . . The time is coming, when an impartial posterity . . . looking from this generation to his sacrifice, will recognize in them the Age and the Man.

In the beginning, only the extreme radicals openly endorsed the martyr, but with the coming of the Civil War, the conservative

---

[82] Weiss, *Theodore Parker, Life and Correspondence* 2: 170–78. This exposition was in a letter to Francis Jackson, dated from Rome, Italy, November 24, 1859.

propertied classes did likewise. They did not possess the insight
to penetrate the theoretical implications of John Brownism;—that
to endorse John Brown in inciting a slave insurrection to socialize
the instruments of production in the South should lead logically
to the endorsement of a similar agitator inciting insurrection to
socialize other instruments of production in the interest of free
workers, such as the factories and landed property of the North.
They could see only that the evils attacked were in the South, at
a distance, and affected *other* people, who, as they thought, needed
reforming,—not themselves and their own system.

Emerson delivered three important lectures within a few weeks
after Brown's sentence in which he endorsed Brown. In the lecture on courage, delivered in Boston, he pronounced John Brown
"the new saint awaiting his martyrdom, and who, if he shall suffer, will make the gallows glorious like the cross." At the Tre-
mont Temple meeting, November 18, 1859, for the relief of the
family of John Brown, Emerson favored his admirers with a biographical sketch of the martyr which was false in almost every
detail, but facts never bothered Emerson, the transcendentalist.
He did make nevertheless a significant observation on the universality of the appeal inherent in the John Brown story:

> This commanding event which has brought us together, eclipses all
> others which have occurred for a long time in our history, and I am very
> glad to see that this sudden interest in the hero of Harpers Ferry has pro-
> voked an extreme curiosity in all parts of the Republic, in regard to the
> details of his history. Every anecdote is eagerly sought, and I do not
> wonder that gentlemen find traits of relation readily between him and
> themselves. One finds a relation in the church, another in the profession,
> another in the place of his birth. He was happily a representative of the
> American Republic.[83]

This universality of interest is illustrated by the public letter
written by Victor Hugo in France December 2, 1859. By coincidence it was dated on execution day, but the news had not yet
arrived, and the purpose of the letter was to appeal to sentiment
in France and England to take steps to forestall the execution.
That practically every specific detail concerning Brown was a mis-

[83] It is long since time that scientific biographies were written of Emerson,
who has been so carefully embalmed in a protective legend by his family and
his admirers. Biographies are needed of the group known as the "secret committee of six."

R. V. Harlow, *Gerrit Smith* (1939), is the only such biography of any one
of the group.

statement of fact only made it more effective as an atrocity story illustrating the results of the slave system. When the word came that John Brown had been hanged Hugo drew his famous picture of Brown on the gallows and inscribed it "Pro Christo sicut Christus." He attempted no depiction of the scene at Charlestown nor portraiture of Brown. He had no data for such details and that type of realism would not have served the purpose. It was drawn out of pure imagination, a gibbet and a vague human form hanging by a rope. The remarkable artistic power and emotional appeal lay in this shadowy indefiniteness which suggested but which left the imagination free to supply the detail.[84]

It is scarcely sufficient to dismiss John Brown as most scientific historians have done merely by pronouncing him insane. Not only the United States, but Europe as well, was nearing the end of a cycle bringing economic collapse, and the climax of social reform, the national unification movements by means of blood and iron in Italy, Germany and the United States. A frustrated generation of youth found its opportunity in an outpouring of emotion upon a cause or a man. Not only had most of John Brown's followers at Harpers Ferry come under his influence as boys and young men, but his biographers, Redpath, Sanborn and Hinton, were aged respectively, 21, 23 and 24 in 1854 when the Kansas crusade opened and 26, 28 and 29 at the time of the Virginia raid. The Civil War was the climax of the cycle in the United States and it was American youth which caught up the banner of nationalism and abolition. John Brown became its first Hero, and had no serious rival until the assassin's bullet added the martyred Lincoln.

[84] The present author has not been able to trace the sequences of publication and translation of either the Hugo letter or drawing. It was printed in the London *Star*, however, then reprinted from that paper in the New York *Express* and drew a reply by Ann S. Stephens dated December 27, 1859 published in the New York *Express* and both were republished in pamphlet form by Irwin P. Beadle & Company, New York, 1860. Redpath reprinted the Hugo letter from the London *Star* version in his *Echoes of Harpers Ferry* (1860). In France a pamphlet edition of Hugo's letter was published by M. E. Dentu and Mm. Dusacq et Cie., Paris, 1861. The drawing was published in two sizes; a large and expensive one, and a small cheap one for the populace. Letter from Gen. C. F. Henningsen in reply to the Letter of Victor Hugo. . . . Pamphlet. 32 pp. New York. Davies & Kent, 1860.

CHAPTER XI

THE REDPATH PERIOD IN JOHN BROWN BIOGRAPHY

The extraordinary public interest in the Virginia raid induced various types of purely commercial exploitation of the event which contributed to the satisfaction of the appetite of the world for the latest sensation as well as to the promotion of the cause. On October 20, four days after the raid began, D. Appleton and Company advertised a series of stereoscopic views of the Harpers Ferry vicinity.[1] Two portraits and a ballad of John Brown were advertised in New York during the first week of December.[2] Among the most spectacular news stunts was the controversy between *Frank Leslie's Illustrated Newspaper* and its imitator the *New York Illustrated News*. When the *News* published pictures of the execution December 2, the execution of Brown's associates December 16, and the burial at North Elba ahead of *Leslie's* the latter charged that they were faked. With respect to the execution of December 16, the *News* offered proof that it had chartered a special train over the Baltimore and Ohio railroad to Baltimore, which enabled them to print their pictures and distribute them Saturday afternoon before *Leslie's* artist arrived in New York that evening.[3]

Enterprising publishers printed sermons, documentary materials and descriptive matter relating to the affair. One pamphlet compiled by Thomas Drew was published in Boston in defense of Brown, "*The John Brown Invasion, an authentic history . . .* ," with a preface dated December 21, 1859. It included a denunciation of the "slanders upon John Brown," one of which was the letter of Mahala Doyle exulting over his approaching execution. The editor pointed out that such a crime as the Potawatomie mas-

[1] New York *Tribune*, October 20, 1859. See their advertisement in the classified department under the division, New publications.

[2] Charles H. Brainard advertisement, New York *Tribune*, December 5, 1859, and Chailly's Gallery advertisement, New York *Tribune*, December 7, 1859. "The Ballad of John Brown" was advertised by C. E. Hering, with the explanation that the proceeds were for the benefit of Brown's family. The price was 25 cents.

[3] See advertisements in the New York *Tribune* December 6–19, 1859, of the rival papers. New publications section of classified advertisements.

sacre was contrary to the tenor of Brown's whole career; he had
denied it as well as many witnesses in the territory, Redpath's
Tribune letter, the letter of Brown's brother, and Hinton's *Evening Traveller* letter.   Altogether, the arguments and the documents
published made an impressive array.

Among the proposed biographies was one by Lydia Maria
Childs, the announcement declaring that the proceeds would go to
the Brown family.[4]   The Topeka *Tribune,* January 14, 1860, ma-
liciously advised Mrs. Childs regarding the gathering of materials
for her life of the *Brigand Chief,* specifying that she not overlook
Mrs. Mahala Doyle, then living at Chattanooga, Tennessee, who
"is in possession of some *thrilling facts* that Lydia Maria can weave
into her work."

The first man to qualify as Brown's biographer was James Redpath, born in Scotland, who began his education for the ministry
but turned to printing and in 1852, at the age of nineteen, had become a writer on the New York *Tribune.*   Highly emotional in
temperament, he was always involved in some reform.   He was a
perfect agitator type as he possessed a gift of vivid language and
a complete disregard for facts.   As one Kansas acquaintance said
when he reproached Redpath for inaccuracy, the latter replied that
it "sounded better as he reported it, and would have a more telling effect in the East."[5]   He had traveled in the South and became involved in the Kansas controversy, all of which led up to
the publication of a book March 5, 1859, entitled *The Roving Editor, or talks with slaves in the Southern States.*[6]

The talks recorded were not in themselves particularly sensational, but Redpath's pronouncements were bold to the point of
rashness.   He dedicated it "To Captain John Brown, Senior, of
Kansas.   To you Old Hero, . . . To you in due homage for first
showing how, and how alone, the gigantic crime of our age and
nation can be effectually blotted out. . . . You, Old Hero, believe
that the slave should be aided and urged to insurrection, and hence
do I lay this tribute at your feet."   He held that Brown had gone
to Kansas to have a shot at slavery, and that is why he himself

---

[4] *Herald of Freedom,* December 10, 1859. Mrs. Childs's book was not published.

[5] O. A. Carpenter to Charles Robinson, March 5, 1885. Lawrence *Herald-
Tribune.*

[6] This book was published in New York by A. B. Burdick. The announcement of its publication is found in the New York *Tribune,* March 5, 1859, New
publications section of the classified advertisements.

went. Redpath's rationalization was that the Kansas question would bring the North and South into conflict, and that the result would be the abolition of slavery. His function in Kansas was to bring on such a conflict, a plan which the conservative republican statesmen defeated. But he argued that "the South committed suicide when it compelled the free squatters to resort to guerilla warfare, *and to study it both as a mode of subsistence and a science.*" The mountains and swamps of the South, he believed, would provide an ideal setting for a slave insurrection led by young men "trained in the art in Kansas ravines." He believed a slave insurrection was possible, but it must be with the aid of white men, and that there were "men ready for this holy work." He closed his chapter on "My objects" with the appeal: "Will you aid them —will you sustain them? Are you in favor of a servile insurrection? Tell God in Acts."

When the attempted insurrection occurred and failed in October 1859, less than seven months after the publication of this book, Redpath rushed to John Brown's defense in his Boston *Atlas and Daily Bee* articles and in his attack on G. W. Brown for ventilation of Kansas history. G. W. Brown took cognizance of the announcement of Redpath's biography by charging that of all persons, Redpath was best qualified to "make him appear as a saint, and a pattern of meekness, humility, etc.," adding that the editor had a mass of facts which ought to go into such a work.[7]

The first work on "the life, trial and conviction of Capt. John Brown of Kansas" was announced in prospect through the New York *Tribune*, October 20, 1859 by stating merely that arrangements had been made for the publication of a verbatim report of the trial by Robert M. DeWitt of New York, and orders would be filled as received. The first announcement of the full title appeared November 11, with a price of twenty-five cents for a complete life, verbatim report of the trial, and correct portraits of John Brown and his associates. Apparently it was ready for distribution about November 26, when an advertisement described it further as containing one hundred pages, eight engravings and a portrait, and solicited agents who were assured that "a smart active man can sell one hundred copies in a day." A new and enlarged edition was announced in the *Tribune* December 15.[8]

---

[7] *Herald of Freedom,* November 19, 1859.

[8] The enlarged edition had a slight change of title, the word execution was substituted for conviction. It contained 108 instead of 100 pages.

The enterprise of this publisher challenged Thayer and Eldridge of Boston who had arranged with James Redpath for a biography of John Brown. On November 14, therefore, they ran an advertisement promising their book by January 1, with a steel engraved portrait, and begged their public to "Wait and get the best." By December 9, their agent in New York, S. T. Munson, advertised in the *Tribune* that the book would be four hundred pages, published by subscription, and solicited orders at one dollar a copy. An advance subscription of 10,000 copies was announced December 20 of "the great book of the day." A week later the *Tribune* advertisement averred that this was the "only genuine and reliable biography, authorized by, and for the benefit of the family." In proof of this it offered the text of letters of endorsement from Mrs. Brown and Salmon Brown. A new feature was announced in an autobiography of Brown's childhood and youth. The rivalry of the DeWitt book, which must have been stealing the market, was recognized in a warning: "Be not deceived. Beware of spurious 'Lives of Brown.' Wait and get the best, the only authentic and reliable work, written by Brown's old comrade in Kansas. . . ." The public was assured that the book was then in press, and would be issued immediately, and that the advance subscription had reached 20,000 copies. This advertisement drew a reply in the *Tribune*, December 27, in which DeWitt declared his "the only illustrated and reliable history of the Harper's Ferry Insurrection. Its correctness and genuineness have already secured a sale of 40,000 copies." Redpath's book was not ready until January 10, 1860, and was noticed in the new book column of the *Tribune* January 21.[9]

The humorous aspect of the aspersions cast by Thayer and Eldrige on the authenticity and reliability of the DeWitt book lies in the fact that the DeWitt life of Brown was cribbed verbatim, for the most part, from James Redpath's *Atlas and Daily Bee* articles. In other words both were Redpath books.

In Kansas a card was published in several newspapers announcing that Redpath and Hinton were preparing a life of John Brown and appealing for information, anecdotes and reminiscences of conversations with Brown, and promising a complimentary copy of the book to the editors who printed the notice and to all persons making contributions of materials. In the Manhattan *Express*,

[9] An edition of the book was printed in England, identical in text, but in smaller type on 294 pages, n. d.

December 24, it was stated that the purpose was to vindicate the
Old Hero in connection with Kansas affairs. The Lawrence *Republican*, December 1, expressed the opinion that "it will undoubtedly be a correct and valuable book . . . and will unquestionably
refute, upon unassailable evidence, the monstrous slanders set afloat
by the Democratic enemies of Brown." Such verdicts could not be
expected to attract but one kind of response from Kansas correspondents.

Two of the letters written in answer to this appeal have been
preserved; that of C. G. Allen, a Christian preacher at Cottonwood
Falls, undated, and that of James Hanway of Shermanville (Dutch
Henry's Crossing) dated December 5, 1859.[10] Allen was under the
impression that Mrs. Childs was to write the book, but he authorized Redpath and Hinton to use his letter as they saw fit. He
had arrived in Kansas after the spring troubles and consequently
his reminiscences were limited to the last few days of August and
early September, 1856. He first met John Brown at Lawrence
buying mules from Eldridge, and shortly afterwards, on appeal
from Osawatomie, went with the Lawrence troops to give aid. They
found Stanton and Osawatomie deserted of families, but at the
latter the leaders were consulting about defenses against the expected attack from the northeast. Brown was among those present, and the discussion turned on the use of the river as a first
line and the block houses as a second line of defense. Sometime
later, but dates were not given exactly, John Brown came in from
an expedition with a herd of stolen cattle. At another time an
expedition went out to intercept a pro-slavery party and attempt
to capture John E. Brown, the pro-slavery sheriff of Linn county.
As the Lawrence troops had overstayed their time before the expected major attack on Osawatomie occurred, Allen was not present when the Ried forces circled the town and attacked it from the
rear August 30. Later John Brown appeared at Lawrence, asking for troops to use against the border ruffians, declaring that "I
have suffered from Free State men every indignity that they could
heap upon me, yet I am determined to serve through the war."
Colonel Harvey, to whom he was talking, discouraged his expectations. While in Lawrence, on the first Sunday in September, a
council of free-state leaders was being held and Allen reported
that Brown was invited to attend and speak, but refused. The

10 *Hinton Papers.* Kansas State Historical Society.

letter contained, however, a damaging piece of evidence: "I heard several say that they thought Capt. Brown to be insane after the battle of Osawatomie."

Hanway's letter opened with commendation of the plan for a biography: "This is right & well timed; the book will sell, and everybody will feel an interest in knowing something about Old John Brown. There are but few men, even in Kansas, who know realy the character of John Brown. I hope your efforts to spread the incidents of his life, and the motives by which he was prompted to act, will place him in his true light before the world."[11]

In regard to the exit of the Doyles, Wm. Sherman and Wilkinson (the postmaster), who, lived on Potawatomie creek, I could perhaps give you the correct facts in connection with this 'tragedy'—but I presume you know them. *Never perhaps have as many various statements been published on any event as on this event.* [The sentence in italics was omitted by Hinton.] However, I can give you Brown's opinion of this event. In conversation with him, he remarked (about a year ago) that it was a just act, to take the lives of those five pro-slavery ruffians. That it had saved the lives of many good men, that he knew it was the intention of the border ruffians to 'clear' the creek of every free-state man, by driving them off by threats, burning and taking of human life. [Surveyor story at this point.] John Brown received the information directly from these pro-slavery banditti; and he only took the advance upon them, and thus blasted their hellish designs. The old settlers, almost unanimously, justify this tragic act, and they feel as if a debt of thanks was due to John Brown and his confederates in checking the hand of the border ruffians in that section of the country.

In this letter, Hanway developed only one specific instance of pro-slavery threats, the case of the storekeeper Morse, who he said was warned by the Doyles to leave in three days. Hanway defended Brown also against the charge of revenge against the pro-slavery men, Martin White in particular, quoting the Old Hero as saying that he acted from principle alone,—"to rescue human rights." He defended Fred Brown against the charge of insanity,—he was only "excitable in debate." The identification of John Brown with Puritanism was firmly established in Hanway's mind;—"John Brown is the Oliver Cromwell of America," but he was possessed of more humanity.

Although these letters were filed away and preserved among Hinton's papers they were not used in the Redpath biography. At

[11] This letter was printed in Hinton's *John Brown* (1894) with omissions which were not indicated. The opening paragraph of the letter which is quoted above was omitted.

this time the two men were cooperating, but no explanation has been forthcoming concerning the details of their working arrangement. In the New York *Tribune* advertisements, Redpath alone was credited with the book, but in the Kansas newspaper card both were announced as authors. There was one other collaborator at this time, about whom also information is deficient. Sanborn had some association with the enterprise.[12] It would be enlightening to know for certain to what extent these three were familiar with the Allen and Hanway letters, and whether they discussed the evidence, and why Redpath chose to ignore completely the facts. Of course, Redpath had been in Kansas at the time of the difficulties of 1856 and there is every reason to believe that he knew the facts without the reminder of these letters, especially the Hanway letter in which so definite a confession was made that John Brown was guilty of the Potawatomie tragedy, the only concern on the part of the author being to present a convincing statement of reasons why it was justifiable. In the above letter Hanway stated for the first time his settled opinion of John Brown, and as Hanway was to have a very great influence in the Brown controversies, the exact ground on which he stood has been emphasized for future reference, as well as to furnish a check upon Redpath's unreliability.

In one sense it was a remarkable feat for Redpath to gather his material, write his book of 407 pages and have it published by January 10, 1860. The title of the volume is *The Public Life of Capt. John Brown,* but the original plan had been to include his private life and correspondence as well as an account of his associates. If Redpath's explanation in the preface is to be trusted, the reason for narrowing the limits was the loan by the Brown family of hundreds of letters which made possible a more detailed treatment of his public life and opened the way for a prospective second volume. Redpath avowed that "I have written the book, because I could not resist it." He avowed positively that "I think John Brown did right in invading Virginia and attempting to liberate slaves. I hold God in infinitely greater reverence than Congress, and His holy laws than its enactments." When the first news of the raid was received and people called Brown a madman, Redpath felt that "now, or never, was the time to defend my friend,"

---

[12] F. B. Sanborn to James Redpath, April 2, 1878. *Hinton Papers.* In the preface Redpath acknowledged only the aid of Thomas H. Webb, Hinton and his own wife. It would be interesting to know whether Webb gave Redpath access to his voluminous scrapbooks of clippings, now in possession of the Kansas State Historical Society.

but before his series of newspaper articles was finished "the highest talent of the nation was marshalling to the rescue of the conquering prisoner of Charlestown jail. . . . I withdrew myself from the conflict for a time—for, a guerilla skirmisher only, unfitted both by habit and nature for a place in any regular army, I did not care to fight under any General, or to fire except where I wanted to kill." Redpath ostentatiously repudiated the republican party, saying that he was offered the opportunity to write a life of Brown as a campaign document, but declined the offer of a New York publisher because "I would not help to light cigars from the fire above the altar." He accepted the "nobler request" of his publishers, however, because "they wished to do him [Brown] justice; they desired to assist his destitute family." The book was dedicated to Wendell Phillips, Emerson and Thoreau, that "highest talent of the nation" to whom he referred in his preface, those men "who, when the mob shouted, 'madman,' said, 'Saint!'" Redpath received the endorsement as historian of Mrs. John Brown and of Salmon Brown, the latter stressing particularly his truthfulness.

The general spirit in which the book was written was to justify the militant type of abolitionism and equally to condemn, in as offensive a manner as possible, all types of hedging or evasion on the question of the Virginia raid and the procedure it represented, or as he put it in the preface, that as a guerilla, he fired where he "wanted to kill."

Redpath handled the story of Brown and the Wakarusa war by quoting the story of his arrival in Lawrence as given by G. W. Brown in the *Herald of Freedom*, October 29, 1859, and elaborated upon John Brown's part in the events that followed. Brown was credited with taking a party out "to draw a little blood" but desisted at the earnest entreaty of Lane.[13] He was invited to the council of war, but refused. When the treaty of peace was announced, he attempted to address the people, "but a desire was manifested to prevent his speaking." He demanded to know what the terms were and was assured that no concessions were made: "The politicians feared the old man, knowing that neither cunning nor duplicity would please him. Hence their desire to prevent his speaking; hence their determination to keep the Treaty secret; hence their unblushing announcement that nothing had been conceded. . . . This Treaty when published justified the old man's suspicions."

13 This episode has no corroboration so far as the present author has found.

The matter referred to was the compromise on the matter of obedience to the laws, without specifying whether it meant the federal or territorial laws, and Redpath represented Brown as regretting both that he had yielded to Lane's entreaties not to "draw a little blood" and to the acceptance of the treaty. In sppport of this contention Redpath quoted the New York *Tribune* correspondent, probably meaning William A. Phillips, who declared that Brown later lamented having lost his chance.

In spite of the fact that the connection of John Brown with the Potawatomie massacre had been quite fully exposed, both publicly and privately, Redpath gave his own version, a product of his fertile imagination.

I have spoken of the rumors of midnight murder in the Potawatomie region, and stated that Capt. Brown was accused by the invaders of having done the deed. The charge is false. It was first made by his enemies, who feared him, and desired to drive him out of the district, and subsequently repeated by a recreant Free State journalist, who sold himself to the Federal Administration for a paltry bribe of public printing.

After denying so positively that Brown had anything to do with the affair, he proceeded to defend the killings as a stern act of justice such as was necessary in a new western country, and charged specifically that "free state men were daily robbed, beaten and killed," that the Missourians had matured a plan for clearing the region of free-state men, that John Brown learned of the plan by posing as a surveyor, that a meeting was held which decided on summary punishment, that the grossest indignities were offered John Brown's daughter and daughter-in-law, that the story of the slaying had been told to him by two of the participants, not members of the Brown family, and that John Brown endorsed the act although he had no part in it. Redpath insisted that John Brown was twenty-five miles from the scene of the crime. Redpath did not claim that the Potawatomie massacre saved Kansas from slavery as Sanborn was to do later, but he insisted that the general effect was beneficial, and "every one in Kansas at the time admitted that fact, although many of them deny it now."

Redpath's chapter on the battle of Black Jack followed substantially the contemporary John Brown account, and the same source was utilized for the battle of Osawatomie. In dealing with Martin White, Redpath charged that the story of the summer of 1856 about the killing of White was a hoax planned by the proslavery men to discredit the free-state cause. He pictured White

as having "laughingly described" to the pro-slavery legislature of
1857 how Fred Brown "toppled over" when he shot him, but
"Poor Martin White, when the session was finished, proceeded to
his home. But he never reached it . . . his corpse was found stiff
and cold on the prairie—with a rifle ball in it." Unfortunately
for Redpath's veracity again, Martin White must have had three
lives, if not nine like the proverbial cat, because in 1860, after the
publication of Redpath's book, he was alive enough to write another
vigorous defense of his own Kansas career.[14]

A chapter was devoted to the defense of Lawrence in September
1856. According to Redpath, about four o'clock on Sunday afternoon, Lawrence saw that Reid's force was coming and "It was
no sooner known that Captain Brown was in town, than he was
unanimously voted general-in-chief for the day," and Brown addressed the people in the street opposite the postoffice. The speech
was quoted, as it was reported by Hinton, but without credit to
him. Brown was then pictured as visiting every portion of the
town, planning for defense and placing troops, and arming them
even with pitchforks. About five o'clock, four hundred horsemen
appeared south of the town, and Redpath had Brown order out
all the men with Sharps rifles, forty or fifty, and as darkness closed
in the firing became general, a brass twelve-pounder was sent out
to give support, but the armed and mounted southerners had fled
in panic before thirty or forty footmen. And to complete his full
measure of falsehood, Redpath closed the chapter with a fanciful
poem written by Richard Realf, vouching for "its historical accuracy, literary merit, and an indication of the range of intellect
which the brave Old Hero gathered around him." One part of
Realf's poem is sufficient:

> And all throughout that Sabbath day
>   A wall of fire we stood,
> And held the baffled foe at bay,
>   And streaked the ground with blood;
> And when the sun was very low,
>   They wheeled their stricken ranks,
> And passed on, wearily and slow,
>   Beyond the river banks.

[14] Martin White's letter was dated January 14, 1860 and was published in
the Bates County (Missouri) *Standard*. Undated clipping in John Brown
Scrapbooks, Volume I. Kansas State Historical Society. The letter was in
reply to August Wattles's defense of Brown.

In his biography Redpath presented John Brown as the hero who had saved Kansas in spite of the compromising politicians. However that may be, it was a different interpretation of Kansas honors from that he had given in 1857 when he declared that it was to Eli Thayer "more than to any other person, or party of freedom, that the Free State party is now indebted for its existence." [15]

Redpath appreciated the propaganda value, in that mid-Victorian era, of emphasis on religion, and described Brown's guerillas, a part of whom had just committed the Potawatomie murders, and all of whom had engaged in the stealing of horses, cattle and other plunder: "In this camp no manner of profane language was permitted; no man of immoral character was allowed to stay. . . . He made prayers in which all the company united, every morning and evening; and no food was ever tasted by his men until the Divine blessing had been asked on it. After every meal, thanks were returned to the Bountiful Giver."

Redpath's major offense was not that he was biased in favor of Brown and wrote a eulogy, rather than a biography. The unforgivable in his record was that scarcely anything in his book was true, either in general effect or in detail; that he falsified the documentary record itself, inventing freely both incidents and details. He was not content with coloring and interpreting facts, he attempted to establish a false record, allegations of fact, as a basis for history.

The only extended contemporary review of the book was that of C. E. Norton in the *Atlantic Monthly* in which he declared that "it would have been well, had this book never been written. . . . He [Redpath] has shown himself incompetent to appreciate the character of the man whom he admires, and he has, consequently, done great wrong to his memory." Norton pointed out that he had not collected all the letters available, but the chief grievance of the reviewer was that "he has written in the worst temper and spirit of partisanship . . . in the spirit and style of an Abolition tract"; as though Brown was "little more than a mere hero of the Abolitionists." In contrast, Norton's view of Brown was that "he belonged to the same class with the Scotch Covenanters and the English regicides." [16]

Not only had Redpath missed his opportunity of writing a biography of John Brown, but Norton had missed his in failing to write

[15] *Herald of Freedom*, April 18, 1857.
[16] *Atlantic Monthly*, 5 (March 1860) 378–381.

an adequate review which would have attacked Redpath on the merits of the book as history,—the soundness of its factual foundation. Instead, Norton's criticism had been directed primarily against Redpath's point of view or interpretation. Norton failed to understand that the thing that gave Brown so broad an appeal as a symbol was the highly contradictory character of his writings, sayings, actions, and the anecdote and folklore that had already come into existence. With so varied a material for the imagination to work upon, men of most every shade of opinion might find something from which each could rationalize Brown's career and set up for himself a hero in his own image. Norton failed to realize that Redpath had the same right as himself in this matter, and after all, Norton's review went only a little beyond a contrast of his own heroic creation with that of Redpath. One of Brown's friends was not disposed to permit Norton's interpretation to pass without protest, because he also had his own heroic image to set up for the admiration of the world. F. B. Sanborn wrote a strong letter condemning the magazine for printing Norton's review.[17] Although not printed, here is a significant foretaste of aggressive warfare which Sanborn was to carry on against anyone who dared to differ with his peculiar version of the John Brown Legend. This was Redpath's hour, Sanborn's was to come.

Some others of the inner circle of Brown enthusiasts differed also from Norton but expressed themselves otherwise. Mrs. E. A. J. Lindsley wrote March 3, 1860 to A. D. Stevens, one of Brown's men awaiting execution in the Charlestown jail: "The life of Capt. Brown is bought and read by all parties and all creeds, he is speaking in thundering tones although his body lies mouldering to dust through the mercies of Va it gives a new impetus to the great cause of the oppressed of our country that and Helpers impending Crisis advertised by congress has done more than all the abolition Lectures in America."[18]

The Redpath biography of Brown was followed quickly by a second book, not the promised private life, but a compilation entitled *Echoes of Harpers Ferry,* "comprising the best Speeches, Sermons, Letters, Poems, and other utterances of leading minds

[17] This letter without date is in the T. H. Higginson Papers, K. S. H. S. Apparently Sanborn hoped Higginson would have it printed.

[18] *Hinton Papers.* K. S. H. S. Mrs. Lindsley's use of the phrase "his body lies mouldering," a phrase which was used a few months later in the John Brown song, is only a coincidence, but it is a reminder that folksongs must spring spontaneously from the common speech and thought of the people.

in Europe and America, called forth by John Brown's invasion of Virginia. . . ." [19] The preface was dated April 14, and it was published May 9, 1860. The advertising matter pointed out that "It is also valuable for circulation as a presidential campaign document." [20] By this time the publisher claimed that the sale of Redpath's biography had reached 40,000 copies.

The purpose of the new book as explained by the compiler was "first to preserve in permanent form, the memorable words that have been spoken of Captain Brown; second, to aid the families of the blacks and the men of color, who recently went to heaven via Harpers Ferry, or who were murdered, with legal form, at Charlestown, Virginia." But the object was not so much these things as "the hope that I may thereby fan the holy flame that their action kindled. . . . Agitation is a good thing when it ultimates in action; but not otherwise," and in that spirit he offered a toast: "Success to the next negro insurrection."

In Kansas the democratic *Weekly Leavenworth Herald* in commenting on Redpath's biography declared that "an extensive review and exposure of the book is useless, as the readers will perceive its rottenness themselves. But the spirit of the work deserves more than a passing notice. . . . There is a studied design . . . to make more 'heroes of Harper's Ferry.' " The editor charged flatly that Redpath, an unnaturalized foreigner, was avowedly plotting to destroy the Union which he hated:

An appeal is directly made to the partisan feeling now existing—opposing sections are hissed on to strife—abolition, by servile insurrection, advocated and planned—John Brown endorsed and canonized—and the existence of another similar conspiracy divulged.

As the presidential campaign of 1860 began to take more definite shape the same editor expressed foreboding on the permanency of human government:

Again—a united South against a united North is the rallying cry on each side of Mason's and Dixon's line. But one more Harper's Ferry raid will bring civil war and disunion. Yet again—we view another sign. Here in Kansas a spirit of disorder and lawlessness broods over the land; fostered, and anon fanned to flames by the dominant party. This may be regarded as a lingering relic of border life; but its birth and nursing in the cradle of politics give it a more significant and startling interpretation.

The time has come when every man must act upon his own impressions. The duty of a patriotic citizen in this day of secedings and irrepressible

[19] New York *Tribune*, April 20, 1860.
[20] New York *Tribune*, April 20, 1860.

conflict, is too delicate to be trusted to the sway of agitators and demo-
gogues. The danger of the Union is just now too eminent, for the avert-
ing power to be delegated to other hearts and heads than those most interested in its preservation. Let Americans look to their country.[21]

The next biography of John Brown was prepared by Richard D.
Webb, an Englishman, entitled *The Life and Letters of Captain John
Brown . . . with notices of some of his confederates*, and was published in London in 1861. Emerson had said that the only way in
which the public would be satisfied about Brown was when Brown
spoke for himself. Norton had made the same point. In this book
Webb designated himself not as author, but editor, with a view to
permitting Brown to tell his own story so far as possible. Webb was
severe in his condemnation of Redpath's book; it was overbur-
dened with comments and epithets, inappropriate scripture texts,
and minute particulars of events in Kansas. Further criticisms
were that the arrangement was unsatisfactory and the nomen-
clature of the books and chapters was more calculated to mystify
than to assist the reader. Webb's interest in Kansas was slight.
His view of Brown placed the emphasis upon Harpers Ferry;
"just before Brown's enterprise [slavery] seemed as firmly established as the everlasting hills," but the Virginia raid prepared
the North sooner than otherwise "to defy the slaveholders by electing a republican President." He hoped that the American Civil
War would result in the abolition of slavery, and if so, then Brown
would have been "as the instrument in the hands of Providence"
in accelerating the attainment of that objective. Webb was of
the opinion that Brown's agency in the Harpers Ferry raid would
not alone entitle him to a biography, but that his conduct afterwards was such as to make him worthy of a permanent record.

Apart from Brown's own words, Webb acknowledged that
Redpath was his principal source of information about Brown.
In so doing he was recognizing that his objections to Redpath were
limited to his methods rather than to his allegations of fact. In
view of this kind of dependence upon Redpath, there is no reason
to present here a detailed analysis of the content of the book.

This chapter has been designated the Redpath period in John
Brown biography. There had been, first, Redpath's articles in the
Boston *Atlas and Bee;* the DeWitt *Life* cribbed primarily from

---

[21] *Leavenworth Herald*, February 18, May 19, 1860. During this period
the editor was William H. Gill, who had succeeded L. J. Eastin as editor on
November 19, 1859.

these newspaper articles without acknowledgment; Redpath's own books, the *Life* [22] and the *Echoes;* and finally, the Webb book, frankly based on Redpath. In spite of the severe criticism of the Redpath brand of biography, the outstanding fact is that none challenged his supposed facts, and all paid him the compliment of repeating his falsehoods, and no other book-size biography of Brown was attempted until Sanborn's in 1885. What was there to prevent the Redpath version from exercising a major influence in moulding the Brown Legend during the first twenty-five years?

The first crystallization of the Brown Legend was given its capstone in the North by the events of the Civil War;—the John Brown song and the abolition of slavery. There are almost as many versions of the origin of the song as there were free states, but the one most fully authenticated is that in April 1861, soon after the firing on Ft. Sumter, the second batallion of Massachusetts infantry was ordered to Fort Warren, in Boston harbor. One of the songs sung around the camp was an old Methodist tune, "Say, brothers, will you meet us?" There was a John Brown in the organization and he became the object of jokes; among them one about him being dead and his body mouldering in the grave. The words became associated with the tune, and the song was born. An attempt was made to substitute the name of some military hero, but the name John Brown stuck. The song was printed without music in May 1861 and sold on the streets of Boston as a penny ballad. The second edition was with music arranged by C. B. Marsh, the application for copyright being dated July 16, 1861. The song almost immediately became immensely popular as a marching song, and the public association of the name John Brown was of course not with the Massachusetts private at Fort Warren, but with the John Brown of Harpers Ferry.[23] Here again is another of the accidents when transfer to him of the song bearing the common English folkname became the means of spreading abroad the reputation of the John Brown of Harpers Ferry. It seemed to be his luck to fall heir to other men's fame. In Kansas he had been credited with fathering R. P. Brown, the victim of the Easton election brawl. On several occasions he was

---

[22] The *Life of Brown* had been published in both an American and an English edition.

[23] George Kimball, Origin of the John Brown Song, *New England Magazine*, New Series, 1 (December 1889) 271–377. This article is fortified by photographic reproductions of the first and second editions of the song and by the copyright records.

credited with the activities of his eldest son, and finally the title
"Osawatomie Brown" was transferred to him from O. C. Brown,
the founder of the town of Osawatomie. Later in 1859 the old
song "Old John Brown had a little Injun" was transferred to him
by the simple process of substituting the word nigger for injun,
and finally the Fort Warren song was similarly made the property
of the John Brown Legend. Even the phrase "his body lies mouldering" was not new as applied to Brown, because it had appeared
in Mrs. Lindsley's letter to A. D. Stevens, March 3, 1860.

The crystallization of the John Brown Legend was being effected, therefore, partly through deliberate falsification of the
record, and partly through a most astonishing succession of accidental associations. The fact that this uncanny process was taking place was not altogether lost upon contemporaries. The editor
of the Illinois *Weekly Mirror* (Mt. Carroll), August 6, 1862, wrote
an extensive editorial about it:

> The apotheosis of old John Brown is fast taking place. Someone has
> said: 'Permit me to write the songs of a people, and you may make its
> laws.' The utterance is true. The living sentiment that inspires a people
> finds expression in song.
> One of the most wonderful songs, in this respect, ever written is the
> Old John Brown song. . . . All over the country it may be heard at all
> times of the night or day in the streets of Chicago and all our other cities;
> it is the pet song among the soldiers in all our armies; more than a thou-
> sand verses have been composed and sung to the tune of old John Brown's
> soul is marching on.
>
> * * * *
>
> Our better judgment pronounced the verdict of the jury, which con-
> demned him to the gallows, to be just and right. Neither do we intend
> now to justify old John Brown or any action of his in Virginia. But
> there is no use denying that we have always had kind and sympathetic
> feelings towards the old hero—the very same feelings, which are now
> animating the masses of our people, when they sing the old John Brown
> song, or applaud it, when sung by others. . . . This is the reason that the
> apotheosis is set to music, and sung by millions in the land—millions whom
> no one ever charged with being Abolitionists.
> Let no one misconceive the spirit of this article. We do not intend it
> as a eulogy upon Old John Brown; we simply intend to look at the causes
> and effects of this old John Brown song.

The abolition of slavery in the United States came during the
Civil War. This is a fact no one can dispute, but the worshippers
of the Old Hero jumped at the unjustifiable conclusion that it
came because of the war, that the war came because of John Brown,

and, therefore, John Brown abolished slavery. In this manner the
failure at Harpers Ferry was transmuted into success and rationalized;—John Brown was not an insane man and a failure; he
was a prophet and a martyr. That facts ran to the contrary was
just unfortunate for the facts. It ignored the generation of anti-
slavery agitation which had preceded Harpers Ferry, as well as
the operation of natural forces, independent of propaganda, which
were restricting and diminishing steadily the geographical extent
of the peculiar institution.

The rounding out of the Brown-abolition dogma for the Civil
War period came after the conflict, when the victors were ration-
alizing their conquest. Survivors of the marching armies and
particularly the relatives of those who had died in action, had been
convinced that they had participated in a holy cause. The war
had not brought much in tangible return to the rank and file, and
the turmoil of post-war economic depression, hate, greed and dis-
illusionment brought many to question whether the war had not
been fought in vain. And yet, a highly sentimental generation,
in want of a more tangible token, must needs find some moral compensation. In devotion to the rites of Hero worship they and theirs
partook vicariously in his martyrdom, and thus experienced emotional fulfillment. In celebrating his apotheosis they tended the
clear white light upon the altar of their own war sacrifice.

CHAPTER XII

HANWAY'S CHALLENGE TO THE JOHN BROWN LEGEND IN KANSAS

James Hanway was the first friend of John Brown to make a determined effort to establish the facts with regard to him in Kansas, especially those touching the controversial Potawatomie massacre question. He believed that the facts did not discredit Brown, but, on the contrary, justified the act. Hanway was an Englishman born September 4, 1809, whose father was a philanthropist and whose mother was a Quaker. Upon attaining his majority he emigrated to Darke county, Ohio, married, raised a large family, wrote voluminously for the newspapers on most all subjects, scientific, social, economic, literary and political. He was active in the anti-slavery movement and in the organization of the republican party. In the spring of 1856, he migrated to Kansas settling in Potawatomie township, in the southeast corner of Franklin county, on Potawatomie creek, a region which became the home of a number of settlers from the same county in Ohio.[1]

James Hanway was a prominent local leader, holding local office, was a member of the Wyandotte constitutional convention in 1859, of territorial senate in 1860, and of the state house of representatives in 1864 and 1869. Without question, he was held in the highest esteem by his neighbors. He died May 9, 1882.

During the year 1856 Hanway kept a little memorandum book in which he entered various kinds of items without any rigid system or dates, a casual type of little book in which to record an idea which he might use in his writing or with which he might refresh his memory. On page two a pencil entry was made and then crossed out, but the most of it can be deciphered:

[1] He stated that in 1856 he pre-empted the northeast quarter of section five, township 19 south, range 21 east (*First Biennial report* of the Kansas State Board of Agriculture, 218), but he received a patent June 1, 1860 for the southeast quarter of section five. He claimed for his son, John S. Hanway, the northwest quarter of section four, and in the spring of 1857 built a log cabin on it, living there himself for two years (Andreas-Cutler, History of Kansas, 605). This is the cabin that was to figure in the propaganda of the seventies as that of John Brown. The patent to John S. Hanway was issued, however, for the northeast quarter of section four.

Started on 20 of May 1856.
Arrived at Middle fork the same night—then traveled to Shores.   we passed Toy Jones rendevous stayed 2 nights at S [hores] then to Palmyra —stayed 2 nights there on the S [anta] F [e] road then traveled to [?] the morning of [?] then returned home on Thursday evening.

A long entry begins on page three, running through pages four, five, six and about half of page seven, or four and a half pages, also in pencil. The context determines positively that it was written after May 26. The reference to the release of Morse and the absence of any mention of the battle of Black Jack or of the raid on Osawatomie June 7 suggests that it was written about June 1:

Killed in Saturday night May 24, 1856
3 men of the name of Doyal—Wm Sherman & Wilkinson—The latter received 6 wounds each one would have proved fatal. Old man Doyal was shot through the head & stabed in the heart, & his two boys where desperately cut about the hands—the younger boy's hands were mangled as if he had held up his hands to defend himself from the blows of the saber—Sherman's head was cut by a saber blow, and others [one line blank] five men murdered on one night enticed from their houses with the promise of being kept from violence, as prisoners of war—lead a few rods from their doors then killed. one was flung in the creek down the bank (Wilkinson) he was postmaster—The murderers inquired for Henry S, but he was away from home hunting up his cattle this saved his life— At Shermans they seized 3 other men with him took them all out from the house asked them their names, told them to go back again. The question now is who has performed this frightful tradagy [sic] men names are whispered—no positive knowledge—Mrs. Doyal describes 2 of the men, which description is exactly that of Mrs. Wilkinson—a man who lives at Shermans for several years says he did not know any of them, altho he has lived here 2 yrs and knows most people on the creek. The settlement is plunged into a perfect commotion. a meeting of the settlers was held on the 26 and they mutually agreed to protect each other from foreign or internal foes all men of real good sense, condemned this midnight assassination and also the killing of men who are attending to their concerns—one murder by the opposite side, only makes another on the other— — The supposed causes which made the Doyal family the victims, is that the old man & his sons, called on a man who kept a store near Sherman's—and told him to pack up his goods, moved off his claim in five days or they would kill him. Morse did not move but is still at home, he was arrested by a body of men & as there was no evidence against him he is at large. Sherman it is said as repeatedly threatened to shoot & exterminate free state men, and at the news of the fall of Lawrence raised a red flag: which was said he meant to intimate that war was commenced & he was in for it—Wilkinson appears to have been a very violent & imprudent man making threat of killing & burning & his wife is a fine woman, sick at the time of the murder and told the Dr that she has frequently urged him to be more quiet—but could not do it—it appears

from general opinion that they were extreme men, and very obnoxious to
the free state men—thus violence breeds violence. Again. No sooner the
news of the destruction of the Hotel at Lawrence and the two printing
presses than the "Border Times a violent paper published at Westport
after given a short statement of the pillage and destruction of Lawrence,
comments thus, it says—"This is right, nuisances should be suppressed"
and then recommends the pro-slavery party of the Ty to drive and exterminate every "black hearted abolitionist and drive them from the Ty."
They advocate assassination and now that 5 persons have been murdered
on their side perhaps they will learn that such hellish sentiments when
carried into effect, will work equally to the destruction of the pro-slavery
men of the territory Such men are the immediate instigators of all such
bloody tragedies as we have witnessed—they should be held responsible at
the bar of public opinion.

Following this extended note are several miscellaneous entries
and on page 8 occurs the first dated entry, August 8. Near the
middle of the volume are entries that refer to the battle of Osawatomie and subsequent events:

> 5 men killed, Brown, Bunda Garrison
> Gardiner & Dayton [crossed out]
> 2 store burnt. Winers & Jho Brown Sr & son house, letters stolen &
> read in the Pota Cr—several of the Bogus Officers in this act—Toy Jones
> house burnt & shot at.—
> Election today
> Investigating commt report
> Will K be a slave state.

These last entries are puzzling, because if his memory was accurate Hanway had left the Potawatomie country August 10 with
a friend Allen Jaqua to return to Ohio to settle up business and
prepare to bring his family to Kansas in the spring of 1857. They
were in Lawrence between August 12 and 15, because Hanway
remembered that it was after the battle of Franklin and prior to
the attack on Washington creek, and he was at Leavenworth when
the news was received of the capture of Fort Titus August 16.
He was in Ohio when the battle of Osawatomie was fought. The
entries must have been made after his return in the spring or
from letters or newspaper reports. But the second part of the
entry is confusing, because it is usually stated that the Brown
houses were burned just after the Potawatomie massacre, and here
the statement is sandwiched between two items for August 30.[2]

---

[2] Hanway's account of his trip east is contained in a letter to H. Miles
Moore, February 11, 1882. *H. Miles Moore Papers.* Kansas State Historical
Society. The Wiener store might have been one established in Osawatomie
instead of the one on Mosquito creek.

In view of these uncertainties about the notebook it is clear that there are limitations on its use as evidence, but whatever the exact dates and circumstances of the entries, the text is of outstanding importance. Made without thought of its historical consequences or any idea of the outcome or implications of the events, this contemporary record is of the very essence of history. Remembering that he had arrived in Kansas only that spring and had resided there only a few weeks at most, he was describing a community event in language which implied that he was not acquainted with the principals: "3 men of the name of Doyal"; "Wilkinson appears to have been a very violent & imprudent man"; "it appears from general opinion that they were extreme men"; he condemned "the killing of men who are attending to their concerns," and repeated only what were the "supposed causes" of the killing of the Doyles, and the evidence against the Shermans was hearsay introduced by the phrase "it is said." The detailed description of the dead bodies is positive evidence of the brutality of the proceeding; six wounds any one of which would have been fatal to Wilkinson, and the mangled condition of the younger Doyle boy. It is further evident that Hanway condemned the murder, but at the same time he was trying to find a basis for justification, and it seems not too much to say that as he wrote the entry he was making progress toward a rationalization. All the local allegations were hearsay, however, and except for the Morse store incident, were general charges, the most specific offense was the distant *Border Times* newspaper article relating to the raid on Lawrence and that would not have reached the community until after the massacre. It is not a matter of wonder that he was having difficulty in coming to a satisfying conclusion that so fiendish a crime was warranted.

A letter appeared in the Cincinnati *Commercial* July 23, 1856, written by a Kansas settler under the date of July 4, but the evidence points to Hanway as the author although the name was withheld by the editor for his protection.[3] "It is true, I have sent

---

[3] The editor stated that the author was from Ohio, and the writer admitted that on passing through Cincinnati on the way to Kansas he had promised to write and was fulfilling that promise. He was a member of the company which had marched to the assistance of Lawrence. He recounted the panic in the community after the massacre giving details nearly exactly as Hanway's signed writings did later. The visit to the officer commanding federal troops is also a stock Hanway story of later date. Hanway stated later that he had written a letter to the Cincinnati *Commercial* giving a full report, and understood that it had been printed. (Letter to Redpath, March 12, 1860.)

several letters, giving the particulars of the Potawatomie tragedy, the causes which probably led the perpetrators to commit the deed, &c, but up to this date I know not whether they have been seen by anyone outside of Missouri or the Territory.'' He reviewed briefly the march to Lawrence and return, ''and since then the Squatters have been in a continued state of alarm. The five persons murdered by some personal enemies, who had been quarreling and making threats one towards another, was the first local difficulty we have had.'' He then described the settlers' meeting condemning the crime, promising to bring the murderers to justice, warrants for arrests, and the man hunt with the excesses accompanying it, the taking of fourteen prisoners, pillaging of homes, the carrying of seven prisoners to Lecompton for hearings, and the release of all but two. At this point in the narrative he arrived at the significant conclusion that ''men who have heretofore advocated obedience to the mandates of the United States District Court of this Territory, are no longer to be found. The practical operations of the Court are nothing more or less than the worst system of despotism.'' He then commented on the federal troops, admitting that they had been of some service in preventing conflict, but they were mostly pro-slavery sympathizers. He quoted rumor that Captain Woods was only sorry that the whole town of Lawrence had not been burned, but he checked up on the federal officers stationed in his neighborhood by visiting their camp, finding that the captain was a fireeater and consequently he was convinced of the truth of the other reports.

In comment on the general community situation, he reported that: ''Within the last ten days some ten families have moved off the creek, both free state and proslavery, but chiefly the proslavery stamp. Some of the proslavery men, who have left their homes from fear, are honest and quiet men, who condemn the conduct of their border friends.'' He admitted horse-stealing on both sides, but insisted that the enemy had started it. ''Parties soon commenced a system of retaliation and this demoralizing system is now in full blast. . . . Innocent men are the doomed sufferers.'' He closed with the story that within a few days the wife of the postmaster had burned all the letters addressed to free-state people.

Another letter, also unsigned in the printing, was published in the *National Era,* September 25, 1856, dated September 6 at Castine, Darke county, Ohio, the town of which Hanway had been mayor prior to coming to Kansas. The author must have been

Hanway. He sent greetings to the Quaker editor of the *National Era* from his friend, the Quaker Richard Mendenhall, of Osawatomie, and emphasized the great suffering and destitution which prevailed in Kansas among both pro-slavery and free-state people who were prevented by the troubles from planting crops. A considerable part of the letter, however, was devoted to a review of the man hunt described in the former letter, and in much the same way. In justification of the free-state men being held by the courts, John Brown, Jr., and H. H. Williams, he maintained that "they had committed no offence against the laws of God"; they had merely taken up arms to defend themselves.

If the identification of the author of these letters is correct, it is clear that he had not yet arrived at a satisfactory justification of the Potawatomie crime, but made one of the most damaging admissions possible, that it "was the first local difficulty we have had." Some advance toward the basis of a theory of justification was made in recording the newly crystallized unanimity of sentiment against the federal courts, and in making a case against the federal officers in command of troops.

The first identification by Hanway of John Brown as the murderer of the Potawatomie came in the letter to Hinton of December 5, 1859, but in that letter the admission was indirect. After the publication of the book, Redpath sent Hanway a copy according to the promise to contributors, and what he found there occasioned great surprise and moved Hanway to write a long letter of protest March 12, 1860.[4]

Shermanville, Franklin Co. Kansas Ty.
March 12, 1860.

My dear Sir.

Your note and the order to Thayer & Eldridge has been received and the book read by my family. It has given us much interesting matter, and on the whole is I doubt not a correct life of the old man—many of the incidents in Brown's Kansas life, of course we who have lived here during the troubles, know to be as recorded.

But my dear Sir, I am sorry to see that you have fell into a very common error, with most of those friends of Brown who live at a distance in stating that "The old man declared that he did not, *in any way*, participate in their execution; but thought here, in jail, as he had believed in Kansas, that the act was just & necessary" page 374 alluding to the Potawatomie affair.

On page 117 it reads "on the 23 of May John Brown left the camp of his son, at Osawatomie &" this ought to read at Ottawa Creek. On page

[4] *Hanway Papers*, Kansas State Historical Society.

118 in regard to the conduct of the ruffians to Browns daughter & daughter in law, we on the creek understand that this affair was *after* the killing of Doyle Wilkinson &c and not before. Mr. Adair at whose house they fled says this is all news to him.

Permit me to give you a short outline of facts, which I am knowing to personally. I was a member of John Brown Jr company, we had started to protect Lawrence. We received a dispatch from Lawrence, containing the news of it being sackt &c and also requesting us not to come to Lawrence till further orders. Our military company camped on Ottawa creek, near Capt Shores residence for 2 or 3 days Old John Brown & I think 7 others of our company formed a camp of their own. And left us to go to the Pottawatomie Creek. John Brown *Jr* and Jason remained with us. Frederick Brown & the Thompson and another son, were I think in the company. They started in the afternoon; and 3 cheers were given to the success of Capt Brown & his men. Now sir, what I am going to relate to you, I have never mentioned to but one man living. And that is, one of the party made a proposition to me to join the company, and also gave me such information in regard to their contemplated enterprise as to satisfy my mind that they were the chief actors in the Pottawatomie tragedy.

A few days after we received the news of the killing of the pro-slavery ruffians. It was on Sunday afternoon; I was outside of the guards, in company of Jason Brown when the news arrived. Our camp march to Ottawa Jones the same night. About 1 oclock A M old John Brown & his party arrived. I spoke to the old man, he asked me, if there was any news. I told him of the report received from the Pottawatomie. He wanted to see his son John, who was sleeping in Jones house.

The next morning John Brown Jr resigned his office of Captain, and we elected another person in his place. That portion of the company who resided near the Sherman's on the Pott Creek, recognized several horses which belonged to the ruffians—And several of our men remarked that they hoped they would not take them in the neighborhood of Osawatomie &c because they were well known—one was a stallion.

The parties started towards Osawatomie—John Brown Jr accompanied the Osawatomie party, and those belonging to the Pottawatomie Rifle Company separated near Middle Creek—the old Man Brown & his sons & a few others remained at North Middle Creek, where his sons had taken claims, and resided.

Two of my neighbors, who are still living here, called on me as soon as I arrived home from camp duty. They asked me various questions about the dress of old John Brown—his leather cravat—light coat &c &c one of these men remarked, 'I am perfectly satisfied, it is impossible to be mistaken' I inquired more fully into the matter, and they informed me that they had just arrived from Kansas City; and the morning after the killing of these men—they called at Wilkinsons for mail matter. Wilkinson's wife was sick in bed, and she informed them that she feared that her husband was killed &c They found the body, and buried it; in company with several other neighbors. They also assisted in the burial of Doyle & his two sons.

The description of the dress of 'the old man who appeared to be leader' was described by Mrs W. & by other women & men at Shermans. And all I have to say is, that it agreed precisely to that worn by John Brown Sr. Of this there is no doubt.

The testimony under oath as published in the investigating Committee, page 1193 & 4,5 is not all true. Testimony to the contrary might be obtained on this head.

I was personally acquainted with the Doyals, Wilkinson & sherman, and I am fully satisfied, as everybody else is who lived on the Creek in 56; that a base conspiracy was on foot to drive out, burn, and kill;—in a word the Pottawatomie Creek from its mouth to its founded head was to be cleared of every man woman, or child who was for Kansas being a free state.

I will give one item, which has never been published, and perhaps I may be considered as infringing on private conversation; but the importance of the question demands it. When the party called at the house of the Shermans, Mrs Harris who was living there—commenced getting breakfast, believing that the party who had arrived, were friends who were expected from Missouri to carry out the border ruffian plan of clearing the Creek of Abolitionists. This important fact alone is evidence that John Brown was correct in his predictions. This incident came through a moderate pro-slavery man, who was astonished to hear that such a plan was under consideration. Names I am not permitted to give, but the facts are undisputable.

The remarks you have made in regard to the causes which lead to the killing of these men, are correct. I have personal knowledge of these facts. Threats were made to various persons Squire Morse, John Grant & his family, Mr Winer & others. And I will add, that the absence from home saved the lives of other pro-slavery men on the creek.

My dear Sir, I will sum up the whole question of the Pottawatomie Matter in a few words.

Old John Brown was at my house several days, at various times in 1858. We had a long talk over the political difficulties of Kansas. He asked me 'how do the people on the Creek, regard the killing of the Shermans &c at this time' My remark was, that I did not know a settler of 56, but what regarded it as amongst the most fortunate events in the history of Kansas—that this event saved the lives of the free state men on the creek: that those who did the act were looked upon [as] our deliverors &c. The old man remarked, that the first shock frightened the free state men, almost as bad as the ruffians, but he knew when the facts were understood that a reaction would take place. He then remarked, 'if the killing of these men was murder, then he was an accessory.'

This remark did not surprise me, because I heard his brother in law, Revd Mr Adair, say that the old man had said the same to him.

The question is how can we reconcile the various reports which have been published on this Pottawatomie affair? In the first place, it was a matter [on which] the old man did not think prudent to communicate his thoughts, to everyone. He could truly say 'I did not kill them. I was not present when they were killed &c &c' Because from the best of evi-

dence which I can obtain he did not kill any of them.   The old man understood the examination, and others carried out the verdict.   They were all
taken from the premises & slain.   By a cap being discharged, the signal
was given to retreat.

I could give you many other circumstances in connection with this
affair, but I deem I have said enough to convince you that old John Brown
& his party knew all about the affair; and I may add that no man in this
section of the country but feels confident that Brown was the chief leader
in the Pottawatomie affair, and *honors him for it.*

This incident in the life of Capt Brown may 'shock' men who have
passed their lives in Eastern cities &c but we in Kansas who have known
John Brown for many years, and have warm friendship for his memory:
do hope that the *Whole* facts may yet be published in his life.

I have heard one of the Shermans declare that he would rather take the
life of certain men on the creek, than kill a rattlesnake—I heard Squire
Morse relate the threats made by the Doyals and also by the Shermans,
because he sold some powder & lead to our military company.   I have
heard frequently the violent threats which Mr. Grant and his whole family received from the two Shermans.   Also Mr Winer, because he gave
provisions to the free State organizations:—& in this case they burnt his
store house and its contents and narrowly escaped with his life, by being
fired on several times while detained by high water on the Osage River.
Take in connection the fact of John Brown running in the border ruffian
camp with his surveying instruments and there hearing the plans on foot
to drive out and exterminate the settlers on our Creek—And I think we
have good & sufficient testimony to believe that our lives were in danger,
and that John Brown and his little band saved us from a premature grave

you may ask, why has not this matter been examined into before.   it
has been; but one fact I do know that various Repn papers in the fall of
56 objected to publishing the corrected version—thinking it would act
prejudicial to the Repn nomine & party.   I sent a full report in 56 to
the Cin-ti Commercial and altho I never saw it myself, I understood the
article was published.   It was difficult to receive mail matter in the fall
& summer of 56 in Kansas.

Miss Mary Partridge has engaged quite a number of names of the life
of Brown.   Your friend H called on me a few weeks since, and obtained
incident of Browns men who fell at Harpers Ferry.   He also took notes
on the subject matter of this letter.

In conclusion if there is any matter which you deem would be of interest to your future publications, and I can aid you in any way, I shall
most willingly comply to your request

There is one remark which I will now make, and that is, that many of
our citizens who knew something of the Pottawatomie affair has said but
little about it, outside of a certain circle as they did not wish to be brought
up as witnesses before the courts, or do anything to injure those who they
believed acted in the matter.   Some have now fell at Harpers Ferry, but
still others are living—whose names *at* better [had – be] kept from paper.
~~The following names could~~ [crossed out in MSS]

I send this to your publishers, not knowing your address. I should like to receive a line from you, and have your opinion on the matter of this letter

your respectfully

Jas Hanway

[Note written at head of last page]

John Browns sons & his son in law took claims in Franklin Co not in Lyki.'s Co—as stated in your book. We have 2 middle creeks. one is called North Middle Cr Franklin Co the other South Middle Creek which is in Ly'ins Co.—thus the mistake—we claim the Brown family for Franklin.

As this letter is found only in *Hanway Papers,* a question might arise whether it was sent. The probabilities are that it was and that the document in the *Hanway Papers* is a copy because Hanway frequently kept copies of what he wrote for publication and frequently used his copies when he had occasion again to write on the same subject. It should make little if any difference, however, to Redpath's subsequent career as a defender of Brown, because near the close Hanway stated that H[inton] had called recently and "took notes on the subject matter of this letter." Of course, there is little doubt but that both Redpath and Hinton knew the facts from their experience in Kansas during 1856 as newspaper correspondents. This correction of their writing on the subject should have served as a warning, however, that if they did not make the correction themselves, there were those, whose loyalty to the memory of Brown could not be questioned, who would expose them eventually. Redpath must have received this warning prior to the writing of the preface, April 14, 1860, to his *Echoes of Harper's Ferry,* but gave no hint of any modification of views.

From the standpoint of Hanway historiography the letter is an important land mark. He had taken an important step in justification. With regard to the victims of the massacre, he was able to say "I was personally acquainted with" them; "I have heard one of the Sherman's declare"; and in regard to evidence from others he could say "I heard Squire Morse relate threats"; and "I have heard frequently the violent threats" to the Grant family; "also Mr. Winer," because he gave provisions, his store was burnt and attempt made to shoot him. The first two items show that he had gone a long way since writing the entry in the memorandum book in 1856. In the reference to the Grants and to Wiener there is some confusion of chronology; exactly how much is impossible to determine, but almost certainly the Wiener incidents came after rather than before the massacre. He still used the argument of general danger to the whole community of being murdered, used the surveyor story and added to it the story of Mrs. Harris making breakfast preparations, but neither of these has any specific bearing on the principals in the massacre. Such general threats against each other were commonly indulged in by both sides during the border strife, and were published in the papers, but were never carried out by either. Historians must not be misled by such bombast, and must not permit it to be associated with the Potawatomie massacre in any cause and effect relationship.

The passage of time did not dim Hanway's interest in John Brown; in fact, the Brown question seemed to occupy a more significant place in his thoughts as the negro question developed through the sixties and Hanway, in his later years, came to live more and more with his memories. In 1863 he made a trip to Lawrence to the burial of Dr. Rufus Gillpatrick, one of the old settlers on Potawatomie creek, the doctor to whom Mrs. Wilkinson had told her story as mentioned in the letter to Redpath. On his return he stopped at Palmyra to refresh his memories of the Expedition of May 1856, located the spot where the camp had been, and referring to the massacre commented: "This is a part of the history of Kansas which has never been correctly recorded." [4] Two years later he wrote to the Richmond, Indiana, *True Republican* that "If Kansas, as a State, is intensely radical, you must remember that the war of Slavery first endeavored to subjugate us to its iron yoke. That the incipient steps of this gigantic rebellion were inaugurated upon the prairies of Kansas." Then, as though he could not write about Kansas without mentioning John Brown, he illustrated his point with the surveyor story:

It was by information thus obtained, that he found out that certain abolitionists were to be burnt out, and driven off or exterminated, on the Pottawatomie Creek. He prevented the consummation, by the timely movement by cutting off these assassins from the community. Here, by the way, is a chapter in the life of that conscientious old man, which has *never been written*. The chapter subtitled 'Pottawatomie' in Redpath's Life of John Brown, is incorrect, hardly a word of truth in it.[5]

[4] Clipping from the Leavenworth *Bulletin,* undated. Hanway *Scrapbooks,* 2: 112. The letter was dated December 6, 1863.

[5] Clipping undated, in the Hanway *Scrapbooks,* 2: 96. The letter was dated from Lane, Kansas, April 30, 1865. At this time Hanway was writing frequently for the *True Republican.*

In this letter Hanway took another step in justification, by becoming more specific. Instead of a general threat against the free-state men on the creek, the threat was against "certain abolitionists," but no one was mentioned by name.

In 1865, the St. Louis *Republican,* a democratic paper, republished a letter of General Hunter to Jefferson Davis, dated in September 1862 which was a panygeric on John Brown, as an example of the excesses of republican radicalism, and in reply republished an article from a monthly magazine *The Old Guard* containing portions of a speech delivered in the senate by President, then Senator, Andrew Johnson, on December 12, 1859, in reply to Senator Doolittle. Johnson's speech was based on the *Herald of Freedom* ventilation of Kansas history and the affidavits on the Potawatomie massacre published in the minority report of the committee which investigated Kansas troubles in 1856.[6] These things came to the attention of Charles A. Foster, of Osawatomie, who was in St. Louis at the time. He wrote an immediate reply, which was published through the rival St. Louis *Democrat,* July 3, 1865, denying that John Brown was present or participating at the massacre, but justifying those who were. He developed the general theme of the impending danger to the free-state community, but introduced specifically the Georgian camps near Stanton and southeast of Osawatomie as the centers of the menace. By surveying a line through their camp John Brown found out that they were going to raid the Browns for their fine stock. He maintained that the Georgians then moved over into the Potawatomie creek country and commenced depredations; that William Sherman made advances towards a daughter of a free-state man and that she appealed to Fred Brown for protection. When the Lawrence news arrived, Brown counseled delay, and it was several days before they started, the Potawatomie Rifles going on a day ahead of the Osawatomie company, who met Old John Brown's party at the Osage crossing returning Friday morning. He related that H. H. Williams had been left behind by the Potawatomie Rifles to get lead, and at Morse's store heard the warning to Morse to leave, and on rejoining his company on the road gave them the information. The news of the massacre reached the expedition near Prairie City, on their way back Sunday afternoon, through James Harris whose story was of the opposite tenor to that given in the committee affidavit. With regard to the massacre,

6 St. Louis *Republican,* July 2, and 3, 1865.

Foster insisted that when Old John Brown returned to Middle
creek the houses of his sons, John and Jason, were closed and deserted, also Mrs. Thompson (his daughter Ruth) was gone.[7] He
inquired of a neighbor, who related the threats and that the women
had gone to Osawatomie with the oxen. Brown then found the
burning homes of three squatters, among them Jacob Benjamin,
who accused the Doyles, Wilkinson and Sherman. However John
Brown and Fred left the party and rejoined them on Sunday, so
they could not have been present or participating at the massacre.
In further support of the argument as to the nature of the men,
he repeated Mrs. Wilkinson's admission to the doctor of urging
her husband to be more moderate. Foster claimed that there was
no cruelty in the massacre beyond what was necessary to kill, but
admitted that it had not been the intention to kill the Doyle boys,
only they had come to their father's aid. He conceded that his
letter was imperfect, because he did not have access to his papers,
but if it was necessary he would return to the question in order
to defend the men engaged in the Potawatomie massacre, so-called.

It is notable how many similarities there were between Foster's
and Hanway's justifications. The legend had become pretty well
established on certain points. The differences were significant
also; the fact that the Osawatomie company were a day behind
the rest, the meeting with Brown on his return, the details of the
treatment of the Brown women and the three burning cabins, together with Benjamin's specific accusation. If these were true,
then the process of justification of the massacre was complete. Just
how the introduction of the Georgians fitted into the justification
is not so clear.

The next stage in the development of the story was inspired
by the publication of J. N. Holloway's *History of Kansas* in 1868.
Holloway was an Indianan, who had tried his hand at preaching
and teaching, but without much success, although he did seem to
have a capacity for making enemies. He migrated to Kansas in
hopes of new prospects, settling for about a year at Ottawa where
he taught school. Finding that there was no history of Kansas
he conceived the idea of writing one, and after investigation, decided he could make it pay. As he put it in his journal: "I finally
decided as my way in other directions seemed hedged up to make

---

[7] Foster was in error as Ruth had not accompanied Thompson to Kansas.
The wives of John Jr., and Jason were in Kansas.

an attempt and run the risk."[8]   He financed the venture mostly
on borrowed money, and moved to Topeka late in January 1867
to gather material and write. By December of that year the book
was off the press, printed privately, and he arrived in Topeka
with the books during the session of the legislature, in January
and February, 1868. He recorded that he made about fifty dollars per week during the session and then took a horse and buggy
and set out to sell the book from house to house and "at night
I would camp out, do my own cooking, and sleep in my buggy."
By the end of the year he had paid off about one thousand dollars
of his debt and returned to Indiana. It is clear from this story
that the author had no qualifications for writing the history of
Kansas, and that one year was too short a time to collect material
on a subject that was strange to him, write a book of 584 pages,
and put it through the press. Nevertheless, this was the first book
that pretended to be a history of the state of Kansas. What was
the quality of the product? The newspapers reviewed it as kindly
as possible, complimented the author, but agreed that the history
of Kansas was still to be written.[9] The *Western Home Journal*
admitted that "partisan prejudice and passion are not yet ready
to hear or believe the truth."

James Hanway thought, nevertheless, that the public should
have the truth as he saw it, and wrote a three column article for
the Ottawa *Western Home Journal*, April 23, 1868, correcting
Holloway on the Potawatomie tragedy. He admitted with the
author that "the history of Kansas is a difficult one to write" as
the "facts were so perverted and differently represented by contemporary writers, that the searcher for truth is often lost. . . .
Much, too, . . . has never been written." Both of these comments fit perfectly into Hanway's thesis. He blamed especially
the New York *Tribune* and the St. Louis *Democrat* for contemporary falsification in connection with the Potawatomie affair,
charging that their reports "are almost destitute of truth." Later
writers had followed the first writers and no one, to his knowledge,
had attempted to correct those first reports. He admitted that
"some will no doubt consider my effort in the present case to correct history, as very impolitic. 'It will do no good, but injure

[8] Holloway's *Journal* is in the possession of the Kansas State Historical
Society. The entry is for April 15, 1868 summarizing the period after February 6, 1867, when the last entry had been made.
[9] Ottawa *Western Journal*, January 23, 1868, and the Leavenworth *Commercial* reprinted in the *Western Home Journal*, March 12, 1868.

the party,' and other objections will be urged, as has been done heretofore.'' After making the necessary corrections in connection with this affair, Hanway promised his readers to tell the story in his next communication of the abolitionists and Judge Cato's court, which had been omitted by Halloway. But there was no next in the *Western Home Journal* and the historian is left to surmise whether Hanway's first had convinced the editor that such history would hurt the party or the circulation of the paper.[10]

The publication of history must wait a favorable opportunity, but Hanway would write it anyway. He remarked to Adams when his doctor ordered him to quit writing that "Life without Literature is death."[11] During the following year he arranged with the Ottawa *Republic* to publish his "Reminiscences of Pottawatomie township, Franklin County, Kansas," beginning with the issue of November 18, 1869 and running through eight numbers. As originally planned, the Potawatomie affair was treated briefly, but for some reason the article of 1868 was reprinted, giving the longer version a second time. Two years later he revised the series and published it in the Ottawa *Herald* in twenty-one numbers.[12]

By piecing together these three versions Hanway's history of the year 1856 and early 1857 can be presented in complete form as follows:

[10] This paper was edited by I. S. Kalloch, a notorious anti-slavery minister in Boston in the fifties who was tried and acquitted on adultery charges and who had migrated to Kansas, engaged in politics, railroad and land speculation and in newspaper work which would promote all three. Few, if any, personalities in Kansas history have stirred up more controversy than the "Sorrel Stallion of the Marais des Cygnes." Cf. John H. Shimmons, The shame and scourge of San Francisco; or, an expose of the Rev. Isaac S. Kalloch . . . n. p. 1880.

[11] *Hanway Papers*, Kansas State Historical Society. Hanway to Adams, February 28, 1878.

[12] In later years Hanway rewrote parts of all of these reminiscences and republished them in other newspapers. In 1875 three papers were published on John Brown in the Lawrence *Western Home Journal*, correcting Sanborn; a "Potawatomie Valley" series, probably in the Paola *Republican* in 1879. [The clippings, not fully identified as to paper and date, are in the Hanway *Scrapbooks*.] An article on "Old Border Ruffian days" in the Paola *Western Spirit*, April 5, 1878, two articles in the *Kansas Monthly Magazine* in 1880, and finally a series of "Early Reminiscences" in the Osawatomie *Times* beginning August 5, 1880 in thirty-four numbers. Besides these Hanway wrote numerous letters and short articles on special phases of the John Brown problem, especially after the new controversial period began late in 1879. Of course, he had little to say that was new in the later communications and in the heat of controversy said some things that had better been left unsaid.

[1869 version]

In the month of January, 1856, an election was held for State officers; 39 votes were cast for Governor at this election. The Ruffians did not attend the polls. We find on the poll books, John Brown Jr., Frederick Brown, Owen Brown, Henry Thompson (son-in-law of Old John Brown.) Why the old man did not vote I know not. He brought with him, early in the morning, a basket containing revolvers and dirk knives, thinking it possible that the legal voters might need them. This was the first introduction of Old John Brown on the warpath.

In the spring of 1856, a considerable number of emigrants settled on Pottawatomie creek, both on the north and south fork, extending into Anderson county. During the month of April a great many claims were taken, but in a short time the peaceful avocation of the squatter was changed by the call for volunteers. The rumble of a distant storm soon convinced them that, if they intended to settle in Kansas, they must fight for their homes—that what was called "squatter sovereignty" in the States was "slavery, or your life," in the Territory.

It became, therefore, necessary for the Free-State men to organize for mutual safety. We therefore formed ourselves into a company, known as the Pottawatomie Rifle Company; John Brown, Jr., was elected captain.

We now come to an important epoch in the early history of Kansas. I allude to what was termed by the government organs as an "abolition outrage," "breaking up Judge Cato's court by armed men" &c. As this event is passed over by Mr. Halloway in his History of Kansas, I will attempt to fill the omission, as I had the honor to be one of those charged with this grave offence. Meetings were frequently held for drilling and and for purposes of consultation. It was at one of these meetings that a series of resolutions were adopted, which were afterwards passed by similar organizations. The Herald of Freedom pronounced them to have the "right ring."

After these resolutions were adopted, a vote was taken by the company to visit Judge Cato's court, then in session in the log house of Henry S. Sherman, a pro-slavery man, whom I shall have occasion to speak more about hereafter. Our fire-arms were left in a log cabin, which still stands on the farm of John T. Hanway, a mile to the southwest of the Court House. Our object in paying this visit to the court of Judge Cato was to satisfy ourselves in regard to the position the judiciary intended to pursue in relation to the laws passed at the Shawnee Mission, by those who were elected by the slave-holding rabble from Missouri, the year before. Our company proceeded to the spot, we found Judge Cato delivering his charge to the grand jury, which was filled up with several boys under age. The room was small and only a few of us could obtain entrance. We were about thirty in number. Our visit, doubtless, was unexpected; for it proved what in parliamentary language might be called a lively sensation. But as we came as citizens, without any of the outward signs of war the court continued its charge. After Cato concluded his charge, Captain John Brown, Jr., and a few others who had obtained entrance, left the house, and J. B., Jr., remarked that the instructions to the grand jury were as he expected; that the laws passed at the Shawnee Mission were

to be enforced and recognized as the statutes of Kansas. Your correspondent remarked that he thought the Court had said nothing in his
charge to the jury but what were recognized principles of the common
law—that he had not referred to the "bogus laws." As this led to a conversation, J. B., Jr., remarked it would be best to have that point decided.
So he again entered the court-room and wrote on a slip of paper: "We,
the citizens of this part of the Territory, would thank the court if he
would state if he intended in his charge to the jury, to be understood as
recognized and enforcing the acts or laws of the Shawnee Mission, so
called?" Cato took the paper and read it; flung it to the Sheriff across the
table, and evidently was much agitated, and said, "The Court cannot permit itself to be disturbed by outside issues." Capt. J. B., Jr., in the yard
before the court room, cried out with a loud voice, which no doubt was
heard by the court and the packed jurymen, "The Pottawatomie Rifle Company will meet at the parade ground." There was no person, I am convinced, of our party, who made any threats, or in any way disturbed the
court, further than what is related above.

As soon as we assembled on the parade ground we formed ourselves
into a meeting of public safety, for it was evident that if the government,
aided by the pro-slavery Ruffians, intended to enforce the bogus laws that
trouble would follow.

The resolutions, which I have referred to were voted by the company
to be sent to Judge Cato for his instruction. I think H. H. Williams (now
of Osawatomie) and one of the Brown family were appointed to deliver
them. A copy of these resolutions would be instructive at this time.
They may, perhaps, be found in the Herald of Freedom for the month of
April, 1856. They declared that the acts passed at the Shawnee Mission
were "bogus," a gross violation of public right, and to attempt to enforce
them on the citizens of the Territory was an act of usurpation, and if
any persons attempted to do so it would be at their peril.

The next morning the Judge, the jury, the Sheriff and all his subordinates had fled toward that pro-slavery bastile, Lecompton. This was the
first and *last* of the bogus courts attempting to administer *justice* to the
settlers in this part of the Territory. That Cato and his Border Ruffian
clan got frightened by our visit, and by receiving the resolutions of our
military company, there can be no doubt. There was no intention to
disturb the sittings of the court; but there was a fixed determination that
if the court attempted to enforce any of the bogus laws on the Free-State
men, that they would resist them. This is the simple history of Judge
Cato's court on the Pottawatomie. That "an armed mob of 150 abolitionists" threatened it with extermination, and broke it up, was all false. The
servile organs of the administration had this falsehood in their weekly issues as one of the crimes of the Free-State party of Kansas.

[*Cato's Court, 1871 version*, additional comment]

This action on the part of the free-state men of this township may at
this time be looked upon as revolutionary, but let it be remembered that
we had to deal with a set of men who had repeatedly threatened our lives;
a mob upheld and counterbalanced by the pro-slavery administration at
Washington.

[1869 version resumed]

Only nine months previous, on this very spot of ground, a drunken rabble from a neighboring State, might be seen depositing their votes at an election authorized by Gov. Reeder for the purpose of electing members of the Legislative Council. They came armed, took possession of the ballot-box and deposited 199 votes, while the whole district did not contain fifty voters, and most of them through fear, never showed themselves at the polls; and this unparalleled outrage of the elective franchise was passed over without a word of disapprobation by these venal echoes of the then administration. History does not afford a greater mockery than this. The spring of '56 will long be remembered by the settlers who at that time took an active part in the proceedings of the Territory. It was a time that tried men's souls. Isolated as the Territory was, from its geographical position, from its friends in other sections of the country, was a serious disadvantage to the Free-State element: a mere handful of settlers had to contend against a populous State on its border, and the whole power and patronage of the administration.

A few miles to the northeast, on the Miama lands, there was a camp of Georgians, imported by Col. Bufort. Another encampment was located on Pottawatomie creek, under the charge of a Ruffian by the name of Mitchell. Our post-office was the head-centre of the pro-slavery element. It was called Shermanville, after Henry Sherman, a German who, many years prior to the Kansas-Nebraska bill, had settled and taken a tract of land while the Pottawatomie Indians had possession of this country.

This notorious and well known individual took an active part to prevent this portion of the country from being settled by Free-State men. One of his first acts was to burn down the few old cabins on the creek which were left by the Indians. He frequently made threats of extermination to the Free-State settlers. He was looked upon as an ignorant tool of the slave power, and the feeling towards him was not the most cordial. In the spring of 1857 he was shot by two Free-State men while traveling the public highway. This act was not approved even by many of his most bitter enemies.

[Killing of Henry Sherman, 1871 version]

In the spring of 1857, in the month of March, he was shot by two free-state men while travelling the public highway. He died a few days after. This act was almost universally condemned by all classes, free-state as well as pro-slavery. It was prompted by private malice; emigration was pouring in by the thousands, and he was no longer an instrument in the hands of the pro-slavery element, that could possibly work evil.

[1869 version resumed]

To return to the post-office. It was deemed somewhat unsafe to go to the post-office without company, or being well armed with a six-shooter or a large bowie-knife. On one occasion a settler by the name of John Manace, a man considerably advanced in years, was interrogated by Mitchell and some others of his party by the question, "what papers do you take?" Mr. Manace replied "The New York Tribune," taking a copy from his pocket and handing it to him, observing it was a very good paper. At this remark Mitchell said it was a d —d abolition sheet, an incendiary publication and ought to be burned. At this moment one of the party knocked Mr. Manace down with a heavy ox-whip, and while prostrate and helpless, the ruffians joined together and gave him a most brutal flogging with their ox-gads.

This outrage on an inoffensive man caused considerable excitement in the neighborhood. The next day the military company met, under a previous notice; and as there were more than commonly attended, the report spread that the abolitionists were organizing to retaliate on Capt. Mitchell and his pro-slavery associates for whipping the old man Manace.

Late in the evening, going to my lodgings from the military parade, I saw several wagons making their way across the prairie. The next morning we found out to our great joy that Mitchell and his Georgians had left the neighborhood. They took fright like Judge Cato's court, and fled to parts unknown. The ruffians always believed that on the creek the Free-State men had some 25 or 30 Sharpe's rifles; this notion no doubt saved us much trouble, while, in fact, there was never more than five or six at any one time.

About the middle of May, rumors arrived from Kansas City, that the various encampments under Buford and others, which had been rendezvouing [sic] in and around Westport, most emigrants from the various Southern States, were ordered into the Territory. The Free-State men were tolerably well posted in regard to the designs of these maurauders. Our military company was ordered to rendezvous at Winer's store, on the Mosquito creek. At this place we landed with good supply of provisions; our destination was Lawrence. About two miles on the east side of North Middle Creek, Old John Brown and three or four of his sons joined the company. He had a large basket filled with revolvers; those he loaned to such of the company who had none, taking their names with the promise that they should be returned to him after the expedition. We crossed the Marais des Cygnes about 1 o'clock that night, when a courier informed us that Lawrence had been sacked and burned. We camped next morning a few miles from Prairie City, on Ottawa creek; and while there we received word that Lawrence was short of provisions, and did not need our assistance. We remained there two days to see what might turn up. It was at this point that Old John Brown and several of his sons, his son-in-law and a few others organized themselves into a company to pay a visit to the Ruffians on Pottawatomie Creek. A neighbor came from that locality and reported that the Ruffians were going to drive off certain Free-State men from their homes, and that they wanted assistance to ward off the attack of the Ruffians. Our company next changed its camping ground to the locality called Palmyra, adjoining Baldwin City.

[1868 version, substituted for short 1869 version]

Mr. Redpath, in his life of John Brown, says: "On the night of the 24th of May, 1856, an old man of the name of Doyle and his two sons, Wm. Sherman (brother of Dutch Henry Sherman,) and Wilkinson, the latter an acting Justice of the Peace and member of the bogus Legislature, were taken from their homes and killed. They all resided on the Potawatomie creek, near to the Dutch Henry crossing. All the published accounts written by free-state men say that John Brown was not knowing to the facts till *after the occurrence.*" Mr. Redpath, page 119, after stating that Brown *denied* having any participation in it, quotes him as making the following remark: "But remember," says Brown, "I do not say this to exculpate myself; for although *I took no hand in it,* I would have advised it had I known the circumstances. I endorse it as it was." And again, "Time and honest verdict of posterity," says he in his Virginia cell, "will approve of every act of mine." "I think," says Redpath, "it will endorse all the acts he endorsed; and amongst them this righteous slaughter of the ruffians of Potawatomie. John Brown did not know these men were killed until the following day; for, with one of his sons, he was twenty-five miles distant at the time;—he was at Middle creek."

Mr. Holloway, in his late history of Kansas, page 351 says: "While Brown went north for aid, on the night of the 24th of May, Mr. Doyle and his two sons, Mr. Sherman, and Mr. Wilkinson, were taken from their homes and murdered. The act had been precipitated in consequence of certain outrages committed by the above mentioned parties the day before. Old Brown, who was absent at the time, fully sustained and approved the deed."

The words attributed to John Brown by Mr. Redpath, "I took no hand in it—I would have advised it had I known the circumstances," are certainly contrary to the general character of John Brown, as I shall prove from his own testimony addressed to me. Whatever faults John Brown may be charged with, duplicity was not one of his failings; he was one of the most conscientious men I was ever acquainted with. Why this studied attempt to excuse him from being an actor in the tragedy, when, by all accounts, he frequently asserted that he "endorsed" the deed?

With these preliminary remarks, I will now proceed to give such testimony in this case as fell under my own knowledge and observation. A messenger was sent from the north to inform Capt. John Brown, Jr., that Lawrence was likely to be attacked by the pro-slavery invaders. The Potawatomie Rifle Company were notified by the Captain to meet at Winer's store, four miles from Dutch Henry's crossing. It was evening before we left this place of rendezvous. That same evening John Brown Sr., and his sons, and Thompson, his son-in-law joined the party. We camped that night on the site of Mount Vernon, on Middle creek; but before day-light we started towards Lawrence. While crossing the Marais des Cygnes, we first heard that Lawrence had been sacked. We hurried on, and took breakfast on Ottawa creek. Here a messenger arrived from Lawrence stating that the ruffians were leaving, and the town short of provisions, and requested us not to advance towards the fated city.

It was at this place, and not at Osawatomie, as Mr. Holloway states, that the company took a vote whether to go on towards Lawrence or go into camp. At first the company voted with old John Brown to go on towards Lawrence; but on a motion to reconsider, the vote was carried against his proposition. The old man became considerably excited; and remarked that he would rather be ground in the earth than passively submit to pro-slavery usurpation and wrong. But the next day he said to me, "I believe it was well that you moved a reconsideration of the vote yesterday—it was a providential circumstance. I am glad you did it."

We went into camp near the residence of Capt. Shore on Ottawa creek. We remained there, I think, but one day. A messenger arrived from the Potawatomie settlement with the information that the pro-slavery men in the neighborhood had ordered Squire Morse, who had a small store near the crossing of the creek, to leave his house by Saturday evening, as a punishment for furnishing our military company with ammunition on our trip to Lawrence. The messenger also reported that Mr. Grant, who now lives four miles south of Lawrence, and others were ordered to leave, or abide the consequences. This aroused "old Brown." A short consultation was had, and in a short time he commenced packing up his camp equipage. Eight others composed the party. Few there were who knew the object of the expedition, and much speculation in camp. An old gentleman who seemed very much alarmed at the movement, and knowing the views of old Brown on the "peace policy," as it was called, ventured to ask Brown what movement was now on foot. He replied that he was going to regulate matters on the Potawatomie. "Well, Capt. Brown," said the old gentleman, "I hope you will act with caution." The Captain suspended his packing arrangements for a moment, looked the stranger in the eye, and said: "Caution! Caution!—These are always the words of cowardice." From the firm and deliberate manner in which these words were spoken, no person ventured to question his course. All knew the determined spirit of the old Captain, and I think I may safely say that every one in camp expected to hear of some bold stroke at the pro-slavery ruffians. I was frequently solicited to ask Capt. Brown the object of this new movement; but after I heard his remarks to the old gentleman, as above stated, I thought it useless to approach him. But I did venture to approach one of the eight, and from him I learned the whole contemplated movement. In fact, I received an invitation to accompany the party, and being unwilling to consent before learning the object, I was made acquainted with the whole programme. It shocked me. I begged my informant to desist, alleging that such a course would bring us additional troubles, the settlement on Potawatomie would be wiped out, etc. Just here let me add that Henry Sherman, brother of the one who was killed, and one of the marked ones, but being away from home that night his life was spared to the spring of '57, at which time he was shot while traveling on the highway, but not by one of the Brown party. And I could mention another name which was on the list of doomed men, but as he is now living it is perhaps best to let his name be forgotten.

In a short time old Brown loaded up his camp kettles and started from our camp in a wagon, and not as represented in the wood cut of Mr. Holloway's history, of "John Brown starting out to begin the war," with "sword upraised, calling upon all who were willing to begin the war in earnest to follow him." It is a pity to destroy an interesting picture, but truth must be vindicated.

The next day we marched to the town of Palmyra, on the Santa Fe road. We were joined by a number of recruits from Osawatomie, and the company under Capt. Shore. The object of taking this position was, if possible, to rescue Gov. Robinson, whom the ruffians had captured on a steamboat near Lexington, Missouri, and who was expected to pass this point on his way to the Bastile of pro-slavery proscription, Lecompton; but they took him by the way of Leavenworth.

[Slave Liberation Episode, 1871 version]

Several of our party left camp [Palmyra] one night, to procure provisions. They came across a pro-slavery man with his family and teams, loaded with his household goods on his way to Missouri. He lived at Black Jack. He was also a slaveowner, and had with him several negroes, He was brought into camp, this was about one o'clock at night. The negroes were told by the party who captured them, that they might remain in camp, and become free; one of them consented. The slave owner and family were passed through the camp, and journey on their way towards the Missouri border. This bold movement of taking a slave from under the nose of a master and setting him free, produced a great excitement in camp. Our Captain, John Brown, Jr., was for giving the negro his liberty; Captain Shore (a former resident of a slave-state,) and most of his men remonstrated, and many of them threatened if the slave was not immediately restored to the owner, they would leave the camp.

It became evident, that here was an element of discord, which would if persisted in ultimately break up the military organization. The parties were about equally divided, most of the eastern men sided with Brown, and the western men, with a few exceptions, with Shores and his party, the final result was, the negro was conducted back to the master, whom they overtook some five miles from camp, on his way to Missouri. The pro-slavery papers rejoiced over this event. They charged that the abolitionists had the will, but not the courage to carry out their sentiments; under the circumstances which then existed, there can be but little doubt, that the action of the company was the most prudent, although the radical element of the anti-slavery party, who live *afar off*, denounced it as wrong and cowardly.

[1868 version resumed]

On Sunday we changed our camp to "Liberty Hill" near Prairie City. It was there that we first heard of the affair on the Potawatomie creek.— Three men came into camp that evening and reported that at least one dozen of the ruffians had been dispatched. It did not seem to produce that degree of astonishment which might have been expected, which proved that most everybody was prepared for strange news. That night we camped at the residence of John T. Jones. About 12 o'clock that night John Brown, Sr., arrived. He came to the tent of his son John, and enquired if he was there. I knew his voice, and told him his son was in Jones' house. He then asked me if there was any news? I replied, only the Potawatomie affair; I suppose you have heard about that? To which he made, as I thought, rather an evasive reply, and left to see his son John. The next morning those who had accompanied old Brown were in our camp. Our Captain, John Brown, Jr., resigned his command and H. H. Williams, now of Osawatomie, was elected in his place. We marched that day towards the Potawatomie, and each man went home. The store of Mr. Winer, who was a member of our company, with its contents, was burned to the ground.

As was anticipated, the military, with the numerous escort of border ruffians, came to ferret out the affair. They arrested numerous persons on suspicion, but finding no evidence against them, discharged them. But Capt. H. H. Williams and John Brown, Jr., were too valuable prizes to be set at liberty. They were taken to Lecompton. This law and order posse stole horses both from the pro-slavery and the free-state men. All communication with the river was stopped, thus cutting off supplies, which produced no little distress and inconvenience. In fact, it was unsafe for a long time for any member of the military organization to be seen on the highway.

I will now investigate the point on which we are told all "free-state men agree," that John Brown Sr., was absent at the time and knew nothing of the event until the following day. The morning after I arrived at the residence of Mr. Elbridge Blunt, on the west side of Potawatomie creek, (Mr. Blunt is now a resident of Ottawa, and I refer to him for corroborative testimony to my statement,) an intimate friend, the late Dr. R. Gillpatrick, called to see me. He had heard that I was with young Brown's company on the trip to aid Lawrence, and he asked me how old Brown was dressed at the time he left his son's camp on Ottawa creek. I told him, for I perfectly recollected a black military stock he always wore. After I had given him the information, he replied: "I am satisfied—your description is identical with that I received from Mrs. Wilkinson."

The morning after the pro-slavery men were killed, Dr. R. Gillpatrick and Mr. Elbridge Blunt were on their return from Kansas City. They had camped the night before a little north of the house of Wilkinson. The Doctor stopped at the house for mail matter. No person had been there that morning, or since her husband had been taken in custody. Mrs. Wilkinson was sitting up in bed crying. She said that she was fearful some evil had befallen her husband, and then related the circumstances of his being taken prisoner by free-state men. The doctor asked her if she knew any of the men. She said she did not, but thought she had seen one of them before, after mail matter; but after she arrived at Westport, Missouri, a week or two afterwards, she then stated that she knew old John Brown and his sons. (See Investigating Committees Report.)

Although she did not at that time know old man Brown, she could describe his person and dress precisely. If I needed any other evidence to convince me of who composed the party who waited on these pro-slavery men and despatched them, this conversation the day after with Dr. Gillpatrick and Elbridge Blunt was full and convincing, notwithstanding Mr. Redpath says "other witnesses have testified to the contrary, who told him they were with the party."

There is a living witness, who was with this party, who has told me the whole programme, and much of his testimony is known by other witnesses, who says old Brown was the Captain of the party and conducted the expedition. No old settler on Potawatomie creek ever doubted it.

But as this is a controversial point, I will adduce other evidence, which must be conclusive to any reasonable man. It is not proper on ordinary occasions to relate private conversations which take place between friends, but the present occasion seems to warrant it. In the fall of 1859, during his last visit to Kansas, John Brown tarried at my house about a week. Of course, we conversed on the troubles of '56. One evening he asked me, "What do the old settlers on the creek think now of the punishment inflicted on the Shermans, Doyles, etc.?" I replied that a considerable change in public opinion had taken place; many who condemned it at the time now endorsed it, and consider that it was a justifiable act under existing circumstances. "Oh," said the old man, "knew the time would come when people who understood the whole circumstances attending it would endorse it." He repeated several times, "*If* it was murder, I am not innocent. The life of a good man is worth more than the life of a bad, wicked man." At one time he became quite excited on the subject of slavery, and walking the room with a quick step, he stopped and said, "I tell you, Mr. Hanway, that [it] is infinitely better that this generation should be swept away from the face of the earth, than that slavery shall continue to exist." He related the information he had obtained while he was on a surveying expedition, by setting his compass so that he could obtain access into a camp of pro-slavery men without causing suspicion,—for all United States surveyors were deemed pro-slavery and members of the democratic party. It was in one of these ingenious expeditions that he became convinced that the ruffians intended at some time to "clear out the creek," and drive all free-state men from gaining a residence, and especially old Brown and his sons.

That John Brown and his party had sufficient evidence to convince them that a deep laid plot was on foot to kill certain obnoxious free-state men, destroy their property, and otherwise break up the settlement on the creek, is beyond controversy.—Lawrence, Osawatomie and other places had been threatened long before they were burned and destroyed, and judging from the past, it was reasonable to suppose that similar threats in other quarters would in time be carried out.

A little incident took place at the residence of the Shermans, which is good evidence in support of our suspicions. After the party had arrived at the house, which was at the dead of night, the women commenced preparing breakfast, supposing that the Brown party was a party just arrived from Missouri, and having traveled a long distance, needed refreshments. This movement of the women caused surprise, and to ascertain the reason, a pro-slavery woman, (one who had but little sympathy with the ruffians however), was employed to call and ascertain the facts. She brought us this information and stated that they (the Shermans) were expecting friends from Missouri who were going on an expedition up the creek. I know the parties who gave me this information, and I believe them to be reliable.

[1869 version resumed]

On the return of our company from Ottawa creek, we found that the storehouse of Mr. Winer has been burned during our absence. It was at this place we laid in our supplies. It contained a good supply of provisions, and was a great loss to the owner, as well as to the neighborhood. Mr. Winer was a German, and a radical Free-State man, and was very obnoxious to the pro-slavery element. He was absent at the time, having joined the expedition in defence of Lawrence.

The pro-slavery men in the neighborhood became wonderfully alarmed, not knowing to what extent the new order of proscription might extend: the Free-State men were no less excited; for they anticipated a visit from the Government officials and their Border Ruffian allies. It was therefore deemed best to call a public meeting, which was called a "conciliation meeting," and was held at a spring on what is now known as Partridge Branch. The object of this meeting was to exchange opinions and if possible live in harmony together. Many of the Free-State men did not attend, believing it was a ruse to kidnap them, but the pro-slavery element turned out to a man. This meeting by a vote condemned the recent act of violence in killing the five pro-slavery men, also pledged themselves to discountenance all outside interference in the affairs of the Territory, &c. In a few days the Marshall and his posse of "law-and-order" men— 150 in all—traversed the country over, took in custody every Free-State man they could hunt up, confiscated or pressed in the service every horse their eyes beheld and even took work cattle and teams with them.

It was at this time that H. H. Williams (now of Osawatomie), who, acting as Captain of our military company, was kindly taken care of and sent to Lecompton, where he remained for several months, in company with Gov. Robinson, Deitzler, Jenkins and John Brown, Jr. Several of our citizens were taken to Paola, Miami county, and after an examination by the "powers that be," were permitted to depart in peace.

Those who had side-arms or Sharpe's rifles were divested of these warlike weapons as unnecessary appendages to a "squatter sovereign."

For weeks these maurading parties traveled up and down the creek; but the Free-State men were on the alert. Many a day and night were spent in the bushes, not deeming it safe to sleep in the usual place of abode.

A few Sharpe's rifles were of great service to the cause of freedom. The Ruffians had heard most wonderful reports of these new instruments of warfare; they believed that an expert with one of these guns could hit a pane of glass 8x10 one mile distant. This made them extremely careful; they seldom ventured far into the thicket, and never without a competent force. In fact, it is not too much to say that Sharpe's rifles, called by the Ruffians "Beecher's bible," and Colt's revolvers, "Joshua R. Giddings' prayer book," were what saved the Free-State men in the year of 1856 from being driven from the Territory. These carnal weapons saved Kansas from Border-Ruffian rule.

During the summer months of 1856 rumors of war kept the squatter in a perfect state of excitement. Those who in early spring intended to raise a crop had to give up the idea. Not a week passed over but a call for assistance came from Ossawatomie or some other place. Many of these reports were of course unfounded, and a lot of cattle seen in the distance traveling across the high prairie would be the foundation for rumor. A few strangers enquiring for claims would sometimes cause suspicion that they were spies from the enemy's camp. Thus was the settlement kept in commotion. No person ventured to a neighbor's house without being well armed. Neighbors would frequently avoid the beaten roads, and if they witnessed a person approaching in the direction they were traveling, would turn off and make a circle to avoid a personal meeting. Many amusing incidents occurred by friendly neighbors avoiding each other on the open prairies or in the woods.

Soon after the tragic event of the Pottawatomie the Government ordered a company of dragoons to encamp in the neighborhood, to keep order and enforce the laws. It was under command of one Capt. De-Saucer, a native of Charleston, S. C. The Company was composed of men of Southern proclivities, but it was the policy of the Free-State men to pay due respect to Uncle Sam's military servants; and fortunately there were a few in the company who sympathized with the cause of freedom. Therefore, whenever a detail was ordered for a night's excursion the information would be secretly reported to the Free-State men, and in every attempt they had to return without making any arrests. This became so extremely annoying to the officers that they finally gave it up. They performed no considerable service for the pro-slavery party, for the Free-State men, knowing the country, would avoid them in their military movements.

This same Capt. DeSaucer was the individual who figured in the first movements of the war in the taking of Fort Moultrie and Fort Sumpter.

As every article of consumption had to be hauled from Kansas City, or some place out of Kansas, it became a serious question with the Free-State settlers how to supply this want. The roads to Missouri were blokaded by the pro-slavery party; Free-State men were frequently robbed and their teams taken from them, on the public roads. Flour, bacon and other necessary articles of consumption became very scarce. Occasionally a team from Kansas City loaded with these articles would pay us a visit and sell at high prices; but this did not supply our needs.

Towards the close of summer many of our Free-State [men] concluded, as the enemy would not sell them provisions, that rather than starve, they would live on beef. This was an article readily procured. Many of our pro-slavery men had large herds roaming over the prairie, and under the circumstances they had no scruples to kill a beef whenever needed. These cattle owners were not long before they opened the roads to Kansas City: at least this class of men were permitted to trade in Kansas City and haul provisions to the settlers. This was the best means to save their beef. The fine spun theories of ethics did not enter into the programme of '56;—Free-State men were compelled to adapt themselves to surrounding circumstances, retaliation is so natural in man that we have often been surprised that the Free-State men were so moderate in their proceedings.

In the month of August the struggle between the contending parties was fast coming to a focus. It was evident the Ruffian element was encircling a chain around the friends of freedom. In all parts of the Territory they were concentrating all their forces; block houses were erected and well provided with provisions, &c. One of these was located a few miles from the Pottawatomie creek, on the Miami lands. A meeting of several leading Free-State men was held, and it was concluded that it be destroyed. The Georgia rendezvous was one of the first attended to. Many of our citizens joined in the undertaking. As soon as they arrived on the spot they found it was abandoned, as the Georgians took flight before the arrival of our forces. Several barrels of bacon and flour were loaded in wagons, and the building burned. It contained a large supply of the necessaries of life, much needed at the time; but as there was no way of saving it by hauling it off it was destroyed with the building.

[1871 version]

After the difficulties we passed through, during the month of May and June, 1856, to which I have related in the former numbers, we were much annoyed from the lack of almost every article of consumption, for everything had to come through by the way of Westport, from Kansas City. It became at times a serious question with the free-state settlers how to supply our wants. The roads to Missouri were blockaded by the pro-slavery party; free-state men were frequently robbed and their teams taken from them on the public highway. Flour, and other necessary articles of consumption became scarce, and brought high figures. Occasionally a team from Kansas City with these articles would pay us a visit but this did not supply our wants.

Necessity it is said knows no law, and it was amusing to witness how the most tender hearted and conscientious amongst us, adopted that proverb. Towards the close of the summer many of our free-state men, in council assembled, concluded as the enemy would not sell or permit us to obtain provisions, that rather than suffer, they would live on beef by "pressing" it. Many of the most obnoxious pro-slavery men had large herds grazing on the prairies, and therefore, under the circumstances, they had no scruples of conscience to kill a beef whenever needed. These cattle owners were not long before they advocated the opening of the roads to Kansas City; at least this class of men were permitted to trade in Kansas City and haul provisions to the settlers. The fine spun theories of ethics did not enter into the programme of '56; free-state men were compelled to adapt themselves to surrounding circumstances, and retaliation is so natural in men that we have often been surprised that they were so moderate in their proceedings.

In the month of August the struggle between the contending parties was fast coming to a focus. It was evident the ruffian element was encircling a chain around the friends of freedom. In all the southern portion of the Territory, they were concentrating all their forces; block houses were erected, all well provided with provisions, etc. Mr. Gihon, private secretary to Gov. Geary, says in his work on "Geary and Kansas," "the pro-slavery mauraders south of the Kansas river, had established and fortified themselves at the town of Franklin; at a fort thrown up near Osawatomie; at another on Washington creek; twelve miles from Lawrence, and at Col. Titus' house on the border of Lecompton. From these strong holds they would rally forth, 'press horses and cattle, intercept the mails, rob stores and dwellings, plunder travellers, burn houses and destroy crops. The fort near Osawatomie, in consequence of outrages committed in the neighborhood, and at the solicitations of the settlers, was attacked by a company of free-state men from Lawrence on the 5th of August."

The attack on the Georgian party, by agreement was to have taken place the night previous, but the Lawrence party lost their way on the prairie, which caused a delay. The signal to be given of their coming, was the firing of the prairie, south of Stanton, on the south side of the river; several of the free-state men who remained on the Potawatomie, rendezvous that night on the high prairie, on the claim occupied at this time by Mr. David Baldwin; from this place we could see across the valley; and the high divide of the Marais des Cygnes river. We looked in vain for the sign, no fire illuminated the north. Our boys who had volunteered their services returned homeward, not knowing the cause of the failure. A few hours after the intelligence reached us, that the attack would be made that night, and they again marched towards the enemy. As soon as they arrived on the spot they found it was abandoned, the Georgians took flight before the arrival of our forces. Several barrels of bacon and flour were loaded in wagons and the building burnt. It contained a large supply of the necessities of life, much needed at the time; but there was no way of saving it by hauling it off, so it was destroyed with the building. This Georgian encampment never returned to this neighborhood, but retreated to the fort at Washington creek, where they were on the 15th again routed by Gen. Lane and his forces from Lawrence.

A short time after this event, the ruffians made another raid on this settlement. They burned the house of a free-state man of the name of Kilborne, also the residence of Benjamin Crockrin, with every article they contained. They captured and carried off with them George Partridge, who was sick at the time, and confined to his bed; they took the prisoner to their camp on South Middle Creek. They were followed up by several small companies, under the charge of Capt. Anderson, Shore of Prairie City, and Stewart, (the fighting preacher.) Dr. Gillpatrick was visiting some patients on the east side of South Middle creek, the afternoon previous to the fight which took place the next day, and noticing an encampment at the crossing of the creek, and hearing of what had transpired in the neighborhood on his return home, immediately spread the news. Thus the free-state men rallied from various quarters. Anderson and his party came from Anderson county. Plans were laid for the coming conflict, some crossed the creek to intercept their passage at daybreak, while the ruffians were preparing their breakfast; the signal was given, and the free-state men rushed upon them, which produced a panic in ruffian camp, each man attempted to make his escape the best he could. Many of the ruffians were wounded and others taken prisoners. Mr. George Partridge was set at liberty. There is a high mound about one mile from the crossing of Middle creek, sometimes called "potato mound," but the old name should be retained which is "battle mound," and so named on the old maps of Kansas. Let me correct a slight error which Redpath and some other writers have made. They give to old

John Brown the honor of this victory, this is incorrect. Brown and his men were on the Pottawatomie creek at the time; he heard of the burning of Mr. Kilborne and Crockrin's houses, (the latter was a member of his party,) and he went in pursuit of the ruffians who had committed these acts, but Brown did not arrive at Middle creek till the fight was over.

The day after the fight on Middle creek, the battle of Osawatomie took place, from which old John Brown received the name of "Osawatomie Brown." Many of those who took part in the Middle creek fight did not participate in the battle of Osawatomie; not knowing that an enemy was so near at hand, they had left for Lawrence. This circumstance accounts for the small number who were engaged with Brown, against the forces of Gov. Reid, whose force was about 300, with one piece of artillery. Dr. Updegraff had a small force under his charge, and those who had joined Brown at Middle creek, composed his whole force, between thirty and forty men. The fight lasted about three hours. Brown and his men retreated towards the timber; superior numbers forced him to abandon the unequal conflict. In crossing the river George Partridge, who I have stated was released as a prisoner from the ruffian camp, was shot while fording the stream, others received various wounds; but the ruffians from the best accounts that could be gathered, lost over thirty men killed, and many more wounded.

Frederick Brown, the son of John Brown was killed on the public road, near the house of the Rev. J. S. Adairs, about one hour before the battle commenced in the morning. He was shot by the Rev. Martin White, who boasted of this exploit the next winter while a member of the legislature. Mr. Cutter, now of Douglas county, was also shot and left on the road for dead, at the same time and place. Mr. Garrison was also killed by the ruffians, early in the morning before the fight commenced.

The remains of George Partridge, Frederick Brown and Garrison were deposited in a cemetery which the citizens of Osawatomie set apart for this special purpose. A monument should be erected over their remains. It has been talked about for the last fifteen years, but it appears there is not sufficient public spirit, or interest manifested in the past history of those early days in Kansas troubles, to donate by subscription a tablet to mark the last resting place of these martyrs of human liberty.

These frequent inroads of the ruffians into the Territory, produced a retaliating spirit on the free-state men. Many who had heretofore interposed objections to this system of warfare, gave their assistance and aid, as the only means to check these marauding expeditions from the border. A man of the name of Holmes, collected a few resolute fellows, several from this township, and under his lead, entered the border counties of Missouri, and retaliated on those whom they learned had been aiding and assisting the marauding expeditions into Kansas. In some cases the offenders were storekeepers; they would surround the premises, put a guard on every person they found, and take as prisoners those that came to purchase or trade for goods; while others would be selecting and packing up such articles as they deemed most valuable to them. These were packed on the extra horses or mules they had taken for the purpose. They were not forgetful to inform them that so long as they (the Missourians) sent marauding parties into Kansas to plunder and destroy property, that they would continue their visits. These movements, however objectionable they might be considered in a strict moral point of view, produced a very salutary effect on our troublesome neighbors. They sent a dispatch to Gov. Geary, informing him of the difficulties which had occurred on the border. He immediately ordered a detachment of soldiers under Deputy Marshal Preston, "to proceed to the southeastern section of the Territory, and protect the peaceable citizens of Missouri, who had been plundered by Holmes."

Governor Geary, the newly appointed governor, was a man who endeavored to do what was right between the two political parties. His object was peace. His task was a difficult one. The administration of the courts was a mere mockery and a farce, more detestable than the Spanish Inquisition ever was under the administration of Loyola and the Jesuits. Geary admitted that the courts were partial, and did not aid him in his administration. Even in this case he ordered the marshal "to protect the peaceful citizens of Missouri." Who were the peaceful citizens, we might ask? One of these stores which was plundered by "the horse thieves under Holmes," as they were termed, was owned by a man who was one of the ruffians at the rendezvous on Middle creek, on their way to assist Gen. Reid in the sacking of Osawatomie. This man mounted his horse as soon as the free-state men attacked the camp. He was ordered to "halt," refusing he rushed past the picket guard and was shot by a ball discharged from a colt's revolver, which carried away the greater part of his nose, which disfigured him for life. The free-state man who it is believed inflicted the wound on this "peaceful citizen," whom Gov. Geary was anxious to protect, is now an honorable citizen of Anderson county.

The result of this military posse under deputy marshal Preston, is thus reported: "The deputation sent on the 8th (Nov.) inst, in pursuit of a band of alleged marauders who were committing depredations in the southeastern section of the Territory, returned to Lecompton, and made a lengthy report of their proceedings. They succeeded in arresting seven notorious characters, one of whom, James Townsley, confessed to having been a member of the party that murdered Wilkinson, Sherman and the Doyles, on the Potawatomie creek. Others were examined and committed for felony. The five prisoners committed were carried to Tecumseh, and there held in custody to await the action of the grand jury."

Such is the wording of the official report. These "notorious characters," at least five of them, the writer could speak of from personal knowledge. The said James Townsley, lived a few miles from this neighborhood, and being one of the first settlers is very generally known. He lives on the same farm he was residing on when he was arrested, and as for his "notorious character," save the facts of his being one of the party above referred to; he has so far as my knowledge extends, borne a character that stood fair. Two others have since died, and no person ought to say any thing against them, but the testimony in their favor would be that they were good reliable free-state men, and were respected. The other two are still living, and have followed an honest calling since their release from Tecumseh.

It was once remarked by the great Montesquieu to a friend who was conversing with him on the importance of the study of history, that he had as much faith in the record of an old almanac, as in most histories; and certainly when we read the official records of the history of Kansas, during the trouble under the democratic administration of Pierce and Buchanan, it is not even entitled to as much respect as an old almanac; because if we would desire to arrive at a more correct history of those times, we must transpose the phraseology of such expressions as "law and order men," to mean pro-slavery desperados, who boasted that to kill an abolitionist was a virtuous act. "Abolition thieves," to mean men determined to protect themselves and their property from being "pressed" into the service of the ruffians. "Negro-thief," we must understand to apply to a man who refused to assist in returning a fugitive slave to his master. "Notorious characters," to read characters who have become known, by their daring exploits in stemming the current of pro-slavery ursurpation. If we adopt this rendering, we shall be able to understand the official records of those times. If not, an old almanac is a more reliable and worthy document. Still these records should be preserved for future reference; for "history is philosophy, teaching by example." Before me are the "bogus" statutes of Kansas. People even at this day, ask, "is it possible that a law ever existed in Kansas, which made it an act of felony to call in question the right of persons to hold slaves in this Territory, to imprisonment at hard labor, not less than two years." There it is, published by order of the government.

[1869 version, resumed]

The winter months of 1856–7 will long be remembered by those who resided here at that time. Many have said it was the most uncomfortable period of any in the Kansas troubles. The fall campaign had been closed but it left an impress of doubt and insincerity that could not be solved for the future. Many settlers from Missouri had in the first settlement of this country taken claims along the creek; which, by the way, were very valuable. Most of these settlers were pro-slavery in sentiment, and had an awful antipathy against Yankees and free negroes. This class of persons was respected and they were protected in their rights as squatters, so long as they did not give aid and assistance to their ruffian brethren of Missouri, when they visited the Territory on marauding expeditions. That the sympathies of this class of our settlers, were more in favor of the slave power and the administration, was natural and to be expected.

During the trials of the winter season some few of this class, thinking no doubt that the ruffian element was in the ascendancy, acted on the sly with their old friends and neighbors. In all cases that became known to the Free-State men, the parties were notified that they should not remain in our midst and act as spies for the enemy. Some moved back to Missouri, but in many cases they returned the following spring and summer. Hence arose the difficulty in the land of "proving up claims." Whenever a squatter left his claims through fear of personal injury, the land office generally recognized the right of the squatter, although he had left it and resided in another state during the time. In Linn county the ruling of the land office was more in favor of the Free-State men than pro-slavery men, but in our Radical neighborhood more pro-slavery men left their claims than Free-State men.

Early in the spring of '57 emigration came pouring in by the hundreds and thousands, to the great joy of the friends of freedom, who had for two years baffled the storm of pro-slavery proscription: it was the day of Pentecost to them. Assistance had so often been promised by the North that when it came, like an avalanche, it seemed more like a fiction than a fact. The Presidential election the fall before had spread the facts before the people. Many Kansas men who had been eye witnesses of the trials and difficulties which surrounded the party of freedom, returned to their old homes and testified to what they knew. The great heart of humanity responded to the call.

The Missouri river, which had been blockaded the previous summer and fall, was now opened to the citizens of all the States. The citizens of Massachusetts and Ohio were granted the boom of traveling by the way of the river to Kansas. No Inquisitor General stopped the traveler and asked, "What State are you from?" Steamboats were loaded down with human freight. Six hundred were landed at Kansas City from one boat. On every line of communication people came by hundreds.

The contest between freedom and slavery was decided, so far as making Kansas a slave State was concerned. I was at Westport, a short time after two boats had discharged their passengers at Kansas City. The border ruffian town turned out to witness the influx of immigration; a menagerie of wild beasts could not have attracted greater interest. Desirous to hear the opinion of its citizens I mingled with the by-standers, and near the office of Hy Pate some of the leaders of the border ruffian clan had assembled. One of them with true depth of feeling, remarked: "My God! The cause is lost." The reply was: "I'll be damned if it don't look like it."

The great majority of those who immigrated to the Territory in the spring of 1857 were what are justly called "carpet baggers"—many of them young men who were induced to visit Kansas from the excitement growing out of the election of James Buchanan to the Presidency. Most of this class came to the Territory with very crude notions: they had never experienced the privations necessarily incident to all new countries. They generally formed themselves into companies of six or more. Anxious to see the soil on which contending political parties had the two previous years been in bloody conflict, contending for supremacy. With hurried gait and enthusiasm sufficient for a crusader in the time of Peter the Hermit, entered the Territory determined to explore its vast plains and winding streams. But, alas! disappointment met them at the threshold.

Having to travel through the Shawnee Nation, they found no tavern to rest at night, no restaurants to fill their hungry stomachs;—nothing but a vast expanse of prairie, with scarcely a house to convince them that the country was settled by some one of the genus homo.

Many of them found their feet were becoming sore; by forced marches they found a resting place at Paola; and after a few days rest they retraced their steps to Kansas City, bidding adieu to the Territory.

Others, with a little more enthusiasm, crossed the Marais des Cygnes and tarried at Ossawattomie; some, however, were grievously disappointed in not finding it a large city, for it had been named so frequently that they supposed it must necessarily be a place of great importance. The desolated ruins of the previous year, caused by the ruffian raid, did not fill their expectations. What were a dozen houses sacked and burned to the frequent references made by stump orators in the Eastern States to the historic town of Ossawattomie. Tired and disgusted the patriotic enthusiastic "carpet bagger" turned around, retraced his solitary way to the banks of the Muddy river, took boat with the determination to see his father and mother and enjoy the peaceful avocations of sweet home.

But still a large number remained, took claims and are at this hour dwelling among us; and I am happy to say that most of them are doing well and enjoying life. The first trials of a frontier life are passed over. Railroads, school houses, churches and other improvements which mark the progress of civilization we now enjoy equal to many portions of the older States.

The Pottawattamie settlement, after the spring of '57, witnessed no more troubles and disturbances. In Missouri, all along the line, our settlement had established a most awful name. Emigrants were especially instructed to avoid the settlement around Dutch Henry's Crossing. The name of Kansas was odious; but the abolitionists from Ossawattomie were reported as the worst class of Gentiles.

It would be out of the question to summarize all of Hanway's miscellaneous writing on these topics of early Kansas history. He realized to some extent how voluminous his work was becoming and in attempting to correct the John Brown cabin story expressed the fear that he had written too much "for I am an enthusiast on everything relating to the reminiscences of John Brown's pilgrimage in Kansas, having camped with him, slept with him, and passed many an hour of social intercourse." [13] The cabin in question was one that he himself had built for his son J. S. Hanway, but in which he had lived for two years, 1857–1859, and in which John Brown, Jr.'s, company had stacked their arms on the day of their unceremonious visit to Judge Cato's court April 21, 1856. He believed also that John Brown had written his famous "Parallels" there. The cabin became notorious as a result of a photograph made of it by an Ottawa photographer printed in C. C. Hutchinson's book *Resources of Kansas* (1871) prepared to promote immigration to Kansas. The picture was labelled John Brown's cabin, and sold in large quantities separately from the book. As in most of the John Brown yarns, the truth could not catch up with the

[13] Lawrence *Journal* clipping, undated, in *Hanway Scrapbooks*, 2: 200. Letter dated December 26, 1871.

falsehood, and Hanway spent several years trying to convince the purveyors of the Legend that John Brown never owned a cabin in Kansas, and that the only associations with John Brown were through visits while the Henway family occupied the place. Hanway's son had proposed to tear down the old building but his father intervened because of the associations.[14] It is not strange that this elderly man should have felt the importance of the John Brown associations, because he commented upon the number of visitors, some from as far away as New England, who made the pilgrimages to this isolated region to see the cabin. He explained that these votaries, in visiting the shrine, took away with them, as relics, pieces of wood from the cabin itself, bark from the trees around it, and even earth upon which John Brown had walked when in Kansas. He felt that a truer and more authentic John Brown relic would be a photograph of Frederick Brown's grave at Osawatomie, and proposed that one should be made,[15] but apparently the public, loving myths better than truth, preferred the mislabeled cabin picture.

[14] Two letters, partly duplicating the essential information about the cabin, appeared in the Lawrence *Journal* December 26, 1870 and January 27, 1871.

[15] *Miami County Republican,* July 1, 1871.

CHAPTER XIII

SANBORN AND THE LEGEND; THE OPENING OF THE SANBORN PERIOD IN JOHN BROWN BIOGRAPHY

Franklin Benjamin Sanborn was graduated from Harvard in 1855 at the age of twenty-four, and established himself at Concord where he opened a school. Theodore Parker and Emerson were then his guiding spirits. He quickly became involved with abolitionism, and served as secretary of the Massachusetts State Kansas Committee. Early in 1857 he met John Brown, becoming one of the "secret six" who backed him in his pretended Kansas work which ended at Harpers Ferry. During the winter following the Virginia raid, he fled to Canada on two different occasions. During the Civil War he became editor of the Boston *Commonwealth* leaving that paper for the Springfield *Republican* with which he was connected in some capacity during the remainder of his life. Aside from the John Brown Legend, his ruling passion was social reform. His real claim to fame is in the rôle of pioneer in applied sociology, although his radicalism, his often offensive contentiousness compromised his influence.[1]

When Sanborn committed himself to any cause he made no compromises, and he was so constituted that he had to have not only a cause but a hero. He first met John Brown in January 1857, and the strange friendship ripened rapidly. On April 16 John Brown gave Sanborn a little autographed notebook containing his "Articles of enlistment, and By-laws, of the Kansas Regulators" and other Kansas memoranda.[2] From Brown's side this gift suggested that, whatever his plans may have been, the door was already closed on his Kansas work,—the act carried with it an air of finality. In itself—for Brown—the little book no longer possessed a practical value, but recognizing Sanborn's weakness, he sensed that in sealing the affection of this emotional youth, it

---

[1] Cf. article F. B. Sanborn, *Dictionary of American Biography*. Edward Stanwood and Lindsay Swift in *Proceedings* of the Massachusetts Historical Society, 50: (1917) 209–13 and 51: (1918) 307–11.

[2] F. B. Sanborn, "The Virginia Campaign of John Brown," *Atlantic Monthly*, 35: (February 1875) 224–233.

signified an incalculable investment in sentiment and loyalty. By April 26, Sanborn had pledged the remainder of his life, sixty long years, to the cause of John Brown. He never revealed publicly any consciousness of regret, and neither did he divulge to his public the fact that he was bound by a most solemn vow to John Brown to defend his memory against any who attacked it;—a blank check drawn on the future which might involve even his own honor:

I thank you for remembering me as you have done, and I shall prize anything from you as a momento of the bravest and most earnest man it has been my fortune to meet. You need not fear that you will be reckoned an unprofitable servant. Your name will be handed down as long as those of Putnam and Stark. Your friends here will take a deep interest in your future career, and hope they shall meet you again in better times.

For my own part, I hope so most earnestly, and should we never meet in this world we shall certainly seek each other out in the other; and should you fall in the struggle, I will take it on myself to see that your family is made comfortable and your memory defended against any who attack it— and if I can in any way serve you, I shall reckon it an honor to do so.[3]

Sanborn's unprinted protest to the *Atlantic Monthly* in 1860 against Norton's review of Redpath's biography has already been noticed. His determination to defend the memory of his hero was fustrated further by the attitude of Gerrit Smith and his family who instituted libel suits in 1860 and 1865–67 against others in order to silence charges that Smith was implicated in the Virginia raid. When Sanborn proposed to publish a full account in 1872, the Smith family begged him not to use Smith's name, the basis of the plea being that it might bring a return of his insanity. On that account, in part, Sanborn's first two articles on John Brown, published anonymously in the *Atlantic Monthly* in 1872 (April and July), dealt only in cautious generalities; Smith was not mentioned. Of course Sanborn warned his readers in his opening paragraph that "it is too early, perhaps, to tell the whole of the remarkable story of John Brown," but that warning could scarcely be interpreted to excuse misstatements of facts. He claimed that the Massachusetts friends of Brown were not informed that he had engaged Hugh Forbes to train his recruits, that they "knew nothing whatever" about Brown's relations with Forbes until about Christmas 1857. The correspondence shows, nevertheless, that

[3] F. B. Sanborn to John Brown. April 26, 1857. The original of this letter of which the above quotation is only a part, is in the possession of the Library of the Atlanta University, Atlanta, Georgia, with whose permission it is used here.

Your friends here all take a deep interest in your future career, and hope they shall meet you again in better times— For my own part, I hope so most earnestly, and should we never meet in this world we shall certainly seek each other out in the other; and should you fall in this struggle, I will take it on myself to see that your family is made comfortable and your memory defended against any who attack it — and if I can in any way serve you, I shall reckon it an honor to do so —

Yours Ever
F. B. Sanborn

Capt John Brown

Brown did mention Forbes and that Sanborn replied September 14, 1857: "You say Col. Forbes has a small school at Tabor, do you mean a childrens school, or a school for drilling? I am glad you have so good a man with you as he is said to be, and hope his services may be made available."[4]   In this early writing, not only did Sanborn show a lack of candor, but he proved remarkably unfamiliar with his subject in several respects, or else saw fit to create a wrong impression, because, for instance, he stated that John Brown was in Kansas until January 1858.

In Sanborn's second published excursion into the defense of Brown in 1875, he utilized again the *Atlantic Monthly* as his medium.[5]   The first two of the five articles carried the Brown story into 1857. He dated Brown's anti-slavery crusade from 1838, interpreting Brown's Kansas years as a reconnoissance in preparation for the final attack on slavery at Harpers Ferry. Except for the Potawatomie massacre, he omitted most of the controversial points from his treatment of Brown in Kansas, a procedure which is in sharp contrast with his later writing. Again, however, he showed his ignorance of Brown's career in Kansas, a fact which may help to account for the simple brevity of treatment. He mislocated the Brown settlement near Osawatomie in Lykins county, and he had Brown spend three successive summers in guerrilla warfare in Kansas, 1856, 1857 and 1858, a mistake which his own correspondence with Brown should have corrected. It is evident that Sanborn's as well as Brown's Kansas contemporaries required some refreshment of memory before they became involved in the great battle of the Legend soon to break out.

James Hanway, as John Brown's most conspicuous defender in Kansas, challenged immediately Sanborn's *Atlantic Monthly* articles on the Potawatomie massacre issue.[6]   In considering this challenge to his Eastern antagonist, it is important to emphasize the "set of his mind," which can best be accomplished by quotation:

At this time [1856] various statements were published in the newspapers; differing somewhat in detail. These reports gained circulation for they

[4] The original of this letter is in the possession of Atlanta University, with whose permission it is used here.

[5] Sanborn, "The Virginia Campaign of John Brown," *Atlantic Monthly*, 35 (January–May 1875). Five numbers.

[6] James Hanway, "John Brown's Parables," A series of three papers published in the Lawrence, Kansas, *Western Home Journal*. February 4, 11, 18, 1875. The first had no connection with the Sanborn articles, dealing exclusively with John Brown's Missouri slave raid of 1858 and the origin of the "Parallels."

were nothing but flying reports, but they now pass for history. The *Tribune Almanac* of 1857 contains what purports to be a history of this event, which caused considerable amazement to those who knew more about the matter than the writer of the *Tribune Almanac*.

A presidential election was pending, and public opinion, even in radical Kansas revolted at the midnight outrage. Those who justified the act, kept their opinions to themselves. The warmest friends of old John Brown differed in opinion and spoke to each other in a whisper. Brown was always regarded as an extremist, as an ultra abolitionist, and perhaps it is not going beyond the possibility of truth, to admit that the great majority of the free state party in Kansas at that time considered that the old Captain was a detriment to the progress of free-state principles.

Introduced by these remarks, Hanway quoted Sanborn's statements that the Potawatomie "murders" were committed by a portion of Brown's band, but without his knowledge as he was more than twenty miles distant at the time, but that he justified the act. Sanborn insisted that John Brown had assured him "more than once," that he had not taken part in the deed. Hanway then quoted Redpath and Holloway to the same effect. These contentions Hanway countered with the devastating rejoinder, "why this studied attempt to excuse Brown from being an actor in the tragedy, when by all accounts he frequently asserted that he 'endorsed the deed' ?"

Having stated his case, Hanway proceeded to restate the whole narrative, copying most of the material from his Ottawa *Journal* paper of 1868. In closing, he proposed as an explanation of John Brown's supposed denial while in prison of the murders that "there is no doubt that he [Brown] could say he did not see any of these five ruffians slaughtered, but that does not prove that he was not the leader of the expedition which undertook the task." Hanway contended also, that as a principle of historical interpretation, a historical judgment must be rendered according to the standards of the time, and seemed to stake his final justification of Brown's action on the quotation from the Westport *Border Times* demanding that abolitionists in Kansas be wiped out. Instead of the abolitionists being wiped out, "the result of this advice was that Wilkinson, Doyle and Sherman lost their lives by attempting to carry out the plan of their proslavery leaders." The fatal weakness of this clinching argument lies, however, in the fact that Hanway had presented no proof that these particular pro-slavery men were guilty of executing or attempting to execute such an alleged proslavery plan.

Inspired by these articles, two conspicuous free-state leaders, James Blood and Samuel Walker, wrote Hanway letters of commendation. Blood's letter was dated February 7, 1875:

I have read your article in the *Journal* of this date. Why did you not go on and relate the fact of Old John Browns coming into your camp near Jones's on Ottawa creek the next night after the tragedy? and the fact that Capt. John Brown Jr was discovered to be insane within a short time after, and that the next morning the Company elected H. H. Williams Capt—and that John Brown Jr was not captured by Capt Pate as stated by Sanborn, but that he was arrested a few days after by the U S troops and taken to Lecompton, &c. I happened to be in the neighborhood of the tragedy a few hours before it took place and saw old John Brown and his party there.[7]

The Walker letter, dated July 8, 1875 is reproduced as nearly as his orthography and punctuation permit, because his testimony has been inexcusably misused by biographers of Brown. He made three major points: that John Brown was insane in 1856; that during that period of aberration he admitted his leadership in the Potawatomie massacre, but coupled it with the charge that Robinson and Lane were responsible; and lastly that in connection with the rescue proposal, the younger John denounced his father:

I have just been reading your article on John Brown. I am glad that some one had had the courage to tell the truth John Brown has got the credit of doing many things he did not do he was a great man but you and I know he was insane in the summer of 56 Governor Robinson sent me to Nebraska to Pilot Lane's party to Kansas upon the Nemehaw River I ran across John Brown and several others trying to leve the country he joined me ? went to Nebraska city with me and returned to Kansas with me he would always go off and camp by himself I went to wake, him one morning he was sitting leaning against a tree with his rifle across his knees I put my hand on his shoulder that moment he was on his feet his rifle at my breast I pushed the muzzle up and the ball grazed my shoulder in riding along that day I referred to the Pottawatomie murder and said to him I would not have that on my consience for the world he said he had not raised his hand to one of those men but he was in command of the party and ordered theare execution that Lane & Robinson were the instigators of it and now would not sustain him in it but he believed he had done what was for the good of the country When he returned to Lawrence he wished me to carry a message to young John Brown then a prisoner in the U. S. camp that he would be theare at a certain night with men to rescue him John said to me he wanted him to stay away that he was the cause of his arest that he did not approve of his acts and wished to have nothing to do with him. I read your letter with great pleasure.[8]

[7] *Hanway Papers.* Kansas State Historical Society.
[8] *Hanway Papers.* Kansas State Historical Society.

CHAPTER XIV

ORGANIZATION AND SYMBOLS FOR HERO WORSHIP

Many of those engaged in the Kansas controversy of the fifties were possessed of a conviction that they were participating in a movement of heroic historical proportions. Sometimes the historian cannot avoid a suspicion that, in this self-consciousness some of the documents were framed with a view to establishing a record as they thought it ought to appear to posterity. As early as 1859, an association was formed at Osawatomie to commemorate the battle of Osawatomie. During the Civil War it ceased to function, but not before it had taken the important step April 11, 1859 of removing to one place the bodies of the four victims of that engagement, Fred Brown, George Partridge, David Garrison and Theron Powers.[1]

In 1872 a new association was organized and two-hundred-fifty dollars was subscribed toward a monument fund.[2] Only detached scraps of information have been found from which to piece together a part of the story. Hanway was a leader during the summer of 1872 in promoting a John Brown meeting, apparently state-wide in character. The action of Franklin county was taken at a Grant club meeting. Other counties did not report action and a meeting scheduled originally at Hanway's home was postponed pending an opportunity to discuss it further at a Grant rally to be held at Garnett.[3] Another meeting was arranged for October, but again postponed.[4]

[1] St. Louis *Globe-Democrat*, August 31, 1877. Lawrence *Republican*, April 21, 1859.

[2] St. Louis *Globe-Democrat*, August 31, 1877.

[3] Warren Anderson to Hanway. August 15, 1872. *Hanway Papers*, Kansas State Historical Society. Anderson was editor of the Ottawa *Journal*. This was an election year, and General Grant was running for reelection. It is interesting, but probably not significant, that Grant rallies provided the opportunity for the organizers of this John Brown movement to meet each other. The Brown men seem to have been conservative republicans at this time supporting Grant in his campaign rather than radical republicans, who were leading the liberal republican revolt against him.

[4] W. A. Phillips to Hanway, October 6, 1872. *Hanway Papers*, K. S. H. A.

As the participants in the territorial troubles approached old age, they turned naturally to reminiscing about early days. The *Kansas Magazine*, the major literary effort of early Kansas, offered an opportunity for some publication of memories, and among those contributing was Charles Robinson.[5] He reviewed the early part of the territorial conflict and at the proper point referred to John Brown, but without accusing him of the Potawatomie massacre:

> The slave men having the government, would be held responsible for the peace of the country. . . . It was under these circumstances that the announcement was made that eight pro-slavery men had been assassinated, (24th of May) and their bodies mutilated, near Potawatomie creek. It had the effect of a clap of thunder from a clear sky. The slave men stood agast. The officials were frightened. This was a new move on the part of the supposed subdued freemen. . . . Guerilla parties and guerilla war became the order of the day. John Brown was openly in the field, taking prisoners all persons who came from Missouri, and becoming a terror to all slave men.

In Chicago June 9–12, 1874, a reunion of abolitionists was held.[6] Possibly this meeting, which was duly noted in Kansas, was the inspiration for a suggestion made by Hanway that a reunion of Kansas abolitionists should be held.[7] The editor of the Lawrence *Journal* took up the idea and proposed that it be combined with the celebration of the twentieth anniversary of the settlement of Kansas, which was already scheduled for fall.[8] This twentieth anniversary supper was held October 15, and an organization was proposed to arrange for the holding of annual meetings. The press reports made no mention, however, whether Hanway was present or whether the John Brown matter was discussed.[9]

Kansas was much encouraged in hero-worship at this time by the action of a French committee of eleven Brown admirers, the best known of whom was Victor Hugo, who had a gold medal struck in honor of John Brown. It bore the inscription: "To the memory of John Brown, judicially murdered at Charlestown, in Virginia, on the 2nd of December, 1859, and in commemoration also of his sons and comrades who, with him, became the victims of their de-

[5] Charles Robinson, "Ad Astra per Aspera," *Kansas Magazine*, 3 (May 1873) 389–400.

[6] Topeka *Commonwealth*, April 23, 1874, from the Chicago *Post*, announced the meeting. It was reported in the Chicago *Inter-Ocean*, June 11, 18, 1874.

[7] Letter recounting a visit to the Quaker settlement of Hesper. Printed in the Lawrence *Journal*, July 9, 1874.

[8] Lawrence *Journal*, July 9, 1874.

[9] Lawrence *Tribune*, October 16, 1874

votion to the cause of negro emancipation.'' The letter of presentation to Mrs. John Brown was written by Victor Hugo and dated October 21, 1874, William Lloyd Garrison acting as intermediary in transmitting the medal and letter.[10]

Kansas had early undertaken the task of establishing a historical society, the first charter being granted by the pro-slavery legislature of 1855. The free-state men effected an organization of a society in 1859 and started a collection of materials, and again in 1867 a third society was projected. It remained, however, for the Kansas Editorial Association to make the move in April that resulted in a permanent organization in December 1875. F. P. Baker, the first secretary, was editor of the Topeka *Commonwealth*, but soon gave way to a full time executive secretary, F. G. Adams, who took charge February 4, 1876, and held office until his death in 1899. Adams was born in New York in 1824, was admitted to the bar, came to Kansas in 1855, residing a short time in Riley county. He was in Leavenworth in 1856, in Atchison in 1857, and during the next twenty years was never in any one place very long, serving from time to time as lawyer, editor and officeholder. At the time of his appointment as secretary of the historical society, he was a clerk in the state treasurer's office. In point of view, he was inclined to be a reformer, associating himself with anti-slavery, the Granger movement, woman suffrage, temperance and prohibition. He was not an extremist, however, and in his new office in the historical society held the scales fairly well balanced although personally inclined to favor the John Brown Legend. Even those who differed sharply with his point of view appear to have respected Adams during the controversies of the late seventies, when his office served as a clearing house for much of bitter and vindictive argument and when the historical society was not dominated by men of judicial temperament.

A letter written to Adams by James Christian, a life-long democrat, July 1, 1878, throws much light on the status of the Kansas State Historical Society during its early years: ''It always seemed to me (with a few honorable exceptions) an 'abolition *mutual admiration society*.' Nobody could do anything, or know anything,

---

[10] In 1887 the Brown family deposited the medal with the Kansas State Historical Society. The French committee had been appointed in 1870, but the project was delayed on account of the Franco-Prussian war. A duplicate medal in bronze was presented to the Kansas State Historical Society under a covering letter dated February 2, 1878. See *First Biennial Report* of the state board of agriculture . . . Kansas, 1877–78, pp. 88–90.

except he was in some way or manner connected with Old John Brown, a man that I never endorsed, or could admire, although he had many noble traits of character and much to admire.'' [11]

Housed in the state capitol building, the society did not have any funds at first even to pay salaries except from money derived from dues. The close connection between the infant organization and F. P. Baker of the *Commonwealth* afforded some outlet, however, for publication of a few historical articles. During the winter of 1876–77, Adams arranged through a committee for a series of lectures on early Kansas history, Charles Robinson, of course, being on the list.[12] During the early winter of 1878–79 a lecture course was inaugurated at Lawrence, and later in the same winter another at Topeka.[13]

The urge of the old settlers to organize was widespread, and at a meeting in Ottawa September 25, 1875, a Franklin county association was launched with a constitution which limited membership to residents of the county prior to 1860 and resident in the county at the time of application.[14] For settlers of this particular description in Franklin county to meet and not to reminisce about John Brown was unthinkable.

By 1877 the monument committee, made up of men from Franklin and Miami counties, was ready to complete its task. A shaft of Vermont marble, thirteen feet high, was secured and placed in position to be dedicated on the anniversary of the battle of Osawatomie, August 30, to the memory of those who fell in that engagement. On the day of the ceremonies, the village of Osawatomie was crowded with 5,000 to 6,000 visitors. Charles Robinson presided. John J. Ingalls delivered the eulogy on John Brown. W. W. Updegraff told the story of the battle. A colored man, C. H. Langston, delivered the dedicatory address. Although dedicated to those who fell in the battle, the monument was inscribed also to the memory of John Brown. Ironical though it may be, immediately it became popularly known as the John Brown monument,

[11] *Corresopndence* of Kansas State Historical Society, 3: 265.

[12] *Correspondence* of K. S. H. S., 1: 100. Charles Robinson to Adams February 7, 1877, accepting the invitation to deliver one of the lectures.

[13] *Daily Commonwealth*, November 28, 1878. Adams to Robinson November 28, 1878. *Correspondence* of Kansas State Historical Society. First biennial report of the Society, 59.

[14] Ottawa *Triumph*, October 1, 1875. A second meeting was held in 1876 (*Triumph* September 15, 1876) but no record was found of later meetings.

rather than as a shrine commemorating those whose bodies were buried at its base.[15]

In connection with these ceremonies, Robinson made an address which was to haunt him the remainder of his days:

Before proceeding with the order of exercises, I desire to thank your committee for the high honor of being called to preside on this occasion. It is an occasion of no ordinary character, being for no less an object than to honor and keep fresh the memory of those who freely offered their lives for their fellow men. We are told that 'scarcely for a righteous man will one die, yet peradventure for a good man some would even dare to die;' but the men whose death we commemorate this day, cheerfully offered themselves a sacrifice for strangers and a despised race. They counted not their lives dear to them so they might break the fetters of the slave. They were men of conviction though death stared them in the face. They were cordial haters of oppression, and would fight injustice wherever found; if framed into law, if upheld and enforced by the government, then the government must be resisted. They were of Revolutionary stock and held that a long train of abuses had put the people under absolute despotism, it was right and duty to throw off such government and provide new guards for further security. The soul of John Brown was the inspiration of the Union armies in the emancipation war, and it will be the inspiration of all men in the present and distant future who may revolt against tyranny and oppression, because he dared to be a traitor to the government that he might be loyal to humanity. To the superficial observer John Brown was a failure. So was Jesus of Nazareth. Both suffered ignominious death as traitors to the government, yet one is now hailed as the Savior of the world from sin, and the other of a race from bondage.[16]

Ingalls's oration revealed that he knew little about Brown, but that only gave greater freedom to his flow of rhetoric: "He [Brown] believed there is no moral acquisition so splendid as moral purity; no possession nor inheritance so desirable as personal liberty; nothing in this earth nor in the world to come so valuable as the soul, whatever be the hue of its bodily habitation; no impulse so lofty and heroic as an unconquerable purpose to love truth and an invincible determination to obey God."[17]

15 John Brown's name appears on the north side, Frederick Brown's on the west, David Garrison's and George Partridge's on the south, and Theron P. Powers's and Charles Keizer's on the east. The last two were not killed in the battle, but were shot the same day. Of the six names on the shaft, only three were of men killed in the battle proper, and only four were buried there.

16 The Lawrence *Daily Journal*, September 4, 1877, printed what appears to have been the official version of this address. The Lawrence *Standard*, September 7, printed it also. The Leavenworth *Weekly Times* printed a somewhat different version, and several other papers followed the *Times*. Sanborn's *John Brown*, p. 324, followed the *Times* version.

17 Atchison *Champion*, August 31, 1877.

Kansas never could escape the conviction that a man who could command such rhetoric as Ingalls was able to offer must possess a remarkable intelligence, and must be an authority on whatever subject he choose to speak. They did not understand his language, but they felt the spell of his personality, and were certain that such a flow of words must have a profound meaning.

Updegraff's story gave a picture of the battle of Osawatomie somewhat different from John Brown's: The defenders of the town had been under arms continuously for about two weeks; their headquarters was the blockhouse in the town; Brown was across the river guarding his cattle when the alarm was given and was sent for. Obviously there was no surprise in the attack, except the direction from which it came. Updegraff pointed out further that when it became evident that the enemy possessed a cannon, he abandoned the blockhouse as a danger rather than a defense and deployed in the timber with Brown's men. Many who heard this description became convinced that Updegraff, not John Brown, had been the real commander that day.

As early as August 16, 1877, F. G. Adams of the state historical society had written Hanway that the dedication ceremonies would afford a good opportunity to secure the histories of the neighborhood and that there should be a special history of events connected with John Brown. He urged Hanway as chairman of the Monument Committee to suggest a plan of procedure.[18] At the celebration Hanway presented a resolution directing the historical society to collect momentoes of early Kansas history. John P. St. John presented another resolution narrowed down to the collection of personal recollections of the associates of John Brown. This was adopted and September 25 Adams wrote Updegraff that he would be in Osawatomie in a few days to fulfill the objects of the John Brown resolution.[19]

In reporting the dedication exercises, the Lawrence *Journal*, September 6, drew some "lessons and inferences:" ". . . it is evident that unless some industrious, fair minded, judicially bent writer of history took things in hand soon, much of what pertains to early Kansas will be irretrievably lost. The careful listener last Thursday might have heard two or more separate and distinct accounts of almost every transaction of early days."

Those present at the Osawatomie celebration did not stop with

[18] Hanway *Correspondence*, 1: under letter A.
[19] Kansas State Historical Society, *Letter-press books*, 1: 219.

putting reminiscences down in writing. Ingalls made the suggestion in his oration that one thing more should be done in honor of John Brown,—the placing of a statue of him in statuary hall in the National Capitol. The crowd that heard Ingall's oration endorsed the suggestion as offered formally in a resolution sponsored by D. R. Anthony of Leavenworth.[20]   When the next legislature met in 1879, Speaker Sidney Clarke presented a bill to provide statues for John Brown and James H. Lane in recognition of their services to the free-state cause, to emancipation of the slave, and to freedom of the nation.[21]   The committee on ways and means, to which the bill was referred, reported adversely February 10. Another attempt was made in the legislature of 1881, when Senator Harrison Kelley's resolution was enacted providing for a joint committee to procure information and estimates of costs and to report to the next legislature.

The news that Kansas was considering the matter of a statue drew from F. B. Sanborn a letter of inquiry.[22]   In November 1881, the Labor Standard American Auxiliary Association of New York inquired of Governor St. John whether a statue had been sent to Washington, and whether Kansas had erected a statue or monument within the state.   St. John replied explaining the action pending under the Kelley resolution and sent as enclosures cuts of the Osawatomie monument and of the French medal.[23]

On December 2, 1881, the state historical society printed a four-page circular concerning the proposed statue, and appealed for relics of Brown to be deposited with the society.   The cut of the Osawatomie monument was labeled in this circular, "John Brown's monument."   John Brown had not only stolen the monument dedication ceremonies in 1877, but the monument had been appropriated as well.   The Brown statue movement was stranded by a storm of controversy before the legislative committee had completed its work, thereby leaving the issue open to plague the state for a whole generation.

[20] Leavenworth *Weekly Times*, September 6, 1877.   An act of congress, July 2, 1864 had invited the states to place in the old hall of the house of representatives statues, not to exceed two in number, of deceased persons who have been citizens of historic renown.

[21] Manuscript copy of the bill is in the *John Brown Papers*, Kansas State Historical Society, *House Journal*, 1879.

[22] Sanborn to Adams, May 13, 1881.   Adams's reply, May 20, 1881.   Kansas State Historical Society, *Correspondence*.

[23] Letter of inquiry, November 11, 1881.   St. John's reply November 17, 1881.   *John Brown Papers*. K. S. H. S.

Of broader state-wide, or even sectional interest in 1882 was the holding of a John Brown meeting at Topeka, in the rooms of the state historical society, October 21 and 23. The call appealed for the attendance of all former associates of John Brown. A John Brown memorial association was organized with an official title of "The Society of Associates of John Brown," and the objects of the organization were presented in an elaborate set of resolutions. First, it was declared to be the duty of those associated with Brown to "spare no pains in their efforts to hand down to future history such facts and experiences as we had with our worthy leader as will tend to correct false statements and substantiate that which is true concerning one so little understood and appreciated by many of our citizens and the world at large." Secondly, to "hurl back with scorn the assertion . . . that John Brown was insane in his efforts to free four million of bondsmen. . . ." Thirdly, to bring testimony to his purity and nobility of character. Fourthly, to bring forward testimony to honor him and "stamp with condemnation the slanderous calumnies vindictively sought to be fastened upon his character by the enemies of human rights, the devotees of gold, and of such as may be envious of his just fame." [24]

Of course the importance of these numerous organizations may easily be exaggerated, and to off-set such an impression, it should be pointed out that few of them proved of permanent importance. Their significance lies rather in the frequency with which these organization campaigns were launched, and the effect of the numerous subscriptions collected for the purpose of John Brown commemorations. They served to keep alive the agitation and reiterate the John Brown Legend. The effectiveness of the process was attested on numerous occasions, but James Legate probably summed up the popular verdict as pointedly as any:

Men have sought to change the verdict of the people of those days concerning John Brown and others. How futile the attempt! You might as well attempt to overturn the Rocky Mountains with a lady's hairpin for a lever. The verdict has been rendered and is settled, not alone by the people of Kansas, or by the people of the nation, but by the people of the whole world. I conceive it to be our part, as survivirs of those days, to give merited place in history to those men whose heroic conduct made them so richly deserve it.[25]

[24] The call was printed in the Topeka *Daily Capital*, October 17, 1882. The meeting was reported in the Topeka *Commonwealth*, October 22, the *Capital*, October 24 and 25, 1882.

[25] Address before the annual meeting of the Kansas State Historical Society, January 17, 1888. *Collections*, K. S. H. S., 4: 273.

CHAPTER XV

THE POST–MONUMENT CONTROVERSY, 1877–79

No doubt the editor of the Lawrence *Journal* had good intentions when he pointed out the lessons and inferences to be drawn from the dedication of the monument at Osawatomie, the necessary judicially minded person was not available and instead of eliciting facts the opposite versions of Kansas history seemed only to stir up controversy and bitterness of spirit. H. Miles Moore of Leavenworth immediately wrote a letter, to be read at the Old Settlers Meeting at Lawrence September 7, attacking Ingalls's oration so far as it dealt with the defense of Lawrence in September, 1856, insisting that instead of John Brown playing any conspicuous part, it was J. B. Abbott who was in command with Moore in charge of the rifle pit at the south end of Massachusetts street; that Brown came in during the afternoon and stopped at Moore's fortification, but Moore sent out the Sharps rifles to meet the advance guard of the pro-slavery forces in the late afternoon, before the federal troops arrived.[1] In this case there can be little doubt that Moore was as inaccurate as Ingalls.

HANWAY'S WRITINGS ON KANSAS HISTORY, 1878

General James G. Blunt was inspired to write his reminiscences of the flight of the eleven slaves liberated by Brown in the Missouri raid of December, 1858, and subsequent difficulties in southeastern Kansas. Immediately his story was printed by permission of the state historical society, it aroused a barrage of denials and criticisms that left little of Blunt's story standing. Hanway became one of the leading figures in this exposé, and in succeeding months sent to the historical society several papers on a variety of topics of Kansas history.[2] It seemed now that in cooperation with the state historical society, Hanway might be enabled to reach a state-wide audience. His first efforts were a new version of his

[1] The letter, dated September 6, did not arrive in time for the meeting but was printed in the Lawrence *Standard*, September 13, 1877.

[2] A list which includes most of the papers was printed in the *First Biennial report* of the K. S. H. S., 1877–79, p. 36. Others will be designated in the course of this chapter.

reminiscences of Potawatomie township with special reference to
the spring of 1856 and an article describing a projected rescue of
John Brown. These were acknowledged by the secretary, F. G.
Adams, January 19, 1878 and a letter was printed in the Topeka
Daily Commonwealth, January 25 and 26, and in the weekly issue
of the same paper a copy of which was sent to Hanway. Adams
was much disturbed by the Potawatomie article and Hanway's
letter, now lost, which had accompanied it. He hesitated to accept
Hanway's contention that John Brown was present and leader of
the execution squad. Apparently Hanway had mentioned in the
letter that he and Johnson Clark had a statement from a participant testifying to this fact. The full effect of Adams's perturba-
tion is evident only through a careful reading of the whole letter,
dated January 26:

> I am for a moment hesitating about the publication of your evidence
> as to Brown's part in the Pottawatomie creek execution. I desire to con-
> sult Gov. Robinson. And had you not better add a paragraph relating to
> what was just told you and Johnson Clark? The public should if pos-
> sible fully understand how that the execution was a necessity. Gov. Rob-
> inson told us at Paola last fall how necessary that act was. He gave a
> very forcible showing of the conditions of things in the territory justify-
> ing it. It may be he will be induced to write a paper on the subject.
> Your remarks on Montgomery are most timely and just. Your tribute
> to his character shows a true appreciation. You do yourself honor in
> invoking public appreciation of the noble acts of that brave and devoted
> friend of humanity. You do justice to Updegraff too. Let us give to
> history the truth as to the achievements of the great martyr Capt John
> Brown. But let us do justice to all.[3]

Hanway prepared the additional evidence in a six-page statement on February 1, but in his argument only elaborated the
former justifications without adding any vital point. He was specific in a few accusations, previously made only in more general
terms, such as one that he had himself heard Henry Sherman say
that he would as soon kill David Baldwin as a rattlesnake. He
rationalized more specifically the extermination editorial of the
Westport *Border Times* stating specifically that these men thought
after the destruction of Lawrence that it was time to carry out
orders as printed in that paper. His conclusion was also more
specific that "there cannot be a reasonable doubt, that Brown and
his party, took the border ruffians at their word, and considered it
his duty to strike FIRST; a mere question of time," and that al-

[3] *Hanway Correspondence,* 1: letter A.

though the community was shocked at first they came to realize that "he had saved their homes and dwellings from threatened raids of the pro-slavery party."[4] Although emphasizing the time element he did not analyze his evidence to demonstrate that John Brown could have and did read the extermination editorial, virtually a chronological impossibility and highly improbable under the circumstances even if possible. In the original article, the only point that could be called new to Hanway's customary treatment was the quotation of most of Samuel Walker's letter of 1875 repeating John Brown's admission of participation in the massacre. He made a variation in his story of the manner in which the news of the tragedy was received by the Potawatomie Rifles at Liberty Hill that "this report did not surprise many of us, as all who were posted" expected something radical. Later where he introduced a new discussion of the old subject he made a contradictory statement that "for one, I was no way surprised, for the plan as it was made known to me by one of the eight, was carried out in detail. And I may add that I was the only one, who was not taken by surprise."

CHARLES ROBINSON DRAWN IN

Adams was determined not to leave any stone unturned in his search for evidence which would establish the facts, but it is evident that he had a definite preconception that the facts should exonerate his hero, if not of the murder itself, then at least, of any deeds unbecoming a martyred hero. His appeal to Robinson was dated January 31:

I send you a copy of *Commonwealth* containing a paper of Judge Hanway relative to John Brown. We have another paper from him in which he presents reasoning going to show the participation of Capt. Brown in the Potawatomie creek execution,—he sends me a card in which he speaks of a secret interview with one of the participators who states that Brown was an *actor* in the affair. Since hearing your remarks on the subject at Paola, last August, I have been looking for such developments, and I am now fully convinced of the importance of your suggestions then made. I write you now to ask if you will not write out at length the views you then expressed, and especially detailing the facts showing the conditions of the Territory in May 1856, justifying and making necessary if you please the execution of the Doyles and others. No one so well as you can

---

[4] How Hanway could make this final argument seems inconceivable as he had recounted again and again how, after the massacre, the homes of the Browns, Wiener, Benjamin, Kilborne, Cochran and others had been raided and burned.

give a true exhibition of affairs in Kansas and if the policy of murder and assassination which ruled the action of the proslavery party till the affair of which I am speaking checked that policy. You will render history a great service by making a statement now on this subject detailing your own observations and experiences at that period. Will you not do it?[5]

Hanway had written Robinson the day before Adams's letter and Robinson replied February 4 in a letter that was to be historic: "I never had much doubt that Capt Brown was the author of the blow at Potawatomie, for the reason that he was the only man who comprehended the situation, & saw the absolute necessity of some such blow, & had the nerve to strike it. I will improve my first leisure to put on paper my views of the situation at that time & forward them to Mr. Adams."[6] In the meantime Robinson had written to Adams, who assured Hanway February 8 that "When we get the testimony all in we will consult about publication. I will await with interest for the statement of J. T."[7]

Adams's pursuit of facts led him to write to John Grant, living near Lawrence, on February 28 that

There is a growing interest in the public mind concerning the facts connected with the career of Capt John Brown in Kansas, and the state historical society is endeavoring to gather up for the benefit of future history such facts as may be in the memory of those who were more or less familiar with his career and which may not have been written and put in form for preservation. Hon James Hanway, Governor Robinson and others have undertaken to write out statements showing the condition of Kansas Territory, and especially that portion in which Capt. Brown was present in the spring of 1856; and most especially giving facts bearing upon the affair resulting in the death of the Doyles and others on Pottawatomie creek that spring: showing if possible a justification of the killing of those men. Judge Hanway informs me that you are cognizant of threats made by the Doyles and their associates rendering that killing a necessity, for the safety of their neighbors.

You will render the historical society a favor, if you will write up for filing among its manuscripts or for publication a statement of your recollections on this point. It is due to the memory of Capt Brown that all the facts relating to this matter should be recorded.[8]

With the summer Adams received other strange facts about Brown from one S. L. Moore writing from Memphis, Kansas, June 6 that "Old John Brown made his home at my house more than any other house in the State and I now of things about him that

---

[5] *Robinson papers.* Kansas State Historical Society.
[6] *Hanway Correspondence*, 1: letter B.
[7] *Hanway Correspondence*, 1: letter A.
[8] Kansas State Historical Society, *Letter-press books*, 2: 225–26.

none other man liveing nows—I cant give his life in Kas without differing with others esp Gen Blunt. . . .'' Soon after this the historical society was to receive the Hyatt *Papers* which contained a statement from the same man written in the winter of 1856-57 describing his Kansas experiences since his arrival in the territory in August 1855:

Have added to my stock 2 heifers, and one splendid mare: these came into my hands through Capt Brown's party who 'pressed' them from the enemy. I pay for the heifer, I got the other from my brother who 'pressed' her while in service.

JAMES TOWNSLEY SPEAKS THROUGH HANWAY

The publication of Hanway's writings in the papers was bearing fruit. Judge D. M. Valentine, of the Kansas Supreme Court, had first written him February 14, 1877, for historical information in connection with writing upon which he was engaged. Among other things he gave as well as asked information: ''Is the settlement of John Brown & sons as stated in the Ottawa Republican concerning the settlement of Cutler Township correct? If not where did they first settle? I would here state that James Townsley, who lived about a mile above Mr. Gilead, told me in 1863 that John Brown and himself were both present at the killing of the Doyles, and Wilkinson & Sherman.

''I shall visit Franklin county soon to refresh my recollections of what I have seen and heard there: but I shall probably not get down as far as Lane.'' That they had other correspondence is implied in a letter of July 18, 1878, asking for the names of the members of the Potawatomie Rifles and of the John Brown party that left them at Middle creek prior to the killing of the Doyles. Hanway became one of the chief oracles on the Brown question, and there will be occasion to call attention to others who wrote him for some refreshment of memory.

The much discussed statement of James Townsley was forwarded to Adams March 20 apparently, as on that day Hanway wrote that it had been sent and suggested that ''it would be proper to place it with the report I sent you, in case of any dispute which may arise therefrom.'' The statement follows:

On divers occasions, and quite recently, James Townsley has stated to us as follows—to wit:—

That he accompanied Old Capt. John Brown on the occasion of the Pottawatomie tragedy (so called) which occured on the 24th day of May

1856—that he states that he took the party, consisting of Old John Brown, and four of his sons, and a son in law, and one Wyans, and hauled them in his two horse wagon from the camp of John Brown, Jr on Ottawa Creek to Dutch Henry's Crossing where the tragedy occured, and that John Brown, Sr. did command the party and did order the killing of Wilkerson, Doyle and his two sons, and William Sherman, generally known as 'Dutch Bill.'

Lane, Franklin Co   JOHNSON CLARK
Kansas March 1878.   JAMES HANWAY

Judge Valentine informs me, by letter that the said James Townsley also stated to him the same facts as above.

J. H.[9]

SANBORN RE-ENTERS, 1878

While these developments were taking place in Kansas, Sanborn was pursuing eagerly the establishment of his version of the John Brown Legend in the East. His opportunity came when the Rev. Samuel Orcutt published early in 1878 his *History of Torrington, Connecticut*, including a hundred page "Memoir of John Brown" by Sanborn. Some separates of the *Memoir* were printed and distributed to libraries and friends. As Sanborn wrote to Redpath April 2, "it is only a sketch for a fuller biography, which I mean to write this year and next, using the material I have, and what John Brown Jun. will put at my disposal." He complimented Redpath's book and asked for any further material the latter would be willing to furnish. Sanborn felt relieved that through a controversy involving the Gerrit Smith family the facts of Smith's connection with John Brown had become public: "This secret history of G. S. has kept me from writing more than I have, for I could not appear as his accuser." [10]

Sanborn's *Memoir* pictured Brown as seeing the Kansas conflict as the battle ground of freedom and as participating on that basis, not merely as a defense against aggressions. He denied John

[9] The copy of this statement, which appears to be the original, is written in pencil on two half-sheets of rough paper and seems to be in the handwriting of Johnson Clark and is signed in his name in the same hand. Hanway did not sign. This copy is in the *Hanway Papers*, Kansas State Historical Society. The copy which Hanway sent to state historical society is on one sheet of paper written with ink in the handwriting of Hanway, including Johnson Clark's and his own signatures. This bears the date March 1878. It was filed in the John Brown collection K. S. H. S. The pencil original was not dated, but Hanway inserted the date, March 20, 1878, the day he was sending the copy to Adams, who acknowledged receipt of the letter and the Townsley statement March 26.

[10] *Hinton Papers.* Kansas State Historical Society.

Brown's participation in the Potawatomie massacre, and attributed the younger John Brown's insanity to his suffering inflicted by the pro-slavery party. His accounts of the battles of Black Jack and Osawatomie followed closely John Brown's own accounts with the Redpath glosses. Of the defense of Lawrence in September 1856 Sanborn said:

He was asked to take command of the defenses of the town and though he declined, he did in fact command. Between four and five o'clock in the afternoon he assembled the people in the main street, and, mounted on a dry-goods box in the midst of them, he made this speech, which is reported by one who heard him: [Hinton's report of the speech.]

After this fitting speech, which reminds one of John Stark at Bunker Hill and Bennington, Brown sent his small force to the few forts and breastworks about the town and ordered all the men who had the far-shooting Sharpe's rifles—then a new weapon—to go out upon the prairie, half a mile south of the town, where by this time the invading horsemen could be seen, two miles off. After a halt for reconnoitering purposes, the enemy made an advance upon Brown's left, and came within half a mile of his advance guard, just as the sun was setting. Under cover of the dusk some of them came nearer, but the discharge of a few Sharpe's rifles, and the approach of a brass cannon, which Brown ordered up to support his riflemen, caused the enemy to turn their horses and retreat, without any further attempt to take the town.

Hanway wrote Sanborn July 6, but the letter is not available. Sanborn's reply of July 22 indicates, however, somewhat of the contents:

I am under obligations to you for your letter of the 6th inst. and will certainly give all due weight to the evidence you mention concerning the Pottawatomie killing affair. I will write to Mr. Adams as you suggest, asking to see a copy of your communication.

Mr. Redpath to whom I have quoted what you write me, says, "John Brown, Sr, was not at Potawatomie. A man who saw the killings and who took part in them, told me the story, and he said J. B. was not present. But he was only accidentally absent. He was 12 or 20 miles away, at some 'Creek' buying stores, if I rightly remember." This agrees with what Brown himself told me, as I remember it.

I shall be glad however to hear and weigh the testimony on the other side. Mr. Charles A Foster, whom I know, and who met the men who killed the Doyles etc the next day or next but one says that neither John Brown nor John Brown Jr were present at the killing, and add that James Harris also told him so.[11]

Adams sent Sanborn on August 8 newspaper clippings of John Brown articles; almost certainly one or more of them were by Han-

[11] *Hanway Correspondence*, 1: letter B.

way, and stimulated by Hanway's letter and these newspaper clippings, Sanborn acted on Hanway's suggestion that he ask Adams
for a copy of the latter's article "including the testimony of an
eye witness, or a person claiming to be such." [12]   That final phrase
with its insinuation was typically Sanbornesque.   In replying
August 20, Adams fell into somewhat the same spirit at the opening, but veered around in the course of the letter to a painful acceptance of the inevitable, recognizing that the defense must rest
upon justification rather than denial.   As a psychological study
possibly the long letter is worth reproducing in full:

> I send you enclosed a copy of the so called statement of James Towns-
> ley, spoken of to you by Judge Hanway, in reference to the alleged par-
> ticipation of Capt. John Brown in the affair on Pottawatomie Creek.   The
> statement does not appear to me to be in a proper form.   Townsley how-
> ever has made the same statement to many persons.   We have somewhat
> elaborate papers written by Judge Hanway in support of his belief in the
> participation.   The Judge himself was a witness of some of the facts
> stated by him.   I am of the opinion that the weight of testimony here in
> Kansas will be in support of that opinion.   But I have hesitated to give
> publicity to the papers we have till the case shall be more fully made up.
> Gov. Robinson has expressed the opinion that it will be sometime proven
> that Capt Brown was present at the affair.   He thinks the act was a
> justifiable and necessary act: that the act did in fact have the effect to
> check the career of wholesale murder which the proslavery man had en-
> tered upon, intended [to] kill or to drive from Kansas every free state man
> in the Territory.   The Governor has promised to write for our society a
> paper presenting his views on the subject, and exhibiting facts support-
> ing his views.   On that account and in hopes to come in possession of
> other testimony justifying the act I have kept Judge Hanway's manu-
> scripts out of print thus far.   Should they not be published before the
> time you shall need them I will send you copies.   Those of us who were
> witnesses of the acts of the pro-slavery men in Kansas in 1856, can easily
> see that the act of execution at Potawatomie creek could be a justifiable
> one.   But so the world, if possible, should be made to see it before it shall
> be made to appear a matter of history that John Brown was engaged in
> the act.   I hope whatever opinion you may express in your book on this
> subject you will also present full showing of circumstances of the times;
> for did not Capt. Brown say that he approved the act?   And is it not
> possible that you may have misunderstood him, as denying that he was in
> any sense a participant?   I shall be glad to aid you all I can in gathering
> John Brown history.[13]

[12] Sanborn to Adams, August 12, 1878.   K. S. H. S., *Correspondence,*
volume three.
 [13] Kansas State Historical Society, *Letter-press books,* C: 223.

ENTER SARA: THE FEMALE OF THE SPECIES

In November the Springfield (Massachusetts) *Republican* published an article on Richard Realf and his fantastic poetical account of the defense of Lawrence in September, 1856, which attributed it to John Brown. This aroused Mrs. Sara T. D. Robinson to a characteristically vehement reply that John Brown had nothing to do with the defense of Lawrence, that the command was vested in Abbott, and that Deitzler led the skirmishing party with Sharps rifles; that W. W. Updegraff was in command at Osawatomie; and Brown was of no importance at the Wakarusa war; that if John Brown aided in making Kansas a free state it was in the horror at Potawatomie; and that having despaired of making civil war between the North and South in Kansas he turned to Virginia. In accounting for the insanity of John Brown, Jr., she referred to the statement of a witness of an altercation between the father and son over the father's proposal to go back to Potawatomie creek to do the killing and that for months afterwards in the prison camp the son had been insane from mental suffering on account of his father's deed.[14] Possibly Sanborn had been responsible for the Realf article, anyway he replied to Mrs. Robinson through the Springfield *Republican* November 26 in that offensive sneering style he so often assumed when engaged in controversy. Mrs. Robinson and Sanborn seemed to thrive on controversy and this was their first encounter. Neither of them exhibited any spirit of either fairness or common courtesy. Sanborn alleged that Mrs. Robinson had drawn upon her memory instead of consulting contemporary sources. In particular he cited as final evidence John Brown's own account of the defense of Lawrence, of the battle of Osawatomie, and a hitherto unpublished letter written in June in which were described the events of May and June 1856.[15] He did not stop with quotation, but added his own interpretations which went further than what Brown had claimed. Regarding the Potawatomie affair he declared "that Brown was connected with this affair and approved of it, I have never doubted; that he was actually present he always denied to me, and I shall believe him until some eye witness proves the contrary. One eye-witness has told

[14] Apparently the Realf article was printed in the *Republican* November 8. Mrs. Robinson's reply was dated November 18. The clipping in the John Brown *Scrapbooks*, Kansas State Historical Society, is a reprint from the Wichita *Eagle* December 12, 1878.

[15] This notoriously misleading John Brown letter of June 1856 is republished in Sanborn, *John Brown*, 236–241. Cf., Ruth's reply, Chapter 6.

two contradictory stories about it, and nobody has yet made public the whole truth.'' The crowning insult was saved for the last,
of course, when he called special attention to John Brown's opinion that at Lawrence the ''leading men had decided in a very
cowardly manner not to resist any process'' which might be served,
and then concluded (Sanborn speaking) ''if I mistake not, Dr.
Charles Robinson, the husband of your Kansas correspondent, was
one of the 'leading men' whom Brown here censures. This fact,
if it be one, may explain the pains taken by Mrs. Robinson to set
aside the verdict of history.'' Not only was this final thrust in-
excusable, but Sanborn had been untruthful about his own position on the Potawatomie affair, because there is no statement of
his available in which he stated it as his opinion ''that Brown was
connected with this affair.'' His reference to the eye-witness is
also inexplicable because he had in his possession the Townsley
statement to Johnson Clark and Hanway and there is no record of
any other statement by Townsley of that date that conflicts in any
substantial manner.

Mrs. Robinson's reply was dated January 3, 1879 and opened
with the disarming admission that ''no one can question that he
[Brown] was true to his convictions in his warfare upon slavery,
and the moral heroism he displayed commands the admiration of
the world,'' but, and there was the rub, Brown came not to settle
and make Kansas free, but to incite civil war between the North
and the South and the former policy won. She then pointed out
Sanborn's misquotation of Brown on the defense of Lawrence,
and followed that by pointing out that Sanborn's three contemporary records by eye-witnesses disagreed on the defense of Lawrence: John Brown said only a few scattering shots; Redpath general firing at night; and Realf's poem, ''all through that Sabbath
day a wall of fire we stood and held the baffled foe at bay.'' On
the subject of the Potawatomie massacre Mrs. Robinson said:

There is some direct and positive testimony in existence that John
Brown was present at the killing on the Pottawatomie. A large amount
of circumstantial evidence, whether true or false, matters not however,
considering he has acknowledged his responsibility in the matter to various parties. Whether the insanity of John Brown, Jr., was caused wholly
by the knowledge of this fact or his treatment as a prisoner or both, one
thing is certain, during a large portion of the time, I was at the prisoners
camp with him, he was brooding over this terrible massacre.

In closing Mrs. Robinson took account of Sanborn's parting word and called attention to the fact that the allegation seemed to apply to the events of May 1856 instead of November 1855, and at the former date her husband was not at Lawrence at all but was held as one of the treason prisoners, and if Sanborn had been acquainted with contemporary testimony which he valued so highly he would have known this.

Sanborn's attack on Mrs. Robinson did not have a favorable reaction in Kansas. H. Miles Moore wrote Adams January 11 that she had answered him as he deserved. Hanway was astonished and wrote Adams asking if Sanborn had ever sent for his article: "Sanborn, I believe, is writing a Life of Jno B of course he will publish the old foolish falsehood and it will pass for history. I will obtain if possible the affidavit of a man who was present." Adams replied to Hanway March 8 that "I sent Mr. Sanborn a copy of the Townsley statement you sent us, and told him in a general way of what we had on file by you, but sent him nothing of the latter, yet told him I could do so if desired." [16]

CUMULATIVE EVIDENCE

During the year 1878 the Kansas state board of agriculture was preparing its first biennial report, and planned it on a large scale as a document for the promotion of immigration to Kansas. One of the outstanding features of this voluminous work was a historical and descriptive story of each county. That for Miami county, formerly Lykins, was prepared by E. W. Robinson, who gave a succinct review of the events of 1856. He attributed the massacre to John Brown, gave Wiener as the messenger who carried the news of the threats to free-state settlers, described the excitement caused, the arrests, the sacking of Osawatomie in June and the driving out of Buford's men in August.[17] About the same time a commercial publishing house brought out the *United States Dictionary of Biography; Kansas volume,* edited by John Speer. It contained an extended statement of the Potawatomie matter by Johnson Clark on the authority of a Mr. T. who carried the party of killers in his wagon, but who did not take a hand in it himself. Mr. T declared that the Brown boys did most of the killing, with the advice and encouragement of Old John Brown himself, who shot old man Doyle.[18]

[16] *Hanway Correspondence.*
[17] The letter of transmittal was dated December 31, 1878, and the volume was distributed early in 1879. It went through three editions.
[18] This account is found on page 526. The *Dictionary* bears the copyright date 1878, but the imprint is 1879.

CHAPTER XVI

JAMES TOWNSLEY IS HEARD AT LAST, 1879

ELI THAYER TROUBLES THE WATERS

The Old Settlers' meeting of 1877 was held at Lawrence during the week following the dedication of the Osawatomie monument. Hanway was present and talked informally, explaining that he had not been attending the meetings for some years because the last one he attended had too much of a political cast. His historical remarks pertained to his usual list of themes: John Brown, Montgomery and associates. The principal speaker of the occasion was Eli Thayer who gave his peculiar interpretation of Kansas history; that all attempts to limit slavery by law had been futile, "in my philosophy might is right under fair circumstances" and what saved Kansas was the organization of immigration by himself and associates in the New England Emigrant Aid Company. Furthermore this was the first victory in the Civil War which preserved and freed the nation, and without which the national battle would have been lost.[1] To charge Thayer with "stupendous egotism" was futile. It was tried, only to draw from him a cheerful admission coupled with an even more sweeping boast that the public wanted the truth: ". . . . I would like to know what a man occupying my place in the Kansas struggle could have accomplished without egotism, or what is the same thing, an absolute confidence in himself."[2]

Thayer's interpretation certainly left no place for John Brown in Kansas history. Nearly two years later, Thayer was going through his papers, possibly in preparation for his attendance at Lawrence upon the Quarter-Centennial celebration of the opening of the Kansas struggle and came upon some letters which prompted one to F. G. Adams dated May 21, 1879.[3] His argument was that

[1] Report of the Old Settlers' Meeting of September 7 in the Lawrence *Standard*, September 14, 1877. Thayer was given a reception at Topeka September 10 where he related the origin of his New England Emigrant Aid Company. Thayer to Robinson, July 17, 1877 accepting the invitation to attend the celebration. *Robinson Papers*, U. of K.

[2] Letter to Mrs. Charles Robinson, February 2, 1890 on the occasion of a review of his new book, *The Kansas Crusade*. *Robinson Papers*, K. S. H. S.

[3] It was published in the Topeka *Daily Commonwealth* May 30 and the *Weekly Commonwealth*, June 5, 1879.

the real danger to free-state success was that the free-state men might be incited to hostilities against the federal goverenment. He charged Lane in particular with a plan to rescue the prisoners from the United States troops early in September 1856 insisting that the man who prevented that act was the real savior of Kansas. He thought probably Charles Robinson was that man, but persons were still living who could testify and settle the question definitely. He pointed out further that the release of the prisoners removed the danger of rebellion and those who had come to Kansas for that purpose soon left: "The most disappointed of all was John Brown, who, failing to make a Northern rebellion against the United States determined to be that rebellion himself, and we all know the result. It was his way of committing suicide for his disappointment in Kansas."

If Thayer wished to incite violence in Kansas in 1879, he could scarcely have chosen a more certain method. J. H. Shimmons of Lawrence, a Lane man, protested Thayer's treatment of Lane, "[he was] the master spirit that held together the many different elements that made up the Free State party, the organizing of our military forces, and their trusted and idolized leader and who came out of the conflict and without unnecessary shedding of blood, and whose advice was always to the effect that a bloodless victory over the Pro-Slavery forces was the true one." If the savior of Kansas was the man who prevented a collision over the prisoners at Lecompton then that man was Lane, but the troops in charge were border ruffian militia not United States troops. The key to an interpretation of Lane's policies, according to Shimmons, was not to judge him by his *words,* but by his *success.*[4]

One H. L. Jones of Salina wrote Adams June 7 protesting against Thayer's way of casting "ignominy upon the *name* and fame of John Brown:" "The closing paragraph of his letter is an uncalled for and unmitigated slander upon the honored dead, and what should prompt it at this time is past my comprehension."[5]

The old document which started Thayer off was a letter of 1856 written by G. W. Brown, while a treason prisoner at Lecompton. Thayer wrote to the Rockford, Illinois, *Gazette* inquiring whether Brown still lived and elicited from him a reply. Thayer then wrote

4 J. H. Shimmons to F. G. Adams. Lawrence *Daily Tribune,* June 7, and *Weekly Tribune,* June 12, 1879.

5 Topeka *Commonwealth,* June 19, 1879.

him direct informing him of the Old Settlers' meeting to be held in September at Lawrence and stating that he was going to attend.[6]

In the process of refreshment of memory Thayer also wrote George A. Crawford, of Fort Scott, Kansas, July 28, inquiring about John Brown. Crawford had been president of the Kansas State Historical Society when Thayer was in Kansas in 1877. He replied August 4 covering two subjects: the Potawatomie massacre and the Missouri slave raid of 1859 [7] His authority was conversations with John Brown in camp near Trading Post early in January 1859:

> As to the 'massacre' he said he would not say that he was not engaged in it, but he would say that he advised it, and justified it, and was willing to take a full share of the responsibility of it. He said that the death of those pro-slavery men had been determined upon, at a meeting of the free-state settlers the day before; that he was present at the meeting, and I think presided, and that the executioners were then and there appointed. He said that he would not say that he was one of them, but he would say that if it was wrong, he was as much to blame as any.

The Quarter-Centennial, September 15–16, 1879

In 1879 the Old Settlers' Meeting was held September 15–16, at Bismarck Grove (Lawrence), but the fact that it was the Quarter-Centennial celebration had meant that it was carried out on a larger scale than in other years and the proceedings and addresses were assembled in book form, *The Kansas Memorial*, under the editorship of Gleed. In the light of what came before and after one cannot read the addresses as they have been printed without realizing that every faction was conscious of the opportunity presented and had carefully planned for its advantage.[8] Robinson delivered the opening address taking a broad historical view of the anti-slavery and abolition movement; recognizing credit due to the non-resistant abolitionists, the political-action abolitionists and the anti-slavery men, and in the last stage even the conservative anti-slavery democrats. According to Robinson, each contributed an essential part to the victory, but the key to the Kansas phase of the question lay in the

[6] Thayer's letter is in the Rockford (Illinois) *Gazette*, June 11, 1879. Thayer's letter to G. W. Brown of June 10 is in the *G. W. Brown Papers*, K. S. H. S.

[7] *G. W. Brown Papers*, K. S. H. S. It was forwarded to G. W. Brown by Thayer, December 10, 1879 while Brown was publishing his *Reminiscences of Old John Brown* in serial form.

[8] There is no way of determining to what extent the addresses were revised for publication in the light of what transpired at the meeting.

New England Emigrant Aid Company and the men who made its work possible: Thayer, A. A. Lawrence, E. E. Hale, William M. Evarts and their associates. The presentation made one conspicuous omission, the direct-action abolitionists, especially John Brown. Nothing was said to minimize his importance; he was simply ignored. The contrast with the other addresses was so sharp that it must have been the subject of remark during the two-day session. Among those taking occasion to give praise to the Old Hero were J. P. Usher, J. W. Forney, James Legate, James Hanway, James S. Emery, D. W. Wilder, John Speer and E. A. Coleman.

Hanway's remarks on the fictitious John Brown cabin picture inspired George A. Crawford to write him a letter October 9 admitting that although he knew the cabin story was incorrect, he did not understand that Brown never had a cabin in Kansas. He thought it was near the Doyle's and Wilkinson's. He inquired also "whether his wife was with him in those early days, or ever lived in Kansas." Hanway's reply was dated October 18, in which he went over the whole ground again assuring Crawford that Brown never had a cabin, and Mrs. Brown never lived in Kansas.[9] The remarkable thing about the Crawford inquiry was the revelation of his ignorance of the simplest facts concerning John Brown in Kansas, yet he was participating as an authority in the controversy.

Sara's Victory; G. W. Brown Advocatus Diaboli

After the Semi-Centennial celebration of 1904, G. W. Brown wrote Mrs. Robinson an enthusiastic letter in commentary on the differences between that and the Quarter-Centennial. Then (1879) it was all Lane and Brown, but the "defeat of the criminals, so far as the public is concerned, had its origin in *your parlor, where we* converted Gov. Robinson to the truth about Brown, and which he afterwards labored so earnestly to promulgate."[10] For the first time here is an illuminating contribution toward an answer to what has been a question ever since 1879,—why Robinson changed sides on the Brown question. It is only partially satisfactory,

---

[9] Crawford challenged Hanway's story that the "Parallels" were written in the Hanway cabin or read to Hanway prior to publication and insisted the "Parallels" were written in the house of Dr. A. B. Massey, at Trading Post. His story was sent to the Leavenworth *Times* under the date October 29 and printed in that paper October 31, 1879, together with the correspondence with Hanway.

[10] G. W. Brown to Mrs. Robinson, October 27, 1904. *Robinson Papers,* K. S. H. S.

however, inasmuch as G. W. Brown's egotism did not leave room for Thayer's, and after all, it was Thayer apparently who saw to it that G. W. Brown attended the quarter-centennial. And then, closer to Robinson than Thayer and Brown was Sara, his wife, and no one knows the whole of what happened in Sara's parlor.

The reader must not anticipate this explanation, however, in following the story through the months after the Old Settlers' meetings. On September 22, 1879, Robinson wrote an open letter to G. W. Brown, published in the Lawrence *Daily Journal,* and sent a copy to Brown at Rockford, Illinois. Robinson declared that friends of truth wanted to hear from G. W. Brown and the historical society had nothing from him: "One subject seems just now to be uppermost in the minds of writers of history, and that is where to place Gen. Lane and John Brown. . . . It is not eulogy or censure that is desired, but *facts,* for the historian." G. W. Brown replied October 10, his letter being published in the *Daily Journal,* October 17, stating that "your letter . . ., which I first saw in the Lawrence *Journal* is at hand;" as a duty he accepted the invitation and would write a series of articles of about one newspaper column in length each week, providing they were published in the Lawrence and Topeka papers. The title would be "Reminiscences of Old John Brown." J. H. Shimmons joined in a plea for more facts, asking that Brown include Robinson in his history, along with Lane and Brown.[11] "The Reminiscences of Old John Brown" were first printed serially, as indicated in the correspondence, the Lawrence *Journal* publishing the first installment October 24, 1879, and continuing somewhat irregularly until February 1, 1880 and then in pamphlet form with corrections resulting from criticisms. The introduction to the reprint is most interesting as G. W. Brown explained his supposed feelings and thoughts during the quarter-centennial celebration:

He heard repeatedly, during the two days the convention was in session, the principal character in these pages, lauded as the person of all others to whom Kansas is indebted for her rescue from slavery. He learned that a monument had been erected to his memory, at Osawatomie, and that it was proposed to send a statue of him to Washington, to adorn the National Capitol, and perpetuate his renoun. He saw all around him the *real* heroes in the strife. . . . [G. W. Brown thought to himself.] The time has come, if it ever will come, when the TRUTH of history must be vindicated. [Soon after returning home the Lawrence *Journal* came with Robinson's letter.] I read, and was startled with his proposition. [Did

[11] Lawrence *Daily Journal,* October 16, 1879.

he have the same feeling that had haunted G. W. Brown?] Wonder if, as he looked over that vast assemblage, as its presiding officer, and back over the darkened history of Kansas, and thought of the mouldering who laid down their lives that Freedom might live, and heard eulogy on eulogy, the sweet voice of song, and the loud tramp of Fame, all enlisted in favor of a single person whose name is hardly worthy of preservation—wonder if he felt as I in regard to that character.

So far as the essential facts were concerned about John Brown in Kansas, G. W. Brown had practically no information additional to what he had printed in the *Herald of Freedom* in 1859. He did have a keen enough sense of historicity, however, to appreciate something of the process by which the John Brown Legend had grown and reviewed with telling effect the inconsistent and contradictory stories the legend-makers had written from the time of Hinton's and Redpath's fables of the fifties. In addition to his old materials, Brown was in a position to use the E. W. Robinson account just published in the *First Biennial report* of the State Board of Agriculture. In spite of the absence of new material the *Reminiscences* proved to be a landmark in John Brown historiography, because G. W. Brown possessed an innate capacity to infuriate people, and furthermore, in accusing John Brown of the massacre, he refused to admit that there was any justification. In taking this ground he united both the Sanborn and Hanway schools of thought against him. When both of the latter were in grave danger of losing their Old Hero altogether, they could hardly afford to quarrel over Tweedle-dee-dee and Tweedle-dee-dum, yet Sanborn's perversity almost forced just that outcome.

ATTACKS ON G. W. BROWN AND ROBINSON

The attack on G. W. Brown and Robinson was led by "Honest John" Speer who criticized Robinson first on two counts. The initial installment of the *Reminiscences* left the impression that Robinson in his capacity of President of the Kansas State Historical Society had asked Brown to write the series. As a director of the society Speer protested at such misuse of that organization. His second count was that, as G. W. Brown had been the bitterest of enemies, it was bad taste to have him write such history and in addition he insisted Brown had made errors in statement of facts.[12] These criticisms of the first installment of the *Reminiscences* were

[12] Lawrence *Weekly Tribune*, November 13, 1879.

an earnest of the running fight Speer intended to wage.[13] He conceded that John Brown was present at the massacre but insisted that he was justified, repeating most of the stock stories such as insults to the women, outrages on free-state men, notices to leave; "Free State men had hung to the limbs of trees till the buzzards pecked their eyes out." He declared also that the congressional investigation committee was justified in rejecting the Potawatomie affidavits in May 1856 on the ground that these events occurred after their appointment, and he pronounced Mahala Doyle's letter to John Brown at Harpers Ferry a forgery because she could not write. Speer was in a peculiar position with regard to the Potawatomie massacre, because as editor of the *Dictionary of United States Biography, Kansas Volume,* published within the year he had accepted Johnson Clark's version of "Mr. T's" confession in the matter.[14] Mr. T had given only one instance of threats, and that was to the Grants who had sent a son to the camp of John Brown, Jr., to get help.

Robinson replied to Speer regretting "that Mr. Speer, who is noted for his modesty, should be shocked at the lack of it in himself," and cleared the decks for action by declaring further that Speer's "unsupported word is not proof positive in this community." He claimed the same right for G. W. Brown to write history as Speer had to write his series of articles on Jim Lane, and insisted that in calling on Brown he had spoken only in a private capacity. Robinson explained his reasons for specifying Jim Lane and John Brown as the subjects of investigation because he wished to prepare the way for giving credit where it belonged; to the settlers and the free-state party. As for himself he disclaimed any pretensions to heroism. As to his relations with G. W. Brown he pointed out that they had quarreled and had been estranged during the latter part of the territorial period. Robinson challenged some points in Brown's story of the Wakarusa war, deny-

[13] Other attacks appeared in the Lawrence *Daily Journal,* November 14, November 25, December 16 and 17, and usually appeared in the *Weekly* edition following the printing in the *Daily.* In spite of all the venom displayed the thought persists that possibly this controversy was not so bitter as it appears. Could it be possible that in the beginning at least the affair was arranged beforehand to while away the long dull winter months, and that as the show proceeded unexpected developments turned what had been intended as entertainment or farce into something deadly serious? The basic fact must be remembered that the essentials of Townsley's story were already before the public and had not precipitated particular bitterness.

[14] Cf. Chapter 16.

ing that any insubordinate movements by John Brown had ever been reported to headquarters, but "it was reported one night that General Lane was about to take 100 men for the same purpose," but the expedition was prevented. James Blood had told Robinson, however, that after the peace John Brown had attempted to raise an expedition which Blood stopped and did not report. Robinson also suggested that Blood could give some important facts regarding the Potawatomie massacre and suggested that as the Grants were made to figure in the existing controversy John T. Grant, who helped bury the victims, might have something of interest to say. And finally in connection with the Speer-Lane matters Robinson struck at the reputation of both by dragging out into the open the Speer-Lane embezzlement charges arising out of Speer's service as collector of internal revenue.[15] Of course, in one respect this was a resort to the controversialist's trick of changing the subject to confuse the issue, but it did have an indirect bearing on the controversy in exposing Speer's personal interest in suppressing facts and protecting the Lane-Brown legends. Speer protested that it was John Brown's personal history, not his own, that was the subject of discussion, nevertheless he made denials of the Robinson charges.[16]

Blood's response to G. W. Brown's call for facts was a letter dated November 17, published early in December.[17] In May 1856, returning to Lawrence from the East by way of Westport and Osawatomie, he wrote that he had found that most of the men, both pro-slavery and free state, had gone from Osawatomie to Lawrence; he had met John Brown's party in a wagon, one man riding a horse, headed toward Potawatomie creek upon a secret expedition, and talked with Brown who was greatly excited. Blood quoted George Partridge, who was with the younger Brown's company at Palmyra, as saying that the only provocation was a spring election when Brown and Doyle both expressed themselves on the negro question and threats were made by both. Blood claimed that the Lawrence committee had sent Samuel Walker to investigate the Potawatomie affair at the time and that he could probably tell more.

[15] Robinson's replies are in Lawrence *Journal, Daily* edition, November 16, 30 and *Weekly* edition, November 27 and December 4.

[16] Lawrence *Daily Journal*, December 9, 1879. Robinson's answer was delayed in publication but appeared December 31, 1879. It dealt only with the Speer scandal.

[17] The Leavenworth *Weekly Press* printed it December 4 and the Lawrence *Journal* (*Weekly* edition) December 11, 1879.

After the first few installments of the Brown *Reminiscences* the Kansas *Tribune* declined to publish more explaining editorially November 13 that the motto conspicuously displayed at the Bismarck Grove reunion had been "With malice toward none and charity for all"; but that the numbers on hand were "ghoulish";

The graves of Free State and pro-slavery men, dead for more than twenty years, are invaded, and their bones and reputation dragged into the arena, with an animus suggesting the scramble of jackals and hyenas over the bones of a dead lion. . . .

We never saw John Brown but once, but our knowledge of the old man is supplemented with a knowledge of his work, and complemented by the world-wide influence for good of the old martyr's reputation. His fame is the property of the world, and John Brown one of its idols. His canonization has been informal, but complete, and we cheerfully accept the popular verdict. Our hands shall not aid in divesting his name of the halo surrounding it, nor, if we can prevent it, shall sacrilegious hands disturb the old man's rest." [18]

G. W. Brown gave this editorial special attention in a reply that was unique but characteristic of his controversial talents. He agreed that the canonization had been quite informal, in fact too much so, and according to the ecclesiastical law there were fatal defects in the procedure.

First. The candidate must have been dead fifty years, else the claim of his friends for his beatification could not be considered.
Second. He must have had a reputation through all those years for superior sanctity and supernatural gifts.
Third. A long and minute investigation must be made into the candidate's merits. An *advocatus diaboli* is appointed, who recites the dead man's wicked deeds. This is followed by a eulogist who praises the dead. Then comes the verdict, and, if favorable, the canonization.
But my vituperist wishes to set up a statute of limitations of only twenty years; wholly dispense with the 'Devil's advocate,' allow the eulogist to recite the good deeds of his candidate, estop further inquiry and then pronounce the words of beatification.

Brown insisted that the people were ready to listen to facts and might render a verdict "more in harmony with an enlightened judgment." [19]

Refusing to print the G. W. Brown *Reminiscences* the Topeka *Commonwealth* took the ground that

[18] The clipping of this editorial in the *Robinson Papers*, K. S. H. S., contains a pencil notation at the end, "Speer." Such an identification is not final. The editors were N. Z. Strong, C. F. Strong and H. W. Pinneo, but none of them figured personally in the Brown controversy.
[19] Lawrence *Daily Journal*, November 20, 1879.

the Old Settlers' Meeting at Bismarck was run with an attempt to belittle Republicans and Republicanism and to glorify Democracy, especially Pennsylvania Democracy. . . . But John Speer, . . . is showing Dr. Brown up in his true colors. They are the most scathing articles we have seen.[20]

The St. Joseph *Herald* declared that

Geo. W. Brown is the same liar and mercenary politician that he was twenty years ago, and the Lawrence *Journal* is hardly to be excused for publishing his venom. Brown hates the cause and the men he betrayed. He is not trying to write history, but to make a rogues gallery of the Kansas pioneers.[21]

Under the fury of the enemy the Lawrence *Journal* admitted November 30 that the articles were not what had been expected, but they were part of the material of history. The facts were important, and important ones had been brought out, but the opinions expressed were not binding, and the *Journal* did not share the opinions. J. H. Shimmons took similar ground, admitted John Brown's responsibility, fell back on justification and declared that "He [Brown] died for an idea, therefore his name is immortal." [22] He repudiated, however, "the popular belief that Dr. Brown's history is a put up job between the Doctor and Governor Robinson, got up during the old settlers' meeting. . . ." Robinson denied that Shimmons was correct in interpreting John Brown and pointed out that Kansas history thus far was mostly "romance" written around heroes. Sanborn credited his hero with only two events in Kansas, he said, Potawatomie and Black Jack, and as Shore shared equally the honors at Black Jack it left John Brown with only one exclusive claim to credit. As for Lane, Robinson insisted he had not commanded at any engagement in 1856, all battles being led by others and Lane given the credit. As for himself, Robinson admitted he had been given credit for things he did not deserve; "it is time for sensational history to give place to history based on facts, and that is why it is important to strip the romantic heroes of their borrowed plumes that they may be put upon the persons to whom they rightly belong,"—the free-state settlers. The *Kansas Weekly Press* of Leavenworth, of which James Legate was an editor, insisted that John Brown "was a HERO not a MURDERER," and

[20] Topeka *Weekly Commonwealth*, December 4, 1879.
[21] Reprinted in the Lawrence *Journal*, November 30, and the *Weekly Commonwealth*, December 4, 1879.
[22] Lawrence *Daily Journal*, December 4, 1879.

rendered the verdict that "John Speer is nearly as far wrong in his admiration as Brown in his hatreds." [23]

SANBORN'S "DASTARD" AND "INGRATE" ATTACK

John Brown was being attacked, and by a master hand in controversy and true to his written pledge to the Old Hero, Sanborn, like a modern Don Quixote, rushed in to do battle:

The anniversary yesterday of John Brown's public murder in Virginia makes as good a time as any to consider the attacks now making in Kansas upon his memory, by Charles Robinson and his friends. These attacks are no new thing,—the old hero was always in the way of politicians. Dr. Robinson has been a politician most of his life, and in Kansas acted the politician's part. . . ."

Next came a comparison between John Brown and General Grant in the matter of shedding blood with a view of maintaining that if Brown was a murderer then Grant was likewise:

That John Brown was such a patriot-warrior, and is so honored by the world, few men outside of Kansas would attempt to deny. But in Kansas, ungrateful men and women, for one reason and another—old grudges, new hopes of a statue at Washington, or the natural antipathy that always exists between heroes and dastards—have undertaken the task of pulling down John Brown's reputation and setting up Charles Robinson's in the place of it. It is a dirty job, and has been with great propriety committed to another Brown—. . . . Mud and filth are freely discharged by the combatants on both sides—but, in the course of the billingsgate encounter, some historic facts emerge from obscurity, and at least one historic doubt is in a fair way to be cleared up. . . . It is settled now, as to its main point—that John Brown did direct and approve the execution. . . . That he committed the deed with his own hand was never seriously maintained, and all that is now asserted by the malevolent ingrates of Kansas, is that he led the party which did the execution, and shot the first ruffian with his own pistol. This is the only important new charge made, and it rests on the second hand testimony of a certain 'Mr. T' . . . , doubtless, James Townsley. . . . There is no question that he is a very important witness, and in some degree an eye-witness. . . . He has not always told the same story, we understand he was himself a party to the execution, and therefore not an indifferent witness; and it is more than twenty-three years since the events took place. [Quoted the Johnson Clark statement from the *United States Biographical Dictionary*.] This account is intrinsically probable, in its main statements,—quite improbable in some of its particulars.

[23] *Weekly Press*, December 11, 1879, and Lawrence *Home Journal*, January 15, 1880 quoting from the *Press*.

Sanborn stated specifically that the Townsley charge that John Brown shot Doyle was in "every way improbable" as John Brown repeatedly stated that he took no part in the execution:

The other declaration quoted as Brown's by Redpath, Sanborn and others, that he was not actually present at the execution, must, we think, be modified by the concurrent testimony of several witnesses, that he was at least in command of the party, and was near the place at the time. It is to be noticed that the men executed lived some distance from each other and it may have happened that Brown sent detachments to arrest the ruffians. and dispatch them, while remaining himself apart from the actual deed. Brown's statements on the subject to the late Dr. Webb, of Boston, to James Redpath, to F. B. Sanborn and others, may have been understood by them in a broader sense than he intended.[24]

Negotiations Leading to the Townsley "Confession"

James Townsley had told his story twice through Clark and Hanway, but Sanborn and men of his type were not willing to accept it in that form. G. W. Brown's *Reminiscences* forced the issue because of the bitterness he aroused. John Hutchings, a Lawrence lawyer, put the question squarely, together with a review of the controversy and a copy of Johnson Clark's *Dictionary* article, closing with the inquiry: "Will not some of these 'living witnesses' in the interest of historical truth, give the facts to the public over their own signatures? . . ."[25] The editor of the *Journal* endorsed Hutchings's plea and called upon Redpath to produce his witnesses.[26] Hanway wrote Hutchings, November 24, calling attention to his *Journal* articles in 1875, and to the story he had submitted to the historical society but which had never been printed. He called attention also to the article in the *United States Biographical Dictionary, Kansas Volume*, page 77, which referred to his historical views and endorsed the Johnson Clark article in the same volume, pointing out that he and Clark had conferred when it was written. He had talked several times with "Mr. T." of the Clark article, there could be no doubt of John Brown's participation in the expedition, and only Eastern people denied it. In referring to what he had written for the historical society he suggested that "perhaps if there was a request from you or Mr.

[24] Springfield *Republican*, December 3, 1879. Reprinted in Topeka *Commonwealth*, December 18, 1879. The article was not signed, but the authorship is unmistakable and was recognized at the time.

[25] Letter dated November 17, printed in the Lawrence *Daily Journal*, November 18, 1879.

[26] *Weekly Journal*, November 20, 1879.

Thatcher, Mr. Adams might feel inclined to publish it while the subject is being ventilated." [27]   The next day Speer was writing to Hanway that "I think you ought to contribute something in defense of the old hero. I know you must feel like it." [28]   The day following, November 26, Hutchings answered Hanway's letter stating that it would appear in the *Journal* the next day. He approved the suggestion of getting a statement from Townsley, over his own signature, urging that it should be done before Sanborn wrote his book. Incidentally he was forwarding to Sanborn copies of all the articles appearing in the *Journal*.[29]   On the same day Johnson Clark was writing to the *Journal* in answer to Hutchings's letter and the editorial, stating that

I am satisfied the evidence can be obtained which you desire. . . . I suggest that a reporter be sent by G. W. Brown or some other parties, and the facts be had and the question settled whether in fact John Brown was there or not. In this vicinity there is but one opinion. . . . I have not nor do I wish to argue the question of the expediency or justice of the affair, but I will only say that I believe Brown *thought it a duty*, and that the blow must be struck in the interest of Freedom.

In printing Clark's letter, the *Daily Journal* said that "we shall have this Potawatomie business brought to a historical certainty.[30]

The arrangements indicated by the *Journal* were communicated to Hanway by John Hutchings November 29 and best explain themselves:

After consultation with Mr. Thatcher [the editor of the Journal] I have consented to visit Mr. Townsley for the purpose of procuring his statement in relation to the Potawatomie tragedy over his own signature. Mr. Johnson Clark has given Mr. Thatcher Mr. Townsley's name and advises that some one come down. When I go I want you to go with me. We will call on Mr. Clarke and have him present also. I will write you what day I will be in Osawatomie. Where can you meet me? [31]

In the meantime the pot was kept boiling. A Dr. W. D. Hoover was quoted by the *Miami Republican* (Paola) December 5 as saying that he was in the vicinity at the time of the massacre and confirmed Johnson Clark's statements. The Lawrence *Daily Journal* on December 6 and 7 published a long article from Hanway, telling his oft-repeated justification story yet again. His rationali-

[27] Lawrence *Daily Journal*, November 27, 1879.
[28] *Hanway Papers*, Kansas State Historical Society.
[29] *Hanway Papers*, Kansas State Historical Society.
[30] *Daily Journal*, November 30, and *Weekly Journal*, December 4, 1879..
[31] *Hanway Papers*, Kansas State Historical Society.

zation was new, however, and interesting as a contribution to the philosophy of history of the period. "Mankind in general judge from the effects or results which follow, they do not trouble themselves about the abstract question of right and wrong. They inquire what were the consequences growing out of it. It was this view of the case which reconciled the minds of the settlers of the Potawatomie." This was unquestionably the opposite of the usual view of John Brown which rested his case on devotion to the principle of right, and martyrdom to an idea. Hanway's case is a reminder that the most conscientious of men do strange things when engaged in controversy. He indulged in still another vagary in an article a short time later where he again marshaled his evidence in justification and then he must have felt unsatisfied with the defense, for he tacitly abandoned the Kansas case in declaring that it mattered little what opinion of John Brown was held in Kansas, as his martyrdom outshone all other deeds.[32]

Coincidence often plays an important part in history, and while waiting for Hutchings's return from the Townsley mission, George W. Grant came in from California to visit his brother Henry C. Grant who lived near Vinland, a few miles south of Lawrence. On account of Johnson Clark's reference to John T. Grant having been warned to leave the Potawatomie community and having sent his son George to John Brown's camp, the editor of the *Journal* had been anxious to get some statement from a member of the family. Meeting the Grant brothers on the street the morning of December 4, the editor invited them to his office to answer a series of twelve questions formulated for the purpose of the interview. The questions and answers were printed in full December 5 and, although signed by both, the interview was really with George.[33]

He had been with John Brown, Jr's., company on the Lawrence expedition and now denied outright that he had served as the messenger who carried the story of the outrages against free-state people. After the news was received by messenger from Lawrence that the town was sacked, Grant said that the elder Brown called for volunteers who would obey his orders. The son protested weakening the force by taking a detachment away, and when his father persisted, warned him against any rash act. Grant enumerated the men who volunteered and camped apart to prepare

[32] Lawrence *Daily Journal*, December 20, 1879.

[33] Henry had been but eleven years old in 1856 and too young to participate.

for the expedition and commented that on their return they had
one of Henry Sherman's horses. When asked what effect the news
of the massacre had on the younger John Brown, Grant replied:
"a very marked effect. He showed great agitation and gave up
the command of the company to H. H. Williams."

The next question was put in a challenging form: "it has been
asserted that there was no provocation given by these pro-slavery
men. What do you know about that?" Grant's reply was vigorous, "The assertion is not true." He accused the Georgians in
camp four miles from the Grants of committing outrages [but
named nothing specific] and asserted that a courier carried mes-
sages from the Georgians to the pro-slavery men. When the Lawrence crisis came the free-state men prepared to go, sending Fred
Brown to buy lead at Morse's store south or southwest of Dutch
Henry's and on his return to Grant's he passed Dutch Henry's
with the lead and was questioned by the pro-slavery men. The
lead was made into bullets on Sunday, and, according to his chronology, the company started to Lawrence on Monday. The next
was necessarily hearsay so far as Grant was concerned, that—In
their absence Wilkinson, the Doyles and William Sherman went
to Morse's store and threatened him with a rope, later with an
axe, finally consenting to give him until sundown to leave; Morse
and his little boy fled to Grant's and hid in the bush near by, and
shortly became ill and died. Dr. Gillpatrick was quoted as saying death was caused by fright. Henry Sherman came to Grant's
and warned them also to leave, and under these circumstances they
did not know at what moment the Georgians would descend upon
them. Curiously enough at this point Grant was asked specifically if he was the messenger sent to inform the absent company
of the crisis and he denied it explaining that he was with the company, but no question was put whether there was a messenger or
who the messenger was.

The next question was regarding "evidence of a premeditated
assault upon the Free-State men on the creek." To this he replied that Mrs. Wilkinson had told his father and Gillpatrick that
the last thing her husband had said the night of his murder was
"that there was going to be an attack made upon the Free State
men, and that by the next Saturday night there would not be a
Free State settler left on the creek." In answer to the question
what sort of man Wilkinson was, Grant replied, "He was a dangerous man. Everybody feared him. He was the most evil-looking

man I ever saw. He abused his wife shamefully. . . .'' Grant denied mutilation of the bodies, other than what occurred in the killing with swords.

The identification of John Brown as the principal in the affair was admitted by Grant on the testimony of Mrs. Wilkinson's description of his clothing; "nobody on the creek doubted that John Brown was the leader of the party. As to the killing, it was the current story that Brown shot Doyle, but personally did nothing more. . . .'' On the effect of the massacre Grant declared, "there was no more killing on either side in that neighborhood.'' [34]

It is clear that the questions were framed, consciously or unconsciously, with a view to making a case for justification. Several pertinent questions were omitted altogether. The historian can only wonder what Grant would have replied to some questions that should have been asked, what he would have done under cross-examination, or what he would have told if he had been left to relate his story in his own way, undirected by set questions. In support of part of Grant's story Judge Thomas Roberts of Miami county confirmed the messenger story and the dispute between John Brown and his son over the expedition.[35]

In publishing the full text of Townsley's statement, popularly referred to as his confession, almost three columns in length, the *Daily Journal,* December 10, 1879, announced that "We are enabled to lay before our readers, this morning, the most important contribution ever made to Kansas history.''

Townsley had arrived in Kansas, settled in Anderson county, about one mile west of Greeley, in October, 1855. As a member of the Potawatomie Rifles he went on the Lawrence expedition and while camped near Shore's house, May 23, about noon, John Brown went to him saying he had just received information that trouble was expected on the Potawatomie and Brown wanted him to take him and his boys back in his wagon. Townsley consented and they started about two o'clock. Near Dutch Henry's crossing, a camp was made in a ravine and there after supper John Brown

---

[34] When Sanborn printed the text of part of this interview in his *John Brown* (1885) he omitted the questions; in fact, he did not explain that the statement was in the form of answers to set questions; also, he omitted without marks the answers to three questions in the early part of the interview and seven at the end. In his book the two answers printed were "run on'' as a continuous narrative.

[35] La Cygne *Journal,* December 20, 1879, quoting from the Paola *Citizen,* December 13, 1879.

first told Townsley what he intended to do. Townsley refused to guide the party to the forks of the Potawatomie and make a clean sweep of pro-slavery men coming down. On this account the action was postponed until the next night, Townsley being prevented from leaving. Saturday night the party set out toward the upper part of Mosquito creek. [T. does not bring out that this is in the opposite direction from the Forks and meant a complete change of program from that first explained. His hearers probably understood this matter of geography clearly.] They got no response at the first cabin, so proceeded down the creek to Doyle's, John Brown shooting the elder Doyle and the boys using swords. Next came Wilkinson and then Sherman. During the killing Townsley, Fred Brown and Wiener stood guard. Other persons on Brown's list, but who were not found, were Henry Sherman and George Wilson, probate judge of Anderson county.

Townsley admitted that he did not approve of the killing and considered it terrible, but Brown insisted that it was necessary for the protection of the settlers. He always understood that George Grant was the messenger who carried the news to Brown, but it was only hearsay as he did not know Grant. The remainder of the statement traced his wanderings during the latter part of the summer and fall. After the battle of Black Jack, he was at Lawrence for some time, going into Iowa in July where he remained until fall. Townsley was confronted with Redpath's statement that two squatters, not members of the Brown family, who participated, told him that John Brown was not present. He, Townsley, declared that Redpath's statement was false, as the only members of the party under this description were Weiner and himself, and as for himself he said nothing of the kind to Redpath.

The Lawrence *Journal* gave the history of the document, reporting that Hutchings left Lawrence on December 4, arriving at Lane the same day, staying at Hanway's home. In response to an invitation Johnson Clark was present and Townsley came to Hanway's home, where after several hours of discussion, he dictated the statement to Hutchings. Townsley read it and signed. It was dated December 6, 1879. W. H. Ambrose, writing about twelve years later, gave a list of all who were present when the document was signed. In addition to himself and those mentioned already he listed Helen Hanway, John S. Hanway, Brougham Hanway and Sarah Hanway.[36] There is a special interest at-

36 *W. H. Ambrose Papers*, Kansas State Historical Society.

tached to this group, because G. W. Brown charged that these
"over-zealous friends" of John Brown, by their "importunate
insistence" influenced Townsley in that part of the statement which
dealt with the messenger.[37] In this connection possibly another
version of the Townsley statement is of importance; the one given
Hanway and Clark, August 3, 1882, for the Andreas-Cutler *History of Kansas*, which omitted the messenger story and emphasized
that Townsley acted under duress, being kept guarded constantly
in camp and being guarded by Fred Brown and Wiener while on
the expedition.[38]

AFTERMATH

The Paola *Republican*, December 12, republican in politics, defended Brown and condemned the G. W. Brown *Reminiscences* as
conceived in malice. Its democratic contemporary, the *Western
Spirit*, sneered "Some other [falsehood] must be invented if his
friends would satisfy the impartial judgment of posterity that he
was justified in committing this great crime. As the case stands
now, Brown and his sons are shown to have committed a wanton
and brutal murder upon five unarmed and unoffending citizens of
this country."

The Garnett *Plaindealer*, December 12, edited by Sol Kaufman,
one of the guerillas of 1856, stated that Townsley had told him the
same story soon after it occurred. The Garnett *Journal*, December
13, declared that the editor knew John Brown and that:

he was the prime mover, if not the most active participant in these cold-
blooded, dastardly murders, we never doubted. . . . Henry Sherman, a few
weeks prior to his own murder [1857], told us that he and his brother were
not 'Pro Slavery nor Free State,' as he expressed it. They were Dutch-
men and came to Kansas to make a home and not to engage in politics.
. . . As we recollect the man today, we do not believe he was a character
to interfere with any one, and certainly not in the way of murder and
bloodshed.

Now let the Lawrence *Journal* hunt up testimony as to the character of
the men murdered by Brown for 'opinion's sake,' for no overt act on their
part, save an attempt to scare the store keeper at the 'crossing,' is alleged
against anyone on the creek.

In printing the Townsley statement, December 11, the *Daily
Journal* summed up the status of the Brown problem and defined
the next issue to be cleared up, the messenger story, and suggested

---

37 G. W. Brown, *False Claims corrected*, p. 72–77.
38 Andreas-Cutler, *History of Kansas*, 603–604.

that ''Mr. Weiner is still living we believe in Kansas, and we may possibly hear from him on this and other points.'' Probably this article was written by Hutchings because two days later he wrote Hanway.

Lawrence, Kansas, December 13, 1879.

Friend Hanway: Yours with article for the *Journal* just received. I will hand the article to Mr. Thacher in the mornnig. The Townsley statement is being extensively copied and it is being generally conceded that it settles the question of Brown's connection with the Potawatomie affair. Mr. Clark's statement has been copied with a column and a half of comments, by the Springfield (Mass) *Republican.* The *Republican* goes for G. W. Brown, also Robinson, but recognizes the importance of Townsley's statement as historic evidence. After I left Lane the other day, and while in Paola, I became satisfied that Winer was the party who went up to Middle Creek to notify John Brown of the threats of Sherman Wilkinson and the Doyles instead of George Grant. When I got home I learned that Grant had stated to Mr. Thacher that it was not l.im. I have found out exactly where Winer lives and shall go and see him soon. I shall be greatly pleased if you can go with me. Our stopping off point will be Fontana on the Mo River, Fort Scott and Gulf road. The thing for you to do would be to meet me at Paola. I will try to let you know in season what day I will start. If there was a telegraph station at Lane I would dispatch to you. You remember that Townsley persisted in the statement that he met John Brown Jr in Nebraska going out with his father. You thought it impossible as did I then but I learn since coming home that J. B. Jr did accompany the old man out of the Territory at that time. G. W. Brown states the facts in his article published in the Journal today.

Respectfully yours,

JOHN HUTCHINGS.

The following day he wrote again after seeing Speer who showed him Hanway's last letter saying the latter had received the Springfield *Republican* containing Sanborn's dastard and ingrate article. Hutchings asked Hanway to show it to Clark:

Upon the whole I think the comments of the Republican are contemptible. It virtually stigmatizes every one of us as ingrates who do not agree that John Brown was innocent of taking any part in the Potawatomie massacre. I have no doubt the article was written by Sanborn himself, and the difficulty with him is, that, if Brown is shown to have been present and to have participated in the killing, either Brown told a falsehood in denying it, or Sanborn has lied about what Brown said to him about it.

D. W. Wilder was vindictive about the Townsley confession and sneered at Townsley's soft-heartedness—a man who had spent five years in the army fighting Indians—why didn't he tell the story before all the others were dead? To this the Lawrence *Daily Jour-*

nal reminded him that Wiener was living in Kansas and Owen Brown in Ohio, and both could correct Townsley.[39] The *Journal* might have added three names to the list of the living: Salmon and Owen Brown and Henry Thompson. In reality, only three of the original eight were dead.

The next contribution to justification was from John B. Manes who charged also that the Grant family had been warned to leave, that Mary Grant had been threatened and that his father had been knocked down for having a copy of the New York *Tribune* and his house and his brother-in-law's house had been burned, and the authors of these outrages were the victims of the Potawatomie massacre. Here was some more fiction, but no one exposed it.[40]

WIENER SILENT

Once the matter was opened up it is surprising from how many sources information came on one point or another. Already Wiener's presence in Kansas and Hutchings's purpose in seeking an interview had been mentioned and the La Cygne *Journal* took up the Wiener question and gave a fuller identification of him, saying that he was the brother-in-law of Jacob Benjamin, formerly of that city, and at the time was living with the Benjamin family near the edge of Linn county north of La Cygne. Wiener's whereabouts and identity seemed quite well known at this time. In spite of the fact, however, no biographer of John Brown ever traced him except to say he fled from Kansas, to Texas or Louisiana or elsewhere.[41]

[39] Lawrence *Daily Journal* quoted Wilder from the St. Joseph *Herald* and replied at the same time. December 19, 1879.

[40] Garnett *Plaindealer*, January 9, 1880. The Manes statement was dated December 29, 1879. The Lawrence *Daily Journal* copied it January 22, 1880. James C. Malin, ''John Brown and the Manes incident,'' *Kansas Historical Quarterly*, 7 (November, 1938) 376–78. Cf. Ch. 9.

[41] Sanborn gave no information about Wiener in his *John Brown* (1885) although he knew his whereabouts. August Bondi had written him December 26, 1883, that Wiener was then living at LaCygne, Linn county, Kansas. The letter is in the *John Brown Collection*, Kansas State Historical Society. Villard followed Bondi only so far as to have Wiener leave Kansas for Louisiana in June, 1856. Villard, *John Brown*, p. 210. Leon Hühner said Wiener served in the union army and reported that he died in St. Louis in 1906 [he would have been 86 years of age], being buried in the Jewish cemetery. Some Jewish associates of John Brown, *Publications* of the American Jewish Historical Society No. 23 (1915), pp. 55–78, at 75. Also B. W. Blandford, Jewish friends of Old John Brown, *American Hebrew*, April 15, 1927. (Based largely upon

Salmon Brown tried in later years to make it appear that he was a bad character, a blood-thirsty Austrian looking for a fight. August Bondi related the story of the summer of 1856 in a form that is neither consistent within itself nor with other versions. Wiener and Bondi went on the Lawrence expedition donating two wagon loads of supplies rather than have them fall into pro-slavery hands while Benjamin and wife were delegated, according to Bondi, to load into wagons the most valuable goods and take them to the Marais des Cygnes timber for hiding. The remainder were stolen or burned after the massacre along with the store building which was on the Benjamin claim and belonged to him. Wiener left the territory according to Bondi, without telling him specifically who did the killing, going to Louisiana to sell four thousand acres of land and Benjamin and Bondi undertook to care for Wiener's salvaged goods. The pro-slavery enemies located them however, and on attachment for debt seized the dry goods and sold them. Although much of the detail of Bondi's story does not agree with other evidence, this sale of goods under attachment proceedings was confirmed in the contemporary press under the name of Wines, which might easily have been a printer's error for Winer as most non-German people seem to have written the name.[42]   In December the three, according to Bondi, together with Cochran and Manes entered the townsite of Greeley, Theodore Wiener being represented by power of attorney. However this may have been, the patent when issued ran for Benjamin, Bondi and Herman not Theodore Wiener. Bondi claimed to have visited Wiener July 1–3, 1857, at his home at Washington, Iowa, and mentioned his temporary return to Kansas in April, 1859.

The story of that visit to Kansas is explained by the act of the territorial legislature of 1859 which set up the Hoogland commis-

Bondi and Hühner.)   Hühner and Blandford were interested primarily in Jewish propaganda and did not recognize the unreliability of Bondi as a witness.

There were two Wiener brothers, Theodore and Herman, and Jacob Benjamin and August Bondi and possibly others, all Jews radiating from St. Louis, who were associated in varying combinations from time to time in land speculation, townsite promotions and mercantile enterprises. Theodore Wiener, Benjamin and Bondi, with St. Louis financing, were associated in the Mosquito creek land claims and store, 1855–56. Herman Wiener, Benjamin and Bondi were later associated in the Greeley (Walker) Townsite promotion and under the townsite law the land was patented to George Wilson, Probate Judge of Anderson county in trust for the unincorporated members of the town company. See Records of Register of Deeds. Garnett, Anderson county, Kansas, for the east ½, section 30, T. 19 east, R. 20 south.

[42] New York *Tribune*, August 11, 1856. Cf. Chapter 9.

sion to hear and determine the validity and amounts of claims of citizens of Kansas for damages suffered during the troubles. According to his affidavits of May 11, 1859, Wiener was a resident of Anderson county, Kansas, having returned to the territory April 9. The claim was for the whole stock of goods valued at $4500.00 of which he was absolute owner and which he maintained was taken and destroyed by a mob. In explanation of his part in the Lawrence expedition Wiener declared that ''I left to go and defend myself as threats had been made, I thought it more safe to keep in camp. I left my business in charge of Jacob Benjamin, . . . and if I should get killed I should leave no widow, . . .'' and later in the summer ''I thought it advisable to leave the territory for my own safety; when I left I intended to return, and have always intended to do so.'' He reported hearsay evidence that Little opened a store in Ft. Scott with his goods and that Weightman peddled his goods through the country during 1856. Bondi swore that he had just arrived in Kansas seeing the goods for the first time May 18 or 19, 1856; that on May 21 he went on the Lawrence expedition; and that the goods were worth $4000. Benjamin's affidavit maintained that he clerked for Wiener from February to June 1856 and being a family man was left to keep store. Although his chronology was indefinite in this affidavit, to save themselves he loaded his family and some of the goods from the store into a wagon and fled to Potawatomie creek where he was captured, turned over to Captain Wood, and taken to Osawatomie past the smoldering ruins of the store. In Bondi's claim for damages for goods of his own worth $1,148.00 Benjamin stated specifically that he left them at the store June 2 or 3 and that they were taken or destroyed June 6 or 7. Apparently he fled after the battle of Black Jack and the store was looted by the Pate or Whitfield or other parties returning from that region after being dispersed by the United States troops. Benjamin put in a claim for the building, livestock and equipment on the claim valued at $1,085.00, property destroyed about June 6, 1856.

The Hoogland commissioners were skeptical of these claims and of the veracity of the principals, each of whom made affidavit to the other's alleged losses. They certified $862.50 on the Benjamin claim without comment, and $1,000.00 on Bondi's, adding the qualification ''with many doubts, but governed by the proof.'' Wiener's claim was thrown out on the ground that he was not a resident of Kansas but they questioned the veracity of the affidavits citing the testimony of two witnesses, John Chockey and Amos Alderman, who convinced them that the "petitioner's agents, Bondi and Benjamin, had saved out of the stock quite a large amount of goods, and retailed them for many months in Osawatomie [and Greeley] a fact of which they were oblivious when they gave their testimony. . . ." [43]

WIENER'S KANSAS RESIDENCE

The Kansas residence of Theodore Wiener is established by both the Kansas census and land records.[44]   He was listed in Scott township, Linn county, in 1870, 1875 and 1880, but not in 1885 although his son Theodore, Jr., was then working there as a farm hand. On November 15, 1869, J. G. Blunt deeded a large block of land to Elizabeth Benjamin, wife of Jacob Benjamin, and she deeded 160 acres of it in two detached parcels March 3, 1870, to Theodore Wiener, the consideration not stated.[45]   Wiener sold the southwest 40 acres of his 120 acres on January 30, 1872, and lost the detached 40 acres as the result of an adverse judgment of law July 17, 1875. He held the remaining 80 acres, the east half of the southeast quarter of section 23, until February 23, 1883.[46]

According to the census of 1870 one is led to the conclusion that Wiener was just moving to the farm, no production being listed for the previous year, 1869, and only ten acres were improved. His

[43] Hoogland, *Kansas Claims*, Public doc. 1106–1107. Theodore Wiener claim No. 249, pp. 1144–50. Jacob Benjamin claim No. 253, pp. 1059–63. August Bondi claim No. 262, pp. 1079–81.

[44] Kansas census records, K. S. H. S. Federal census of 1870 and agricultural census of 1880. State census of 1875 and 1885. Land records are in Register of Deeds office, Mound City, Linn county.

[45] The principal body of land was 120 acres in the southeast quarter, section 23, T. 19, R. 23, and the second parcel was 40 acres, the southeast quarter of the southeast quarter of section 24. This land lay four miles south and thirteen miles east of Dutch Henry's Crossing (Lane Postoffice), or seven and one-half miles south and six miles east of Osawatomie, or three and one-half miles west and two miles north of La Cygne.

[46] The census shows that until 1865 Jacob Benjamin, August Bondi, Poindexter Maness and James G. Blunt lived near each other in Anderson county, southwest of Dutch Henry's Crossing. According to August Bondi, *Autobiography*, pp. 66, 68, Jacob Benjamin married Elizabeth Maness in 1857, a second wife. The Benjamins moved to Scott Township, Linn county, after 1865. The La Cygne *Journal*, December 20, 1879, said that Wiener and Jacob Benjamin were brothers-in-law, but there is no clue to the basis of such a relationship. They were associated, however, as Wiener's name appeared several times in the papers of the estate of Jacob Benjamin, 1870–72 (Miami county, Probate Court, Case 27). It is evident that the acquaintances of 1856 had not been wholly interrupted.

livestock consisted of two horses and a cow. He was fifty years of age, born in Prussia, and was a citizen of the United States. His wife Maria was thirty-eight and was born in Mississippi. Of his three children: Susan, thirteen, was born in Arkansas; Ernestine, nine, in Missouri, and Theodore, Jr., five, in Missouri. It is noteworthy that Susan was born in 1857 in Arkansas when Bondi said Wiener was in Iowa, the year after the Massacre, and the other two in Missouri which would place the family residence there from 1861 to 1865 at the minimum. The Jacob Benjamin family was listed in the same township with a 640 acre farm, but the mortality schedule listed Jacob, a merchant, 43 years old, as having been killed in February, 1870, from falling off a wagon load of lumber while crossing a creek and being run over by the wheels.

Hutchings made the trip as planned to interview Wiener, but Hanway was unable to go, which is fortunate for the historian, because Hutchings was then obliged to write Hanway a detailed report, January 20, 1880, which has been preserved in the *Hanway Papers:*

LAWRENCE, January 20, 1880.

Friend Hanway:

Yours of the 13th came duly to hand. I went down to LaCygne the day I wrote you from Kansas City that I should go and found on my arrival that Weiner lived several miles in the country. I hired a buggy and took in James P. Way Esq. an old resident and many years treasurer of Linn County, and drove out to Weiners house. We found the old man quite courteous. He invited us in and we made known our errand. He said John Brown was dead and wanted to know what good there was in raking up that old matter now. We explained that G. W. Brown's letters had raised a discussion on this subject and that to get the exact truth and publish it would be beneficial to the name and memory of Brown as well as to the good name of all those who participated in the early struggles on the Potawatomie. We explained to him that no danger would come to him in consequence of his revealing the whole facts within his knowledge; that the legislature had passed amnesty laws covering all alleged crimes committed during those days, and then read him your letter, Blood's letter and Townsley's statement. At first we thought he was going to tell us what he knew. He admitted being in the battle of Black Jack and that he saw Redpath in their camp near Prairie City as Townsley stated, but when we quietly asked him if John Brown accompanied them on the expedition against the Doyles, Wilkinson & Sherman, he said he didnt know anything about that matter. I then said, 'you dont say you were not along do you? The evidence shows that you were with the party and Col. Blood saw you with the others within two miles of where you camped, and Townsley says you were there.' He replied that it must have been some other Weiner. I said further that 'Col. Blood knew you and saw you with them, Judge Hanway knew you and saw you start with the party—the evidence all goes to show that you were there.' At this he became a little excited and said "gentlemen let me say to you in plain English that all your evidence dont amount to hell-room." "I tell you I know nothing about the matter." This amused Way very much, but it was evident that we were "up a stump," so we came away. He remarked courteously when we left that he was sorry he could not give us the information we sought, but he could not. Winer is evidently a man of good education and understands himself pretty well. I think if you were to see him and talk with him he might be disposed to tell what he knows. I have not given up trying him again.

Truly yours

JOHN HUTCHINGS.[47]

This is the end of the trail as far as available data is concerned, but the historian cannot escape the conviction that Wiener must have revealed somewhere his terrible secret. Because he did not speak out to defend himself, the Brown legend has made of him a coward and a monster in spite of the fact that for many years he lived peacefully within about ten miles of the Dutch Henry Crossing. His silence speaks eloquently, however, to the effect that he was one of the Potawatomie killers who was never duped by the Brown Legend into believing himself a Hero.

A curious aftermath of the Townsley confession episode is a letter by Johnson Clark to Charles Robinson:

STONEWALL FARM, LANE P.O.
FRANKLIN CO., KANSAS.
December 10, 1879.

GOVERNOR CHAS ROBINSON:

Dear Friend

I am thinking of getting up a lecture on John Brown, and his Potawatomie Tragedy, for the purpose of delivery in the cities and towns from Kansas to Maine.

I want some change from the hard work of years, & hope to *make it pay* by a small admittance fee in order to finish & furnish my new House, get a Piano &c &c. Now I know of none so capable of advising as yourself. Please tell me if you think it will pay. By the time you get this you will see the statement from James Townsley which I have been years in getting and at last pursuaded out of him with the help of Jas. Hanway, and which has been put in good shape by John Hutchings, Esqr *one of your friends*. I did not say anything to Mr. H. when he was here, as I wished to get your opinion first.—Living in the vicinity since the winter of 56 and spring of 57, acquainted with Townsley and some of the Browns, knowing Dutch Henry, and being the first man in Kas. that published a

[47] James P. Way was listed in the census of 1875 as a farmer in Scott township, the same one in which Wiener lived. He was then 48 years of age.

statement of the facts from an eye witness—perhaps setting aside my want
of ability as a public speaker, it might not be altogether out of place in
me to get up such a Lecture and it appears to me it would pay something
more than expenses.

I can get the skull of "Dutch Bill" (William Sherman) which has two
long swoard [sic] cuts in the top—part of it—his brains having been
washed out at the time of the killing in the creek where he fell.

Now as this is a private matter, I beg pardon for troubling you, and
promise as a part remuneration, to write up some items that may be valuable in your *proposed History* of Kas. which Mr. Hutchings told me you
was going to write. Allow me to congratulate you and all good & true
Kansans upon the prospect of a true history of Kansas. The "true in-
wardness" *of some things ought to be written up,* and you are the man
to do it.

I hope you will accept my apology for trying to make some money out
of a lecture on the ground that I need it.

The only question with me is would it interest the people? Would it pay?
I am glad the history of Kas, is being, and in time likely *to be* righted
up. The d—d *lies* of Redpath & others are a disgrace.

With special regard to Mrs. Robinson, I am very truly yours,

JOHNSON CLARK.[48]

Robinson's reply to this letter has not been found and no record
has been discovered of the proposed lecture tour, or of any public
display of the skull of Dutch Bill, although Clark did talk on Brown
to local settlers' meetings.

[48] *Robinson Papers,* K. S. H. S.

CHAPTER XVII

ROBINSON, ADAMS AND SANBORN CHANGE POSITIONS, 1880

Repetition, elaboration and controversy over the Townsley statements, the G. W. Brown *Reminiscences* and Sanborn's offensive reprisals all interacted to force reconsiderations and realignments. With the opening of the year 1880 the controversy entered a new phase. Charles Robinson decided to reply to Sanborn's "dastard" and "ingrate" article and, in doing so, to announce his new position.[1] By way of introduction he made an unprecedented confession:

Unfortunately for me, Mr. S. some time since had a tilt with Mrs. R, and he has seemed to owe me a grudge ever since. It was not my fault. I advised her to leave Mr. S. alone in his publication and worship of heroes, as he seemed to be happy in his ignorance, and it would be folly to disturb his peace of mind with the truth. But, as usual, she would have her say, and I have to suffer the consequences.

Robinson took the ground that John Brown was not a competitor for the statue because the law required that the person must have been a citizen of the state. Reviewing the Kansas struggle along his usual lines, he adopted Sanborn's epithets "dastard" for the peace party and "hero" for the radical or revolutionary party. On the crucial issue of the controversy he declared that

John Brown's massacre on the Potawatomie was a most terrible and revolting butchery, utterly undefensible in the 19th century, but it was an incident of the civil war, inaugurated by S. J. Jones at Lawrence. . . . The threats of the men massacred, as claimed, even if made, could not justify it, and John Brown did not put his defense on that hand, as, according to Mr. Townsley's testimony, he proposed to slaughter all the proslavery men of the region—those who had made no threats as well as those who had, if any. But was John Brown at heart a murderer in this butchery? I think not. . . . John Brown seemed to believe he was the special messenger and servant of this [ancient Hebrew] God, and he may have been as sincere as was Abraham, when he stretched forth his hand to take the knife to slay his own son. . . .

[1] His letter was dated December 20, 1879, and was published in the Topeka *Commonwealth*, January 3 and 4, 1880.

The paper closed with a resumé of the remainder of the civil war of 1856, the rôle of John Brown and Jim Lane, including Lane's proposal, late in the fifties, for wholesale massacre of pro-slavery men.

Robinson-Speer Feud

Speer opened the new year by publishing what he called "John Speer's New Year's Compliments to Charles Robinson," reviewing all the swindles charged to Robinson from his California days to his alleged blackmailing of a large farm from the Union Pacific "from under his sister Martha's petticoats," and the alleged robbery of widows and orphans.[2] A few days later he replied to Robinson's article on Sanborn with a view to defending Lane.[3] Near the close he took a personal thrust at Mr. and Mrs. Robinson by quoting the former's confession that she must have her say: "In his frenzie he seems at war with God and man even his wife is found fault with. . . . Oh hear! From old Adam to old Robinson, 'the woman thou gave me did it,' and, then, the impious old man takes a tilt at God. . . . Is the man deranged? Must we get up a new God and a reformed humanity to suit him?"

The other exchanges had only incidentally to do with the Brown matter,[4] but one paragraph drawn from Robinson furnishes an interesting sidelight on the relations of Robinson with G. W. Brown:

I called out one person who is infinitely above Speer in integrity, truthfulness, and every other trait, as I believe. He did not pursue precisely the course I supposed he would, but what he has written is very valuable and more truthful, to say the least, than Speer's articles in the Kansas City papers, or Sanborn's histories or romances. For doing this Speer jumped into the arena and commenced impugning my motives, etc. I deemed it my duty to place him where he belongs, in the same catalogue of crime as I would a witness in court.[5]

One of Speer's articles attacked G. W. Brown's account of the defense of Lawrence in September, 1856. The conflicting witnesses were marshaled first; Jacob McGee said Sam Walker commanded, Mrs. Speer said Cracklin; and in summary Speer added that James Blood took a small command and reconnoitered and that Walker,

---

[2] Lawrence *Daily Journal*, January 6, 1880.

[3] Topeka *Commonwealth*, January 9, 1880. 3 columns. The article closed with an obscene reference aneñt the statue question.

[4] Robinson letter January 8, in Lawrence *Daily Journal*, January 13, and *Weekly Home Journal*, January 15, 1880. Speer in *Daily Journal*, January 8, 1880. Robinson, A Correction, *Commonwealth*, January 13.

[5] Lawrence *Daily Journal*, January 13, 1880.

Cracklin, O. E. Learnard, J. B. Abbott and others had small commands, so several men commanded. But the real point was based on William Crutchfield's account which concluded that "In this manner, under his [Brown's] direction or suggestion, with Capt. Cracklin in command of the main force, the pro-slavery forces were held at bay until Gov. Geary sent soldiers from Lecompton to avert bloodshed."[6]

A year later the defense of Lawrence question arose again when the Lawrence *Tribune* attributed the stone fort on the hill to John Brown. Again Robinson reviewed the matter; no one sent for Brown, he just came in unannounced; the forts were built in the fall of 1855, Wakefield superintending the one on the hill and Judge Smith the one near the intersection of Massachusetts and Henry (Eighth) street; Abbott was in command, and other leaders, Cracklin, Moore, Walker, Deitzler, went out to meet the enemy, who with Governor Geary deserved the credit for saving Lawrence; the pitchforks with which some defenders were armed were furnished by Duncan and Allen's hardware store, and not by John Brown. The editor, L. D. Bailey, admitted frankly that he had not arrived in Lawrence until April 1857 and was only repeating statements made to him by others supposing they were reliable, and commented on "how a little fact may become the foundation, or occasion, for an enormous growth of fiction" like Mrs. O'Leary's cow and the Chicago fire.[7] This friendly interchange had the effect of bringing out Captain Joseph Cracklin's own story in two letters. The Lawrence forts had been built by order of Lane; "he was engineer and director, but I regret to say there was little engineering skill displayed in their construction. They were built for a temporary purpose, and served for the time being." The circular mud fort at the north end of Massachusetts street he attributed to Judge Smith, and the one at the Henry street intersection to Lyman Allen, while the one on the hill was built by Wakefield out of loose stone banked with earth on the outside, being good against small arms, but against artillery it would be more dangerous inside than outside. Cracklin maintained that Lane had given him command shortly before this crisis and in order to accept he had resigned his position as Captain of the Stubbs, Cut-

[6] Speer's article, Lawrence *Daily Journal*, January 16, *Weekly Journal*, January 22, 1880. Wm. Crutchfield, *United States Biographical Dictionary, Kansas Volume*, 506.

[7] Robinson's letter and the editor's reply were printed together. Lawrence *Tribune*, April 16, 1881.

ler taking his place there and going with the Stubbs against orders
to Hickory Point. On Robinson's orders Cracklin said that he
arranged his small remaining forces at the Henry street fort, his
own house on Rhode Island street and at Roberts's box factory.
When the alarm was given Cracklin led this last named small band
of Wabaunsee boys out toward Speer's house, stopping on the top
of the ridge awaiting the advancing force and fired when within
range. By this time other supporting bands came up making in
all fifty-eight. With some more skirmishing and firing the invaders returned to Franklin and the next day the federal troops
were in control.[8] Cracklin then took up the earlier engagements;
the attack on the Georgians near Osawatomie early in August, on
Franklin, on Fort Saunders and on Fort Titus. In the first two
Cracklin claimed the command, pointing out that John Brown was
in Nebraska and in the others Cracklin and his Stubbs took part.[9]
The editor commented in conclusion of the exchange that John
Brown never claimed these things himself, but a "small coterie of
eastern men seem to have taken it into their heads to make history
in accordance with their notions, and if the facts fail to agree with
their statements, 'so much the worse for the facts,' as the French
philosopher said." Sensing unconsciously, perhaps, the power of
reiteration to overcome facts a correspondent evidently felt that
something more ought to be said to repair any damage that may
have been done:

> If there is a lesson for us in the life and character of John Brown, it is
> that *loyalty* to a principle, moral integrity and self-denial even to death,
> insures the general acceptation of the soundness of the principle and the
> immortal glory of his faithful adherents.[10]

The Brown Family

As Robinson had put it crudely, Townsley had revealed that
the Browns did not kill the five men on the Potawatomie because of
particular crimes or outrages or threats of such, but simply as an
act of proscription of pro-slavery men for opinion's sake. This
threatened ruin to the carefully marshaled argument of justification. Earlier the Brown family had participated little in the controversies, but at this juncture, whether it was a carefully prepared
plan or just the idea of an enterprising reporter at Akron, Ohio,

[8] Lawrence *Daily Tribune*, April 18, 1881.
[9] Lawrence *Daily Tribune*, April 19, 1881.
[10] Lawrence *Daily Tribune*, May 21, 1881.

Jason Brown was interviewed for the *Beacon,* and thus the family began to be drawn into the feud. Jason had been on the Lawrence expedition but had not been taken by his father on the killing foray. He admitted that Townsley's statement was correct so far as he had first hand knowledge, but he had no direct information about what had happened to his father's party. At the first reports, Jason confessed, he was horrified: "The thought that it might be true . . . nearly deprived me of my reason for a time." When he asked his father, Jason thought he said he did not do it, but approved it, but Jason admittedly could not be sure what his father said. Certainly anyone as honest as Jason was a bad witness for the defense, even though he admitted approving the murders after he learned the facts. Reviewing the evidence to explain this changed opinion he omitted, significantly, most of the alleged outrages advanced by others and staked his whole argument in a few points. A version of the surveyor story was used in which "every one of the damned Browns" were to be killed, but this statement was made supposedly by the Georgians, not Doyle, Wilkinson and Sherman. He reviewed the earlier meeting of settlers at which the differences cropped out between white free-state men and the abolitionists as he called them. He quoted Martin White's statement that when White heard John Brown declare that he was a "dyed in the Wool Abolitionist" that "it was enough for me," and interpreted it as meaning that White had then and there put his father on the "death list." The third line of justification was the whole series of conflicts, both before and after the massacre, which he argued was adequate evidence that his father was merely acting in self-defense. Again Jason was a bad witness for the defense, and it is evident that he had not been adequately coached by the keepers of the Legend.[11]

John Brown, Jr., had taken more of an interest in the controversies over his father than the less aggressive Jason, and at this time was connected in some way with activities somewhat obscure for rehabilitating the family reputation. Charles Leonhardt, who had been associated with the elder Brown at one time, was on a

[11] Akron (Ohio) *Beacon,* January 21, 1880, reprinted in the Lawrence *Daily Journal,* February 12, 1880.

Hanway endorsed Jason's description of the Lawrence expedition, but did not comment on the justification. Hanway to Adams, February 17, 1880. *Correspondence,* Kansas State Historical Society. Adams thought him "clear and candid." Adams to Hanway, February 19, 1880. *Hanway Correspondence,* K. S. H. S.

mission to Kansas during the summer of 1880 and wrote John Brown, Jr., from Osawatomie, June 22, acknowledging Brown's last letter and reporting on the success of his Kansas mission by saying that "I have found *the* key to unlock the unproven conspiracy of our foes on the Pottawatomie not only to kill your family, but also your uncle, Rev. S. L. Adair, Chesnut and Richard Mendenhall." Leonhardt's informant claimed to have come into Kansas with a pro-slavery teamster, Henry Sherman [Dutch Henry], who told him the whole plot.[12] Leonhardt's information was without foundation, and is of no importance to this story, but the point that is outstanding is the frank confidential admission, as between Leonhardt and Brown, that the alleged conspiracy against the Brown family was "unproven," and Leonhardt's admission to Kansas was to find proof. Did not these correspondents have faith in the elder Brown's own surveyor story or the versions of it told by others?

Adams's Change in Views

F. G. Adams had seemed to take a moderate view of the controversy when it opened and seemed willing, at least, to discuss new evidence, but by the time G. W. Brown's *Reminiscences* were complete he was fully committed to the Brown legend, even to the point of outright misrepresentation. Writing to Mrs. George L. Stearns, April 17, 1880, he said:

I thought of you while the stir was being made by the Geo. W. Brown publication, but doubted if you would care to read what was published on either side. I will if you desire send you one of Brown's pamphlets. But really I don't think you ought to read it. It has done no harm to the memory of John Brown. Very few of the people of Kansas have any feelings but that of execration of the spirit which prompted that pamphlet.[13]

Adams's relations with Sanborn developed to the point that he read proof on Sanborn's *Life and Letters of John Brown*, published in 1885.[14]

Hanway

The controversy appealed to a large enough body of readers to make a substantial demand for John Brown material for publication. L. D. Bailey, who was editing *The Kansas Monthly*, ap-

[12] *Brown Papers*, Kansas State Historical Society.
[13] Kansas State Historical Society, *Letter-press books*, C. 911–912.
[14] Letters to Sanborn, April 1 and 15, 1885. K. S. H. S. *Correspondence.*

plied to Adams for good manuscripts and after examination selected Hanway's *"Reminiscences of Pottawatomie township,"*
which had been submitted to Adams in January, 1878, and which
Adams had suppressed. Its publication in the January, 1880, number of the *Kansas Monthly* was in the nature of anti-climax at that
stage of the controversy, but it was in this manner that Hanway
had been deprived of his proper place in pioneering the newer view
of Brown. As George Grant had already denied being the messenger and H. H. Williams offered himself in that capacity, Hanway "corrected" his article in the next issue by supplying "the
missing link." [15]

Robinson's *Commonwealth* letters struck Hanway a most severe
blow. His first expressions were of astonishment and then anger.[16]
The *Miami Republican* (Paola) January 30 and February 13, 1880,
published two letters signed "Osawatomie" which sound like Hanway. The author pointed out with some bitterness Robinson's
changed attitude but agreed with him in the general position
taken that the credit for Kansas belonged to no one in particular,
or even to a small number, but to the free-state men as a body.
He condemned particularly the eastern men who had done John
Brown so much disservice by idolizing and deifying him. He
commented on Mrs. Robinson's hand in Robinson's new position,
saying that "To cripple Sanborn the Governor attempts to cast
away [*sic*] every conceivable odium on Mr. Sanborn's 'hero,' old
John Brown. If he can accomplish this, of course Mr. Sanborn
has no longer a hero in the person of old John Brown."

The renewed interest resulted in the organization of another
Old Settlers' Union with a celebration at Osawatomie, August 30,
1880.[17] Hanway made an attack on G. W. Brown's *Reminiscences*
and Johnson Clark delivered the oration of the day. His address
was summarized by the reporter, not quoted, but leaves the impression that Clark was doubtful of John Brown's Kansas exploits, taking the ground "that his traducers may stigmatize his
action while in Kansas as that of a thief and murderer, but that
his name would be handed down to posterity as the man who gave
his life as a ransom for the freedom of the slave." [18]

[15] H. H. Williams lied about being the messenger, either here or in 1856,
in his New York *Tribune* letter published August 20, 1856, in which he represented himself as accompanying the John Brown, Jr., Potawatomie Rifles.
[16] Letter to Adams, February 17, 1880. K. S. H. S. *Correspondence.*
[17] Osawatomie *Times,* August 14, 19.
[18] Osawatomie *Times,* September 2, 1880.

Associated with this organized local interest, the Osawatomie *Times* published a new revision of Hanway's *Reminiscences* beginning August 5, 1880 and running into the spring of the next year. In the issue of April 7, 1881, he told with bitterness of Charles Robinson's change of position on the Brown question, comparing his statement at the time of the dedication of the monument in 1877 with his *Commonwealth* letter. Robinson charged Hanway, and justly, with misuse of quotations. Hanway refused to give consideration to Robinson's point that the Townsley statement changed the whole situation because he held that John Brown proposed to sweep the creek of pro-slavery men regardless of their guilt of any offense, and such a course was not an act of self-defense, but a proscription merely for opinion's sake. In refusing to recognize this point Hanway insisted on comparison of Robinson's statements of 1877 and 1880 and inquired offensively why Robinson had accepted Hanway's invitation to preside at the dedication in 1877 if he felt that way in 1880 about John Brown.[19]

SANBORN'S SHIFT OF POSITION

Sanborn had not been willing at the time of the "dastard" article to make a clearcut public admission that John Brown was present at the Potawatomie massacre. He wrote Redpath, however, January 2, 1880, that "you and I must give in that the old hero was at Potawatomie and gave orders. I have this on private assurance of one who knows."[20] In reply Redpath wrote: "I never was more astonished at any statement in my life. . . . Up to the time I read that I never had had the faintest shadow of a doubt that he was not there. The story was told me by a man who took part in the killings." The remainder of the letter-press copy of the document is too faint to be read in full, but enough can be deciphered to be sure that he stated that he had forgotten the name of his informant and that Hutchings had the affidavit of a man [Townsley] who denied having told Redpath Brown was not there.[21]

[19] Hanway's accusation, Osawatomie *Times*, April 7. Robinson's reply, Lawrence *Daily Tribune*, May 19. Hanway's rebuttal, *Daily Tribune*, May 30. Robinson again, June 2. Reprinting of Robinson's *Commonwealth* article of January 3 and 4, 1880 in *Daily Tribune*, June 3. Hanway letter, *Daily Tribune*, June 7. Robinson's closing statements, *Daily Tribune*, June 9 and 10, 1881. On June 3 the editor of the *Tribune* warned both parties that the exchange must be terminated so far as the *Tribune* was concerned.

[20] *Hinton Papers*. Kansas State Historical Society.

[21] Letter-press copy of letter, Redpath to Sanborn, January 8, 1880. *Hinton Papers*, Kansas State Historical Society.

In spite of this "private assurance" and this private admission on his part, Sanborn still declined to permit the matter to rest. In the summer of 1882 he made a trip to Kansas, and for the first time in his life saw the country about which he had been writing and visited Topeka, Lawrence, Osawatomie, Lane and vicinity and Atchison.[22] One document which he saw on his visit to the Hanway home he must have read with mixed feelings, Hanway's letter of 1860 to Redpath giving corrections of his life of John Brown and the mention that the same material had been given to Hinton.[23] Sanborn admitted that it gives "the earliest account I have seen of the Potawatomie affair as it really was." Could Sanborn have been so obtuse as not to realize that Redpath and Hinton had duped him and that Old John Brown himself had deceived him? Or had Sanborn once also known the truth and, knowing, lied?

What passed between Sanborn and John Hutchings is not known, except that they talked over the matter of the Townsley statement and Sanborn must have agreed to visit the Browns and report. However that may be Sanborn wrote to Hutchings, August 29, 1882, from the post office address of John Brown, Jr., Put-in-Bay, Ohio, and for once in his life, at least, expressed himself briefly, and without evasion or attempt at justification: "I have talked with the Browns about Townsley's statement. In the main it is true." One cannot but feel some sympathy for Sanborn, because, regardless of the issue of conscious earlier fabrications, it is difficult to doubt his sincerity on the main issue at this time. The cases of Redpath and Hinton are not so clear. Sanborn, and possibly the others, had come to believe in their own romancing.

[22] Hiawatha *World*, August 31, 1882, summarized his visit and the persons he saw and did not see. He missed Robinson, H. H. Williams and Hanway, who had recently died. There is no indication in the records whether he met Townsley.

[23] Sanborn to John S. Hanway, a son of James Hanway, dated Atchison, August 24, 1882, commenting on the letter to Redpath and asking for a copy. *Hanway Papers*, K. S. H. S.